*Architecture in the Scandinavian Countries*

# Architecture in the Scandinavian Countries

*Marian C. Donnelly*

**The MIT Press**    **Cambridge, Massachusetts**    **London, England**

This book was set in Gill Sans and Janson by DEKR Corporation and printed and bound in the United States of America.

Library of Congress Cataloging-in-Publication Data

Donnelly, Marian C. (Marian Card)
    Architecture in the Scandinavian countries / Marian C. Donnelly.
        p.   cm.
    Includes bibliographical references and index.
    ISBN 0-262-04118-9
    1. Architecture—Scandinavia—History.  I. Title.
NA1201.D66   1991
720'.948—dc20                                    90-24720
                                                        CIP

# Contents

*Preface*

In 1958 Thomas Paulsson published his pioneering book *Scandinavian Architecture*. This was the first serious attempt to set forth a unified history of building in Denmark, Finland, Norway, and Sweden from the Iron Age to the years following World War II. Eleven years later I began teaching Scandinavian art and architecture at the University of Oregon, an undertaking that owed much to Paulsson's comprehensive view of the Nordic building arts.

Now it seems appropriate to carry his work a few steps farther. Cities and countrysides alike have been enriched with many distinguished new buildings. New investigations and publications have not only synthesized previous studies but have also provided much valuable material for ongoing scholarship. Some points of view have changed, bringing certain areas, especially prehistoric and vernacular building, which were generally left to archaeology and folklore, much more into the realm of architectural history. Now that the age of postmodernism has arrived, bringing with it the question of what terminology can be devised for its successor, a new review of the history of architecture in the Scandinavian countries may prove useful.

According to the factors of climate, natural resources, and the ever-changing forces of history, periods of greatest vigor in Scandinavian building have varied in time and place. An introduction of the kind offered here is necessarily highly selective. Readers familiar with the Scandinavian countries may well find some of their favorite buildings or favorite architects missing. Some of the author's favorites are missing as well. The effort here has been to achieve a reasonable balance among the accomplishments within the several nations, bearing in mind that the national boundaries have not always been what they are today. Another subject that has been omitted is the activity of Scandinavian architects outside the Nordic countries. This is a very interesting story in itself that deserves much fuller treatment than is appropriate in the present work.

It will at once be evident from the notes and bibliography that some of the examples chosen have been the subjects of extensive investigation and publication, while others have as yet received little attention. I have omitted some references to materials published in local historical society journals, but they are cited by authors quoted in these pages and can be found in Scandinavian libraries. The bibliography is not intended to be all-inclusive but rather to provide guidance to the principal sources of information.

The illustrations have been assembled from a variety of sources. I have been fortunate in being able to travel from Imatra to L'Anse aux Meadows and from Hamburg/Altona to the Lofoten Islands. The skies have not always been friendly, and perhaps it is just as well that the sterner aspects of climate and weather in these countries be represented. For those sites and buildings for which a personal visit has not yet

been possible, the acknowledgments below and in the illustration captions indicate other sources of photographs. For some buildings, contemporary views have been chosen in order to increase the sense of the times in which they were constructed. The drawings that were prepared especially for this book are the work of Sally Donovan and Cheryl S. Martin.

The Graham Foundation for Advanced Study in the Fine Arts has generously provided assistance toward the costs of publication, for which I am very grateful. I also very much appreciate encouragement and good counsel from the editors of the MIT Press.

Finally, there is a debt to scholars in the Scandinavian countries that can never be adequately acknowledged. In Denmark invaluable help has come from Elisabeth Munksgaard and the staff of the National Museum, Hakon Lund and the staff in the library of the Royal Danish Academy of Art, and the staff of the Royal Library in Copenhagen. In Helsinki Kristina Nivari has helped especially with materials from the modern period, and Halldór J. Jónsson has helped with the resources of the National Museum of Iceland. Norwegian materials have been generously made available by Luce Hinsch in the State Archives and Elisabeth Seip in the Norwegian Museum of Architecture in Oslo. In Stockholm much help has come from Ragnar Jonsson in the architect's office of the Royal Palace and also from the staffs of the City Museum, the Historical Museum, and the Nordic Museum. To all of these my warm thanks for much counsel and persistent and good-natured help in finding elusive materials.

Marian C. Donnelly

| | |
|---|---|
| 1 Reykjavik | 11 Copenhagen |
| 2 Bodø | 12 Stockholm |
| 3 Trondheim | 13 Uppsala |
| 4 Ålesund | 14 Turku |
| 5 Bergen | 15 Tampere |
| 6 Haugesund | 16 Helsinki |
| 7 Stavanger | 17 Porvoo |
| 8 Oslo | 18 Kotka |
| 9 Ribe | 19 Imatra |
| 10 Odense | |

*Architecture in the Scandinavian Countries*

# **1** *Prehistoric Scandinavia*

## *The Stone Age*

Long before the present national states of Denmark, Finland, Iceland, Norway, and Sweden began to take form, glacial ice lay deep over the lands of these modern countries. Three times in the Paleolithic period the ice descended here and three times retreated, doing much to shape these territories, which in their turn formed the settings that would have much to do with the nature of buildings upon them for over 10,000 years (figure 1.1).[1]

Flaked tools from c. 250,000–200,000 BC during the next-to-last interglacial period show that hunters were active in Denmark in this warm interlude, but nothing has yet been found of their dwellings. Remains of shelters from later continental European sites suggest huts of poles or even bones set in the ground and lashed together to make a framework for skin coverings, and a hut so constructed might shelter one or two hearths.[2] In the last interglacial period, c. 50,000 BC, people are known to have been hunting on the present Jutland peninsula, but it was not until the ice began to retreat for the last time that a more regular hunting culture could develop.

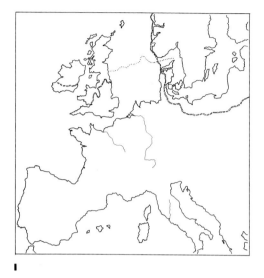

I

--- Limits of last inland ice

···· Northern limit of post-glacial tundra

From c. 14,000 BC there was a landscape of tundra over which reindeer grazed and which could support a modest initial human population. By c. 8400 BC the climate had become much warmer, with forests of birch and pine starting to develop. Settlement sites were still not permanent but seasonal, and again no traces of shelters have yet been found.

The retreat of the glaciers did not leave a fixed geological situation. As the lands were relieved of the weight of ice and the seas received water from melting ice, exchanges were made between land and water for several hundred years. In this Mesolithic period, before the introduction of agriculture, Denmark was connected to England and south Sweden by land masses until c. 6000 BC. The Baltic Sea meanwhile was in turn an ice lake, a bay of the Atlantic Ocean, and a fresh water lake until the opening of the English Channel and the Danish sounds.

Two major concentrations of people from this era have been observed. The earlier, or Maglemose, period, c. 7500–6000 BC, saw hunters and fishers settling at lakeside sites, such as Ulkestrup and Holmegård on Zealand and Ringsjö in Skåne.[3] The Danish examples yielded traces of huts, about 15 by 20 feet, with hearths about 5 feet in diameter in the centers. The walls were made of posts set in the ground and probably covered with rushes or reeds woven into mats, without clay daubing. Birch and pine bark were spread as floor covering (figure 1.2).

The later, or Kitchen Midden, period, c. 6000–4200 BC, saw the growth of the huge rubbish mounds that now give so much information about the diet and implements in these settlements. A few traces of hearths remain, and the shelters were probably seasonal.

With the coming of agriculture and stock keeping, c. 4200 BC, the picture changed dramatically. Hunting and fishing were not discontinued, but food could now be produced at will, comparatively speaking. Forests were cleared to allow for more fields, which could be abandoned when the soil was exhausted. People began to settle together in villages for mutual protection and to share the work of food production, and some traces of their dwellings have been discovered (figure 1.3). From the foundations of these dwellings, c. 3900–3600 BC, at Stengade on Langeland in Denmark, two proposals have been made as to how the stones might have been used (figure 1.4).[4] Both suppose the houses without side walls, the rafters sloping to the ground and covered with some kind of thatching material. In the one case two internal rows of posts set in stones are indicated, while in the other the rafters are shown as set in dry walls of stone.

**2**

1.1 Map of last glaciation. (After Stenberger, *Sweden*, figure 3.)

1.2 Ulkestrup, Zealand. Maglemosian hut foundations. c. 7500–6000 BC. (Knut Andersen et al., "Maglemose hytterne," figure 6, p. 87.)

1.3 Stengade, Langeland. Neolithic house foundations. c. 3900–3600 BC. (Knut Andersen et al., "Maglemose hytterne," figure 6, p. 87. Courtesy Langelands Museum, Rudkøping.)

**3**

**4**

**5**

1.4 Stengade, Langeland. Proposals for reconstruction of Neolithic house by Jørgen Skaarup (left) and Peter Brogaard (right). (Brogaard, Lund, and Nørregård-Nielsen, *Danmarks Arkitektur. Landbrugets huse,* p. 16. Courtesy Gyldendal Publishers.)

1.5 Hjerl Hede, Jutland. Conjectural replica of a Neolithic house.

1.6 Pitkäjärvi, Finland. Neolithic hut. Conjectural drawing of frame. c. 3000 BC. (Helsinki, National Museum of Finland.)

Remains of a more substantial kind of dwelling were found at Troldbjerg, also on Langeland.[5] Here there was a long multifamily house, the roof carried on posts set in stones. The walls were made of wattle, thin withies woven between slender uprights, and daubed with clay. The reconstruction of a Stone Age longhouse at the Hjerl Hede open air museum on Jutland suggests the appearance of such a building (figure 1.5).

The people of these Danish settlements are associated with megalithic burials, to which we shall return. There are, however, other house types from the Neolithic period. At Vrå in Södermanland, foundations of short rectangular buildings, about 12 by 15 feet, have been found from the Funnel Beaker culture, c. 4000 BC. These have stone floors but no trace of hearths, and whether they were used as houses has been questioned.[6]

In Norway a group of three houses was found at Kråkerøy on the east shore of the Oslo Fjord.[7] One was a large rectangular structure with stone foundations and walls of wattle and daub between posts. Two smaller oval houses were also paved with stone, and posts supported the roofs of all three. This site is associated with the Pitted Ware people, c. 3300 BC.

Farther north, Stone Age cultures persisted much longer than in southern Scandinavia, and at Karlebotn on the Varanger Fjord an orderly village of 250 houses was established.[8] These had walls of earth with openings toward the land side, and most had hearths within. From c. 1250 BC, showing the long persistence of this hunting culture by the Varanger Fjord, comes the site of Grasbakken. This was also a village of oval and rectangular houses, many of the latter with two long hearths.[9] The rectangular houses, apparently of a newer type, were half below level, entered by a sloping ramp.

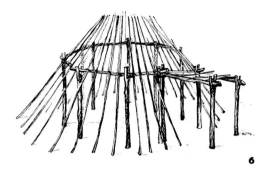

**6**

Other dwellings in Finland were conical tents made with poles leaning against a horizontal frame, then covered with brush, bark, or skins (figure 1.6).[10]

Up to this point we have been concerned with houses for the living. Although the traces are meager and the houses at best very simple, clearly the people who ventured north into the Scandinavian territories in the wake of the glaciers soon found a variety of solutions to their fundamental problems of shelter. But what of houses for the dead? The double row of foundations found at Barkaer on Jutland from c. 3500 BC were long thought to be the remains of row houses, but recent opinion is more in favor of their having been successive burials.[11] This discussion will be confined to the megalithic graves known as dolmens and passage graves that dot the landscape in Denmark and are also found in smaller numbers in southern Sweden. Up to c. 3500 BC the dead had been buried individually in the ground, sometimes in graves lined with stone. These customs, which include the use of grave goods, seem to belong more to the realm of anthropology and will not be elaborated upon here. Dolmens and passage graves are another matter.

**7**

The hundreds of dolmens that are an integral part of the landscape in Denmark and to a lesser extent in Sweden bear witness to the importance of the cult of the dead in this early population. A dolmen is built as if a house for the dead, characteristically consisting of large flat boulders set upright and covered with another block, forming a chamber over the burial itself.[12] This is then surrounded by a curb of boulders and if mounded over with earth would rise to about 6 feet high (figure 1.7). The burial became a memorial and a sacred place for worship and sacrifice. The glaciers had left abundant material, the heavy stones probably being brought to the site and maneuvered into place with the aid of tree-trunk rollers. This type of tomb is found over the large area extending from the Mediterranean lands to the British Isles and was brought to Denmark by migration and trade.

Even more numerous than the round dolmens are the long dolmens, extending in one case to over 500 feet.[13] More frequently they range from 20 to 100 feet and are 6 to 8 feet wide, often including more than one chamber within a rectangular curb (figure 1.8).

From Saxo Grammaticus to the designer of the Danish 50-kroner note, the dolmens have excited awe and admiration. In his *Danesage* of c. 1200 Saxo wrote: "In the far-distant past there lived giants, an ancient people to whose existence the massive roof-stones over dolmens and burial chambers bear ample witness. Should anyone doubt that these are the work of giants, let him say who else could have maneuvered such enormous blocks of stone into position."[14] An interesting revelation, indeed, of the outlook of a learned man whose contemporaries were using heavy masonry for such churches as Ribe and Viborg cathedrals. In post-Renaissance time growing antiquarianism and romantic tastes led to the adaptation of

**8**

JULIANE HOI

9

the dolmen form for a monument at Jaegerspris on Zealand, the Julianehøj of 1775 (figure 1.9), and many representations in drawing and painting by early nineteenth-century artists such as Johann Thomas Lundbye (figure 1.10).

A second great period of megalithic building began c. 3000 BC, when the passage graves were introduced.[15] These are also built of enormous upright stones and capstones, set to form chambers about 15 to 18 feet long, 6 feet wide, and 6 feet high, entered by narrower and lower passages (figure 1.11). Some of these are made double and some have additional chambers. In contrast to dolmens the passage graves were usually completely mounded over, with the entrance on the east or southeast side and upright stones placed before the entrance or even all around the mound. The interiors were intended for multiple and successive burials and

1.7 **St. Elme, Zealand. Dolmen. c. 3500 BC.**

1.8 **Troldkirken, Zealand. Long dolmen. Plan. c. 3500 BC. (After Glob, *Danish Prehistoric Monuments*, figure 17, p. 60.)**

1.9 **Jaegerspris, Zealand. Julianehøj. 1776. Print by Wandel, 1783. (Copenhagen, National Museum.)**

10

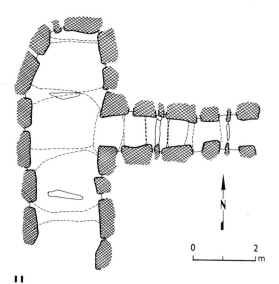

11

1.10  Refsnaes, Zealand.
Painting by J. T. Lund-
bye, 1844. (Copen-
hagen, State Museum
of Art.)

1.11  Raevehøj, Zealand.
Passage grave. c. 3000
BC. Plan. (After Glob,
*Danish Prehistoric
Monuments*, figure 25,
p. 81.)

are even more impressive than the exteriors (figure 1.12). Although much less numerous than the dolmens, only about six hundred being known in Denmark and a little over three hundred in Sweden, the passage graves indicate a further development of the cult of the dead, expressed by massive communal undertakings.

One reason to conclude that the emotional energy of these Neolithic people went into reverence for their immediate ancestors and provision for the dead is the scarcity of other ceremonial sites from this period. It is scarcity, however, not absence, because a small number of "temple" buildings have been identified by their contents of pits and vessels for sacrifice. In one instance the foundations are in a horseshoe arrangement with an opening to the northeast and a pit in the middle (figure 1.13).[16] This has been interpreted as the house of a god or goddess.

The perishability of materials for house construction makes it unlikely that we shall learn to what extent the Neolithic builders attempted refinements of construction or even ornament on their dwellings. The elegant pottery vessels and finely worked tools and weapons that have survived from this period suggest that already these northern people wished to surround themselves with objects that were pleasing to the eye. While the full architectural aesthetic of Stone Age Scandinavia may remain unknown, we can at least observe that the builders of this period had developed several distinctive types of housing and had also been purposeful and skillful enough to construct some of the most impressive mortuary structures of northern Europe.

12

13

1.12  Raevehøj, Zealand. Passage grave. Interior. (Copenhagen, National Museum.)

1.13  Tustrup, Jutland. Ceremonial site. c. 3000 BC. (Højberg, Moesgård Prehistoric Museum.)

## The Bronze Age

The Passage Grave culture did not last. It was overtaken by the Battle Axe people c. 2000 BC, herdsmen who invaded through the Jutland peninsula, with their ultimate origins in Central Asia. Instead of building the megalithic graves just described, they buried their dead in single or mass stone graves. Some of the earliest resembled the dolmens and passage graves in the use of large stones for cists that were then mounded over.

By this time trade with central Europe had already introduced the new materials of copper and bronze into the North, bringing another change in technology and culture as dramatic as that of the introduction of agriculture. Yet while the Bronze Age people of Scandinavia produced tools, weapons, and articles of personal adornment of astonishing brilliance, their structural accomplishments did not, for the most part, equal those of their Neolithic predecessors.

Of dwellings in the Bronze Age little is known. Excavations at Vadgård on the Limfjord in Denmark revealed postholes and stone foundations of several houses.[17] For more enlightenment on houses and settlements we would probably have to consult the evidence from continental Europe of the same period, and then only with caution. Differences in the kinds of timbers available and differences in the kinds of climatic stress to which structures built of them would be subjected could well bring about differences in details of construction, however close the similarities in plan may have been.

For now some note should be made of the most obviously impressive structures of Bronze Age Scandinavia, the large barrows (figure 1.14).[18] As with the dolmens and passage graves, these must have been the work of an organized society. Containing one or more burials, the barrows loom imposingly in the landscape, as they were undoubtedly intended to do. They are found not only in the Scandinavian lands but also in Germany, and taken together they are visible reminders of the extensive north European Bronze Age cultural area. Their survival in such abundance owes much to the careful method of their construction, not random, but of grass turfs built up with internal layers of stone supports. From the oak coffin burials in some of these mounds have come the remarkable garments and accessories that shed so much light on Bronze Age technology and culture.

Another kind of prominent landmark appeared on the coasts of Sweden during the late Bronze Age, the "ship setting" burials (figure 1.15).[19] They were especially popular on the island of Gotland, as might be expected from its seafaring people. The graves are in stone enclosures from 18 to 60 feet long, planned in the outlines of ships. Whether intended for burials or in some cases simply as memorials, they fulfill the latter function admirably, calling attention to the importance of the ship in a visible manner, unlike the later actual ship burials in which the ships were concealed under mounds.

14

15

1.14  Bakkeberg, Zealand.
Bronze Age barrows.
c. 1500–800 BC.

1.15  Boge, Gotland. Ship
setting. c. 1500 BC.
(Stockholm, Antikvar-
isk-topografiska ar-
kivet. Photo: Mårten
Stenberger.)

## The Iron Age

1.16 **Grøntoft, Jutland. Iron Age village. c. 500 BC. Plan. (Becker, "To landsbyer," figure 1, p. 211. Courtesy the author.)**

1.17 **Lejre, Zealand. Iron Age house. Reconstruction.**

If our efforts to understand the dwellings of the Bronze Age are frustrated by the lack of extensive archaeological materials, such is not the case when we come to the Iron Age. This period of thirteen hundred years is usually regarded as having three major divisions, the Celtic, Roman, and Germanic or Migration, according to the peoples who successively dominated continental Europe from c. 500 BC to c. AD 800.

From the early or Celtic period, up to the beginning of the Christian era, the finds of settlements are scanty in Sweden and Norway but are sufficient in Denmark to furnish considerable information about how houses were built and farms and villages organized. At Grøntoft in Jutland a village lasted about three hundred years by moving itself about from time to time. In one stage it consisted of houses 35 to 90 feet long, several with room for up to eighteen cattle, the group enclosed with a palisade (figure 1.16).[20] With the longhouses, including byres, an important farmhouse type was established that was to persist into postmedieval times, being adapted over the years with

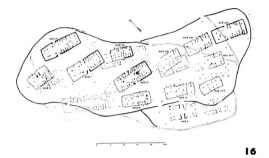

16

17

changes of material and refinements of construction until as late as the seventeenth century. The houses were built on stone foundations, with threshold stones for doors on one side and perhaps some stone paving within. Doors on the south sides would admit a maximum of light. The walls were of turf, as much as 3 feet thick. Two rows of posts, about 3 feet from the walls, supported the roofs, which were probably covered with reeds or heather. Hearths were located on the clay floor toward one end of the houses, with holes in the roofs to let smoke escape. Posts and stone curbs marked stalls for animals in the other portions. Thus people and their animals lived under one roof, sharing each other's warmth and protection (figure 1.17). Foundations of such houses were also found in the extensive excavations at Vallhager on Gotland between 1945 and 1950,[21] and this kind of dwelling was characteristic of northern Germany and the Netherlands as well.[22]

Villages were not characteristic of Iron Age Norway, where the individual farm was more often the rule. When a tract of land had been cleared for grazing and cultivation, often by burning, it was usually enclosed with low stone walls. Houses about 25 to 27 feet wide and from about 65 to as much 300 feet long might accommodate more than one family; they had one or more hearths, no chimneys, and rows of posts supporting the roofs. Such a farm dating from c. 350–500 in the late Roman period was excavated at Ullandhaug near Stavanger in Rogaland in 1967–1969, and here three of the four buildings have been rebuilt.[23] The height of the walls has been estimated from portions remaining after the entire complex was destroyed by fire in the late sixth century. Roofing materials and the interior vertical planking are likewise conjectural. The posts supporting the roofs and the rafters are fashioned and joined in different ways from one building to another, providing a good illustration of the dilemmas involved in attempting reconstructions of this kind. The longest building yielded pottery fragments that suggest that this was the principal dwelling and byre (figure 1.18). Two small buildings, probably for storage, and a long building possibly for guest quarters and additional byre space completed the original group.

Some of the villages appear to have been partly fortified, either against flooding or against marauders. The village remains from c. 100 BC at Borremose in Jutland are notable for the road built across the bog to a slightly elevated site, which has an irregular surrounding ditch and walls (figure 1.19).[24] The road itself is well constructed on a stone foundation, with borders of large stones and paving of small stones, similar to a Roman-period Iron Age road at Ellemose on Zealand (figure 1.20). The houses at Borremose were of the type found at Ullandhaug, oriented east-west, with the dwelling portions in the west ends.

**1.18 Ullandhaug, Rogaland. Iron Age house. c. 350–550. Reconstruction.**

**1.19 Borremose, Jutland. Iron Age village. c. 100 BC. (Copenhagen, National Museum.)**

A later and much more strongly fortified
site is at Ismantorp on Öland, dating probably
from the Swedish Migration period in the fifth
century (figure 1.21).[25] Measuring about 350
feet in diameter, it has limestone walls rising as
high as 15 feet. More than eighty rectangular
foundations have been discovered, arranged radially and divided into four quarters by streets
like the spokes of a wheel. Little evidence of
prolonged habitation has been found here, and,
like certain Viking sites to come, Ismantorp
may have been intended to be more defensive
than residential.

A third group of buildings shows still another approach, this time in a Norwegian village at Varhaug in Rogaland, c. 100 (figure
1.22).[26] Of a type apparently unique to this
area, this consists of about twenty longhouses,
radially arranged but here around the perime-
ter of the site with a central open space. Lack
of provision for cattle suggests that, like Ismantorp, its purpose was probably defensive. Several of these camps, if they may be so
designated, are known in Rogaland and northern Norway and may have been established to
protect the lively trade routes to Denmark and
the Continent. We might be reminded of the
Neolithic Tripolye villages such as Kolomys-
czine in Russia and the medieval Wendish villages such as Satemin in Germany.[27]

20

1.20   Ellemose, Zealand.
       Iron Age road. c. 200
       BC.

1.21   Ismantorp, Öland. Iron
       Age village. 5th cen-
       tury. Plan. (After Sten-
       berger, "Öland," p.
       236.)

1.22   Varhaug, Rogaland.
       Iron Age village. c. 100.
       (Stavanger, Archaeo-
       logical Museum.)

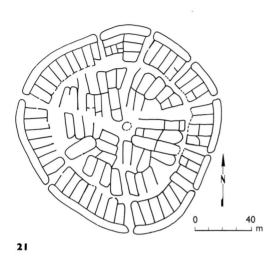

**21**

**22**

## The Viking Age

1.23 **Jarlshof, Shetland. Viking house foundations. 9th century.**

1.24 **Jarlshof, Shetland. Viking settlement. Conjectural drawing. (Hamilton, *Jarlshof*, figure 51. British Crown Copyright, Department of the Environment.)**

The last two centuries of the first millennium of the Christian era were ones of profound change for inhabitants of the Scandinavian territories. While still not yet writing their own history, and therefore technically prehistoric, these people made such an impact in so many directions that their exploits were recorded by their history-writing contemporaries, especially in France, Germany, and England.[28]

The famous remark in the *Anglo-Saxon Chronicle,* referring to one of the earliest Viking episodes, that "the harrying of the heathen miserably destroyed God's church in Lindisfarne by rapine and slaughter," surely reflects the sentiments of many victims of Viking raids. Yet piracy was not all. Search for new agricultural lands and extensive peaceful commerce led to the growth of strong trading centers and settlements far from home. From the remains of both much can be learned about the houses and towns from which the Vikings came.

Remains of dwellings have been found in several places where the Vikings settled as they pushed their activities westward. One of the best known early settlement sites is at Jarlshof

**23**

**24**

on the main Shetland island, which had already been inhabited since the late Stone Age. For the Vikings, arriving from Norway probably c. 800, the natural harbor and adjacent fields made it as attractive as it had been to their Bronze and Iron Age predecessors.[29] Unlike the latter, however, their first dwelling, while certainly comparatively long (extending to 70 feet), had no byre but consisted simply of a long living room and short kitchen (figure 1.23). The walls were slightly curved, with the house 18 feet wide toward the middle and 12 feet wide at the ends.

The method of walling would be used much later: inner and outer layers of stone with an earth core. Whatever the advantages of the site may have been, no one who has experienced a gale at Jarlshof will wonder why the north wall was made especially secure with alternate courses of stone and turf. The roof was supported by two rows of posts, set about 2 feet from the walls. Together with buildings that have been interpreted as a bathhouse, or possibly a family shrine, a smithy, a byre, and another small building with a hearth, the main dwelling made up the first farmstead at Jarlshof (figure 1.24).

Two hundred miles to the north and west of the Shetlands the Faroe Islands rise, shrouded in rain and fog, where thousand-foot cliffs plunge from treeless slopes and the sheep, for whom the islands are named, outnumber the humans. Many problems arise in the interpretation of the early Icelandic histories of the Faroes, but it seems clear that Irish hermits were taking up their lonely abode there c. 700, to be followed by Viking settlers c. 860.[30] One of their dwellings was found at Kvívík on Streymoy, the largest island, in 1942 (figure 1.25). Several others have been excavated, revealing houses similar to that at Jarlshof, with thick stone and turf or gravel walls, the walls slightly

curved, and stone-lined hearths in the centers. Here also wood was used to line the interiors. The climate of Iceland was enough warmer then to allow for the growth of some birch and willow, and perhaps this was then possible on the Faroes as well. Otherwise timber for the interior posts and paneling would have to be imported or salvaged from driftwood. As at Jarlshof, the byre at Kvívík was a separate structure.

Nearly three hundred miles northwest of the Faroes is Iceland, where Ingólfur Arnarson from Norway was the first to settle, at Reykjavík in 874.[31] By the late ninth century settlement had begun in the Thjórsárdalur valley of southern Iceland, which had developed to a substantial settlement a century later. The disastrous eruption of Mount Hekla in 1104 left about twenty houses covered with ash. Modern excavations have made possible not only a clear

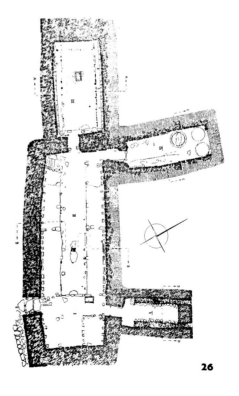

25

1.25 Kvívík, Streymoy.
Viking house
foundations.

1.26 Stöng, Iceland. House.
9th century. Plan.
(Stenberger, ed., *Forn-
tida gårdar,* figure 37,
p. 78. Courtesy Munks-
gaard Publishers.)

1.27 Stöng, Iceland. House
reconstruction. (Reyk-
javik, National Mu-
seum. Photo: Gísli
Gestsson.)

27

idea of how the Vikings built their houses in Iceland but also some clarification of houses described in the later sagas. The house at Stöng is one of the best examples (figure 1.26). Thanks to the studies of Hörthur Ágústsson, a reconstruction based on certain principles of the later Icelandic turf houses was undertaken near the excavations (figure 1.27). The original building differed somewhat from the Viking house at Jarlshof. The walls were over 4 feet thick, built of turfs laid on a stone foundation. The principal room was a long hall, running approximately east-west, entered near the southeast corner. The walls were lined with wood paneling, and there was a long hearth in the center. At the west end there was a smaller chamber with central hearth, while on the north there were two narrow projecting rooms, one evidently a dairy and the other variously identified as a bathhouse or a household shrine. Separate byre, storage, and smithy buildings completed the farmstead group.

**1.28 L'Anse aux Meadows, Newfoundland. House reconstruction.**

Then by the beginning of the eleventh century the Vikings had carried their attempts at settlements to their westernmost limits. Erik the Red's famous arrival in Greenland in 982 led to the establishment of farms and churches in the Eastern and Western Settlements.[32] The houses were similar to those in Iceland, long halls built of stone and turf, sometimes with interior paneling. In response to the climate they later became more complicated, multiroomed to be compact and give easy indoor access from one part to another. As at Stöng, the byre might be separate and thickly insulated with turf. The storehouses, on the other hand, were built of dry stone walling for ventilation, much like the cliets of the Scottish islands today.

From Greenland, partly by accident, the Vikings made their way to the shore of North America. The first examination in 1960 of low mounds of earth on a terrace at L'Anse aux Meadows off L'Épaves Bay in Newfoundland suggested a Viking settlement there.[33] Helge and Anne Stine Ingstad soon found structural remains and artifacts that are now generally accepted as evidence of a Viking occupation. Subsequent excavations from 1973 to 1976 confirmed these findings, up to now the only reliable evidence for Viking settlement in North America.

Three dwellings of Norse turf-walled construction had been built in a curving line now well back from the shore. Each consisted of a long hall with central hearth and one or more small rooms attached. A reconstruction has been attempted nearby (figure 1.28). Evidence for interior posts and paneling in the original buildings is, however, lacking, and it has been suggested that these were temporary shelters.[34] Five other small structures were found, one of which was a smithy, the sure evidence that this was not an Eskimo settlement. Bog iron may still be found in the marsh here. Even a brief encounter with the bleak landscape shows that promise for long-term forage and agriculture was limited. Although the climate was probably milder then, the lines back to the homelands were long and the natives increasingly unfriendly; the project was soon abandoned. It would be just over six hundred years before Scandinavian settlers attempted once more to build in North America.

By the time of the settlement at L'Anse aux Meadows, the first Christian church had been built at Brattalid, Erik the Red's settlement in Greenland. No such structures have been found in Newfoundland, and we can only speculate whether the new faith was carried that far. This brings us, however, to another important aspect of the Viking period, that of the gradual appearance of Christianity. Since the remains of early churches in Greenland come from the later or medieval period of settlement, these will be considered with the

early Christian churches of the homelands.

We may also note that while these first settlements in Greenland were the result of organized expeditions, buildings specifically for public assembly were not erected. The Thing, the assembly for consultation and settlement of disputes, met on open ground first at Brattalid and then at Gardar after the first bishopric was established there in 1126. For festive social occasions, however, the long halls of the wealthier farmsteads could accommodate large crowds of people, as the later sagas so eloquently attest.

Another kind of Viking building was the hut built over a sunken floor, such as those at Lindholm Høje in Jutland.[35] These were 9 to 15 feet long and had posts in the middle of each short end to support the ridge poles. Here there were no walls, the roofs sloping directly to the ground. This sunken dwelling, or *Grubenhaus,* was common on the Continent, in England, and in the Nordic countries. Different

patterns of postholes in the excavated remains of these buildings indicate more than one possibility for superstructures, which is a matter for some debate.[36] The presence of spindle whorls and loom weights in the Lindholm Høje hut indicates that this was a weaver's hut. In other places such huts were for potteries, smithies, bakehouses, and the like, usually in connection with a larger rectangular dwelling.

A structure apparently unique to Lindholm Høje was a nearly square courtyard house, similar at least in plan to the type of farmstead that was to become popular in southern Scandinavia in later years. The use of the several parts remains unknown. It is tempting to think that it was built not so much as a farmstead but as a "villa," possibly in imitation of one that its owner had seen in England or on the Continent.

The dwellings grouped into various kinds of settlements in the Bronze and Iron Ages were built by members of a primarily agricultural society. When the trading enterprises already in operation in these years blossomed into the vigorous and far-flung commercial ventures of the Vikings, more extensive merchant towns accordingly developed.[37] One of the largest about which it has been possible to learn a considerable amount was Hedeby, or Haithabu, on an inlet of the Schlei Fjord, near the modern town of Schleswig.[38] A fort had been built to the north, but the town was also defended by a semicircular rampart enclosing about sixty acres. Fresh water was obtainable from a brook running through the enclosure.

A number of houses have been found in the excavations of the center of the town, some fairly large, about 18 to 45 feet, placed with the gable ends toward the street. Some were walled with wattle and daub, others with halved tree trunks set upright in palisade fashion. Most had central hearths and probably

thatched roofs. Some later smaller houses were hardly more than huts, 10 to 12 feet wide and 12 to 15 feet long, the floors sunken, walling of wattle and daub, and hearths in the corners. Some of the finds included evidence of production of bronze, iron, cloth, and other goods, and a conjectural restoration shows a busy port (figure 1.29).

The trading house types survived into modern times, the rows of gables being a familiar sight in Netherlandish, German, and Danish port cities today. The little houses with corner fireplaces were prophetic of the "Swedish house" type that was transported to America with the early Swedish settlers. Jasper Danckaerts, the Dutch traveler and diarist, described Swedish houses in New Jersey in 1679, saying that "the chimney stands in the corner."[39] The persistence of this arrangement in America is attested by the report of the Swedish scientist Peter Kalm, who saw Swedish houses with the fireplaces "built in one corner" in his travels in America in 1748–1751.[40] This is an especially forceful example of the strength of vernacular tradition over hundreds of years and through profound cultural and political changes.

While Hedeby was a home base town for the Vikings, other urban sites have been discovered farther afield. Some of these have been more difficult to interpret, since, unlike Hedeby, they lie below modern cities. To the east, Viking remains in such places as Staraja Ladoga and Novgorod have aroused much speculation and considerable controversy as to whether some Russian cities had actually been founded as Viking towns.[41] Stronger evidence of Viking urban settlement abroad has come from some western sites, particularly Dublin and York, where excavations over the last twenty years have revealed much of the life of these towns.

The Vikings began raids on Ireland at the end of the eighth century and appear to have made two settlements at what is now Dublin, one in 841 and a second c. 914–917.[42] Excavations in 1962–1963 and again in 1967–1980 yielded an enormous quantity of artifacts, showing the vigor of the town until the early twelfth century.[43] As at Hedeby, many of the houses found proved to be those of woodworkers, metalsmiths, leatherworkers, and the like. The larger ones, about 6 by 10 meters, had walls of wattle and daub, with four internal posts to support the roof, benches on either side, and a stone-lined hearth in the center. There were also some smaller, nearly square buildings, storage pits, and one small sunken building, walled with vertical planks.

Similar excavations at Coppergate in York from 1976 to 1981 revealed not only the Viking but the Roman, Anglo-Saxon, and Norman predecessors of the modern city as well.[44] From their seizure of York in 866 through development in the tenth century until the departure of Erik Bloodaxe in 954, the Vikings plied their trades, crafts, and industries much as they were also doing at Hedeby and Dublin. A distinctive, though not unique, feature of York's history was the establishing of tenement boundaries, marked by wattled fences. In the early tenth century the buildings that housed the various workshops were walled with wattle, but late in the century some of these were rebuilt with sunken floors and walling of horizontal oak planks.[45] It is apparent that the sunken floor type of small building was in use in the trading towns as it already was in the more agricultural villages in northern Europe. Certainly these buildings were traditional in England.[46]

Again a comparison can be made to similar constructions in more recent times. In 1650 Cornelius van Tienhoven wrote that the Dutch settlers in New Amsterdam "dig a square pit in the ground, cellar fashion, six or seven feet

**29**

**30**

**1.29  Hedeby, Schleswig. Viking settlement. 9th century. Conjectural drawing. (Århus, Flemming Bau.)**

**1.30  Trelleborg, Zealand. Viking camp. 10th century. (Copenhagen, National Museum.)**

deep, as long and as broad as they think proper; case the earth all round the wall with timber, with the bark of trees or something else to prevent the caving in of the earth; floor this cellar with plank, and wainscot it overhead for a ceiling; raise a roof of spars clear up, and cover the spars with bark or green sod."[47]

The most spectacular and enigmatic kind of construction remaining from the Viking Age is the "fortified camp." Whether built to house troops in readiness for raids, as has long been thought, or to consolidate the power of Harald Blue-Tooth, as is more recently held, each camp that remains is a striking feature in the landscape (figure 1.30).[48] Four are known, one of them, Nonnebakken, now overgrown by the city of Odense on Funen. The other three, Aggersborg and Fyrkat in Jutland and Trelleborg on Zealand, share several characteristics of plan, though they are not all the same size. Each consists of a circular rampart enclosing groups of boat-shaped buildings arranged in squares. The camps are divided approximately north-south and east-west by "streets" paved with timber, leading to four gates. Trelleborg has been recently dated to 980–981 and Fyrkat close to 976.[49] They were laid out geometrically, with evidently some precise knowledge of surveying.

The buildings, which may have been barracks, are long structures with curved walls, comprising a central hall with hearth and a smaller room at each end. A reconstruction attempted at Trelleborg in 1942 has been shown to be faulty, with the exterior postholes now interpreted as evidence for buttresses rather than an exterior gallery.[50] The walls were of vertical planks and the roof of trussed rafters, supported by the buttresses, making these houses similar to the other medieval hall types in northern Europe.

What is provocative about these "barrack" buildings is the regularity of their construction and placement. Harald Blue-Tooth has been described as having a sweeping vision for his reign and the energy to realize much of it.[51] Had he found what today would be called a military engineer who knew something of the precepts of Vitruvius and Vegetius, whose writings were known and used in the early Middle Ages?[52] These Viking sites are distinctive, and perhaps they represent a conflation, so to speak, of the Vitruvian town plan, recommended to be round, and the Vegetian army camp, which could also be round.[53] At Fyrkat the buildings have been discovered to have housed workshops and storehouses as well as dwellings, suggesting other than purely military use. The precision, however, suggests a trained theoretician.

Finally, although much is known about the Viking pantheon, little is known of actual places of worship. Structural evidence for one aspect of Viking belief is, however, abundant. From the Norwegian ship burials have come the dramatic finds of the vessels themselves. These were not meant to be seen except as mounds, as in earlier times. In Denmark, on the other hand, ship settings were again built, from single examples such as the one at Glavendrup on Funen to the great cemetery at Lindholm Høje (figures 1.31 and 1.32). Whether they were erected in conscious imitation of the Bronze Age monuments on the coasts of Sweden in order to invest their builders with the authority of tradition or simply to display the vital importance of the ship we shall probably never know. To the modern viewer they are strong reminders of the vigorous people within whose ranks rose those who led the Scandinavians into the beginning of their historical period.

31

1.31  Glavendrup, Funen. Ship setting. 9th century.

1.32  Lindholm Høje, Jutland. Ship settings. 9th century.

32

# 2  *The Middle Ages*

## *The Romanesque Period, c. 1050–1250*

From the raid on Lindisfarne in 793 to the battles of Stamford Bridge and Hastings in 1066, the Norsemen spread their adventures to western Europe and across the Atlantic, leaving buildings in those places where they were able to settle. These first attempts led to permanent settlement in Iceland, whereas in Greenland the Norse colonies were abandoned by the end of the fifteenth century. We have seen how short-lived was the little outpost in Newfoundland. But during the Viking Age the Scandinavian countries were being invaded in their turn by Christian missionaries. These determined churchmen gradually won converts, and as the national states of Denmark, Sweden, and Norway were beginning to form, the Church became established as well.

None of this took place overnight. In 827, early in the Viking period, St. Ansgar of Bremen founded churches in the commercial towns of Hedeby, Ribe, and Birka. No traces of Christian structures remain from this time, but a significant beginning had been made. More than a century elapsed, however, before dioceses were established at Hedeby, Ribe, and Århus in

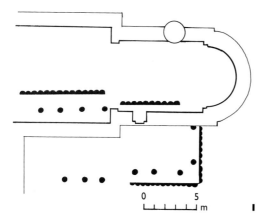

```
0        5
└┴┴┴┴┘ m
```

948, under the Archbishop of Bremen. The baptism of King Harald Blue-Tooth at Jelling, c. 965, brought the secular authority in Denmark into the Christian orbit, as the proud boast on the Jelling Stone asserts that Harald "made the Danes Christian." King Olav Slöt-kuning of Sweden was baptized at Uppsala in 1000, the year in which Iceland allowed Christianity to be adopted along with the worship of the pagan gods. Shortly thereafter another Christian king of Denmark, Knud the Great, became king of England in 1014. The wheel had come full circle. In the late eleventh century the Church was established in Norway under King Olav Kyrre, with dioceses at Bergen, Oslo, and Trondheim, also under the Archbishop of Bremen. Yet it was not until the middle of the twelfth century that the Swedes took the Church to the Finns, nor did the Church become dominant in Iceland until that republic came under the Norwegian King Håkon IV in 1262–1264. By the end of the eleventh century the ecclesiastical system of sees and parishes was in place in Denmark, Sweden, and Norway, resulting in the system of tithes and the obligation of the parishes to build churches.[1]

As a result of these conversions the northern countries put on a "robe of churches" like that which cloaked continental Europe after the year 1000, but the northern robe was at first probably more brown with wood than white with stone. From the hundreds of churches that remain from the Romanesque period, only a modest number can be presented here to illustrate the variety possible among the parish churches of wood, stone, or brick, the larger town churches, the abbeys, and the centralized churches. The early eleventh century began a period of intense building activity in the smaller towns, and by the late twelfth century more ambitious programs were being undertaken in the larger towns and cities.

In the preceding chapter it was shown that, largely as the result of excavation, a considerable amount has been learned about housing in the Scandinavian countries in the pre-Christian eras. In spite of the literary traditions concerning the Nordic gods, however, little is known of buildings for worship in pagan times. The new faith brought a new building need. The first chapels built by the missionaries have disappeared, but were probably single cells, furnished with simple altars. The next step would be to differentiate the nave, or place of assembly, from a smaller chancel, or sanctuary, containing the altar, following the axial arrangement characteristic of western European church planning. The remains of S. Maria Minor in Lund show this type of plan, with walls of vertical halved logs and inner rows of posts around nave and chancel (figure 2.1).[2] Built c. 1000–1020, this little church is one of the earliest examples of one kind of "stave" church construction, the uprights set directly into the ground palisade fashion, the posts carrying the roof. The little church from Holtålen in Trøndelag, built in the twelfth century (now in the museum at Sverresborg,

**2**

2.1   Lund. S. Maria Minor. c.
      1000–1020. Plan. (After
      Ekhoff, *Svenska stav-*
      *kyrkor,* figure 123, p. 150.)

2.2   Holtålen, Trøndelag.
      Church. c. 1050. (Now in
      museum at Sverresberg,
      Trondheim.)

2.3   Hemse, Gotland.
      Church. c. 1100. Conjec-
      tural drawing. (Ekhoff,
      *Svenska stavkyrkor,*
      figure 103, p. 125.)

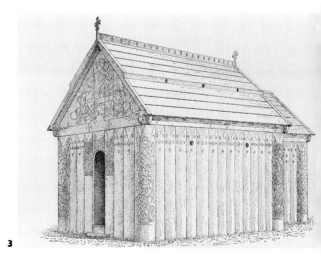

**3**

**4**

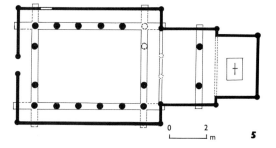

**5**

2.4 **Urnes, Sogn. Church.
1125–1140. Drawing by
J. C. Dahl, 1844. (Oslo,
Riksantikvaren.)**

2.5 **Urnes, Sogn. Church.
Plan. (After Ekhoff,
*Svenska stavkyrkor*,
figure 7, p. 50.)**

2.6 **Gol, Hallingdal. Church.
Early 13th century.
(Now in Norwegian Folk
Museum at Bygdøy,
Oslo.)**

**7**

The church at Urnes in Sogn is considered to be one of the earliest remaining of this kind (figures 2.4 and 2.5).[7] The present building, c. 1130, appears to be the third on the site. It is a small structure, about 28 by 21 feet, resting modestly at the foot of a sheltering hill. The basis for its construction is a "raft" of four timbers, two lengthwise and two crosswise, laid on a bed of stones and crossed with their ends projecting about 4 1/2 feet from the points of crossing. The major upright posts or staves, sometimes called "masts," are tenoned into this raft and joined at the top with horizontal plates. Cross and quadrant braces are used to strengthen the posts. The roof is constructed of rafters and purlins, strengthened by scissors braces and collar beams. Sills for the outer walls are fitted into the projecting ends of the raft to form the basis for an ambulatory. The walls are of vertical planks set into the sills, with a pent roof abutting lower beams between the posts. A short clerestory wall rises above this roof, and the whole assemblage results in the familiar stepped pyramidal appearance of the stave or "mast" church.[8]

To this formula could be added surrounding open porches and turrets or belfries. Two of the grander examples date from the years 1200–1250. The church at Gol was moved from its original location in Hallingdal to King Oscar II's collection of Norwegian antiquities at Bygdøy near Oslo in 1884.[9] It is now a major attraction of the Norwegian Folk Museum (figure 2.6). The Borgund church remains in its original location in Sogn (figures 2.7 and 2.8).[10] Without artificial illumination these churches are dark, having only the smallest of clerestory and chancel openings. The naves rise cavelike, and the orientation remains toward the altars. The few that are left demonstrate the soundness of well-seasoned timber and the ingenuity of the system with which they were built.

Trondheim), has heavy posts set on a sill at the corners of the nave and chancel, with the planks of the palisade wall also grooved into the sill. The sill rests on a stone foundation, which helped to protect the timbers from rot and hence gave the church a better chance for survival (figure 2.2).[3] Fragments from the church at Hemse, Gotland (now in the Historical Museum, Stockholm), show how such timbers might be carved with patterns carried over from Viking times (figure 2.3).[4]

Most of the more than seven hundred wooden churches built in Norway in this period are now gone, about thirty remaining. They were mostly of the type just described, as were the wooden churches of Romanesque Denmark and Sweden.[5] Another kind is the "mast" type of stave church. This is a particularly interesting phenomenon in Norwegian architecture, the significance of which has been a subject of controversy for nearly a century.[6]

**2.7** Borgund, Sogn. Church. Early 13th century. Interior. (Oslo, Riksantikvaren.)

**2.8** Borgund, Sogn. Church. Plan. (After Dietrichson, *Norske stavkirker,* figure 2, p. 8.)

**2.9** Råsted, Jutland. Church. Early 12th century.

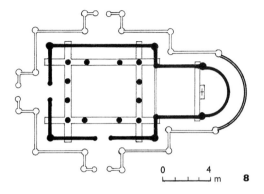

0    4
m    **8**

9

10

Probably more would have survived had they not been razed to make way for larger buildings.

After 1814 a wave of enthusiasm for Norway's cultural heritage arose, otherwise the stave churches remaining then might not have survived at all. Our knowledge of them would have been limited to representations in painting or other arts, which would have been enigmatic at best. Much of the credit belongs to the painter Johan Christian Dahl (1788–1857), who in addition to painting the Norwegian landscape took great interest in the preservation of Norwegian architecture. In order to save the stave church at Vang in Valdres, Dahl

**2.10  Råsted, Jutland.**
**Church. Interior.**

**2.11  Volsted, Jutland.**
**Church. 12th century.**

persuaded King Friedrich Wilhelm IV of Prussia to buy it, and it was dismantled and reconstructed at Bruckenberg in Silesia (now Biertonice in Poland) in 1842–1844.[11] In 1836 Dahl had written an essay on the wooden architecture of Norway, and the widespread interest now being aroused led to the founding of the Society for the Preservation of Ancient Monuments in Norway in 1844. Dahl's view of Urnes has been chosen to illustrate this church as it was in the 1840s.

Since the "mast" type of stave church is so different from the more familiar nave and chancel type that is found also in stone and brick, questions have arisen as to the origins of their design. Opinions range from Lorenz Dietrichson's theory that they are conversions from stone Romanesque basilicas to Kristian Bjerknes's theory that they perpetuated a now-vanished type of pagan temple, and the matter is not yet resolved.[12]

As for ornament for embellishment or didactic purposes, a few fine examples of carved portals have survived from the stave churches, some now in museum collections. Those now seen at Urnes were saved from the previous building and incorporated in the present church. These are of the so-called "Urnes" style, the last of the great Viking ornamental styles. The mingling of pagan and Christian motifs on these portals shows that the adoption of Christianity in the North was by no means immediate and automatic and that the incoming clergy were wise enough to respect and make use of local traditions.

In Denmark and Sweden the church builders turned soon to stone and in the twelfth century to brick. Perhaps the earliest stone church in these countries was that built by King Svend Estridsen at Roskilde on Zealand, c. 1030.[13] Extant foundations indicate that it was a simple nave and chancel structure. It was built of calcareous tufa, which is abundant on Zealand and widely used for these early stone churches in Denmark. Seventeen to eighteen hundred had been built in Denmark alone by c. 1250, many of which still exist, mostly in the smaller communities.

One notable example in Denmark is the little church at Råsted on Jutland, which still has much of its original character. It was probably built sometime before 1150 as a simple nave and chancel church of limestone, to which the south porch and west tower were added in the Gothic period (figure 2.9).[14] The entrance to the parish church in Denmark and Sweden was normally on the south side, for this side got the most sun and shelter from the wind. The porch gave additional protection by keeping the wind, rain, and snow from entering the nave directly. It is called the *våbenhus* or "weapon-house" in Denmark, because weapons were to be left here before their owners entered the church. If a second door was added, it would be on the north side, since the women sat on the north and the men on the south. The tower was a landmark in the countryside and could serve as a watchtower and a stronghold for church or town valuables.

At Råsted the nave and chancel are still covered with flat wooden ceilings, as were so many of the Romanesque parish churches originally. On the east wall of the nave, the arched entrance to the chancel, and the chancel walls there has survived one of the finest remaining cycles of Romanesque wall paintings (figure 2.10).[15] Such paintings, as we shall see, flourished in Denmark, Sweden, and Finland for nearly five hundred years, giving a colorful *Biblia Pauperum* painted *al secco* with mineral pigments.

We have already noted the carvings on the Norwegian stave churches, with their combination of pagan and Christian symbolism. The portals of stone churches might also receive such carvings, usually in granite. A particularly vigorous tradition developed on the Jutland peninsula, where some of the individual carvers can be identified. One of these was Master Goti, who did the portals for the church at Volsted, built early in the twelfth century (figure 2.11).[16] This is another typical small parish church, set apart from the center of the village in a walled churchyard. Until 1873 the carvings were on the original south portal. Then the *våbenhus* was built and the carvings moved to it (figure 2.12). These are in the typical low relief, depicting an episode from the Creation cycle and here an unusual portrayal of a bishop. Volsted is a simple nave and chancel church, the nave covered still with a timber roof and the chancel now covered with a Gothic half-vault. A similar parish church in Sweden is Botkyrka in Södermanland (figure 2.13).[17]

Although wood predominated for early churches in Norway, some parish churches there were built of stone. The church at Tingelstad in Hadeland as now restored may resemble the first little stone church at Roskilde (figure 2.14).[18] Here is a simple stone building, with nave and rectangular chancel, round-headed doors and windows, covered with a steep wooden roof, which is crowned by an octagonal turret. The east gable is filled with masonry, the west gable with timber.

From this detail of the church at Tingelstad we may turn to a brief mention of the early medieval churches of Iceland and Greenland. Settlement of both places was primarily by the Norse, and it is thought that the earliest churches built in Iceland were probably of wood, similar to the nave and chancel type of stave church.[19] These have disappeared, and the wooden churches and very few turf churches that we see today were built much later. Then in Greenland in the late Viking period Erik the

12

2.12   **Volsted, Jutland.**
    **Church. Portal.**

2.13   **Botkyrka, Söderman-**
    **land. Church. 1176.**

2.14   **Tingelstad, Hadeland.**
    **Church. c. 1100. (Oslo,**
    **Riksantikvaren.)**

**13**

Red's wife Thjodhilde became converted to Christianity and built a little church near the farmstead at Brattalid.[20] No trace of this remains, but traces of several parish churches have been found in the Eastern and Western Settlements. By c. 1100 Christianity was more firmly established in Greenland, the first bishop being appointed in 1126. His residence was fixed at Gardar, where the house and the outbuildings of a major estate were built, including a large festival hall.[21] The cathedral church was more elaborate than the parish churches, having north and south chapels. Like other Norse churches in Greenland, it had a timbered west gable. Most of the parish churches that spread over these territories in the twelfth century were, like their contemporaries in Iceland,

**14**

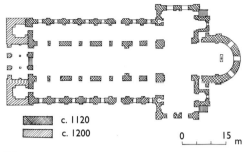

c. 1120
c. 1200

0     15
       m

**17**

**15**

**16**

2.15   Tveje Merløse, Zealand. Church. c. 1125.

2.16   Lund. Cathedral. Early
12th century. East end.
(Copenhagen, National
Museum.)

2.17   Lund. Cathedral. Plan.
(After Anker and
Aron Andersson, *Art
of Scandinavia,* volume
2, figure 13, p. 38.)

hardly more than private chapels by individual farms.

The more ambitious cathedral at Gardar was characteristic of the trend to more splendid churches as the bishops and their royal and noble patrons reinforced their claims and strengthened the position of the Church in the Nordic lands. By the last quarter of the eleventh century Bishop Svend Normand saw King Svend Estridsen's little church at Roskilde as inadequate and on its foundations built a larger three-aisled church of limestone, which is thought to have had western towers, a transept, choir, and perhaps apses.[22] It probably looked very much like the present church at Tveje Merløse, begun c. 1125, which is about 30 kilometers west of Roskilde on the main road to the medieval town of Kalundborg (figure 2.15).[23] Across the Sound in Skåne a new bishopric had been founded at Lund by King Svend Estridsen, who died in 1074, and under one of his sons, King Knud the Holy, a small cathedral was built in the 1080s.[24] It consisted of nave and aisles, transept, choir, and apse, with its remains now forming the crypt of the present building.

Then in 1104 King Erik Ejegod was able to get Lund elevated to an archbishopric, which was intended to serve all of Scandinavia. Although by this event the Church in the Nordic countries was no longer under direct German control, the artistic ties between Denmark and Germany remained strong throughout the Middle Ages and indeed beyond. We shall see that in Norway, on the other hand, strong artistic impulses came from England.

To celebrate the new status of Lund a great cathedral was begun, for which the consecration of the several altars was not completed until 1145 (figures 2.16 and 2.17).[25] An entry in the cathedral death rolls for the period between 1130 and 1140 refers to "Donatus architectus, magister operis hujus obiit," and it is thought that he was an Italian, possibly brought to Lund via Speyer. The original plan of the cathedral consisted of a four-bay nave, separated from the aisles by an alternating system of piers, a transept with projecting chapels and stair towers, choir, and apse, the east end of the building corresponding in part to the predecessor over which it was built. The western tower complex was not part of the original conception but was added under Archbishop Absalon early in the thirteenth century. The aisles were groin-vaulted from the beginning, but the nave had a wooden roof to start, as did probably the transept, and the choir and apse were vaulted. The present vaults were first built over the nave after a fire in 1234 and were rebuilt during restorations in the nineteenth century. So much restoration has been done, in fact, that little of the original surface of the stone is visible.

The exterior of the east end of Lund is justly famous, for apparently here the rich Rheno-Lombardic vocabulary of ornament was introduced into Scandinavia. As extensively restored in the nineteenth century, it has a massive base with round-headed windows opening into the crypt, a story of blind arcades with double arches rising from consoles, a second story of alternating blind panels and round-headed windows, framed by applied colonnettes carrying arches, and a shorter third story of a blind gallery formed by a dwarf arcade. A strong Italian-derived spirit is evident in the portals, with their series of recessed columns and in part classically derived carvings.[26]

Such a magnificent project, unprecedented and the prime ecclesiastical building in Scandinavia until the establishment of an archbishopric in Trondheim in 1152, could hardly fail to have its imitators. The Rheno-Lombardic systems involving applied colonnettes or pilasters, arched

18

corbel tables, blind galleries, and the interplay
of these elements applied in contrasting scales
are to be found on many succeeding Romanesque parish churches. One notable example is
the church at Vä in Skåne, begun c. 1140, perhaps under royal patronage, and taken over as a
Premonstratensian abbey c. 1160 (figure
2.18).[27] It was begun with a flat east end, but
this was changed to a semicircular apse, finished
with an arched corbel table and pilaster strips
separating the window bays. By 1160 the apse
and chancel had been vaulted, and the fine Romanesque paintings on these vaults have
survived.

For the western Danish diocese a new cathedral was begun at Ribe on Jutland c. 1130
(figures 2.19 and 2.20).[28] As planned originally
it consisted of nave, aisles, transept, and apse.
There is no choir, and the transept chapels of
Lund are reduced to niches in the east walls.
The brick northwest tower was added c. 1250
and rebuilt c. 1620, while the aisles are Gothic
and were probably added early in the fifteenth
century. The southeast, or Maria, tower was
rebuilt in 1896. The Jørgen Roed painting
shows how the building once loomed up in the
now crowded town. It also shows it in a different stage of color, with the Rheno-Lombardic

19

2.18 Vä, Skåne. Church. Begun c. 1140.

2.19 Ribe, Jutland. Cathedral. Begun c. 1130.
Painting by J. Roed,
1836. (Copenhagen,
State Museum of Art.)

2.20 Ribe, Jutland. Cathedral. Interior. Painting
by J. Roed, 1836. (Co-
penhagen, State Mu-
seum of Art.)

20

arcading emphasized by white-washing of the flat walls behind. Today the brown-gray stone is seen throughout the exterior, contrasting with the brick additions.

Roed's painting of the interior (actually a study for a painting now in the Hirschsprung Collection, Copenhagen) shows the triforium above the aisles, which was omitted at Lund. The German-inspired domed-up vaults, added after a fire in 1242, were then white-washed, and Roed was evidently fascinated by the effects of light upon them. Today more patterns have been painted on the transverse arches and ribs. The pulpit of 1597 has been moved from its more central location on the north side of the nave to a position nearer the transept on the south. The altarpiece of 1597 seen in Roed's painting has been removed to make way for the tabernacle and altar installed during restorations in 1884–1904. While there is abundant documentation and some visual evidence for the changes that these Romanesque buildings have undergone, these paintings give us an especially effective set of exterior and interior views by an artist who saw the building over one hundred fifty years ago.

In the early large Norwegian stone churches, we can see some of the same German-derived features as those of the Danish churches just described, and also some more clearly coming from England. St. Mary's Church in Bergen, begun c. 1130, is still much as it was originally built (figures 2.21 and 2.22).[29] Bergen was one of Norway's first cathedral cities, and in the twelfth century it was in effect the capital of Norway. The cathedral church in the center of town is Christ Church, also begun in the twelfth century, and St. Mary's appears to have been built to serve the community around the castle at the mouth of the bay. It is a basilical church, with two towers rising on the west, the west door opening into the first bay of the

nave. The nave and aisles are separated by cruciform piers, and there is a bifora motif in the triforium that recalls the trifora of Ribe. Also as at Ribe, there is a shallow apse within the wall at the end of the north aisle. The church is vaulted throughout, with groin vaults over the nave. These may have been constructed after a fire in 1198, since they obstruct the clerestory windows of the south wall. The choir was originally only one bay deep, and it was probably lengthened during the rebuilding after another fire in 1248. The builders of St. Mary's may have been brought from Lund or Ribe, but the spiral colonnettes and geometrical patterns on the archivolts suggest that the designers of the south portal may have come from England.

A closer link with English Romanesque architecture can be seen at the cathedral of St. Swithun in Stavanger (figure 2.23).[30] Built under Bishop Reinald, who was brought to Stavanger from Winchester c. 1125, it was damaged in a fire of 1272, after which the present Gothic choir was constructed. The original western

2.21 Bergen. St. Mary. Begun c. 1130. (Oslo,
Riksantikvaren.)

2.22 Bergen. St. Mary.
Portal.

2.23 Stavanger, Rogaland.
Cathedral. Nave. c.
1130. (Oslo,
Riksantikvaren.)

22

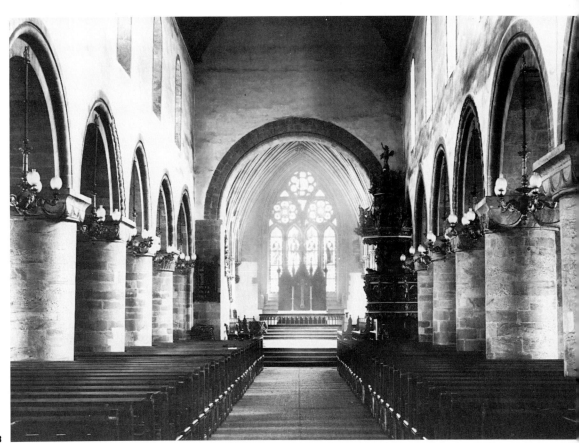

23

tower was also pulled down and replaced by a broad vestibule. The nave, however, remains separated from the aisles by five sets of cylindrical piers carrying a broad arcade. There is no triforium, and the clerestory consists of simple round-headed windows. The cushion capitals with sharply projecting abacus blocks are close to those remaining in the north transept of Winchester Cathedral, 1079–1093.

By far the most impressive undertaking in twelfth-century Norway was the transformation of the old church at Trondheim, then called Nidaros, upon the founding of the archbishopric there in 1152.[31] The town and its church grew from the residence established there by King Olav Tryggvasson in 997. After the battle of Stiklestad in 1030 St. Olav was buried at the second church, which he had begun c. 1016. This was rebuilt as a cathedral church under King Olav Kyrre and called Christ Church. Under the first archbishop, Eystein Erlandson, this building was pulled down and the present one begun, preserving the shrine of St. Olav (figure 2.24). Only the transept was completed during the Romanesque period, but the lower portions that remain are eloquent of the Norman style, with massive walls decorated with wall arcades, rich use of colonnettes with cubical capitals, and zigzag and billet moldings (figure 2.25). Throughout the Viking period Norsemen had carried their culture to England, and now English ideas were being received in Norway.

In addition to the parish churches and cathedrals there were of course the abbeys, and as the different orders established houses in the Scandinavian countries they built their churches according to their own particular traditions. Early in the twelfth century English Benedictine monks were invited to Odense by King Erik Ejegod, but they did not at first build their own churches. Soon after, however, c. 1125, other

English Benedictines built the abbey church at Venge near Skanderborg on Jutland (figure 2.26).[32] It is a small building, with a single nave, transepts with eastern apses, choir, and apse. The semicircular apses are characteristically Benedictine, and the narrow openings into the transepts and choir are in the Anglo-Norman tradition. The church is built of sandstone and originally had wooden roofs over nave and choir. The exterior decoration of the apse is also in the Anglo-Norman manner.

At Venge the rest of the monastic buildings are gone, but from a reconstruction based on foundations remaining at Alvastra in Östergötland we can see the program of the typical monastic establishment (figure 2.27).[33] On the south side of the church there was built a covered passage surrounding a square courtyard. Opening off this on the east side was the meeting room or chapter house, with the dormitory built above. Kitchen and refectory were on the south side, with barns, warehouses, and storage on the west. Alvastra was founded in 1143 by Cistercian rather than Benedictine monks, one of the expressions of this reformed order being the flat east walls of the eastern chapels, as had been established at the original church of the Order at Clairvaux.[34]

While these developments were taking place in stone, a new building material was introduced in the Scandinavian countries, one that was to have a leading role in the architecture of the next several centuries. Earlier, under King Godfred, c. 808, a fortification had been dug across the south end of the Jutland peninsula to protect the Danes from the armies of Charlemagne. In the reign of King Valdemar I (1157–1182) this was further strengthened by a facing of brick, a new manufactured material for which the technology was imported from Lombardy.

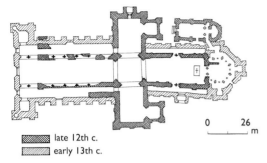

late 12th c.
early 13th c.

24

25

**2.24 Trondheim. Cathedral. Begun 1152. Plan. (After Lundberg, *Bygg-nadskonsten,* p. 200.)**

**2.25 Trondheim. Cathedral. South transept chapel. (Oslo, Riksantikvaren.)**

The Benedictines had built an abbey of tufa at Ringsted in Sorø County on Zealand c. 1080. Here St. Knud Lavard was buried after he was murdered in 1131. A new brick church was begun c. 1160 over the remains of the old, and the nave was nearing completion by the death of Valdemar in 1182.[35] The church has undergone fires and restorations, the fire of 1241 resulting in the Gothic vaulting. In plan it resembles Cluny III, begun 1088, with its broad transept carrying four eastern chapels in addition to the choir and apse (figure 2.28). Although the exterior walls have little surface decoration apart from the arched corbel tables, the plan resulted in a rich complex of masses at the east end. We may well suspect that the builders thought that the application of pilasters, blind arcades, etc., would have created an undesirably busy surface. The interior has breadth of effect, the wide round-headed arches of the nave rising from rectangular piers. There is no triforium gallery, and the nave wall is now punctuated by the corbeled supports for the vaulting ribs.

2.26 Venge, Jutland. Church.
c. 1125. (Copenhagen,
National Museum.)

2.27 Alvastra, Östergöt-
land. Abbey. 1143.
Plan. (After Anker and
Aron Andersson, *Art
of Scandinavia,* volume
2, figure 87, p. 177.)

2.28 Ringsted, Zealand. St.
Bendt. Begun 1160.

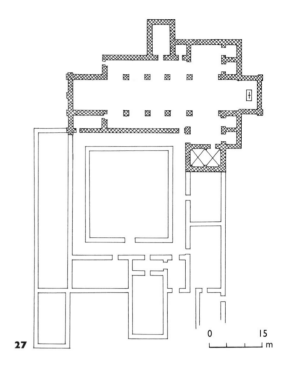

27

0    15
⊢  ⊢  ⊢  ⊣ m

28

At nearby Sorø a new Cistercian abbey was founded in 1162 as a private church for the powerful Hvide family.[36] In some respects the plan resembles that of Ringsted in having nave and aisles, transept, chapels, and apse (figure 2.29). In the nave, however, the bays are square rather than rectangular, and the bays of the side aisles are also square, the whole system based on the Roman rather than the Greek foot used at Ringsted. The transept chapels and apse have flat east walls in the Cistercian manner. The nave was originally covered with a wooden roof, and the vaults were constructed after a fire in 1247. At both Ringsted and Sorø the colonnettes, capitals, and moldings for the ornaments of door and window openings were executed in specially molded brick rather than stone (figure 2.30).

The parish churches, cathedrals, and abbey churches that we have been considering were all planned longitudinally, whether simply with nave and chancel or with the full basilical complex. While this was the most widely adopted plan in Romanesque Scandinavia, another approach was also occasionally used. This was to construct a church around a central vertical axis, using the circle or the Greek cross as the basic plan. A dozen or so were built in Denmark and Sweden, evidently as defensive structures. The southern and eastern shores were menaced by attacks from across the Baltic, and some of the round churches were fortified after the manner of Continental towers.[37]

The most interesting group is that of the four round churches on Bornholm, Østerlars being the most dramatic (figure 2.31).[38] It is a massive building, three stories high, with the roof resting on thick outer walls and also supported by a central pillar. This pillar is actually hollow, a round room formed by six heavy posts that are the inner supports for the annular vault of the surrounding aisle. This room is

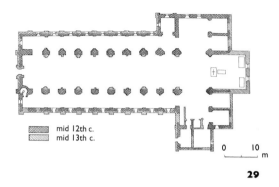

mid 12th c.
mid 13th c.

0    10
          m

**29**

**30**

used as a baptistry, and the choir and apse, also circular, project off the main building. The staircase to the upper levels rises through the wall of the choir. The heavy buttresses that make the exterior so picturesque were added in the sixteenth and seventeenth centuries. Hoardings and machicolations provided the defenses of these churches. Lines drawn on a map of Bornholm will show these churches zigzagging up the island toward the stronghold of Hammershus on the north. The churches are no more than nine miles apart, and signal flares could send quick warning of impending invasion right across the island.

The round churches of Bornholm are all built with a central pier, and there is no conventional nave, only a surrounding corridor. Another approach was to support the vaults of a round church with four central piers, which left comparatively more assembly space at the ground level. The piers rise to five four-part vaults in a Greek cross plan, with triangular vaults to fill out the circle. This system was adopted at Bjernede on Zealand c. 1160 and also at Thorsager on Jutland c. 1200.[39] At Bjernede the church was begun in granite and finished in brick (figure 2.32). The upper portion underwent some changes, and the present pyramidal roof and also the apse date from reconstructions in 1890–1892.

The most spectacular and intriguing of the Romanesque centralized churches is at Kalundborg on Zealand (figure 2.33).[40] It was begun c. 1170 on a Greek cross plan, with an octagonal tower at the end of each arm and a square tower over the crossing. This central tower fell in 1827 and was rebuilt in 1871.[41] The church was probably built by Bishop Esbjørn Snare, brother of the great Bishop Absalon. The massive brick walls and the fortresslike character of the stairs to the towers are appropriate signs of Kalundborg's site on the fjord coming off the

**31**

2.29 **Sorø, Zealand. Abbey Church. Begun 1165. Plan. (After Hermansen and Nørlund,** *Danmarks Kirker. Sorø Amt,* **volume 1, figure 4, p. 24.)**

2.30 **Ringsted, Zealand. St. Bendt. Portal.**

2.31 **Østerlars, Bornholm. Church. c. 1150.**

Great Belt. Modern commercial buildings now
dominate the view from the water, but in the
twelfth century the great church must have
been an impressive landmark. Although the plan
appears to be centralized in outline, the interior is arranged with the altar on the east wall,
opposite the west entrance, creating the effect
of a short basilica with chapels projecting on
north and south. The piers as rebuilt after a
fire in 1314 are more slender than the original,
and the first appearance of the interior (figure
2.34) must have been much like that of
Bjernede, which was built by Bishop Absalon.

With Kalundborg the great age of Romanesque building in Scandinavia was drawing to a
close. A new style was already developing in
France, and with the next major building project in the North, Roskilde Cathedral, the
Gothic would overtake the earlier style.

32

33

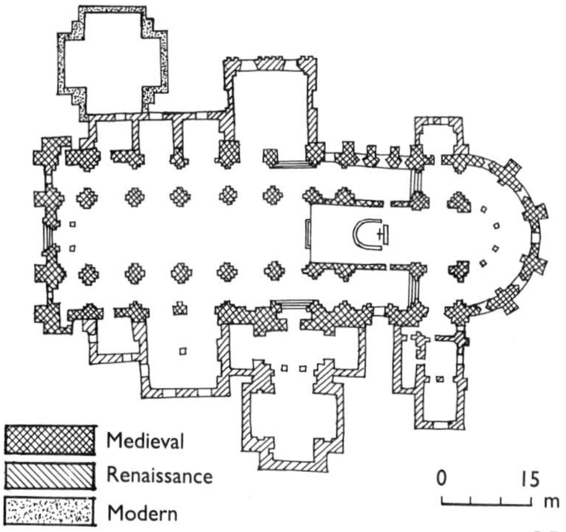
Medieval
Renaissance
Modern
0
15
m

35

## *The Gothic Period, c. 1250–1530*

By the turn of the thirteenth century the Gothic style in architecture was approaching its maturity in France and England. In the Scandinavian countries the new style was sometimes adopted for new construction and sometimes for alteration to existing buildings. Influences came from Germany as well as from France and England. No clear-cut division into regional or national groups is entirely appropriate, but certain tendencies can be observed. In Denmark and southern Sweden brick was especially popular and also to some extent in Finland, with strong relations to German building. Stone was used more in central Sweden and on the island of Gotland, in a mixture of French, English, and German ideas. In Norway and the Atlantic islands building in stone with strong preferences for English details seems to have predominated.

Before turning to some examples of churches from these groups, we should note the transitional character of one of Denmark's most important churches, the cathedral at Roskilde. A campaign to replace Svend Normand's church with something grander was begun by Bishop Absalon c. 1170.[42] He planned it to be a

three-aisled basilica of granite, as some fragments in the present church indicate. The work
was begun at the east end in the Romanesque
style, but fashion changed the plans. Almost at
once the examples of the churches at Ringsted
and Sorø caused a change from stone to brick.
Then when Bishop Absalon was succeeded by
Bishop Peder Sunesøn in 1193 the work was
continued in the Gothic style which the bishop
had encountered in travels in France and the
Low Countries. By 1300 the nave was finished
as far as the west wall, and from then until
1924 no less than eleven additions were made
to the basic plan (figure 2.35). After the court
of Denmark moved from Roskilde to Copenhagen in 1416, Roskilde Cathedral continued to
be the royal burial place, which accounts for its
many chapels. The earlier Romanesque portions
are visible at the east end, and in the clerestory
the windows are still round-headed. The twin
towers that rise at the west end did not receive their slender spires until 1635 (figure
2.36). The Gothic work becomes apparent in
the interior, where the nave is separated from
the aisles by compound brick piers that rise 78
feet to the domical vaults (figure 2.37). Gothic
vaults also cover the aisles and choir. The major
furnishings are sumptuous and include the oak
gallery or pew of Christian IV (1610), the sandstone and alabaster pulpit (1609), the gilt wood
altar (c. 1580), and the organ (1550 and 1654,
rebuilt 1957). These fortunately survived the
fire that broke out during repairs to the eastern roof in 1968.

We should also note one other great transitional church in Denmark, the Cistercian abbey church of Løgumkloster on Jutland,[43] built
on the so-called "Bernardine" plan like that of
Alvastra. Only the chancel and eastern chapels
were promptly ready for use after the building
was begun c. 1200. The remainder of the
church was not completed until c. 1350, which

**2.35  Roskilde, Zealand. Ca-
thedral. Begun 1190.
Plan. (After Moltke
and Elna Møller, *Dan-
marks Kirker. Køben-
havns Amt,* volume 3,
figure 26b, p. 1327.)**

**2.36  Roskilde, Zealand. Ca-
thedral. (Copenhagen,
National Museum.)**

36

accounts for the appearance of pointed arches in the upper portions and the differences in vaulting from one end to the other. According to Cistercian rule a western tower complex like that of Roskilde was omitted. By the time of its completion, however, some of the austerity of the Order was relaxing, and the gable ends were evidently inspired by north German or Netherlandish fashion with their groups of window panels and stepped edges. In contrast the interior is characterized by plain surfaces, with no ribs on the piers and no articulation of the nave wall (figure 2.38). Upon the Reformation in Denmark in 1536 the monastic buildings were largely destroyed and the church itself seldom used until it became a parish church in 1739. Therefore the present altar, pulpit, and font, which the red brick sets off so effectively, are not the original furnishings.

The gables of Løgumkloster bring us to those buildings that may be viewed as belonging to a larger regional group that transcends national boundaries: the "Baltic brick Gothic," which includes the Netherlands, north Germany, and the eastern Baltic countries as well as Denmark and south Sweden.[44] Two cathedrals and two city churches can be noted to demonstrate the vigor of this style in south Scandinavia.

Odense on Funen was the seat of one of the oldest bishoprics in Denmark, founded in 988. In 1086 King Knud the Holy was killed in the small wooden church of St. Alban near the cathedral. He had already begun a new granite cathedral, to which his remains were transferred in 1095 and which was renamed in his honor after his canonization in 1101. This church burned in 1247, some parts now remaining as a crypt, and the present building was begun in the new brick Gothic style.[45] The first five bays of the nave were completed by 1300, then the chancel bays were added, then c. 1450

37

2.37  **Roskilde, Zealand. Cathedral. Interior. (Copenhagen, National Museum.)**

2.38  **Løgumkloster, Jutland. Abbey Church. Begun c. 1200. Interior. (Copenhagen, National Museum.)**

**38**

the two parts were connected without a conventional transept. The west front was given its single tower under Christian III in 1558, and the building was restored in the eighteenth and nineteenth centuries. Unlike the unpainted walls at Løgumkloster, the brick interior has been whitewashed (figure 2.39). The compound piers of the nave carry an arcade with continuous moldings, and these are echoed in the moldings of the triforium and clerestory openings. Vaulting shafts are carried up across the nave wall to the springing of the vaults. The more steeply pointed arches give a stronger vertical emphasis than at Roskilde and Løgumkloster. The whitened brick of the nave provides a setting for the pulpit of 1751–1754 and the royal pew of 1894. The organ in the west end retains its case of 1752, but the most striking furnishing is the great altar by Claus Berg, c. 1520, originally carved for the Gray Friars' Church, and now dominating the raised chancel.

The exterior of St. Knud is comparatively modest, with the plain walls of nave and aisles, simple clerestory windows, and plain salient buttresses. A much grander effect was achieved on the cathedral at Århus on Jutland (figure 2.40).[46] Begun c. 1197, it is the longest church in Denmark, measuring over 300 feet. It started as a late Romanesque church with nave, aisles, a projecting transept with eastern chapels, choir, and apse, similar to Ringsted. The plan as it is now reflects a change at the west front in the fifteenth century, when it was decided to build two chapels flanking a central tower instead of the two towers originally planned. This was followed by raising the nave and changing the vaulting system from three bays to six. The transept was then heightened and the choir rebuilt as a hall church by c. 1482. These changes brought the high stepped gables that give the cathedral its rich exterior. Alterations in the transept included provisions for the religious dramas that were enacted in the cathedral, and the new choir was a fitting stage for the permanent drama of Bernt Notke's great altarpiece of 1498. The building underwent restorations in 1867–1882 and again in 1921–1927.

Copenhagen's old brick Gothic Vor Frue Kirke, or the Church of Our Lady, no longer exists. Under Bishop Absalon a church had been built in Copenhagen c. 1200, probably of limestone.[47] This burned in 1316; a new church was built in brick with granite details.[48] It was a

**39**

2.39 Odense, Funen. St. Knud. c. 1247–1301. Interior.

2.40 Århus, Jutland. Cathedral. Begun c. 1197. (Copenhagen, National Museum.)

three-aisled basilica with eight bays in the nave, no projecting transept, and five chapels surrounding the apse. In plan therefore it resembled Roskilde Cathedral, of which it was then a collegiate dependency. Representations of two coronations give us some idea of the interior. In a print of 1593 commemorating the coronation of Frederik II in 1558, the church was shown in a cutaway view that includes the altar of 1559 and indicates salient buttresses, traceried windows, cylindrical piers, and pilasters on the aisle walls rising to domical vaults (figure 2.41). For the coronation of Christian IV in 1596 the church was shown without the aisle windows and pilasters and with a new altar of 1569, plus the little "swallow's-nest" organ now installed in the southeast corner of the choir (figure 2.42).

Across the Sound in Malmö, Skåne, St. Peter's Church has survived as a fine example of the now fully developed brick Gothic, some-times called the "Hanseatic" style (figure 2.43).[49] It is basilical in plan, with five chapels ringing the apse and additional chapels on north and south. While the transept does not appear as an independent element on the plan, the exterior view shows it rising to the height of the nave. The original west front with its tower collapsed in 1420, its successor in 1442, and yet another burned in 1560. The present tower and spire were built in 1890, and the gables on the transept and chapels were probably rebuilt at the same time, repeating the medieval features of brick paneling and stepped gables. As at Odense, the brick of the interior is whitewashed. The piers are without capitals, in the late Gothic manner, and the vaulting shafts are corbeled, beginning at the springing of the nave arcade. The white interior is generously lit by the large windows of the nave and choir, so that there is a fine setting for the richly carved pulpit of 1599 and the altar of 1611. While

41

42

nearly all the paintings that once decorated the church were lost in nineteenth-century restorations, those of the present baptistry (originally the Merchants' Chapel) have survived and show the delicacy of the late medieval style of c. 1520.

For a major building in the northern extension of this brick Gothic style we can turn to Turku (the Swedish Åbo) in Finland. The bishop's seat was established here in 1229 and a cathedral begun that was not completed until c. 1290. Not long after, in 1318, it was largely destroyed by the Russians and rebuilt in brick as a hall church. Chapels were added on the north side beginning in the fourteenth century. The nave was heightened and the vaults completed c. 1460. The west tower was damaged by fires in 1681 and 1827, after which it was rebuilt in the neo-Gothic fashion (figure 2.44).[50] After the repairs of 1976–1977 we can now see some of the thirteenth-century stonework in the lower parts, particularly in the base of the tower. The later brickwork has the characteristically Finnish whitened decorative panels. The cathedral's growth by addition is evident from the irregularities of the plan (figure 2.45). When the nave was heightened, it was covered by the then popular "star" vaults, springing from corbels in the otherwise plain nave walls (figure 2.46). Corbels for the earlier vaults remain at the springing of the nave arcade. The light and spacious interior created by the rebuilding has also a sharp intellectual quality, fitting perhaps for the cathedral of Mikael Agricola (1508–1557), who brought the Reformation to Finland and made the first Finnish translation of the Bible.

A more varied response to the Gothic styles is visible at the cathedral church of Sts. Lawrence, Erik, and Olav at Uppsala in Sweden, begun c. 1271 (figure 2.47).[51] This is the third cathedral of the archiepiscopal diocese, the first

**43**

**44**

2.44   **Turku. Cathedral. Begun mid-13th century.
(Helsinki, National Mu-
seum of Finland.)**

2.45   **Turku. Cathedral.
Plan. (After Rinne,
*Åbo Domkyrka,* figure
2, p. 13.)**

2.46   **Turku. Cathedral. Interior. (Helsinki, Mu-
seum of Finnish
Architecture. (Photo:
Havas.)**

2.47   **Uppsala. Cathedral.
Begun 1273. (Uppsala,
Upplands Museum.
Photo: Tommy
Arvidson.)**

2.48   **Uppsala. Cathedral.
Plan. (After Boëthius
and Romdahl, *Uppsala
Domkyrka,* figure 250,
p. 203.)**

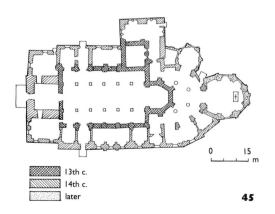

13th c.
14th c.
later

0     15
            m

**45**

46

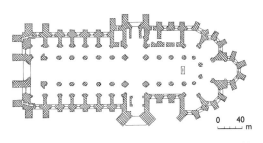

48

47

having been St. Peter at Sigtuna c. 1100 and the second St. Lawrence at Gamla Uppsala, consecrated 1156. The latter was chosen for the burial place of St. Erik after his martyrdom in 1160. By the middle of the thirteenth century, however, it was thought wise to move the site of the cathedral to the trading center of Östra Aros (now named Uppsala). The foundations for the new building were laid probably in 1271, and enough had been constructed for the relics of St. Erik to be moved there in 1273. As originally planned the church had a nave of seven bays with aisles and chapels, a transept, aisled choir, and five eastern chapels, in the tradition of the French High Gothic (figure 2.48). The nave walls are pierced with small roundels, however, the vaults are slightly domical, and the buttressing system does not allow for a full triforium, all of which suggest influence from German brick Gothic in the actual construction.

For continuation of the work after 1287, a letter of appointment (apparently still extant when published in 1719) named "Estienne de Bonneuill, tailleur de pierre," as master builder at Uppsala Cathedral, hence the strong French character of carving in the choir and on the south portal (figure 2.49).[52] Extensive restorations were needed after a great fire in 1702, and then restoration programs were carried out from 1885 to 1893 and again from 1971 to 1976. The cathedral is the largest in Scandinavia, over 380 feet long, and is the national shrine of Sweden, a pilgrimage and coronation church, and a place of burial for monarchs and honored citizens.

One other great brick cathedral that should be mentioned is that of St. Nicholas, or Storkyrkan, the oldest church in Stockholm.[53] The first church of the early thirteenth century burned in 1303 and was rebuilt. Then a major enlargement took place beginning c. 1468, re-

49

2.49 Uppsala. Cathedral. South portal. (Uppsala, Upplands Museum. Photo: Tommy Arvidson.)

2.50 Stockholm. Storkyrkan. 1468–1496. Interior. (Stockholm, Antikvarisk-Topografiska Arkivet.)

2.51 Visby, Gotland. St. Mary. Begun late 12th century.

sulting in the present plan with western tower, nave, and double aisles, but no transept. The interior is rather dark, since the brick piers of the nave and aisles are not whitewashed, and there is no clerestory (figure 2.50). The domical star vaults of the nave spring from vaulting shafts on the piers, and their ribs are sunk into the nave walls without wall ribs. The aisles are covered with square four-part vaults. The liturgical furnishings are the most elaborate in Scandinavia and include the royal pews by Nicodemus Tessin the Elder, designed in 1684 and built by Burchardt Precht, who also designed and built the pulpit of 1698–1701. The central section of the ebony, silver, and gold altar was made in Hamburg in 1652–1654, while the side sections were built in Stockholm. And then there is Bernt Notke's great sculptural group of St. George and the Dragon and the Maiden, 1489.

**50**

In other parts of Scandinavia there was extensive building in stone. As the round churches of Bornholm are a distinctive feature of the Romanesque period, the churches of another principal island, Gotland, occupy a special position among the stone buildings of the Gothic period. Long a center of trade between Europe and Asia, in the thirteenth century its major town, Visby, reached its height of power in association with the Hanseatic League. This came to an end in the fourteenth century, but the time of greatest prosperity left Visby with no less than sixteen churches and nearly one hundred parish churches were spread across the island.

In Visby only the cathedral church of St. Mary remains in use, the rest being in ruins (figure 2.51).[54] It was begun as a three-aisled basilica at the end of the twelfth century. The choir was enlarged c. 1230–1250 and the nave c. 1250–1260, changing the cathedral to a hall church with tall eastern towers, the masons

**51**

coming from Saxony, Westphalia, and the Rhineland. The large south chapel was added c. 1300. Although in disuse for many years after the decline of Gotland's fortunes, the cathedral now again serves the diocese and has recently been carefully restored.[55]

The churches of the countryside fared better. Most have survived to serve their parishes, although changed many times, as for example at Tingstäde (figure 2.52).[56] The church here was begun in the late twelfth century with a wooden roofed nave, a barrel-vaulted choir, and a half-domed apse. Then c. 1230, very likely in imitation of St. Mary in Visby, the nave was divided into four bays by a central pillar and covered with vaults. Having the vaults spring from within the heavy thick walls made buttresses unnecessary, hence the outward simplicity of these churches. Later additions to the church at Tingstäde were the western tower and sacristy, c. 1250–1260. Also characteristic of the parish churches of Gotland are the carved portals, with Biblical scenes and foliage motifs on the capitals.

On the mainland at Linköping in Östergötland the Romanesque cathedral of c. 1130 became outgrown and enlargement was begun c. 1230.[57] The original sanctuary was broadened to form a transept, to which was added a wider choir surrounded by an ambulatory. The slender untraceried windows, shafts banded in the English manner, still rise above the south transept door. Then the nave and aisles were widened and covered with simple four-part ribbed vaults. The work proceeded slowly, resulting in the changing styles of the nave piers (figure 2.53). Viewed from the west end, the clustered piers in the English style are followed by the polygonal piers of the eastern nave bays, and this plainer area forms an introduction to the complex of chapels at the east end. A new ambulatory with three chapels by a German

builder, Gerlach von Köln, was begun c. 1410. The fashionable star vaults of c. 1498 were completed with the help of another German builder, Adam von Düren.

If we turn westward to the Norwegian churches, we will find that the history of Trondheim Cathedral from the Gothic period onward is different.[58] Under Archbishop Eystein Erlandson the rebuilding of the choir and the building of the octagon were begun c. 1186. The archbishop had been in England for several years previously and was evidently much impressed with the English Transitional and Early Gothic styles that he encountered at Canterbury and Lincoln. The work at Trondheim was not completed in his lifetime, and later delays, fires, alterations, and neglect led to a sorry state by the mid-nineteenth century (figure 2.54). A major campaign of rebuilding was undertaken by Christian Christie from 1872 to 1906. He attempted to restore details of construction and ornament according to the intentions of the original builders as they drew ideas from Canterbury, Lincoln, and Westminster Abbey (figure 2.55).

Farther south on the Norwegian coast, at Stavanger, a fire in 1272 brought about the rebuilding and enlargement of the choir of the cathedral of St. Swithun (figure 2.56).[59] The new choir is an extension of the remaining Romanesque nave, raised over the crypt, vaulted in five bays, and lit by large windows traceried in the English manner. The east window is flanked on the exterior by niches for statuary, then by massive towers, and surmounted by a traceried gable, these elements combining to produce an effect more like a western façade.

From these examples of major attempts to build large Gothic churches in the Scandinavian countries it is clear that in terms of a "pure" expression of Gothic architecture in the French, German, or English sense the northern

builders were less than successful. Their enthusiasm for the elements of Gothic structure and
ornament, however, was unmistakable and led
to buildings with their own distinction. One of
the most surprising and least known of these is
the unfinished cathedral of St. Magnus at Kirkjubøur in the Faroe Islands.[60]

While this community is now apparently
out of the way, it was a center of activity in
the Middle Ages when Bishop Erlend began the
cathedral c. 1300 (figure 2.57). Rectangular in
plan, it was to have been vaulted in six bays,
the two easternmost indicated as the choir by
a rise in the floor. A small chapel on the north
side was evidently once vaulted, but the main
body of the church was not, and it may have
been at one time covered by a wooden roof.
Carved corbels indicate the intention for vaulting. The walls are built of Faroese basalt, bound
with shell mortar.[61] Little is known of Bishop
Erlend except that he went to the Faroes from

52

53

2.52 **Tingstäde, Gotland.**
**Church. Begun late**
**12th century.**

2.53 **Linköping, Östergöt-**
**land. Cathedral. Begun**
**1130. Interior. (Stock-**
**holm, Antikvarisk-**
**Topografiska Arkivet.**
**Photo: Rolf Hintze.)**

54

55

56

Bergen. He must have known the sacristy of St. Mary in Bergen, and possibly also the chapter house at Trondheim Cathedral, which might have served as prototypes for the little north chapel at Kirkjubøur. The ornamental details of St. Magnus recall the English-inspired work at Stavanger and Trondheim, but whether they were carried out by local or Norwegian stone-workers is not known.

A new church was built at Hvalsey in the Eastern Settlement c. 1300, whose walls are the most substantial remains of Norse building in Greenland (figure 2.58).[62] Slabs of fieldstone were fairly well dressed and laid up with shell mortar, which was rarely used in Greenland. The 13-foot lintel over the west door and the arched window in the east gable suggest considerable ambition and grandeur. Remains of the house, a large festival hall, barns, and store-houses are nearby. In 1261 the settlers in Greenland, who had been assembling to govern themselves at the Thing at Gardar, agreed to go under the rule of King Håkon Håkonsson of Norway. The bishop at Gardar was then re-sponsible to the bishop in Trondheim, whence stoneworkers may have been brought for the work at Hvalsey.

The major Gothic churches just described are cathedrals or large parish churches. In the 1220s three religious orders were founded that followed the Gothic style in their buildings: the Dominicans, Carmelites, and Franciscans. For preaching purposes some of the houses chose to build hall churches. In the next century a new order was founded by St. Birgitta, c. 1345, and confirmed by Pope Urban V in 1370. The rules that she wrote for her Order include in-structions for buildings. These stipulate lime-stone for the material, sections for monks and nuns, and prohibition of ornament throughout. After St. Birgitta's death in Rome in 1373, her body was brought to the abbey of Vadstena in

57

2.54  **Trondheim. Cathedral.
      Drawing by A. Mayer,
      c. 1836. (Oslo, Riksan-
      tikvaren.)**
2.55  **Trondheim. Cathedral.
      Interior. (Oslo,
      Riksantikvaren.)**
2.56  **Stavanger, Rogaland.
      Cathedral. Choir. 1272.
      (Oslo, Riksantikvaren.)**
2.57  **Kirkjubøur, Faroes.
      Cathedral. Begun c.
      1300.**

Östergötland which she had founded in 1368.[63] Some of the convent buildings remain and have been restored, while the high broad roof covering the nave and aisles of the church rises above them. The nuns' cloister was built on the north side of the church, and the monks' dormitory and chapter house were put in a wing to the southwest. The interior was built as a hall church, the nave and aisles separated by four pairs of octagonal piers (figure 2.59). The absence of decorative carving and the severity of proportion are in keeping with the rule of the Order, although there was perhaps some concession to contemporary style in the star vaults. The Order attracted numerous members and by the Reformation had increased to about eighty houses all over Europe, which usually followed the building instructions of its founder.

The merits of the fire-resistant vaults being raised over these large churches and also the new fashionable elegance of their appearance were not lost on those whose stone village churches still had wooden roofs, and some of the later Gothic parish churches were vaulted from the beginning. At Hyllestad on Jutland, for example, the Romanesque church was given simple four-part vaults, which were painted with Biblical scenes by the Brarup Master c. 1400 (figure 2.60).[64] Hundreds of these small churches were provided with such paintings, based on manuscript and woodcut illustrations and serving as a *Biblia Pauperum* for those who could not read the Scriptures. These vaults are not high, but could be easily reached by ladders or scaffolding for painting *al secco* and were close in the view of the spectators. A great many were eventually covered with whitewash, and much cleaning and restoration has been undertaken in recent years.[65]

Several references have been made to the "star" vaults characteristic of the late Gothic period, which were especially popular in Sweden. At Almunge in Uppland these were

painted by a follower of Albertus Pictor
c. 1490 (figure 2.61).[66] The complex shapes and
surfaces of these vaults offered both opportunities and obstacles to the painters. The mineral
colors have changed over the years so that the
appearance of light and color of these interiors
is now deceptive, but where the paintings can
now be seen in their entirety the sense of
drama, reverent and irreverent, remains.

Mention should also be made of the paintings that were done for the Norwegian stave
churches c. 1250–1300. The structural system
of these churches was not conducive to painting on the buildings themselves. An ingenious
solution to the problem of pictorial cycles was
found in the baldachins, or canopies, that were
built over the sanctuaries and painted with
Biblical or other scenes. Few remain, including
one at Torpo in Hallingdal and one from Ål in
Hallingdal now in the University Museum in
Oslo. They are significant, however, for our un-
derstanding of the original appearance of the
medieval churches. The fresh reds and blues
that have survived on the wooden Norwegian
panels are unlike the brown and beige hues and
present golden appearance of such paintings as
those at Hyllestad.[67]

When Christianity was carried from Sweden into Finland in the early thirteenth century,
numerous parish churches were built in the
Åland Islands and southwestern Finland. Those
built of wood have disappeared. The remaining
churches, built of the local granite under the
direction of clergy coming from the mainland of
Sweden and from Gotland, were usually begun
as simple rectangular structures, with single
naves and sanctuaries with flat east ends. The
first roofs might be of wood, with vaults added
later, as were sometimes porches and towers.

An example dating from the thirteenth
century is the church of St. Mikael at Finström
on Åland (figure 2.62).[68] Here the south porch

59

2.58   **Hvalsey, Greenland.
Church. c. 1300.**

2.59   **Vadstena, Östergötland. Abbey Church.
1365–1420. Interior.
(Stockholm, Antikvar-
isk-Topografiska Ar-
kivet. Photo: Clareus.)**

and the tower with its odd little turrets were added in the fifteenth century. The sacristy on the north side is actually the earliest part, built onto the original wooden church sometime before the beginning of the present building. The walls of the church are laid up with irregular blocks of the local granite, marked by bands of more carefully dressed large blocks.

On the interior heavy piers were added in the fourteenth century to support low vaults, covered with paintings in the fifteenth century (figure 2.63). The arches over the nave are only slightly pointed, while the arch into the tower is more sharply pointed, almost stilted. As in Denmark and Sweden, the Finnish parish churches carry a wealth of carved and painted altars, pulpits, and other liturgical furnishings.

St. Mikael at Finström will be remarked upon again in connection with the Finnish architect Lars Sonck. It also represents another aspect of medieval Scandinavian architecture, the extent to which building practices were not limited by the national boundaries of today. A comprehensive study of the parish churches alone of north Germany, Denmark, south Sweden, including the islands of Öland and Gotland, the Åland Islands, and southwestern Finland has yet to be made.[69]

**60**

2.60  **Hyllestad, Jutland. Church. 12th century. Interior.**

2.61  **Almunge, Uppland. Church. 12th century. Interior. (Stockholm, Antikvarisk-Topografiska Arkivet.)**

62

2.62 Finström, Åland. St.
Mikael. 13th century.
(Helsinki, Museum of
Finnish Architecture.
Photo: Nils E.
Wickberg.)

2.63 Finström, Åland. St.
Mikael. Interior. (Hel-
sinki, Museum of Fin-
nish Architecture.
Photo: Rista.)

63

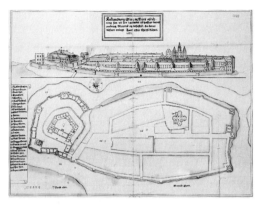

**64**

---

*Secular Building in the Middle Ages*

To turn from religious to secular building, we
find that few individual houses, as distinct from
castles or palaces, have survived from the medieval period in the Scandinavian countries. The
sense of tradition has been strong, and some
habits of building from earlier years can probably be seen in housing from the sixteenth century that will be considered in a later chapter.
Even a brief glance at the history of these
countries from c. 1050 to c. 1530, however,
will reveal the frequent wars that made defenses for the cities and strongholds for the
kings and nobles imperative. Some of the most
notable of these will be described to show how
the Nordic builders responded to these needs.

The towns themselves grew as market
centers for local or international trade as well
as centers of ecclesiastical authority. Studies in
urban history and archaeology, especially since
World War II, have done much to clarify the
development of modern cities in Denmark,
Norway, and Sweden, even from as early as Viking times.[70] For the towns which that enclosed with walls we may, for example, look
briefly at Kalundborg and Copenhagen on Zea-

land and Visby on Gotland.

We have already considered the unique church at Kalundborg, begun c. 1170 by Bishop Esbjørn Snare. The bishop also built a castle there, and these with the town buildings were surrounded by a curtain wall with towers and bastions (figure 2.64).[71] The whole defense system took advantage of the waters of the fjord on the south and the Munkesø or lake on the north; today the latter is filled in and the walls mostly gone.

At Visby, on the other hand, the walls built from the early twelfth to the mid-thirteenth centuries have survived and are among the most extensive of such defenses remaining in Europe (figure 2.65).[72] By 1229 Visby was one of the member towns of the Society of Germans Traveling to Gotland, the Hanseatic League, which came to include more than thirty Dutch, German, and Baltic cities. Having been the center of German activity on Gotland for more than half a century, the original town not surprisingly somewhat resembled Lübeck, with which its merchants were in close commercial relation. In both cities the cathedrals were not so much on formal central plazas as they were placed toward the ends of the towns, with long streets proceeding from them.

As a third example of how such fortifications could be managed we can look at the walls and castle of Copenhagen, built by Bishop Esbjørn Snare's brother Bishop Absalon in 1167 (figure 2.66).[73] Here he hoped to protect what was then a fishing and trading center from attacks by the Wendish pirates coming from Germany. The castle was built on an island, Slotsholmen, and, although it was torn down in 1369, some ruins are now visible under the present Christiansborg Palace. Some of the old streets of the town itself, notably the present series called Strøget and Købmagergade, lead-

**65**

**66**

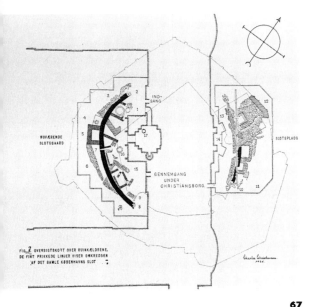

**67**

**68**

2.67  **Copenhagen. Castle. Plan of ruins. (Christensen, *Gamle bygninger på Slotsholmen*, n.p.)**

2.68  **Stockholm. Castle. 13th century. Model. (Stockholm, City Museum.)**

2.69  ***Vädersolstavlan.* Painting, 1535. Stockholm, Storkyrkan. (Stockholm, City Museum.)**

ing to the old bridge to the castle island, survive in the modern plan of the city.

This brings us to the castles. For the twelfth century in Denmark, figures 2.64 and 2.66 show the castles at Kalundborg and Copenhagen to have been typical of European fortresses of that time. There were two lines of defense at Kalundborg, and then the castle with its own towers, formed by five wings around a courtyard. At Copenhagen the castle consisted of a ring wall with at least one, possibly two towers, and there were then buildings inside the wall, with the baking oven of one still in place today. The oldest known seal of the city, from 1275, shows a crenelated curtain wall and two towers, with a castle rising inside with a high central tower and projecting wings. It has been proposed that this depiction is substantially accurate and that the castle was a striking parallel to the church at Kalundborg.[74] The ruins that survived the building of the first Christiansborg Palace in 1733 were excavated between 1906 and 1922 during the building of the present Christiansborg and are open to visitors (figure 2.67).

The thick curtain walls, towers, and heavily defended gateways of such castles were by now well developed all over Europe, partly as a result of the lessons in military architecture learned during the Crusades. These elements were continued in use, in various combinations, for several generations until the introduction of gunpowder in European warfare in the fifteenth century made some of these provisions obsolete.

In the thirteenth century Birger Jarl, regent for his son King Valdemar, did for Sweden what Bishop Absalon had done for Denmark, building a fortress at Tavastehus (now Hämeenlinna) in Finland to establish Sweden's overseas empire and also building Stockholm as a major port for the Lübeck trade. Stockholm's site on

the island of Stadholm was strategic because here Lake Mälar drains into the Saltsjö, coming in forty miles from the open sea. Birger Jarl's castle was dominated by the great Tre Kronor tower, as seen in a modern model and also prominent in early illustrations of the city (figures 2.68 and 2.69).[75] This typical keep, with walls 10 feet thick and a 45-foot diameter, was divided into several stories with a defensive platform on top.

For a more secure royal residence in another great Hanseatic port in the thirteenth century, King Håkon Håkonsson began a new stone castle and walls at the entrance to the harbor of Bergen after the fire of 1248. His own coronation feast in 1225 had been held in a timber boathouse, hardly a royal setting. By 1261, however, when his son Magnus Håkonsson was married to the Danish princess Ingeborg, the new stone hall was ready for the feast (figures 2.70 and 2.71).[76] A seventeenth-century view shows the castle complex at the edge of the water, with the twin towers of St. Mary's church rising just to the right. The hall itself, now called Håkon's Hall, was built much like a German *Kaiserpfalz* such as the famous Romanesque example at Goslar, c. 1040–1050. The ground floor provided storage, the middle story was divided into three parts for council, reception, and private chambers, and the great festival hall was built on the third level. A history of fires and gradual desertion was changed through the efforts of J. C. Dahl, who also rescued the stave church at Vang, but then a tremendous harbor explosion in 1944 brought down all but the walls.

After 1955 a new restoration was begun, and the hall is now made suitable for social gatherings (figure 2.72). The exterior view of the west side shows the normal medieval slit openings on the ground level, larger divided windows in the middle, and much larger tracer-

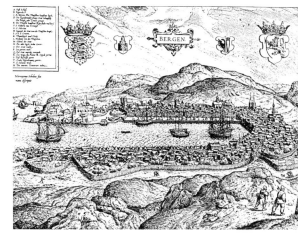

**70**

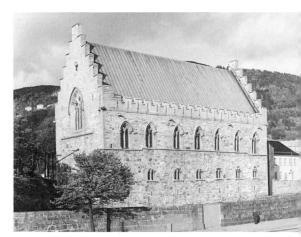

**71**

2.70   Bergen. Scholeus View, c. 1580. (Oslo, Riksantikvaren.)

2.71   Bergen. Håkon's Hall. 1261. (Oslo, Riksantikvaren.)

2.72   Bergen. Håkon's Hall. Great Hall. (Oslo, Riksantikvaren.)

ied windows above; on the interior of the festival hall these window openings come down to the floor, thus providing ample light. The large window in the north wall is built in the English fashion, with three lancets pierced in a thin panel on the inner surface of the wall and four lancets, three quatrefoils, and a roundel in the outer panel. This scheme gave small subdivisions for best support of glass on the exterior and larger openings for better use of light on the interior. A similar double window was built in the east end of St. Mary's church after the fire of 1248, and the same masons may have been employed on both projects.[77]

Magnus Håkonsson built another great stronghold, Akershus, in Oslo. Because of subsequent enlargements, however, we will leave it for later discussion and turn to two important castles of the medieval period in Finland. On high ground overlooking the harbor stands the castle at Turku (figure 2.73).[78] It was begun c. 1280 as two parallel four-story buildings separated by six-story towers at the east and west ends. Among the later additions are the King's Hall built in the top story of the north wing in the fourteenth century, and also the Nuns' Chapel in the east tower, with the first star vaulting in Finland. In the sixteenth century the castle was repaired and embellished to become the center of court life. In later years it housed troops, served as a distillery, was in part a prison, and also housed an embryonic historical

museum. Modern restorations and a full museum installation have followed upon damage by bombing in 1941. These varied uses help point out that this building, while heavily constructed, did not have the curtain walls, towers, and bastions of the other fortresses but was more a massive residence from the beginning.

Probably more satisfying to the romantic mind is the castle of Olavlinna, founded in 1475 by the Swedish nobleman Erik Axelsen Tott (figure 2.74).[79] It was built as a fortress against the Russians, and, like the old Copenhagen Castle, rises dramatically from a rocky island in the Kyrösalmi Strait. By the fortunes of war it fell twice into Russian hands, and was several times enlarged until finally abandoned after the Napoleonic wars. After some time as a prison it was restored in the 1870s and again since World War II. Originally there were three towers, a

2.73   Turku. Castle. Begun c. 1280.

2.74   Savonlinna. Olavlinna. Begun 1475.

main building with living quarters and the Knights' Hall, and ramparts to form a triangular enclosure. Changes in the towers and additions of towers, bastions, and outer walls brought it to its present plan. In spite of many changes and additions since 1475, the castle's basic structure has survived well enough, providing excellent opportunity to observe the heavy outer walls, deep window embrasures, thick inner partitions, and narrow, tortuous spiral staircases with steps of uneven width and depth that characterize such late medieval fortresses.

For the ambitious bishop or nobleman in the late Gothic period a fine stone house could be a matter of pride. One of the best preserved is Glimmingehus in Skåne, begun in 1499 by the mason Adam von Düren for Jens Holgersen Ulfstrand (figure 2.75).[80] The simple blocky building rises above wide moats, with small window openings in the first three stories, larger windows in the top story, and a steep high roof embellished with stepped gables. The building of such imposing and fortresslike noble dwellings had been hindered by the ravages of the Black Death, which swept the Nordic countries beginning in 1349, and Queen Margaret I's prohibition against fortified houses during her reign, 1387–1412. By the end of the fifteenth century times had changed, and Glimmingehus was prophetic, not only in its comparative grandeur but also in the balance of private living and ceremonial quarters on either side of a central staircase. It was traditional in the vertical disposition of its facilities, with kitchens and storerooms on the ground level, living quarters next, and a large open hall at the top, recalling the original scheme of Håkon's Hall.

Up to this point we have been considering ecclesiastical and residential buildings in their

greater or smaller aspects. Growth of towns with their mercantile and civic needs, however, led medieval Europe to the development of the town hall as a separate building.[81] The earliest remaining in Scandinavia is the town hall at Naestved on Zealand (figure 2.76).[82] It now is enclosed with later buildings on either side, and when first built c. 1450 it did not have the steep paneled gable of an enlargement c. 1520. Modest though it is, it too was prophetic, and five centuries later the Nordic countries were to see the construction of some town halls of a much grander nature.

By the time Glimmingehus was built, Alberti had written his treatise on architecture (1452) and Leonardo in the 1490s was making sketches for monumental domed churches in the High Renaissance manner. The Gothic was now outmoded on the Continent. At the same time the voyages of Columbus signaled an immense expansion of geographical knowledge, to be followed by new territorial and commercial rivalries that affected all of Europe. Finally, Savonarola's pleas for religious reform resulted in his death in 1498, less than twenty years before Luther's 95 theses and the beginning of another major religious development. In the next two chapters we shall see how the Scandinavian builders responded to the impact of these events on the ideas of European Renaissance and Baroque designers.

2.75  Glimmingehus, Skåne. Begun 1499. (Copenhagen, National Museum.)

2.76  Naestved, Zealand. Old Town Hall. c. 1450–1500. (Copenhagen, National Museum.)

**3** *The Renaissance in Scandinavia*

Less than a decade after Luther's manifesto of 1517, the acceptance of his reforming doctrine became so widespread in Denmark as to add to the already mounting political and commercial tensions. The oppressive policies of Christian II (1513–1523) caused the dissolution of the Union of Kalmar, losing Sweden to the protesting factions led by Gustavus Vasa. Christian's attempts to reduce the power of the Danish clergy and nobility caused him to be forced into exile in 1523, and his attempt to return in 1532 resulted in his imprisonment for life. Under the system of an elected monarchy his Lutheran-sympathizing uncle became king as Frederik I (1523–1533). Upon his death the Catholics supported Christian's great-nephew Count Christopher of Oldenburg, while the Reformers supported Frederik's son. The ensuing Count's War resulted in victory for the Reformers, the election of Christian III (1534–1559), and the abolition of Roman Catholicism from Denmark in 1536. Church property was confiscated for the Crown, but the nobility still had nearly half the country and the power of election in the Rigsråd, or Council. Oppression of the peasants led to a revolt in Jutland in 1536.

Meanwhile the reign of Gustavus Vasa (1523–1560) brought similarly profound changes to Sweden. Gustavus was elected king in 1523, and in 1544 the monarchy was declared hereditary under the Vasa dynasty. In 1527 properties of the Catholic Church were confiscated for the State, although the Augsburg Confession was not formally adopted until 1593. A smaller proportion of property remained in the hands of the nobility, and a much larger amount was held by the peasants, who also rose in some revolts.[1]

Against this background of conflict and rebellion it is not surprising that building activities in Denmark and Sweden were directed more toward the construction of strong manor houses and castles than toward churches. After all, the Scandinavian countries were by now rich in churches, and the major changes brought by the Reformation were in liturgical furnishings rather than in the buildings themselves. For wealthy landowners, desire for display of wealth and at the same time need for security against frequent turmoil led to the construction of great masonry manor houses having a fortified character. Decorative schemes were now based on Renaissance principles, particularly as they were then being interpreted by imported German and Netherlandish artists. Although technically it is not appropriate to speak of a "Renaissance" in Scandinavia, where classical art and architecture had never existed, the ornamental vocabulary of the "Northern Mannerist" version of the true Italian Renaissance was eagerly adopted, especially in Denmark and Sweden.[2]

Two main approaches to the planning of manor houses can be observed from the first half of the sixteenth century. In Denmark, especially on Funen, the preference was for a rectangular block with the entrance on one of the long sides and with stair towers and corner towers. An early notable example is Rygård on Funen, built for the Councillor Johan Urne (figure 3.1).[3] The first building was the north wing of the present structure, begun probably c. 1530, while the south, east, and west wings were probably added by 1537. The main residence was the north building, a three-story brick house that originally had a stair tower on the north side. Above the vaulted basement is the main floor, then a great hall with beamed ceiling, and a high attic story above with watch gallery and machicolations along the long sides. The timber work for the latter is particularly fine. Built of red brick with no stone trim to soften its broad outer surfaces, the original building rose above its surrounding moat in a clearly defensive manner, as did Glimmingehus. At Rygård, however, there is a difference. The division between the main floor and the great hall is marked by a shallow corbeled arcade as a stringcourse, and on the long sides the machicolations add a second arcade; the result is a sense of horizontality, of layering, that is absent at Glimmingehus and is indicative of changing taste. Two somewhat curious features may be noted. The gables are embellished with paneling in the brickwork, but in patterns that suggest Romanesque rather than Gothic models, as does the thin corbeled arcade of the stringcourse. Was there a conscious archaizing here? Further, there are rudimentary hood molds above the windows of the great hall at the east end of the building, a feature then becoming popular in England. The builder of Rygård must have had some sound training in military construction and perhaps some experience in travel as well. The details of the three additional wings combine to a nearly symmetrical and harmonious whole.

3.1 **Rygård, Funen. Begun c.
1530. (Copenhagen, Na-
tional Museum.)**

3.2 **Hesselagergård, Funen.
North wing. M. Bussert,
attr. Begun 1538. (Co-
penhagen, National
Museum.)**

1

2

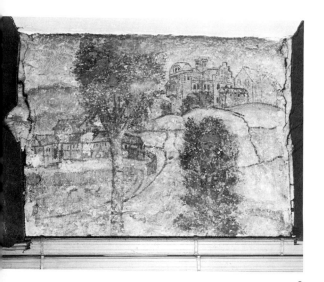

3

**3.3 Hesselagergård, Funen. Detail of wall painting. (Copenhagen, National Museum.)**

**3.4 Egeskov, Funen. Begun 1554.**

In 1538 Christian III's powerful Chancellor, Johan Friis, began his lofty brick manor house of Hesselagergård, also on Funen (figure 3.2).[4] The building consists of a rectangular block with two full stories and an attic story, a square tower on the south, and octagonal corner towers on the north side for effective defense of the walls. Partially surrounded by water and equipped with machicolations, Hesselagergård has a basically medieval aspect. But now the gables are richly ornamented with round-headed window openings and blind arcades divided into four vertical sections separated by applied colonnettes and topped with semicircular pediments, all this being completed c. 1550. The builder was probably the Dutchman Morten Bussert, the royal master builder. For the design of the gables Chancellor Friis may have turned to the painter Jakob Binck. Whether inspired directly from Italy, perhaps via the works of Serlio, or based on gables already appearing on houses such as that of Philip Melancthon in Wittenberg, 1536, which Friis had seen, the medieval stepped and paneled gables of Rygård are here replaced by the distinct motifs of the Renaissance. The new style is also represented in the paintings on the walls of the great "Deer Salon," where a hunting scene and a banquet are shown (figure 3.3). This painting may also be attributed to Jakob Binck.

A third fortified manor house on Funen is Egeskov, begun on an old estate by General Frands Brockenhuus in 1554 (figure 3.4).[5] The name means "oak wood" and comes from the forest that was cut to provide the pilings on which it rests. It is a double building with a double roof, the ridges running lengthwise. It rises directly from the defensive lake, with the land connection on the west, where there is an entrance and stair tower. On the east side there is a round tower at each end, and the present bridge linking the castle to the gardens

**4**

was built in 1883–1884. The upper parts of the
gables were also restored in the same years.
The formal gardens in the French manner were
laid out c. 1730, and the elegant parterre on
the east side in 1962. Egeskov's service buildings now house a restaurant and a car museum,
while the gardens are maintained as exhibit
grounds by local landscape firms. These manor
houses presided over the farm, grazing, and
timber lands that gave them as much self-suffi-
ciency as possible.

In Skåne, then under the Danish crown,
the more popular manor house was that built
with four wings around a courtyard and two
diagonally placed defensive towers. Torup, built
in 1545, is one of the best preserved examples
(figure 3.5).[6] It was built by the wealthy Gjör-
vel Fadersdotter Sparre in the middle of an ar-

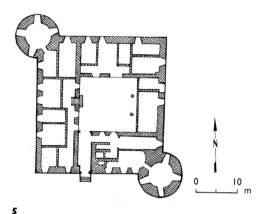

**5**

tificial lake, since partially drained so that it now rises from a small island. The towers are at the southeast and northwest corners, round at their bases. The southeast tower is octagonal above the first level and is the higher of the two. Steps lead up to the main entrance on the south side, through which one reaches the courtyard. The residential quarters are on the north and east sides, with large windows opening into the court. Here the exterior is more severe than at Hesselagergård and Egeskov, with no machicolations or stringcourses and only simple panels in the stepped gables of the attic stories. An arcade on the east side of the court adds a touch of fashion.

A more deliberate stronghold built under the Danish rule in Skåne is Malmöhus (figure 3.6).[7] The city was at that time the second largest in Denmark and an important port. Erik of Pomerania began a fortress here c. 1434, some parts of which remain, and then a new fortress in the Italian manner with moats and round towers was begun in 1536 under Christian III. It was the first of the Scandinavian fortresses for which the central residential portion was planned in a regular manner, and the builder is thought to have been Morten Bus-

sert. The central long rectangular block is four stories high, containing the royal apartments on either side of a central stair tower, with a firing loft in the top story. The round cannon towers stand forward, linked to the main block by wings. The gables here are not yet as Italianate as those of the later manor houses, but are stepped and paneled in the late medieval manner.

Meanwhile Gustavus Vasa was moving to solidify his new kingdom, ruling over the building of Sweden's mightiest and most picturesque fortresses. He began at Gripsholm, where a castle had been built on an island in Lake Mälar in the eleventh century. This had burned, and the new building was intended as a fortified royal country residence (figure 3.7).[8] The architect was Heinrich von Cöllen from Germany, who built an irregular hexagon of brick around a courtyard, defended with four massive round towers. The king's council chamber was located in the Grip Tower on the north, the queen's apartments in the east range, and the hall of state in the west range. Although the rooms look out into the courtyard, this is not spacious, and at best the castle must have seemed cramped. The addition to the west was begun in 1572 by the Duke of Södermanland, the youngest son of Gustavus Vasa who later ruled as Charles IX. Duke Charles's Chamber in the Prison Tower is a richly paneled Renaissance room with an elaborate painted ceiling.

Gustavus Vasa's ambitions for defense did not end with Gripsholm. In 1545 he started Vadstena Castle in Östergötland, on Lake Vättern (figure 3.8).[9] The abbey, which we have already noted, had been an important place of pilgrimage and the town itself a political center, with assizes and meetings of the Diet. A south-central point of defense against the Danes seemed logical here, and Joachim Bulgerin of Pomerania was given the task of designing the

3.5 **Torup, Skåne. 1545.**
**Plan. (After Paulsson,**
*Scandinavian Architec-*
*ture,* **figure 49, p. 107.)**

3.6 **Malmö, Skåne. Malmö-**
**hus. M. Bussert, attr.**
**Begun 1536.**

3.7 **Gripsholm, Uppland.**
**H. von Cöllen. Begun**
**1537. (Stockholm, An-**
**tikvarisk-Topografiska**
**Arkivet. Photo: Oskar**
**Bladh.)**

**7**

**6**

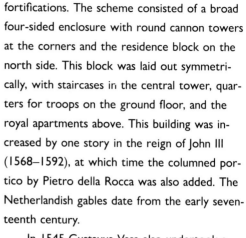

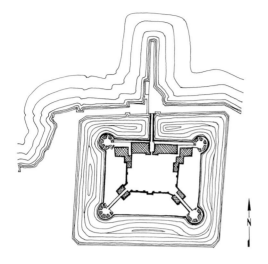

**8**

**9**

fortifications. The scheme consisted of a broad four-sided enclosure with round cannon towers at the corners and the residence block on the north side. This block was laid out symmetrically, with staircases in the central tower, quarters for troops on the ground floor, and the royal apartments above. This building was increased by one story in the reign of John III (1568–1592), at which time the columned portico by Pietro della Rocca was also added. The Netherlandish gables date from the early seventeenth century.

In 1545 Gustavus Vasa also undertook a building project at Kalmar in Småland. Situated on the sound between the mainland and Öland, this had long been a port town, with a castle built in the thirteenth century. The latter was a walled enclosure defended by round and polygonal towers, with the residences built inside the north wall. Gustavus Vasa began a new system of outer ramparts with heavy round corner towers (figure 3.9).[10] These fortifications were also started by Heinrich von Cöllen, but not completed to surround the castle until 1609. Old buildings on the south side were demolished by John III in 1568 and replaced by the present royal apartment block with its massive central tower.

The Chamber of Erik XIV, which he furnished before his reign (1560–1568), shows how the bare castle walls could be concealed with paneling, intarsia work, and a hunting frieze of painted and molded plaster (figure 3.10). It contrasts sharply with the larger, more barren halls. The castle chapel was built for John III by the Italian architect Domenicus Pahr (figure 3.11).[11] Begun in 1586, it is located in a large hall of the south building. It is a long narrow room, the altar at the east end and the entrance originally in the west for the benefit of the royal family, who resided in the north suite. This was not the first chapel at Kalmar,

10

but it is important because of this last point, its
relation to the royal apartments. In the years
to come, the court chapels and also the court
theaters were to be part of the original plans
for new royal palaces rather than, as here, created as well as possible from existing spaces.

For a third project Gustavus Vasa called
Heinrich von Cöllen to Uppsala. In 1545 the
foundations of a new castle were laid on a high
ridge of sand south of the city.[12] This building,
which had a characteristic round tower, was
still incomplete when it burned in 1572. A new
campaign was begun under John III, with Franciscus Pahr the building master (figure 3.12).

11

12

3.11 Kalmar, Småland. Castle. Chapel. D. Pahr. Begun 1586. (Kalmar, Regional Museum.)

3.12 Uppsala, Uppland. Castle. F. Pahr. Rebuilt 1572. (Uppsala, Upplands Museum.)

3.13 Stockholm. Castle. W. Boy. Enlarged 16th century. Painting by Govert Camphuysen, 1661. (Stockholm, City Museum.)

3.14 Stockholm. Castle. Plan, superimposed on outline of Royal Palace. (After A. Lindblom, *Stockholms Slott,* n.p.)

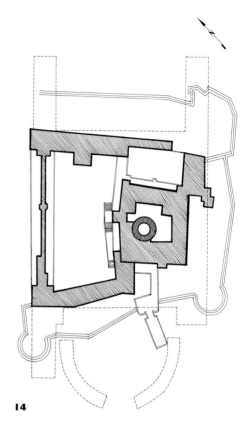

14

13

Royal apartments, chapel, and audience hall
were located in the south range, a rectangular
block four stories high with round towers at
each end of the south facade. A long east wing
was added c. 1640, and a north wing and west
wall appear to have been intended but never
built. Italianate stucco decorative motifs of the
exterior were almost entirely lost in another
fire in 1702. The present castle is largely the
work of Carl Hårleman's rebuilding from 1744,
with restorations by Ragnar Östberg in 1930–
1940.

Finally, the medieval castle in Stockholm
underwent a number of changes in the sixteenth century (figure 3.13).[13] Gustavus Vasa
began a curtain wall around it, complete with
corner towers, and by 1568 a major western
entrance with a drawbridge. Under John III the
old Tre Kronor tower was heightened, new
apartments were built in the east wing, and a
castle chapel in the west wing, the latter a hall
church. The enlarged plan is shown superimposed on the plan of the present palace (figure
3.14). From 1577 until his death in 1592 the
building master was William Boy, a Dutch master who oversaw the embellishment with arcades, window surrounds, and elaborate gables.
A century later Nicodemus Tessin the Younger
was already remodeling the north wing when
the fire of 1697 set the stage for the present
Royal Palace.

In the sixteenth century Norway was still
under the Danish crown, and with no resident
monarchy it was not the scene of such grandiose projects. Two buildings in Bergen, however, deserve our attention, both dating from
c. 1562. On orders from Frederik II the old
medieval tower at Bergenhus was torn down
and a new one built in its place (figure 3.15).[14]
Like Håkon's Hall it was severely damaged in
the 1944 explosion and has been rebuilt. It
now once more rises in five stories, with a

15

16

steep roof and small turret. The restricted window openings in the two lower levels and the
battlements at the top indicate its defensive
function. Its name comes from the governor
who built it, Erik Rosencrantz, who employed
Scottish masons. The Renaissance makes its appearance here only in small details. Rosencrantz
was also responsible for the Wall House, built
as a gatehouse in the walls on the opposite side
of the harbor (figure 3.16). The lower portion
is still used by merchants.

In another Norwegian city a significant
step was taken in the introduction of Renaissance principles in city planning. The Swedes
sacked the ancient town of Sarpsborg on the
Glomma estuary in 1657, and to replace it
Frederik II had Fredrikstad farther to the
southwest built as a fortress town (figure
3.17).[15] The part on the east side of the river
was laid out in grid fashion with an open plaza,
from which streets extend in all four directions. Although the church and barracks now
date from the late eighteenth century, their location at this central drill ground and market
place is probably original. The plan has been
tentatively attributed to Hans von Paeschen, architect to the king, who worked at Oslo on
the defenses of Akershus from 1566 to 1570.
The exact source of inspiration for the plan of
Fredrikstad might be difficult to identify, as the
concept of regular grid plans with squares had
been published by several architects since the
beginning of the century. The ultimate source
was probably Vitruvius, of which a German edition had been published in 1548. While modest
in size and not provided with the outer defenses seen on the plan until 1665, Fredrikstad
nonetheless was an important forerunner of extensive city-planning projects to come.

By 1560 Frederik II had already acquired
the manor of Hillerødsholm, located on a
marshy island in a forested area north of Co-

17

3.15   Bergen. Rosencrantz
       Tower. c. 1562. (Oslo,
       Riksantikvaren.)
3.16   Bergen. Wall house. c.
       1562.
3.17   Fredrikstad, Østfold.
       Plan. H. von Paeschen,
       attr. c. 1570. (After
       Kavli, *Norwegian Ar-
       chitecture*, p. 57.)

**3.18 Hillerød, Zealand. Hillerødsholm. Begun c. 1560. Painting by Th. Vibom. (Hillerød, Nationalhistoriske Museum på Frederiksborg.)**

**3.19 Helsingør, Zealand. Kronborg. H. von Paeschen and A. van Opbergen. 1574–1585. (Copenhagen, National Museum.)**

penhagen. Like Gustavus Vasa at Gripsholm he wanted a country retreat as an alternative to the old medieval castle in the heart of the city. What resulted, however, was much less a fortress than Gripsholm (figure 3.18).[16] The newly named Frederiksborg did, in fact, more resemble an Elizabethan "prodigy house," with the latter's supporting buildings and lands, or perhaps a French château. The manor house itself had been built for the previous owner c. 1550 and resembled Egeskov in consisting of two ranges with parallel roofs and twin gables. This building was little changed. The site was developed into a clear system of three islands by a series of dams and canals, with stables and two round towers on the first, a church and kitchen building on the second, and the manor house on the third. As we shall see, most of this was to disappear not long after Frederik II's death in 1588, but the stables and round towers on the first island, the long pantry wing beside the road, and nearby *Badstuen* or Bathhouse, begun 1580, remain. The painting gives the impression of a comfortable, thriving royal estate.

Frederik II, however, had other responsibilities, not the least of which was to keep the royal coffers filled. In 1570 a peace was concluded in a war with Sweden, and by then the

19

king had already started measures to increase the Sound Dues. These were levied on ships passing Krogen ("The Hook"), a fortress on the promontory that forces the Øresund to its narrowest point, less than three miles from Sweden. Here in 1421 Erik of Pomerania had built an earlier fortress and levied Sound Dues in 1426. Christian III had strengthened the defenses, but it was Frederik II who began the transformation of the old fortress to an imposing castle as a grandiose expression of his royalty (figure 3.19).[17] Kronborg is impressive from the sea, but a view by C. W. Eckersberg shows how commanding it was once from the land side (figure 3.20). As Frederik II developed his new castle from c. 1574 to 1585, his builders followed some of the earlier structures, hence the thicker walls on the west and south

toward the land. From 1574 to 1577 Hans von Paeschen, who had been working at Oslo, served as master mason, and he was succeeded by Antonius van Opbergen, a Flemish builder and military engineer. The chapel, kitchens, and guard rooms were on the ground level, the state apartments containing the king's and queen's apartments in the north wing, and the great Riddarsal, or Knights' Hall, in the south wing. In 1580 the red brick walls built under von Paeschen were refaced in gray sandstone by van Opbergen, and thanks to the leadership of the Flemish master builders the details were carried out by Netherlandish sculptors, especially the north and south portals. The Riddarsal, 206 feet long, is said to be the largest in northern Europe, and it was here that in 1589 the wedding festivities of Christian IV's sister

Anne and James VI of Scotland took place (figure 3.21). Perhaps this even inspired Shakespeare's placement of *Hamlet* in the castle of "Elsinore" (with which the original Hamlet story had nothing to do). Except in the chapel, the original interior fittings were destroyed by a fire in 1629, after which Christian IV undertook restorations and some changes.

One building unique in its purpose was built during the reign of Frederik II. In 1576 the king bestowed the island of Ven in the Sound on the astronomer Tycho Brahe.[18] Although Brahe left for Germany in 1597, having lost the favor of Christian IV and also his funding, he had published illustrations of the observatory that he built on the island, fortunately, for by 1652 the abandoned buildings had all but crumbled away (figure 3.22). Brahe's observatory, which he called Uraniborg, had a symmetrical plan thought to have had a French origin, possibly in a plan by Domenico da Cortona for the château of Blois. The building contained the astronomer's residence in the main block, with guest apartments and student quarters, and a domed observing chamber on top. Towers on the north and south sides carried further observing instruments, and there were also workshops, printing presses, and a library. Some notion of the carvings on doors, windows, and gables may be gained from the contemporary illustrations. Much of the work must have been done under the Netherlandish builder Hans van Steenwinckel the Elder, who studied at Ven from 1578 until he was appointed royal building master in 1583.[19] Uraniborg was surrounded by a formal walled garden, in which were located additional observing rooms. All this was carried out in luxury equaled only by Tycho Brahe's irascibility, and with its many working facilities was prophetic of later scientific establishments. Certainly there was no architectural precedent for Brahe to follow. Though well equipped for

**20**

**21**

its time, Uraniborg set none for the first observatories to use the telescope, invented by Gali-
leo early in the next century.

Up to this point there has been no mention of church building in the Renaissance period apart from the castle chapels. While this
may seem surprising in view of the eagerness
with which the Reformation was adopted in
Scandinavia, several factors made a new wave
of church building unlikely. Thousands of parish
churches were already built and in use, to
which were now added the convent churches.
In addition, the Lutheran reform was less icon-
oclastic than some other strains of Protestantism, Luther in his Preface to the German Mass
of 1526 having said that "The Mass vestments,
altars and lights may be retained till such time
as they shall all change of themselves or it shall
please us to change them."[20] One of the few
churches of this period was the one at Slangerup on Zealand, begun in 1576 from designs by
Hans van Steenwinckel the Elder, replacing an
earlier Gothic church that had become too
small. Even here the building is still fundamentally Gothic, with its high pointed windows, but
the tower and porch gables are in Dutch Renaissance style, probably designed by Steenwinckel as well (figure 3.23).[21] Even more
impressive is the great gable added to the Romanesque church at Valløby on Zealand in 1590
(figure 3.24).[22] In this case the architectural
motifs are further enriched by coats of arms,
herms, and reliefs portraying David and a
warrior.

The coronation of Christian IV of Denmark in 1596 ushered in another lively period
of building in the Scandinavian countries.[23] For
the event the 19-year-old king gave out his
first architectural commission, to have the
tower of Copenhagen Castle heightened and
finished with a spire (figure 3.25).

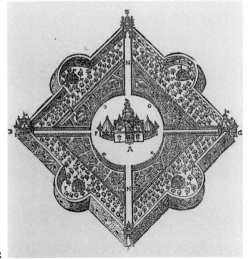

22

In 1599 he turned to the harbor next to Copenhagen Castle where a timber arsenal from 1560 was already in place. A new rectangular basin was dug on the south side of Slotsholmen, and the brick Arsenal was built on the west side, with its vaulted cannon hall 495 feet long (figure 3.26).[24] As it appears on the left of the basin in figure 3.25, it was approached by ship through an opening in the south range of buildings. Opposite was built a warehouse for provisions, including taxes paid in kind. The basin was filled in 1868, and the Royal Library now occupies the site of the south range. The Arsenal now houses the Armory Museum.

As can be readily seen from the 1611 engraving, Copenhagen Castle, surrounded by a moat, with the busy harbor on the south and the dense medieval city on the north, was unlikely to suit the king as a year-round residence. He did, after all, have Frederiksborg, which he had known from childhood. Its old manor house from c. 1550 did not satisfy his ideas of magnificence, and down it came to make room for a more splendid establishment (figure 3.27).[25] The church and other buildings on the middle island were also razed, but the stables and round tower on the south island were kept. In order to have a residence at Frederiksborg during the years of construction the king built Sparepenge ("Save Money") on the north side of the lake. This was taken down in the eighteenth century.

As the new palace was built, an element of symmetry was introduced that gives a more stately approach than that to the fortress of Kronborg. From the plan of the site we can see how the road through the stables on the south island is linked by a curving bridge to the Barbican Gate on the middle island (figure 3.28). When one passes through the gate the Castellan's House is on the left, the Chancellery on the right, while the courtyard created

23

24

by these buildings is dominated by the replica of the Neptune Fountain by Adriaen de Vries, completed in 1624 (figure 3.29).[26] The approach to the palace becomes a drama in itself, as the visitor moves from the comparatively spacious Fountain Courtyard across the narrow bridge over the canal, with terrace arcades on either side of the gateway. Now the opulence to be encountered throughout the palace is clearly stated. The gate by Caspar Boegardt, 1609, is treated as a triumphal arch, with rusticated Tuscan pilasters flanking the arched opening and two sets of armorial bearings above. The arcades rest on Tuscan columns, rising from brackets in the wall of the canal. This somewhat improbable arcade encloses twelve pedimented niches, containing statues of the Olympic gods. The gate, arcade, and niches are in sandstone, contrasting with the red brick walls. The same use of stone and brick is made on the three wings of the palace that surround the inner courtyard. As one enters, the Chapel Wing is on the left, or west, side, the main residence of the King's Wing opposite on the

**3.23 Slangerup, Zealand. Church. H. van Steenwinckel I. 1576. Portal.**

**3.24 Valløby, Zealand. Church. 1590. East gable. (Copenhagen, National Museum.)**

**3.25 Copenhagen. Castle (at center). Detail of Wijk's Prospect, 1611. (Copenhagen, National Museum.)**

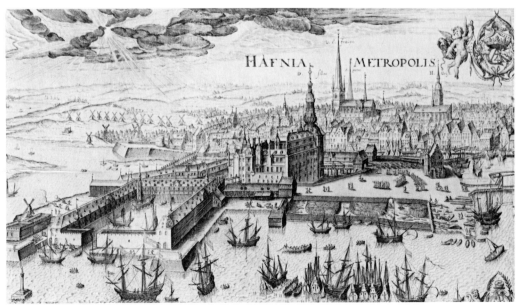

**25**

26

27

3.26 **Copenhagen. Arsenal.
1599. Cannon Hall.
(Copenhagen, Arsenal
Museum.)**

3.27 **Hillerød, Zealand.
Frederiksborg. 1602–
1608. Air view. (Co-
penhagen, Academy of
Art Library.)**

3.28 **Hillerød, Zealand.
Frederiksborg. Plan.
(After Weilbach, *Fred-
eriksborg,* figure 12,
n.p.)**

3.29 **Hillerød, Zealand.
Frederiksborg.
Courtyard.**

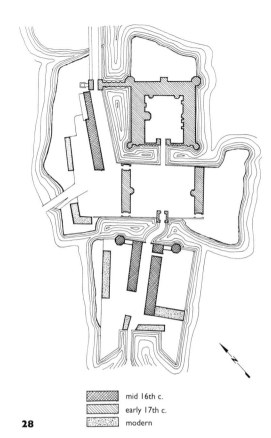

mid 16th c.

early 17th c.

modern

**28**

**29**

north, and the east or Princess's Wing on the right. There is a richly ornamented door to the Chapel, and the King's Wing was made splendid by the addition of the two-story Marble Gallery, with its alternating arches and columned niches and statuary. The warm gray color of this gallery now is deceptive, it originally having had red marble columns and black marble moldings.

The change in color was the result of a great fire in 1859. On the interior of the palace, little survived that disaster except the Chapel (figure 3.30). Even here there is some restoration, especially at the north end, where the original organ of 1614 fell. By great good fortune the organ built in 1610 by Esaias Compenius and given to Christian IV in 1617 was on loan to another palace at the time of the fire. Otherwise, its regular place being at the north end of the Great Hall above the Chapel, it would surely have perished. It now stands in the south gallery, where its fine craftsmanship and wide range of possibilities in performance make it one of Denmark's greatest musical treasures. The Chapel was planned as a long high central space, separated from the aisles at ground level by an arcade with coupled columns before the piers and arcaded galleries above the aisles, all surfaces being richly ornamented. The interiors of the other three wings restored after the fire now house the collections of the Museum of National History.

The overall conception of Frederiksborg cannot be attributed with certainty to any one designer. Hans van Steenwinckel the Elder and the king himself have both been proposed, partly because of certain resemblances in plan to Kronborg.[27] Influence from French château design is evident, possibly coming from the publication of du Cerceau's *Plus excellents bâtiments de France* in 1559. If the plan of the King's Wing, which was built first, is looked at singly, however, it is seen to be a long residence block with octagonal corner towers, a central projecting square tower, and additional projecting octagonal towers on the opposite side—in other words an essentially traditional manor house plan. A similar sense of tradition seems to be revealed in the Gothic tracery of the chapel windows. For the details of completion there are the chapel tower by Lorenz van Steenwinckel, the tilting gate by Hans van Steenwinckel the Younger, and the statues in the terrace by Geraert Lambertsz from the workshop of Hendrik de Keyser in Amsterdam. The Privy Passage across the west canal and the Mint Gate with Audience Chamber on the second level were added about 1614.[28]

For all its splendor and extensive forest surroundings, Frederiksborg is 22 miles from Copenhagen, then a day's journey. It could not be expected to offer an afternoon's respite from the duties and constraints of Copenhagen Castle. The latter was later described by the English traveler Lord Molesworth as "being for the Situation, Meanness, and Inconvenience the worst in the World."[29] In 1606 Christian IV had purchased land outside Østerport, the eastern gate of the city, and began a summer house that would be more readily accessible. It started out as a two-story brick house with a square tower on the northeast side, and was enlarged with two more towers in 1613–1614 and a fourth in 1633. Hans van Steenwinckel the Younger worked here, but the main plans were probably by another Netherlandish builder, Bertel Lange. The exterior surfaces were made lively by stringcourses, window enframements, quoins, and scrolls of sandstone against the brick. In its park setting, with formal gardens laid out in the new French fashion to the south and west, Rosenborg rises like an architectural jewel in the heart of the city (figure 3.31).[30] The interior rooms are finished

30

31

with both original and later paneled walls and
ceilings and now serve as the museum of the
Danish kings.

   Christian IV's building activities did not
stop with Frederiksborg and Rosenborg. With
his encouragement public buildings, churches,
and even city plans were begun or redesigned
at home and abroad. As early as 1608 he had
Copenhagen's old Town Hall, standing between
Gammeltorv and Nytorv, rebuilt with an arcade
on the ground level facing Nytorv, a turret rising above it in the center, and a large Netherlandish scroll gable on either side (figure
3.32).[31] A larger central tower, also flanked by

gables, rose from the street level on the Gammeltorv side. Now it resembled such Continental buildings as the old Town Hall in Amsterdam, but we are not told which of the Netherlandish builders then in Denmark was responsible for it.

The extant commercial building for which Christian IV contracted in 1619 is the famous Bourse (figure 3.33).[32] Lorenz van Steenwinckel was the first architect appointed when the king decided to have a suitable building for the trading companies that he was promoting.[33] On Lorenz's death in the same year his brother Hans assumed the work, and the building was completed in 1640. The king took much interest in the project, especially in the early years up to the completion of the spire in 1625. This somewhat exotic building was rebuilt as a modern stock exchange by Harald Conrad Stilling in 1857 and has fortunately survived fires and bombing. The ground level was divided into warehouse rooms running athwart the building and entered only from the street sides, while

32

3.32 **Copenhagen. Old Town
Hall. Rebuilt 1608.
Thurah, *Danske Vitru-
vius*, vol. 3, plate 41.
(Copenhagen, Academy
of Art Library.)**

3.33 **Copenhagen. Bourse.
L. and H. van Steen-
winckel II. 1619.**

the second level had offices and merchant stalls
and was entered at either end. Along each side
the bays are divided by sandstone pilasters with
herms and strapwork and are further accented
by the scroll gables rising at regular intervals.
The east and west ends are lavishly ornamented
with sandstone carvings against the red brick
walls. The unique spire composed of four inter-
twined dragon tails was apparently based on
firework designs and was planned by the sculptor Ludwig Heidritter.

Christian IV's concern for his overseas
travelers extended to the families of his naval
officers and men. At the north end of town,
midway between Rosenborg and the new citadel of Sankt Annae Skanse, 1627, Nyboder
were begun in January 1631 (figure 3.34).[34]
These were row houses, to be administered by
the Admiralty, ranged in twenty blocks with
over six hundred apartments. As first built they
were single-story yellow brick buildings with
common walls and the ridges of the red tile
roofs running parallel to the street the entire
length of each block. This is different from the
more usual town dwellings with their gable
ends to the street. Nyboder are attributed to
Hans van Steenwinckel the Younger and Leonhard Blasius and are more like workmen's row
houses in Germany and the Netherlands in this
treatment of their roofs, more economical to
build than individual gables and symbolically creating social unity rather than distinction. A vestibule, living room, kitchen, and two bedrooms,
with a stairway to attic storage space, consti-
tuted the interior arrangements. Later second
stories were added, and not all the original
number have survived. We are reminded of the
multifamily Iron Age house, and similar housing
would in years to come be a concern for some
of Scandinavia's most prominent architects.

Before turning to the city plans of Christian IV we may note briefly the kind of house

to which a wealthy individual might aspire during his reign. In Copenhagen, Number 6 Amagertorv was built in 1616 for the alderman Mathias Hansen, who later became burgomaster (figure 3.35).[35] Three stories high, it is impressive in its red brick and sandstone trim, with elaborate gables rising above the large windows of the second and third levels. The ground level has been remodeled for business purposes, but the portal of the passage to the original garden at the back remains. Another well-known example is Jens Bangs House in Ålborg, built in 1623 (figure 3.36).[36] Like the Mathias Hansen House it has its ridge parallel to the street, here finished by three richly ornamented gables that give light to the attic stories. The building is faced with yellow brick and sandstone trim, the ground level quite plain but the three upper stories with abundant strapwork. A stair-

case to an octagonal turret gives access to the main dwelling level, and communication between all four stories is via a conservative staircase tower at the back. For such merchants the lavish exterior ornament of their houses might be matched by that of the interior (figure 3.37). Broad paneling with pilasters, arches, strapwork, biblical or allegorical reliefs, and inscriptions lined the walls, while the ceiling beams were also paneled, a fit setting for the heavily carved furniture of the period.

In connection with the building of Nyboder, reference was made to the defenses that Christian IV had added to Copenhagen. His interest in planning and fortification extended to several other projects, three of which will be described briefly here. An early plan of 1614 was for a new town, named Kristianstad, located on the east coast of Skåne

35   36

3.34   Copenhagen. Nyboder.
H. van Steenwinckel II
and L. Blasius, attr.
Begun 1631.

3.35   Copenhagen. No. 6
Amagertorv. 1616.

3.36   Ålborg, Jutland. Jens
Bangs House. 1623.
(Copenhagen, National
Museum.)

**37**

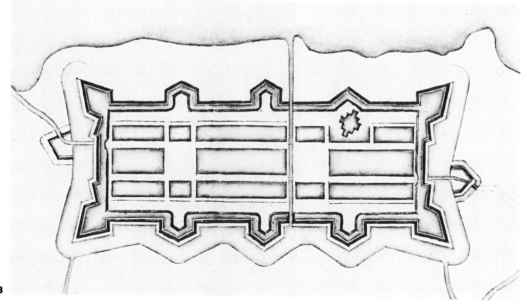

**38**

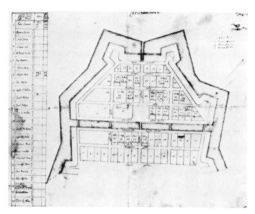

**39**

**3.37  Room from Ålborg,
Jutland. c. 1620. (Co-
penhagen, National
Museum.)**

**3.38  Kristianstad, Skåne.
Plan. 1614. (Copen-
hagen, National
Museum.)**

**3.39  Christianshavn. Plan. c.
1620. (Copenhagen,
Royal Library.)**

**3.40  Oslo. Plan. 1640s. Ak-
ershus at lower left.
(After Kavli, *Norwe-
gian Architecture*, p.
57.)**

**3.41  Oslo. Akershus. Paint-
ing by J. Coning, 1699.
(Oslo, City Museum.)**

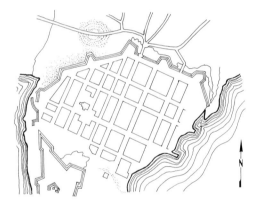

**40**

**41**

(figure 3.38).[37] In this case a rectangular plan was chosen, the length parallel to the shore, with moat and bastions and two inner plazas in addition to the space for the church. A canal separates the main plaza with the royal residence, town hall, and church from the burgher district. The diagonal of the larger plaza was planned to be parallel with the traditional east-west axis of the church, begun in 1617. Kristianstad has since grown out and over the original lines of the walls, a few outlines of which remain on the northern edge.

At home Christian IV planned a new town and defense system at the north end of the island of Amager.[38] The first plan, by the royal engineer Johan Semp, called for a symmetrical design based on an incomplete decagon, with streets radiating from a central square with a church on one side and served by a canal. The final project was based on an irregular octagon, with fewer bastions, the streets on a grid system, a central square, and a canal running across the whole plan in a northeast to southwest direction on the north side of the square (figure 3.39). The basic grid of the plan remains today, including the canal, the square, and the southern portion of the ramparts.

The third town is Oslo, founded in 1048 by King Harald Hardrada on the site of Gamlebyen in the modern city, east of the Aker River. Fires took their toll over the years; after an especially destructive one in 1624, Christian IV set about planning a new and better-defended city which he named for himself, Christiania.[39] He had a residential area laid out on the other side of the river from the old town, where a level site could be walled in and partly defended by the old Akershus on a ridge over-

looking the Pipervik (figure 3.40). An irregular
bastioned wall on the north side enclosed a
grid plan with blocks of varying dimensions and
a plaza for the church that was moved there.
Building the new houses in brick and roofing
them with tile was, not surprisingly, encouraged, although many were also built of half-timber work.

The key to the whole scheme was Akershus.[40] Begun by King Håkon V c. 1319, it consisted of an irregular series of walls, wings, and
courts, with two major towers, the Vågehall
and the Jomfru Tower. By the mid-sixteenth
century the former was deteriorating; its ruins
were incorporated into the east wing during
the rebuilding by Christian IV from 1625 to
1648, when two new stair towers crowned
with spires were also added (figure 3.41). Coning's painting shows how it appeared at the end
of the seventeenth century, rising above the
outer defenses and commanding the harbor, as
did Kronborg on the Øresund. Extensive
changes to convert it to a Baroque palace were
proposed in 1756 but not carried out. No
longer a residence, it has been restored in
modern times and serves as a museum and festival hall. As the visitor climbs up the steep approach and enters through the heavy portals
the impression is one of great fortified
strength.

Christian IV also sponsored a certain
amount of religious building. In 1613 he contracted with Lorenz van Steenwinckel to build
a burial chapel on the north side of Roskilde
Cathedral.[41] This was richly ornamented outside
and in, the windows having Gothic tracery amid
the profusion of Renaissance ornament like
those of the Chapel at Frederiksborg. The
same was done for the church that Lorenz and
Hans van Steenwinckel the Younger built for
the king at Kristianstad from 1617 to 1628 (figure 3.42).[42] Built in brick with stone trim, its

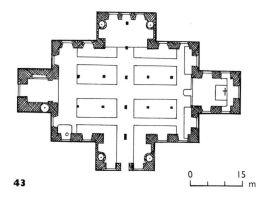

**43**

0    15
⌊__⌊__⌊__⌋ m

3.42  **Kristianstad, Skåne.**
**Holy Trinity Church.**
**L. and H. van Steen-**
**winckel II. 1617–1628.**

3.43  **Kristianstad, Skåne.**
**Holy Trinity Church.**
**Plan. (After Lund and**
**Millech, eds., *Dan-***
***marks bygningskunst,***
**p. 130.)**

generous proportions and Netherlandish ornament give Holy Trinity Church a certain nobility that might seem surprising in a new port
town, some distance from the capital. The plan
at first glance gives the impression of a centralized structure, but this is not the case (figure
3.43). There is an entrance tower on the west,
then a six-bay nave, separated from comparatively wide aisles and terminating in a projecting eastern sanctuary. From the south and
north walls project shallow additions, the width
of the two central bays of the nave, with columns centered in the gaps in the walls to complete the support for the vaults.[43] The aisles
rise to the height of the nave in the traditional
hall church fashion, now given a Renaissance
expression (figure 3.44). The tall windows seen
on the exterior admit abundant light. The
vaults are covered with a cross-gabled roof,
which accounts for the large ornamented gables
on the north and south sides. An especially
valuable piece of the liturgical fittings is the organ case by Johan Lorentz, built in 1630, although the works themselves are modern.[44]

For the capital city the king saw to the
provision for a seamen's church even before
the building of Nyboder.[45] An anchor forge dating from 1563 was converted to a church in
1619 with Leonhard Blasius as the master
builder (figure 3.45). The higher of the two
forge buildings was converted to the sanctuary
of the new church, and three additions were
made to make it cruciform in plan. The walls of
the church are plain, but the gables are ornamented with applied pilasters and moldings. Its
rather curious appearance, rising from the
water of Holmens Canal, comes from its origin
in an entirely different building.

Another church dedicated to the Holy
Trinity was begun in Copenhagen in 1637 after
plans by Hans van Steenwinckel the Younger.[46]
It too is of brick, apparently a hall church from

**3.44  Kristianstad, Skåne.
Holy Trinity Church.
Interior.**

**3.45  Copenhagen. Holmens
Church. L. Blasius.
1619.**

**44**

**46**

the exterior, but without the gables and Renaissance ornament of the church in Kristianstad. The exterior is rather forbidding, very plain, with wall buttresses between the windows rising to the eaves. The interior gives an entirely different impression (figure 3.46). Whereas at Kristianstad the columns are round and support simple four-part vaults, in the Copenhagen church the columns are octagonal and support star vaults over the nave. The aisles are covered with four-part vaults springing from the nave colonnade and corbels in the aisle walls, as had been done at Kristianstad. A comparison with Storkyrkan in Stockholm might be made here, for in that church the nave is covered with star vaults, and the aisle vaults do not rise from wall shafts either. The difference is that in Storkyrkan the shafts emerge from the walls without brackets to support them, in the disintegration of forms characteristic of the late Gothic period. In the two churches dedicated to the Holy Trinity, on the other hand, the clarity of Renaissance principles demanded that at least token support for the aisle wall vaulting shafts be given visible expression.

At Holy Trinity we find the last of Christian IV's buildings that we are to consider, and the most unusual. This is the Round Tower attached to the church at the west end (figure 3.47).[47] It was not the idea of the astronomer Longomontanus to have an observatory in the heart of the city, but the king wanted it as part of the intellectual center of the capital, across the street from the University, whose library was to be housed in an attic story of Holy Trinity. The church was built to be the student church. The astonishing part of the tower is the spiral ramp that winds to the observing platform at the top in eight whorls. The idea was derived from Continental castles in which such ramps were built for riding or drawing up

3.46 **Copenhagen. Holy Trinity Church. H. van Steenwinckel II. 1637. Interior. (Copenhagen, National Museum.)**

3.47 **Copenhagen. Holy Trinity Church. Drawing by C. W. Eckersberg, 1809. (Copenhagen, National Museum.)**

47

gun carriages, and there was already a ramp at the fortress of Varberg in Halland, then under Danish rule. The use of the telescope was then in its infancy, and such towers, without the spiral ramp, were to be the general rule for observatories for many years.

Before Holy Trinity was completed and dedicated in 1656 Christian IV died at Rosenborg Palace in 1648. A map drawn in 1659 shows the legacy he left the city: a new harbor and Arsenal, a Bourse, new defenses for the land side, housing for seamen and their families, a new town on Amager, the palace in the garden that pleased him so much, new churches, and an expanded university quarter (figure 3.48). But old Copenhagen Castle was still there, becoming less comfortable by the year.

In the meantime notable events were taking place in building elsewhere. Queen Christina came to the Swedish throne at the age of 18 in 1644. The years of regency since the

death of her father, Gustavus II Adolf, in 1626, had seen no leadership like that of Christian IV in the arts, and Swedish involvement in the Thirty Years' War did not encourage many large building projects. An attempt was made to colonize in the New World, to be sure, with the settlement at Fort Christina on the Delaware River in 1638. But the fort was built by a Dutchman, Peter Minuit, then in the service of Sweden, and was taken over by another Dutchman, Peter Stuyvesant, in 1655.[48] While the queen did try to encourage commerce and manufacturing after the Treaty of Westphalia in 1648, she was far more interested in presiding over a brilliant court, to which she invited foreign artists, scholars, and philosophers, including René Descartes.[49] Her extravagance and indifference to her people nationwide led to her abdication and conversion to Roman Catholicism in 1654.

The most important works in Swedish architecture at this time actually belonged to the regency. The Makalös ("Nonesuch") palace in Stockholm is known to us only from prints and paintings, having been destroyed in 1825 (figure 3.49).[50] It was built for General Jakob de la Gardie by the German architect Hans Jacob Kristler in 1630. Occupying a splendid site on the water across from Stockholm Castle, near Norrbro, it was a rectangular block with steep roof, corner pavilions in the French manner, and a polyglot ornament. A wealthy merchant, on the other hand, might build a residence like the Petersén House in the Old Town of Stockholm. Built by C. J. Döteber in 1645–1649, rising four stories with gable windows lighting the attic, it is rich with German-Netherlandish ornament (figure 3.50).[51]

Of the several noble estates that received mansions during these years, a good example is Tidö in Västmanland, the palace of the regent Chancellor Axel Oxenstierna, begun c. 1620 and finished 1635–1645 under the architects Simon de La Vallée and Nicodemus Tessin the Elder (figure 3.51).[52] Rising on a height above Lake Mälar, just south of Västerås, it was within easy reach of the capital by water. The main residence is three stories high, flanked symmetrically by two-story wings, with the entrance wing opposite. The palace is especially notable for its rich sculptured doorways by the stonemason Hindrich Blume.

One truly grandiose building for Stockholm was at least envisioned. In 1641 a commission was granted to Simon de La Vallée for the Riddarhus, or House of Nobles, to be their place of assembly in Stockholm.[53] Simon de La Vallée was the son of a French architect working in Paris on the Luxembourg Palace under Salomon de Brosse. The original proposal was for a central rectangular building, with turreted corner pavilions and wings forming large court-

48

3.48 Copenhagen. Map as of 1659. Resen, *Atlas Danicus.* (Copenhagen, Royal Library.)

3.49 Stockholm. Painting by E. Martin, 1787. Makalös palace at right. (Stockholm, National Museum.)

3.50 Stockholm. Petersén House. C. J. Döteber. 1645–1649.

49

50

yards on either side. This plan, along with the proposed details of rustications, balustrades, and segmental pediments all reflected French rather than German or Netherlandish taste. Simon de La Vallée died, however, the same year, with construction barely started, and work was delayed for more than a decade.

When building was resumed in 1653, the new architect was Justus Vinckeboons from Amsterdam, and the style of the Riddarhus was changed from French to Dutch. This did not mean a return to Northern Mannerism, however, but to the now flourishing Dutch Palladianism. The wings, courtyards, and corner pavilions were abandoned, Simon de La Vallée's project being reduced to the central building and two pavilions at the north edge of the site

(figure 3.52). The sandstone pilasters of the monumental order ornamenting the brick building are not rusticated, and the central entrance bays are emphasized by low triangular pediments. A vestige of the corner pavilion design remains in the doubling and coupling of the pilasters framing the end bays, but the whole façades on north and south are unified by the nearly unbroken line of the entablatures. After three years of work on the Riddarhus Justus Vinckeboons returned to Holland, and the work was completed by Simon de La Vallée's son Jean. Now a French touch was added in the round attic windows and the shape of the "säteri" roof, rising in two curving parts with a short vertical part between. If we compare the Riddarhus as finally completed in 1674 with

52

3.51 Tidö, Västmanland.
S. de La Vallée and N.
Tessin I. Begun c. 1620.
(Stockholm, Nordic
Museum.)

3.52 Stockholm. Riddarhus.
S. de La Vallée,
J. Vinckeboons, and
J. de La Vallée. Begun
1642.

3.53 Austråt, Sør-
Trøndelag. Castle.
1654. (Oslo,
Riksantikvaren.)

53

Makalös and Stockholm Castle as it appeared in
1661, we can see that a new taste had been
introduced, mainly by the nobility.

By contrast the only major Norwegian
building at midcentury was not planned on such
theoretical principles at all. In 1654 Chancellor
Olav Bjelke began the transformation of the
medieval church at Austråt in Sør-Trøndelag to
a castle at the entrance to Trondheim Fjord
(figure 3.53).[54] The owner's journeys to Padua,
Madrid, and Vienna probably inspired his conversion of the church to chapel with Riddarsal
above and his addition of wings to create a
courtyard residence, complete with columned
loggia and further Renaissance ornament. Restorations were necessary after a fire in 1916,
but it is still an ingenious example of adaptive
reuse.

The early seventeenth century was not a
time of extensive church building in either
Sweden or Norway. In Stockholm a new
church of St. Jacob had been started as a nearly
square hall church with long choir and apse in
1588. Work was interrupted, and as finished in
1643 by the German architect Hans Förster it
was enlarged by several bays and covered with
late Gothic star vaults of varying patterns (figure 3.54).[55] The portals were carved by Hindrich Blume, who also did the portals at Tidö
(figure 3.55). The church was completed with
side aisles lower than the nave and has none of
the spacious quality of the Steenwinckels'
churches in Kristianstad and Copenhagen.

Another church by Hans Förster was built
at Tyresö in Södermanland.[56] Here there is a
single nave with a three-sided choir, Gothic
windows, and domed-up vaults springing from
half columns on the walls (figure 3.56). Once
again there was the conservatism in the use of
Gothic elements for church building that char-
acterizes the Chapel at Frederiksborg and Holy
Trinity in Kristianstad.

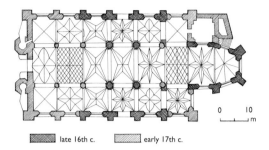

| ▨ late 16th c. | ▨ early 17th c. |

**54**

**55**

By the beginning of the second half of the seventeenth century, then, the royal and noble patrons of building in Scandinavia had moved from the encouragement of a tentative admixture of medieval and Renaissance elements to a much greater reliance on theoretical principles, and some of their most ambitious projects have survived. The change in color from the often monochromatic brick surfaces of the Middle Ages to the lively contrasts of brick with stone carvings was due largely to the contributions of German and Netherlandish architects and sculptors. Apart from the planning of new cities and their defenses, however, much of this activity had to do with individual buildings rather than with large-scale urban projects. More sweeping changes would be made in the cities of Denmark, Norway, and Sweden during the coming years of the Baroque.

**3.54** Stockholm. St. Jacob's Church. H. Förster. Begun 1588. Plan. (After Lundmark, *Sankt Jakobs Kyrka*, figure 59, p. 256.)

**3.55** Stockholm. St. Jacob's Church. South portal.

**3.56** Tyresö, Södermanland. Church. H. Förster. 1638–1640. Interior. (Stockholm, Antikvarisk-Topografiska Arkivet.)

# 4  *Scandinavian Baroque and Rococo*

*Early Baroque, c. 1660–1730*

In the middle years of the seventeenth century a number of political and military events occurred that accompanied and probably hastened changes of direction in Scandinavian architecture. As we have just seen, buildings carrying Renaissance decorative motifs often simply perpetuated medieval ideas of planning; but the later part of the century brought more essential changes, not only for individual buildings but also for city planning.

Before turning to the extensive royal projects of the late seventeenth century, we may find it illuminating to review briefly the personal circumstances of the monarchs of Denmark and Sweden. The Danish kings in the seventeenth century came to the throne immediately upon the deaths of their fathers as young or mature adults. When Christian IV died in 1648 at the age of 71, his son Frederik III succeeded him at the age of 39. Frederik III's son Christian V was 24 years old when he became king in 1670, ruling until his sudden death in a hunting accident 29 years later. In 1699 Frederik IV was 28 years old and lived to rule until 1730.

The situation was different in Sweden. When the great king and military leader Gustavus II Adolf was killed in the fighting at Lützen in 1632, his daughter Christina was only six years old, and Sweden was ruled by a regency, dominated by Count Axel Oxenstierna, for 12 years. Her abdication in 1654 left the throne to the cousin whom she had named her hereditary successor, Charles X. His brilliant military career was cut short six years later by pneumonia when he was only 38. That left his little son, aged four years, to a regency until 1674. In 1697 at the age of 42 Charles XI died, leaving the throne to his son, who became Charles XII at the age of 15, the Riksdag having decided that a regency was not necessary.

Meanwhile Frederik III in Denmark was faced with losses from the wars, and war broke out again in 1657, ending in 1658 with the loss of Skåne, Blekinge, Halland, Bornholm, Ven, and Trøndelag to Sweden. Another war resulted in the return of Bornholm and Trøndelag to Denmark in 1660, and internal politics forced the Council of State in that year to declare the Danish monarchy hereditary. In both Denmark and Sweden the stage was now set for large-scale building programs under absolute monarchies, and neither country was to be disappointed.

These wars meant that town planning was still very much directed toward defense. The fortifications surrounding Copenhagen shown on the map of 1659 (figure 3.48) were besieged by Charles X, and the inner bastions of the citadel were completed by the Dutch engineer Henrik Rüse in 1662–1664.[1] He also laid out the major streets connecting Kastellet with the older portion of the city. Christian IV had intended a new plaza, Kongens Nytorv, to be octagonal with radiating streets, but Rüse evidently thought a grid system to be more efficient (figure 4.1).

A different system was used by Nicodemus Tessin the Elder in his plan for the new Swedish naval base of Karlskrona, Blekinge, in 1680, for which Erik Dahlberg designed the fortifications in 1683.[2] Dahlberg had been trained as a military engineer in Germany and had assisted with Charles X's remarkable march from Jutland across the frozen waters to Copenhagen in 1658. Immediately after the Swedish victory he had strengthened the defenses of Karlshamn, a seaport town in the newly won province of Blekinge. Then in 1680 he built the fort at Landskrona, across the Sound from Denmark. But Karlskrona, founded as a naval base in 1679 and named for the king, was the most forward-looking project of the three.

Whereas Karlshamn and Landskrona had grown from medieval towns with churches and central market places and streets more or less on grid plans, a newer opportunity was presented at Karlskrona. The islands surrounding the town were to be fortified. Tessin's plan for the town itself had the basic elements seen on the plan for fortifications by Dahlberg (figure 4.2). The fortress was to be on the south side of the island, its main building facing a square. Then a principal street was to lead to a second square, and diagonal streets were to lead off the north corners of the first. These, with further diagonal streets, would provide the vistas already adopted in such plazas as the Piazza del Popolo in Rome. Tessin had probably intended a church in the center of the main plaza. Dahlberg's plan, however, shows a church at the east side (the Fredriks Church later designed by Nicodemus Tessin the Younger in 1697), the Town Hall opposite on the west side, and the Church of the Holy Trinity, also by Tessin the Younger, on the south. These streets and buildings form the basis of Karlskrona today.

A plan less ambitious but incorporating some Baroque elements was adopted at Trond-

KØBENHAVNS BYMUSEUM

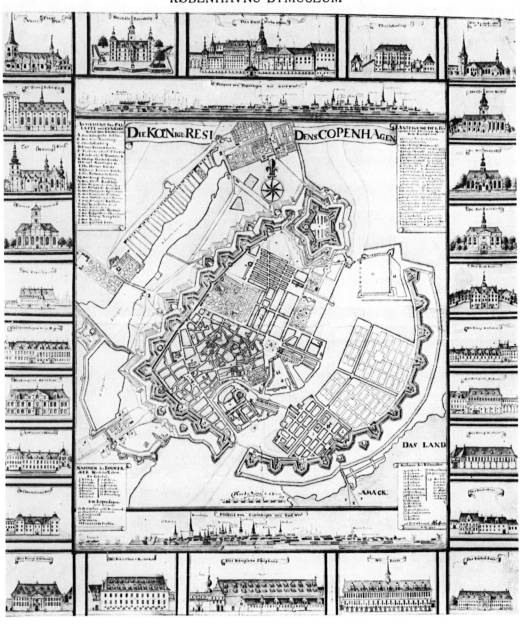

4.1 Copenhagen. Plan by G. Hartmann. c. 1680. (Copenhagen, City Museum.)

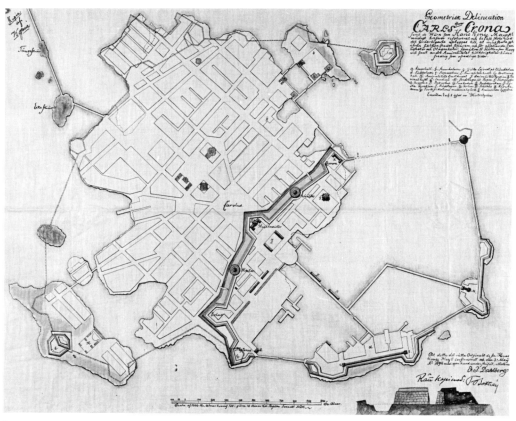

**2**

4.2 Karlskrona. Plan by
E. Dahlberg. 1694.
(Stockholm,
Krigsarkivet.)

4.3 Trondheim. Plan by Cicignon and Coucheron.
1681. (After Kavli, *Nor-
wegian Architecture*, p.
59.)

4.4 Møgeltønder, Jutland.
Slotsgade. 1680.

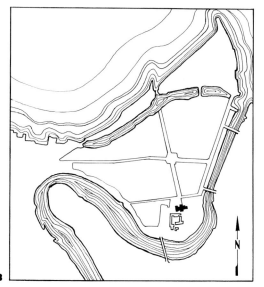

**3**

heim after a fire in 1681 (figure 4.3).[3] The old city was surrounded by water except for a narrow connection with the mainland on the west. Military considerations were foremost in the plans for rebuilding by Johan Caspar Cicignon and Wyllem Coucheron. From the west gate in the wall a broad street was laid across the town, with a central plaza crossed by another broad street, not quite at right angles. The remaining streets were laid out grid fashion, with blocks of varying sizes, the whole much resembling the plan of Fredrikstad from c. 1570 (figure 3.17). The north-south street was laid out to give a line of sight from the Cathedral in the southeast sector of the town through the central square and out toward the island of Munksholmen, where the abbey had been converted to a fortress after the Reformation. If Cicignon's plan did not depend on fully developed Baroque theory, it yet had a certain grandeur of conception.

From this period also dates a small but well-known street, Slotsgade in Møgeltønder on Jutland. General Hans Schack, who had led the defense of Copenhagen against the Swedes in 1659, purchased the medieval castle of Møgeltønder in 1664, razed it, and built a new country house, Schackenborg. In 1680 a street was laid out from the manor house westward beyond the church.[4] Shaded by rows of lime trees on either side, the little brick one-and-a-half-story houses now date from the 1730s at the earliest but still preserve order and tranquility (figure 4.4).

Before the seventeenth century was over, however, at least one truly grand city plan emerged. In Stockholm there had been some regularizing of streets after a fire in the Old Town in 1625. With Nicodemus Tessin the Younger we encounter a strong personality, this time less of a military engineer and more of civil architect. Son of the Royal Architect

4

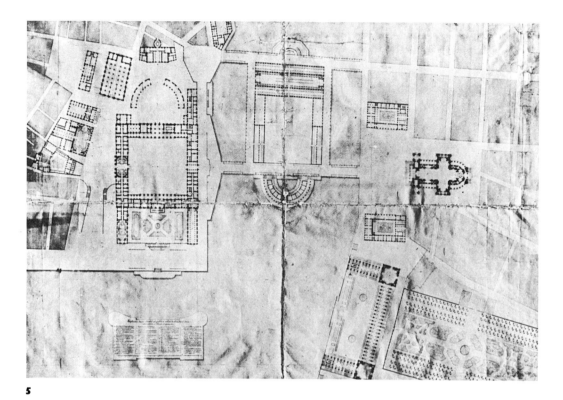

**5**

4.5 **Stockholm. Plan by N. Tessin II. 1697. (Stockholm, Royal Palace Collections.)**

4.6 **Hamina. Plan by C. A. Blaesingh and A. Löwen. 1681. (After Richards, *800 Years*, p. 72.)**

Nicodemus Tessin the Elder, to whose work at Drottningholm we shall return and who had been a pupil of the French architect Simon de La Vallée, he had gone to Italy in 1673 and worked in Denmark in 1678. On his return to Sweden he was appointed Royal Architect after the death of his father in 1681. The major task before him was to modernize Stockholm Castle. As it turned out, a new palace was soon to be required, in connection with which Tessin the Younger developed a plan for a royal city much less dominated by military considerations than Christian IV's plans for Copenhagen. The differences in character between these two cities were doubtless in part brought about by their different geographical locations. Copenhagen lay on the Sound, open to hostile as well as commercial traffic between the North and Baltic Seas. Stockholm, on the other hand, in spite of salt water in her harbor, lay back behind an archipelago, with Sweden's naval defenses in the coast towns like Landskrona and Karlskrona.

A major fire in Stockholm Castle in 1697 provided a clearly welcome challenge for Tessin the Younger, who had seen Rome, Paris, and Versailles. His drawings show a new palace on the site of Stockholm Castle, a rebuilt North Bridge leading to a new square, Normalmstorg, with a massive royal burial church on the central axis, flanked by lesser palaces. To the west, arsenals and government offices were planned symmetrically at the water side, behind which a formal garden, nearly as large as the Royal Palace, extended to the main cross street of the newer city (figure 4.5).[5] Not all the buildings planned were built, but the bridge, the plaza beyond it, and the gardens were carried out and, although modified, are part of the modern city.

One of the last formal town plans of this period appeared in Finland, which was also involved in the wars of this period. The Swedish coastal town of Vehkalahti, near the Russian border, was occupied by the Russians and virtually destroyed from 1713 to 1721. It was then returned to Sweden by the Treaty of Nystad. Renamed Fredrikshamn, or Hamina, it was laid out by the Swedish engineer Carl A. Blaesingh on an octagonal plan with eight main streets radiating from a central plaza, a rare surviving example of an ideal city (figure 4.6).[6] The elaborate bastions on the land side were designed by Axel Löwen, and some traces of them still remain.

While these town planning projects were intended to protect the interests of Denmark and Sweden during many years of strife, the kings and nobles found opportunities to build

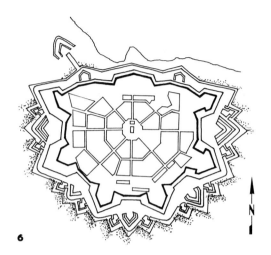

6

**4.7 Drottningholm. N. Tessin I. Begun 1667.**

**4.8 Copenhagen. Old Amalienborg. A. Mathiesen. 1667. (Thurah, *Danske Vitruvius*, volume 3, plate 13. Copenhagen, Academy of Art Library.)**

for themselves in the grand manner. One of the earliest and still most impressive of the royal works is Drottningholm Palace on Lake Mälar near Stockholm, built for Dowager Queen Hedwig Eleanora, widow of Charles X (figure 4.7).[7] It was begun by Nicodemus Tessin the Elder in 1662, and the wings were heightened by Carl Hårleman in 1744. The palace was designed in the symmetrical French style that characterized Tessin's smaller palaces for the nobility. The principal entrance is on the west, or garden side, approached by a double stair. The three large portals give access to an entrance hall with a grand staircase. The State Bedroom and Banqueting Hall lie on either side in the main block, with private residence chambers in the four corner pavilions. The basement story is rusticated, while the walls above have strips of stone between the windows, with a triglyph and metope frieze above. The säteri roof is used on the side portions of the central block and also on the pavilions. Originally the color was pale red with gray trim, very differ-

ent from what it is now. The state rooms were finished with much grandeur. Built on the site of an earlier manor, Drottningholm Palace with its extensive gardens has been called the "Versailles of the North."

Within the next decade two palatial residences were built for members of the Danish royal family, one of which survives, now put to a different use. In 1667 Frederik III's Queen Sophie Amalie of Brunswick-Lüneberg had seen to the planning of a more agreeable palace on a tract of land in the new part of the city, between Kongens Nytorv and Kastellet. The palace is generally attributed to the builder Albertus Mathiesen and was much like an Italian villa in design, with a three-story central block and low wings terminating in pavilions on either side (figure 4.8).[8] The grand curving staircase was also Italian in origin, but the pilasters of the second and third stories, the window surrounds, and the balustraded roof may have been closer to the Dutch Palladianism of Jacob van Campen. The palace was named Sophie

Amalienborg for the queen. A fire destroyed her palace in 1689, four years after her death, but the name was kept for the later palaces proposed for the site.

The city palace built for Ulrik Frederik Gyldenløve, natural son of Frederik III and Governor of Norway, was more fortunate (figure 4.9).[9] It was begun by the Dutch builder Evert Janssen, and some reflection of the Town Hall in Amsterdam has been seen in it. Brick with stone trim, it rises in three stories, with four wings around a courtyard, covered in part by low hipped roofs. Special features are a monumental staircase on the entrance side and a ceremonial hall overlooking the garden. In 1700 Dowager Queen Charlotte Amalie, widow of Christian V, purchased the property, for whom it was then named Charlottenborg. It is now the main building of the Royal Danish Academy of Fine Arts.

After the shock of the Sophie Amalienborg disaster another attempt was made to provide the Danish court with a fashionable

9

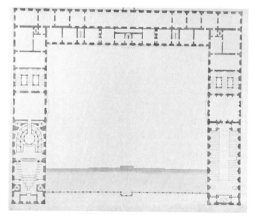

10

4.9 Copenhagen. Charlot-
tenborg. E. Janssen.
1674–1683. (Thurah,
*Danske Vitruvius,* vol-
ume I, plate 42. Copen-
hagen, Academy of Art
Library.)

4.10 Copenhagen. Amalien-
borg. Plan by N. Tessin
II. 1693. (Stockholm,
Royal Palace
Collections.)

4.11 Stockholm. Royal Palace. N. Tessin II. Begun
1697.

modern residence. Lambert von Haven had prepared plans for a new palace to replace Copenhagen Castle, but Christian V was evidently not pleased with them. Ulrica Eleanora, sister of Christian V, had been married to Charles XI of Sweden in 1680 in hopes of strengthening the then more peaceful relations between Denmark and Sweden. Her Royal Architect, Nicodemus Tessin the Younger, was called to Copenhagen in 1693 to plan another palace.

The palace was again to be on the Amalienborg site, in the Italian manner with a central courtyard (figure 4.10).[10] The entrance wing was planned to face Kastellet on the north, and there was to be a chapel in the west wing and a theater in the east, with the main residence on the side toward the castle. A noteworthy feature was the inclusion of a permanent court theater, whereas heretofore the Scandinavian monarchs had had to make do with temporary structures or remodeled halls.[11] Tessin's project came to nothing. He returned to Stockholm and went to work on remodeling the north wing of the castle there. Christian V died in 1699, another war with Sweden started in 1700, and we shall see that Frederik IV had other ideas about royal palaces.

In Stockholm Tessin began the remodeling of the Castle as commissioned by Charles XI. The king, however, died on April 5, 1697, with the work only partly completed. On May 7 a fire broke out and left the whole castle in ruins. Tessin now had the task of building a new palace worthy of Sweden's strength and the confidence of the young new king, Charles XII. The grand urban design that Tessin envisaged with this opportunity was only in part realized, but the Royal Palace itself is still fundamentally as he planned it (figures 4.5 and 4.11).[12]

The palace is composed of four wings around a central nearly square courtyard. The main entrance is on the west from a plaza formed by the curved barracks of the palace guards. The central portion is emphasized in granite with a rusticated Doric applied colonnade on the ground floor, then herms against rusticated pilasters on the next level and Corinthian pilasters and elaborate window pediments on the third level. On the south side the portal leads to the Hall of State on the west and the Chapel on the east. Here an even more imposing effect is created by a triumphal arch motif using six giant Corinthian applied

4.12  **Stockholm. Royal Palace. South façade.**

4.13  **Frederiksberg Palace. E. Brandenburger. Begun 1703.**

columns with niches for statues between and more statues on the attic story (figure 4.12). The central portions of the east and west façades in the courtyard are also in stone, a rusticated arcade at ground level and Corinthian pilasters through the second and third levels. For the overall grandeur of his conception Tessin owed much to his experiences in France and Italy, where with the help of former Queen Christina he met Bernini.[13] So large a project took time to build, and there was an interruption during the Nordic War from 1700 to 1721. Tessin died in 1728, and the palace was completed and furnished under his successors. For the most part his designs were followed, with the notable exception of the court theater intended for the southeast wing but never built. The success of the Royal Palace as it rises above the water of Stockholm Harbor lies in its proportions and the dignity with which the broad walls and the horizontal balus-

trade of the roof hold the richness of the eastern, western, and southern facades in check.

Shortly after this great work was begun in Stockholm, on the death of Christian V in 1699 Frederik IV succeeded to the throne of Denmark. As Crown Prince he had already acquired a half-timbered summer house on land west of the city. He now enlarged the gardens and began a new palace on the hilltop, inspired by the villas he had seen in Italy. The architect of Frederiksberg was the royal building inspector Ernst Brandenburger, who had it essentially complete by 1703. Then in 1708 Johan Conrad Ernst made designs for additions at the ends of the main block, which was built after changes by the general building master Wilhelm F. Platen (figures 4.13 and 4.14).[14] The building is three stories high, with emphasis on the middle story through the addition of triangular and segmental pediments over the windows. On both garden and court facades, the three central bays have the third-story windows heightened and are marked off by pilasters rising to an entablature at the top. Otherwise the exterior is rather soberly finished. Lauritz de Thurah provided the plans for the side wings, built 1733–1738 when the palace was needed to house the royal family during the construction of the new Christiansborg Palace. The original portal to the grounds was rebuilt in 1929. Much of the interior was richly furnished with painting and stucco decorations, especially in the chapel in the east wing.[15] The palace was taken over by the state in 1849 and has been in use as a military academy since 1868. In 1834 the English traveler John Barrow remarked of Copenhagen that "the inland views are also striking, and the palace of Frederiksberg, standing on a well-wooded hill, adds much to the beauty of the scenery."[16]

Mention of Christiansborg Palace is a reminder that the old Copenhagen Castle was

still in use. It had not been much changed since the time of Christian III and still had the gables and balconies that had been added for a touch of Renaissance fashion in the 1550s (figure 3.25).[17] Frederik IV was not partial to city living, but he made an attempt to convert the castle to something more regular. The whole complex was enlarged and the gables and irregularities abolished or concealed as much as possible (figures 4.15 and 4.16).[18] The work was done in stages, from 1710 to 1714 under the builder Christopher Marselis and from 1720 to 1727 under Johan Christian Ernst and Johan Cornelius Krieger. While this was all at best a makeshift solution, one noteworthy detail was the inclusion of a theater, the first to be installed permanently in a Scandinavian royal palace.

The contrast between what Frederik IV was able to do with Copenhagen Castle and what he could do with a fresh start is well demonstrated by comparing the bird's-eye view of the castle with a bird's-eye view of the palace of Fredensborg (figure 4.17).[19] North of Copenhagen and a little beyond Hillerød was a royal hunting park east of Esrom Sø, where Christian V had laid out a radiating system of avenues. Here in 1719 Frederik IV began a new summer palace, whose name (meaning "Fortress of Peace") commemorates the treaty ending the Nordic War between Denmark and Sweden, signed here in 1720. The architect Johan Christian Krieger began with the main block crowned by a dome, which covers a high central hall, the major interior space. The four corner pavilions were added by Niels Eigtved in the 1750s, and the minaret-like turrets were added by Lauritz de Thurah. The buildings of the octagon were raised a story higher by Caspar F. Harsdorff in 1774–1776, and he also opened an entrance to the originally enclosed octagon, making a closer connection between

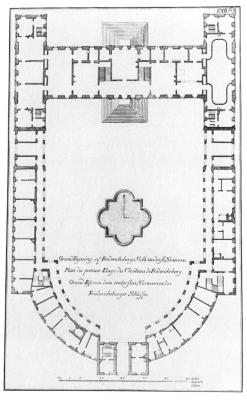

**14**

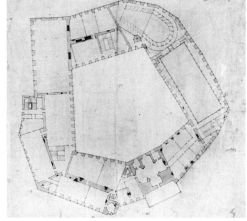

**15**

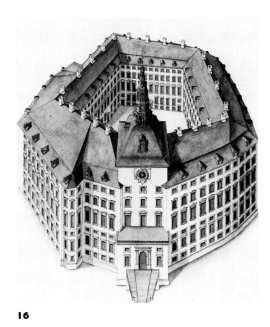

**16**

4.14 Frederiksberg Palace.
Plan. (Thurah, *Danske
Vitruvius*, volume 2,
plate 68. Copenhagen,
Academy of Art
Library.)

4.15 Copenhagen Castle.
Plan of 1728. (Copen-
hagen, National
Museum.)

4.16 Copenhagen Castle.
View by J. J. Bruun. c.
1728. (Copenhagen,
National Museum.)

4.17 Fredensborg Palace.
J. C. Krieger. Begun
1719. Bird's-eye view
by H. C. Lønborg, c.
1730. (Copenhagen,
National Museum.)

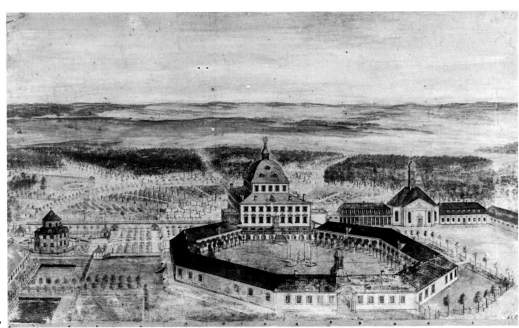

**17**

**4.18 Fredensborg Palace.
Chapel. Interior. (Co-
penhagen, National
Museum.)**

**4.19 Rosendal, Hordaland.
1661–1665. (Oslo,
Riksantikvaren.)**

the main palace and the eight small houses lining the main avenue of approach.

The interior of Fredensborg was provided
with a series of painted and stuccoed decorations by several artists through the 1770s. Especially fine is the chapel in the east wing,
completed in 1725, with its hipped roof, tower,
and elaborate southern entrance. The royal box
is in the west end, accessible from the palace.
Although economy dictated marbleized
wooden columns rather than any more expensive materials, the altar and pulpit by Johan
Friedrich Ehbisch provide the appropriate
splendor (figure 4.18).[20]

Unlike Copenhagen Castle, Rosenborg, and
Frederiksborg, Fredensborg was never isolated
fortresslike by water. Krieger used the hunting
avenues to link the palace with the Sø and forests and to make a basis for the formal gardens
on the south. Much of this has been retained,
with the addition of several sculpture pro-

grams. In its ease of setting and spaciousness
Fredensborg has much in common with Drottningholm, and it is interesting that for a variety
of reasons these royal country estates preceded
the first great urban palaces in both Denmark
and Sweden.

By the time Fredensborg was begun, the
new palace in Stockholm was already under
construction, interrupted by the same Nordic
War from which the Danish estate derived its
name. Before turning to the new palace that
shortly was begun in Copenhagen, however, we
should note first some residences built for less
exalted individuals and also some churches.

In 1661 a barony had been created in Norway that was first held by the Danish aristocrat
Ludwig Rosencrantz, who had married into a
wealthy Scottish trading family. He laid out his
manor farm called Rosendal near Malmanger
Peak in Hordaland in 1661–1665 (figure 4.19).[21]
The residence was built symmetrically around a
courtyard, with a grand curving staircase in the
central portion and a large knight's hall in the
north wing. Some of the original wooden
paneling of the interior remains, but some
rooms were subdivided by later owners. The
property was willed to the University of Oslo
in 1923. As at Fredensborg, a coherent plan
was possible, unlike the earlier piecemeal construction at Austråt.

The comparative modesty of Rosendal in
Norway is not surprising in view of its distance
from the center of court life. In Sweden and
Denmark a number of much more ambitious
manor houses remain, attesting to the wealth
and position of their owners. For a good Swedish example we can look at Skokloster in Uppland on an inlet of Lake Mälar, northwest of
Stockholm (figure 4.20).[22] Like Tidö earlier, it
was built by a powerful nobleman, this time
General Carl Gustav Wrangel, who contributed
his own ideas after seeing castles during his

19

18

**4.20   Skokloster, Uppland.**
**        J. de La Vallée. 1679.**
**4.21   Clausholm, Jutland.**
**        E. Brandenburger.**
**        1693–1699.**

campaigns in Germany and Poland. The architect was Jean de La Vallée, who also had Nicodemus Tessin the Elder working with him. Partly because of the owner's inclinations, the plan of the castle around a courtyard with octagonal towers projecting at the four corners gives the mass of the building a conservative medieval shape. The abundance of large window openings, especially on the ground level, belies any fortress character. The exterior walls are rusticated, with strong horizontal stringcourses and shallow panels surrounding the windows. On the interior, which has been restored, little expense was spared in furnishing with tapestries, stuccoed ceilings, and elaborate tiled stoves.

   In Denmark a similar formality was observed at Clausholm on Jutland, built in 1693–

**21**

1699 by Ernst Brandenburger for Chancellor Conrad Reventlow. (figure 4.21).[23] This is a large manor house, with a central block and wings that form a wide courtyard on the north, or entrance, side. The shorter wings on the garden side were added in 1722–1723. Here the portal, which was redesigned by Tessin the Younger, leads to a wide vestibule with stairs at either end. The rooms in the wings are served by a corridor on the courtyard sides, the doors between them set *en filade*. The dining salon overlooking the garden and the salon above have some of the finest stucco decorations in Denmark (figure 4.22). The gracious family chapel in the west wing was restored in 1931.[24]

Among the city houses of the period, the mansion that Tessin the Younger built for himself in Stockholm across from the Royal Palace reveals something of his own sense of importance (figure 4.23).[25] It is three stories high, the lowest one rusticated. The second and third stories are framed by corner pilasters between which runs a bracketed cornice with an attic story above. A triple-arched portal leads into a columned vestibule across the lower story, which in turn opens out to the garden. Tessin was able to secure enough land to lay out an imposing effect in very little space. The garden walls were purposely slanted to give a perspective effect, with curved elements, niches, columns and pilasters, balustrades, symmetrical planting beds, and sculptures. Since 1772 the house has been the residence of the Governor General.

22

23

4.22 Clausholm, Jutland. Stucco decoration.

4.23 Stockholm. Tessin House. N. Tessin II. 1697.

4.24 Copenhagen. Library of Frederik III. A. Mathiesen. 1665. (Copenhagen, National Museum.)

4.25 Kalmar, Småland. Cathedral. N. Tessin I. Begun 1660. (Kalmar Museum.)

24

25

**26**

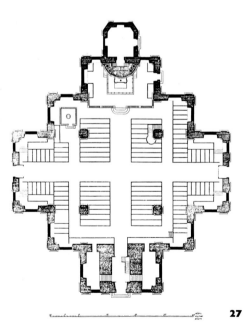

**27**

While the Baroque period was primarily notable for palaces, manor houses, and some churches, one building remains in Copenhagen that was built for a more specialized purpose. In 1665 Frederik III decided to build a library and museum to house the royal collections.[26] The builder was Albertus Mathiesen, on whose death in 1668 the work was completed by Thomas Walgenstein, the city building master. It is of brick, three stories high, located on Slotsholmen on the east side of the former naval harbor, which is now the Royal Library garden. The ground floor was for the storage of field artillery, with the library on the second level and the *Kunstkammer* on the third. A beautiful room was created for the library, paved with marble and lined with galleries carried on gilded Corinthian columns (figure 4.24). All this lasted until 1908, when the building was remodeled to house the State Archives. The paving was salvaged for the floor of the Great Hall in the present Christiansborg Palace.

Baroque church building in Denmark and Sweden was not extensive but partook of the regularity of planning and frequent grandeur of expression that characterized the palaces and manor houses. At Kalmar the old city with its winding medieval streets lay inland north of the castle. Military considerations c. 1640 prompted a decision to relocate the city on the nearby island of Kvarnholmen, offshore to the east, which was fairly well accomplished by 1658. The new city was laid out after several years of planning and was of course regular in design, with a central plaza that was to contain the cathedral. For this Nicodemus Tessin the Elder provided the design. The construction, which took over forty years to complete, was begun in June 1660. The rising land of the island provided a majestic setting above the harbor, although as at Kalundborg the effect is now somewhat obscured by modern buildings. The cathedral is the only major ecclesiastical work by Tessin the Elder, and on it he lavished ideas gleaned from his observations of Baroque Rome (figure 4.25).[27]

To meet the requirements for the congregation-oriented Lutheran services of the time, Tessin began with a Greek cross plan. As it developed, the plan was given east and west extensions, ending in apses. The four massive central piers may have been intended to carry a dome, but one was never built. The principal entrance is on the south side, the upper story with pediment and scrolls perhaps recalling Il Gesù in Rome. The cathedral is colorful, with Tuscan and Ionic pilasters against the pink stuccoed wall surfaces and the copper-green roofs and turrets above. The broad south facade gives a majestic backdrop to the plaza. The interior is made stately by a giant order of paired Ionic pilasters. The pulpit against the northeast pier first captures the attention of those entering from the plaza. The cathedral is not entirely centralized, however, because the main body is clearly on the east-west axis, with the seating directed toward the altar in the eastern apse.

A comparison with Kristianstad, founded in 1614, is instructive here. There the fortified town was laid out in grid fashion, with two principal squares, but the site along the water ran northeast to southwest so that Holy Trinity Church had to be built on a diagonal in relation to the town (figure 3.38). It was not given a central location and its principal entrance was planned on the traditional line with the altar rather than in relation to a major part of the town plan. Entirely apart from the differences in ornamental vocabulary of the two buildings, we can see that forty years later at Kalmar a new concept had been formulated for planning town and church.

In Denmark a modified Greek cross plan was chosen for an important new city church in

28

4.26 Copenhagen. Vor Frelsers Kirke. L. von Haven. Begun 1682. (Thurah, *Danske Vitruvius*, volume 3, plate 61. Copenhagen, Academy of Art Library.)

4.27 Copenhagen. Vor Frelsers Kirke. Plan. (Thurah, *Danske Vitruvius*, volume 1, plate 82. Copenhagen, Academy of Art Library.)

4.28 Copenhagen. Vor Frelsers Kirke. Interior. (Copenhagen, National Museum.)

29

1682. Founded under Christian V as the church
for the Order of the Elephant, Vor Frelsers
Kirke was built in Christianshavn in Copenhagen by Lambert von Haven and completed
except for the spire by 1696 (figures 4.26 and
4.27).[28] The view illustrated here is from *Det
Danske Vitruvius* by Lauritz de Thurah, who was
justly proud of the spire he added in 1749–
1752, based on that of Borromini's S. Ivo della
Sapienza in Rome. On the exterior, brick Tuscan pilasters rise the full height of the building,
with tall round-headed windows between and
an entablature above encircling the church. On
the interior four central piers rise to support
the roof, and the eastern, northern, and southern projections from the main square are shallow enough to give the effect of a hall church
(figure 4.28). The magnificent Baroque altarpiece was designed by Tessin the Younger in
1695 but not finished until 1732.[29] In contrast is
the neoclassical pulpit by Caspar Frederik Harsdorff, designed in 1773. From the original period of building comes the famous "Elephant
Organ," carved by the royal sculptor Christian
Nerger in 1698 (figure 4.29).[30]

Contemporary with Vor Frelsers Kirke is
the Reformed Church in Copenhagen (figure
4.30).[31] The German Reformed worship was
permitted by Christian V in 1685, in response
to the religious preferences of Queen Charlotte Amalie of Hessen-Kassel, and the church
was built by Heinrich Brockam, from Germany
or Holland, in 1688–1689. Unlike the Protestant churches we have seen in the Lutheran
tradition, the Reformed Church was planned
with the principal axis across the breadth
rather than the length of the building. This is
expected on the exterior, where the main entrance is on the center of the long northeast
side. As at Vor Frelsers Kirke, there are pilasters, here Ionic, rising the full height of the
building, with an entablature and a pediment

over the entrance bay. The hip roof has dormers and is crowned by a turret. The interior is arranged in the German/Dutch Calvinist manner with the altar and pulpit opposite the door.[32] The original scheme was repeated in rebuilding after the fire of Copenhagen in 1728.

The late seventeenth century was not a time of extensive church building in Norway. A small number of wooden parish churches were built in an experimental manner, using a Y-shaped plan. One example is the church at Rennebu in Nord-Trøndelag, 1668–1669 (figure 4.31).[33] From the southwest the entrance wing of the church recalls something of the stave churches, with its successive gables, turret, and spire. The interior is arranged with two wings for seating and the third for the sanctuary. This plan did not, apparently, prove to be entirely satisfactory and gained little acceptance.

For the new cathedral in Oslo by Jørgen de Wiggers in 1697 a cruciform plan was chosen (figure 4.32).[34] In 1850 the spire was added by Alexis de Chateauneuf, the west tower having originally been lower with a pyramidal roof. The wide cross-arms make a spacious interior, where the pulpit and altar dating from 1699 dominate. Their design by an anonymous Netherlandish master was important in bringing to Norway the acanthus ornament that spread over the country in the next century in carved and painted decorations for churches and houses (figure 4.33).

30

31

**32**

4.32    Oslo. Cathedral. J. de
        Wiggers. Begun 1697.

4.33    Oslo. Cathedral. Pul-
        pit. 1699. (Oslo,
        Riksantikvaren.)

**33**

## Late Baroque and Rococo, c. 1730–1800

The accession of Christian VI in 1730 brought Denmark a monarch who was somewhat paradoxical in his approach to the arts and architecture. In the years following, the grandeur of the late Baroque and its lively transformation into the Rococo were part of another paradox. Along with an apparent climax of stylistic richness in the visual arts and music went the beginning of major political, economic, and industrial change, some effects of which can be detected in Scandinavian architecture from c. 1730 to c. 1800.

The early years of this period in Denmark were dominated by the building of the first Christiansborg Palace in Copenhagen.[35] The alteration of Copenhagen Castle under Frederik IV placed too great an additional load upon the old foundations, and by 1730 it was clearly time to make a major change. Furthermore the now hopelessly unfashionable irregularity of the castle plan could not be concealed, and the monotony of the new exterior must have been even more forbidding than the castle in medieval times. As Crown Prince, Christian VI had already been involved with the building of

**4.34** **Copenhagen. Christiansborg I. E. Häusser. Begun 1732. (Thurah, *Danske Vitruvius,* volume 1, plate 23. Copenhagen, Academy of Art Library.)**

**4.35** **Copenhagen. Christiansborg I. Site plan. (After Faber, *History of Danish Architecture,* p. 74.)**

**4.36** **Copenhagen. Christiansborg I. Plan. (Thurah, *Danske Vitruvius,* volume 1, plate 10. Copenhagen, Academy of Art Library.)**

Hørsholm Palace, begun for his future queen Sophie Magdalene in 1728, and the rebuilding of a mansion across Frederiksholms Canal from the castle.[36] Although J. C. Krieger was one of the architects for both projects, when it came to a new royal palace the new king chose Elias David Häusser as the general building master.

Häusser was a military engineer, trained in Germany, and had given Christian VI some instructions in architecture. In 1731 his first proposal for the palace was submitted, but it was dull and heavy. A second proposal, dated May 10, 1732, met with more approval, and in the same year the final project was begun. The royal family moved to Frederiksberg, and the old castle was pulled down.

Whether Häusser was the author of the final design is a matter of some question. He wrote on the drawing that it was a copy of one that the king had given him as a model.

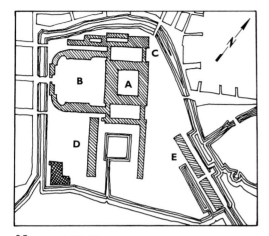

**35**

A. Main Palace
B. Riding Ground
C. Chapel
D. Arsenal
E. Bourse

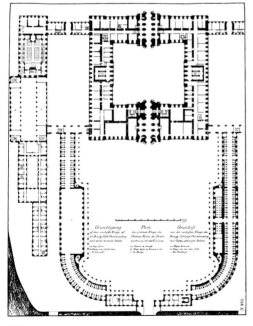

**36**

Here the overall scheme of the palace facade was established. It was divided horizontally by rusticated basement stories, two principal stories, plus an attic, crowned by a balustrade behind which rose three mansard roofs and a central tower.[37] The vertical divisions were marked by three bays at each end separated by giant pilasters rising through the two main stories, and a central portion of nine bays with a modified triumphal arch motif for a projecting portico rising in the center of the basement story. A curved pediment over the central bay and triangular pediments over the end bays, as shown on the drawing reproduced here, were replaced by a triangular pediment in the center and segmental pediments at the ends on the building itself. In the final version the roof line was also made continuous. With its chapel and administrative wings the palace could now overlook its square with a grandeur deriving from the south German and Austrian princely palaces (figure 4.34).

Whoever the designer may have been, the new palace was also laid out so as to form a monumental complex (figure 4.35). The main building consisted of four wings around a central courtyard, with a grand entrance hall on the east, or square, side, another on the west side in connection with the tower, and additional entrances and stairs on the north and south sides of the court (figure 4.36). This plan may have owed something to Lambert von Haven's project for a royal residence or to Tessin the Younger's plan for the Amalienborg (figure 4.10). As at Fredensborg the Chapel was built separately to the north; the Chancellery had already been built by J. C. Ernst in 1715–1720 to the south.[38] Both were connected to the main palace by two-story gallery wings. The west facade looked out to the Riding Ground, which was flanked by the stable wings, ending in curved portions leading to a bridge over the canal. The symmetry that no amount of remodeling could bring to the old castle was now achieved and the whole spatial setting for courtly splendor much enlarged.

So large a project required considerable time for execution, and the palace was in fact not entirely complete in all details when the main building and the chapel were destroyed by fire in 1794. Häusser was primarily a military engineer who undoubtedly used the surveying techniques for fortifications in laying out the plan. He was responsible for the Riding School building in the center of the south wing. He also planned a monumental gatehouse for the entrance to the bridge over the canal, but this was not built. Construction of the main building had risen except for the two top stories by 1736, when Lauritz de Thurah and Niels Eigtved were appointed for the interiors. Häusser was gradually superseded, finally dismissed in 1742, and sent to take command of the fortifications at Nyborg. In the meantime enough had been completed that the royal family was able to move in by November 1740, and the name "Christiansborg" was officially adopted in January 1741. On the departure of Häusser, Eigtved, who by then was much in the king's favor, was appointed the chief architect.

For the nature of the interior designs we may consult a drawing of 1781, which shows the dining salon with its decorations designed by the sculptor Louis-Augustin Le Clerc (figure 4.37). The room overlooked the Riding Ground, and the narrow walls between the windows were echoed by pilasters on the interior wall opposite. The end wall visible in the drawing was rhythmically adorned with alternating wide and narrow panels, with rich pediments over the doors at either side. The cartouches on the pilasters and in the narrow end panels were not placed at the midpoint but just above head level in such a way as to stabilize the height of the room.

How Eigtved and Thurah treated the residential suites we do not know, but in his book *Den Danske Vitruvius* Thurah illustrated the interior of the chapel.[39] This was the work of Eigtved. He combined the French arrangement of the royal boxes at the east end, connected to the main palace as at Versailles, with the German Reformed placement of the pulpit with organ above in the center of the west end, as at the Reformed Church. To the west beyond the chapel lay the coach house and the stables for the horses of the guard and the Crown Prince.

The whole establishment reflected the kind of court life that Christian VI intended. Erecting the palace chapel as a separate building set forth court religious observances as more than private devotions. Further, the importance of horses and riding skills as entertainment is well demonstrated by the broad Riding Ground and surrounding buildings, which survived the fire of 1794. The exterior of the wings is treated soberly, with rustication on the lower

4.37  **Copenhagen. Christiansborg I. Salon. Drawing by J. W. Haffner, 1781. (Copenhagen, Rosenborg Palace Collections.)**

4.38  **Copenhagen. Christiansborg I. Stables. (Copenhagen, National Museum.)**

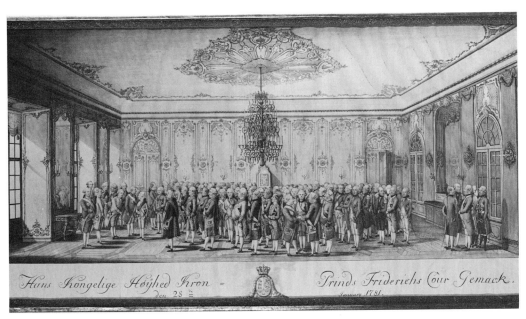

Hans Kongelige Høyhed Kron =

Prinds Friderichs Cour Gemack.

den 28ᵈᵉ                    Januar 1781.

37

38

level and pilasters between the windows above. As shown on Thurah's plan, a colonnade surrounded the Riding Ground, still a welcome shelter from sun or rain. On the north side the lower level was made into stables throughout, with the saddlery in the raised central section. Even the horses were splendidly housed in their marble stalls (figure 4.38). On the south side the Riding School occupied both stories, with the royal box at one end and surrounding galleries carried on curved brackets.

Here was a paradox in the nature of Christian VI and his queen, Sophie Magdalene of Brandenburg. Amid receptions, banquets, balls, musical events, and equestrian entertainments there was no place for theatrical performances, which had been part of Copenhagen Castle's festivities since the time of Christian IV.[40] The king's religious convictions led to the prohibition of all theater in Denmark and Norway in 1738.[41] No theater was included in the palace, in contrast to what Tessin had proposed for the Amalienborg and Stockholm palaces, and in this respect Christiansborg was out of step with the princely palaces of the Continent.

One other major building project came during the reign of Christian VI. The fire of 1728 also devastated Vor Frue Kirke. After several proposals for its rebuilding had been made, that of J. C. Krieger was chosen and the major portion of the work done between 1731 and 1742 (figures 4.39 and 4.40).[42] The church was rebuilt on its former basilical plan but with the side aisles now raised to the height of the nave and separated from it by square piers with flat pilasters. Light came from two ranges of windows in the aisles, the upper range being the taller. The spectacular western tower and spire were built from drawings by the court Master of Ceremonies Vincent Lerche, who based his design on plates in *A Book of Architecture,* published in London by the English archi-

TAB LXI.

Opstilt af vor Frue Kirke     Façade laterale de l'Église     Aufsijt von der Frauen-Kirche
      paa Siden.                      Notre Dame.                      auf der Seite.

**4.39** Copenhagen. Vor Frue
Kirke. J. C. Krieger.
1731–1742. (Thurah,
*Danske Vitruvius,* vol-
ume 1, plate 61. Co-
penhagen, Academy of
Art Library.)

**4.40** Copenhagen. Vor Frue
Kirke. Interior. En-
graving by J. Haas. (Co-
penhagen, National
Museum.)

**4.41** Copenhagen. Frederiksstad. Site plan.
(After Faber, *History
of Danish Architec-
ture,* p. 80.)

**40**

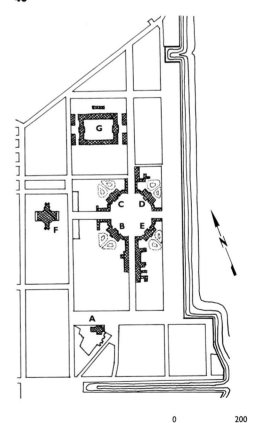

tect James Gibbs in 1728. As to the furnishings,
the pulpit and altar were by Johan Friedrich
Ehbisch, who had done those at Fredensborg.
As finally completed about 1747, the church
stood until the English bombardment of Copenhagen in 1807.

On his death in 1746 Christian VI had had
only five years to enjoy his new palace. His son,
Frederik V, was more fortunate, and further
significant contributions to art and architecture
in Denmark were made during his reign of
twenty years. Born in 1723, he had seen the
great fire of Copenhagen in 1728, the demolition of the old castle, and the building of the
palace. It was for him that Eigtved had built a
new Prince's Palace on the site of J. C. Krieger's remodeled mansion in 1743–1744.[43] Almost immediately on his accession Frederik V
revoked the 1738 ban on theaters, and several
places in Copenhagen were at once fitted up

0         200
              m

A. Garnison Church
B. Moltke's Palace
C. Levetzau's Palace
D. Brockdorff's Palace
E. Schack's Palace
F. Frederik's Church
G. Frederik's Hospital

**41**

*Place Royale de Frederichstadt à Copenhague.*

**42**

with stages.[44] One of Eigtved's first projects in the new reign was the Royal Theater in Kongens Nytorv, built in 1748, remodeled several times, and finally demolished in 1874.[45] Then in 1749 a new project was begun, in the three hundredth anniversary year of the House of Oldenburg.

Where the gardens of the ill-fated Sophie Amalienborg had provided space for military exercises, a new section of the city was laid out and called Frederiksstad (figure 4.41).[46] From the present Sankt Annae Plads to Kastellet, the area between Bredgade (then called Norgesgade) and the harbor was divided by a new street, called Amaliegade, and crossed by another new street, called Frederiksgade. At the crossing a monumental square was created, at the corners of which four prominent noblemen built mansions in 1750–1754. An eques-

**4.42** Copenhagen. Frederiksstad. Engraving by J. M. Preisler after drawing by L.-A. Le Clerc, c. 1740. (Copenhagen, National Museum.)

**4.43** Copenhagen. Levetzau's Palace. N. Eigtved. 1754–1756.

**43**

trian statue of the king was planned for the center of the square, and a church was planned to be the climax of the ensemble as viewed from the harbor (figure 4.42). The attribution of the designs for the site plan and its buildings has not been definitively established for lack of documentary evidence. The German architect Marcus Tuscher and Eigtved both worked on the project; probably Tuscher's role was more with the planning of streets and squares, with Eigtved designing the buildings themselves. Part of the original scheme was to have Amaliegade lined with houses of uniform requirements for façades, but this was not fully observed. On Bredgade the area was given a strong accent at the south end by the Bergentin mansion (now the Odd Fellows Palace) and at the north end by Frederik's Hospital (now the Museum of Decorative Arts), while the beginning of Fred-

eriksgade opposite the church site was flanked by the Bernstorff and Dehn mansions. Perhaps this concept owed something to Tessin the Younger's proposal for a burial church in Stockholm (figure 4.5).

The four palaces with their pavilions surrounding the square comprise the finest expression of the Danish Rococo (figure 4.43).[47] Each palace consists of a central block three stories high, placed diagonally at the corners of the square and flanked by pavilions whose wings partially enclose a garden at the rear. Above the shallow rustication of the basement story the main and upper stories are embellished with a giant order of Ionic pilasters between the windows and crowned by a low balustrade before the hip roof. The three central bays are brought forward, forming a balcony enobled by coupled columns framing the central bay and surmounted by a richly carved gable. There is no longer a grand entrance, as at Christiansborg. Instead, the entrance is now through the short wing connecting palace and pavilion.

At the main level on the interior of Moltke's palace the rooms are arranged *en filade* behind the façade, with similar extension into the pavilions. This is the least altered interior of the four and includes the great salon designed by Eigtved with stucco work and painted and gilded panels between a series of paintings by François Boucher (figure 4.44). Small wonder that when Christiansborg burned in 1794 the royal family under the leadership of Crown Prince Frederik purchased the Amalienborg palaces for their enforced new residence. In the splendor of the palace built by Count Adam G. Moltke, high steward to Frederik V, we see an ornament to the city that was encouraged by the king, a situation contrasting with the jealousy that Nicolas Fouquet's magnificent Vaux-le-Vicomte had provoked in Louis XIV nearly a century earlier.

Two of the principal architects of Christiansborg and Amalienborg were involved with major projects other than their work in design. In addition to the work at Christiansborg, Lauritz de Thurah had designed the palace at Hørsholm, 1728–1744, and the Eremitage in the Deer Park in Copenhagen, 1734–1736. In 1735 Christian VI commissioned him to prepare an illustrated book on the architecture of Denmark.[48] *Den Danske Vitruvius* appeared in two volumes, the first in 1746 and the second in 1749. Materials assembled for additional publications were still in manuscript form at Thurah's death in 1759 and were published as a third volume in the modern edition of 1967. Unlike earlier publishers of maps and views, Thurah presented most of the buildings as architectural rather than topographical subjects,

with elevations, plans, and sections, together with descriptions in Danish, French, and German. These illustrations are especially valuable for buildings that have since been lost or altered. Christian VI had in mind to memorialize the splendors of his reign, but it is probably more Thurah's contribution than the king's that commands our attention today.

The other project was the location of the Royal Danish Academy of Art in the Charlottenborg Palace in 1754.[49] Founded in 1738 and variously housed, the Academy had become the training school for young painters, sculptors, and architects. Eigtved had been named Director in 1751, and on his death a few weeks after the move to the new quarters (which are still occupied by the Academy), the French sculptor Jacques-François-Joseph Saly was chosen to replace him.[50] Trained in the French academies of Paris and Rome, his great work was the equestrian statue of Frederik V for the Amalienborg

4.44 **Copenhagen. Moltke's Palace. N. Eigtved. 1754–1756. Salon. (Copenhagen, National Museum.)**

4.45 **Copenhagen. Town Hall. J. C. Ernst. Begun 1729. (Thurah, *Danske Vitruvius*, volume 1, plate 94. Copenhagen, Academy of Art Library.)**

**44**

**45**

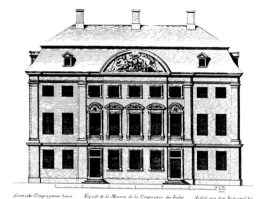

danische Compagnie huus   Façade de la Maison de la Compagnie des Indes   Aufriß von dem Indianischen

**46**

47

**4.46 Copenhagen. Asiatic Company Office. P. de Lange. 1738. (Thurah, *Danske Vitruvius,* volume 1, plate 107. Copenhagen, Academy of Art Library.)**

**4.47 Damsholte, Møn. Church. P. de Lange. 1743.**

square, 1755–1771. Under his leadership Danish art students were brought into an international setting, with strong ties to France. Formal education in architecture was now more firmly established and included the necessary techniques of draftsmanship, lectures from professors, competition in exhibitions, and, if the means could be found, travel in Europe, especially to Paris and Rome. Measured drawings and sketches from ancient monuments and modern buildings followed upon careful observation and gave the young architect a storehouse of models for his own choosing.

Among other notable buildings in Denmark from the reign of Christian VI were the Town Hall begun in 1729 and the Asiatic Company Office of 1738. The former has not survived, having burned in 1795, and is known from Thurah's illustration (figure 4.45).[51] Built on the foundations of the old Town Hall, lost in the fire of 1728 (figure 3.32), it was planned by J. C. Ernst with gables designed by J. C. Krieger. A strong resemblance can be seen to the curved gable and crowning tower of the 1732 design for Christiansborg, and both are thought to be derived ultimately from the works of the

Austrian architect Lucas von Hildebrandt.[52] As houses and shops were rebuilt after the fire, this mansion of the city must have added to pride and determination in recovery.

Surviving, on the other hand, is the Asiatic Company Office, built in 1738 from designs by the Dutch architect Philip de Lange (figure 4.46).[53] Built of brick with sandstone trim, it has a ground-level story above which the principal and attic stories are framed by a giant order of Tuscan pilasters. The central segmental pediment above has sculptures of Neptune and Hermes, patrons of the Company, and the building is covered with a mansard roof. The manner here is Dutch, rather than German as at the Town Hall. Located across the harbor on Christianshavn, it does not occupy a dominant position and is hardly distinguishable from a large mercantile or noble residence.

This points up a contrast between these two nonresidential buildings. The Town Hall fitted in with what was by then a fairly normal pattern: a symmetrical blocky building, distinguishable from a residence by site, ceremonial entrance, and tower. For an individual commercial organization the precedent would be the guild hall, in form similar to the town hall. The merchant's house with shop on the ground floor and residence above, two to three windows wide, with gable end to the street, was familiar enough, such as the houses in Copenhagen and Stockholm that we have already seen (figures 3.35 and 3.50). The Bourse in Copenhagen had been built to accommodate a large number of individual merchants (figure 3.33). But a building for offices was another matter, and Lange's solution is essentially domestic in its outward appearance. This is an early example of the dilemmas that architects in the coming industrial ages were to face in designing appropriate expressions for a whole new set of building programs.

The pilasters framing the principal salon of the Asiatic Company Office also appear on the elegant parish church that was completed in 1743 at Damsholte on Møn from Lange's only complete designs for a church (figure 4.47).[54] It consists of a rectangular nave with a polygonal projection on the west for a porch and another on the east for the pulpit and altar. The roofs of these projections are hipped and set into the hip roof of the nave, with an onion-domed turret over the porch. The brick walls are painted yellow, and the corners are accented with white Tuscan pilasters. The central window in the south wall is further accented with rusticated pilasters and a pediment, carrying the emblem of Christian VI, who provided some of the funds for the church. Damsholte Church is a surprising note of the baroque in a rural landscape more characterized by medieval churches, such as those at Elmelunde, Keldby, and Fanefjord nearby.

Damsholte Church is one of several, starting perhaps with the Reformed Church in Copenhagen, built in 1689 and rebuilt in 1731, whose sources may lie in earlier seventeenth-century Dutch designs, such as those of Pieter Post. Other churches and chapels built in early eighteenth-century Denmark had this characteristic broad façade and hipped roof with central turret. In the Reformed Church the pulpit is on the broad wall opposite the entrance. In other examples the pulpit and altar are on the long axis, as at the Fredensborg chapel. Damsholte Church seems to be a variation, having no entrance through the central bay of the south side and the turret displaced to mark the entrance on the west.

The churches and chapels with entrances on the long sides, hipped roofs, and central turrets resemble nothing so much as town halls, and indeed for some branches of English Protestantism the town hall or market hall was

**48**

4.48 **Sigtuna, Uppland. Town Hall. 1744.**

4.49 **Helsinki. Sveaborg. A. Ehrensvärd. Begun 1745. (James A. Donnelly.)**

**49**

probably the inspiration for church design.[55] Certainly the Town Hall of 1729 in Copenhagen was the grandest to be built, and it had its imitators. The type was familiar, and one much more modest example survives at Sigtuna in Uppland, built in 1744 (figure 4.48).[56] One story high, with a massive säteri roof and dominating turret, the building stood for authority in the town. The turret was much more than a decorative climax, for it could be a watch tower, house the town bell, and also sometimes the town clock. Communication by watchman's cry, by lantern, and by bell were all still needed in the eighteenth century.

A last great fort was nearly contemporary with the Town Hall at Sigtuna. The military engineer Augustin Ehrensvärd was called upon to design new defenses for Helsinki, Finland, then still under Swedish rule. Begun in 1745 on a group of islands at the mouth of the harbor, Sveaborg (Suomenlinna) was completed several years later and became known as the "Gibraltar of the North" (figure 4.49).[57] Ehrensvärd had journeyed to Denmark, Germany, France, Holland, and England in 1736–1738, studying fortifications, and for Sveaborg he followed the principles of the military engineer to Louis XIV, Sebastian de Vauban. The bastions, outworks, and casements withstood bombardment by the British and French in 1855, during the Crimean War, although the governor's residence and officers' quarters were destroyed. Today the fortress is largely a park, with museum, restaurants, and many walkways winding among the high heavy walls. For the visitor to Helsinki who has no time to venture into the country-

**4.50 Svartsjö, Uppland.
C. Hårleman. 1735–
1739. (Stockholm, Läns
Museum. Photo: Ingvar
Lundkvist.)**

**4.51 Ledreborg, Zealand.
J. C. Krieger. c. 1743.
Engraving by J. J.
Bruun, 1753. (Copen-
hagen, National
Museum.)**

side, Sveaborg offers a rich opportunity to see
the wide variety of color available in native Finnish granite, here with the different colors of
stone juxtaposed at random, yet forming a harmonious total picture.

After the Frederiksstad project it was
many years before any further large urban designs were carried out in the Scandinavian
countries. For the work of various architects
and some of the changes in taste that occurred
during the remainder of the eighteenth century,
we may look briefly at several houses and also
churches.

At Svartsjö in Uppland, for example, a sixteenth-century castle was rebuilt for the
owner, Fredrik I, in 1735–1739 by the Swedish
architect Carl Hårleman. He was then in charge
of decoration for the Royal Palace in Stockholm, where work had been resumed. For the
new manor house he created a compact building in two stories with a mansard roof and rusticated exterior, the main salon projecting from
the garden (figure 4.50).[58]

Prospect of Lethreborg
af See fra Haugen Anno 1755 .

**51**

Another rebuilding took place at Ledreborg near Roskilde (figure 4.51).[59] Bruun's view shows that a desire for pomp was by no means restricted to the royal family. Here and at other great noble estates, such as Lerchenborg and Bregentved, the main buildings and their dependencies, much like Palladian villas, presided over great tracts comprising formal gardens and large forests and plantations. About 1743, J. C. Krieger remodeled the old manor of Lejregård for its new owner, Councillor Johan Ludwig Holstein. The long garden façade is rhythmically divided by giant pilasters forming five bays, the central one emphasized by a shallow balcony over the door and a segmental pediment above. The end bays are accented by balustrades at the roof line. Holstein was a bibliophile and collector, and Thurah added pavilions for his private library and museum,

connecting them to the main building with curved wings. A third hand, that of Eigtved, is seen in the decorations of the interior. All in all it had become a splendid estate, including the majestic tree-lined allée, six kilometers long, leading from the main road beyond the gates that originally belonged to the Amalienborg gardens.

A third remodeling was begun in 1759 on a property acquired in 1758 by Chancellor Moltke and later named Marienlyst, in Helsingør (figure 4.52).[60] Frederik II had built a summer house called "Lundehave" on the strand there north of Helsingør, and Moltke had it substantially enlarged by the French architect Nicolas-Henri Jardin. The latter had been called to the Academy by Saly after the death of Eigtved in 1754 and was at work on the Frederik's Church project, to which we

**4.52** Helsingør, Zealand. Marienlyst. N.-H. Jardin. Begun 1759.

**4.53** Copenhagen. Harsdorff House. C. F. Harsdorff. 1779–1780.

**4.54** Bergen. Damsgård. 1770–1795. (Oslo, Riksantikvaren.)

shall return. He brought to Denmark the new classicism of French architecture, promulgating its ideals in his teaching. These are clearly stated at Marienlyst, with its simple blocky mass, clear division of stories, restrained use of ornament, and low-pitched roof virtually hidden behind the crowning balustrade. The surface energy of the Rococo has been replaced by a quieter and more dignified statement, a great contrast to Moltke's palace in Amalienborg.

The French taste now dominant in the Academy was continued by Jardin's student Caspar Frederik Harsdorff, whose teaching emphasized even more the correct use of classical details. As a demonstration of his ideas he was able to build a double house on Kongens Nytorv next to the Academy in 1779–1780 (figure 4.53).[61] The smaller unit, next to the Academy, has a five-bay façade with rusticated ground level, entrance in the central bay, and segmental pediments over the end bays at the second level. The larger unit, intended to house a wealthy owner's offices as well as residence, has a three-bay façade, marked by an applied

**53**

**54**

55

56

temple-front motif with giant Ionic pilasters and a pediment filled with sculpture above. On the interior Harsdorff made use of the curved walls in salons and staircases that were also becoming popular in France and England at this time. Although some of his proposals aroused controversy, the classicism of Harsdorff and his pupils became even stronger in the town houses of Copenhagen, especially those built after the next great fire, in 1795.

While the French classical taste was taking hold in Denmark, the Rococo was more persistent in Norway, where major postmedieval contributions were yet to come. The most striking of the late eighteenth-century Norwegian manors is Damsgård in Bergen, as rebuilt in 1770–1795 (figure 4.54).[62] The original wooden house was enlarged by brick wings on either side of the front and by the addition of a central roof platform and turret. The rather astonishing gables and pediments were undoubtedly inspired by designs in pattern books. Much less exuberant but certainly commanding is the contemporary Stiftsgården in Trondheim, built 1774–1778 for the Commandant's mother-in-law (figure 4.55).[63] Said to be the largest wooden building in Scandinavia, the main building is laid out symmetrically with a central reception salon and flanking lesser salons and chambers. Service quarters extend as wings at the back. It is a northern château in wood. The main façade, seventeen bays long, is potentially hopelessly monotonous in spite of the pilasters and pediment framing the entrance and above these a pediment interrupting the roof line and extending over the three central bays. An illusion of greater height than is actually the case was achieved by building a 6-foot space between the ceiling of the ground floor and the floor timbers of the next level. Then the eight bays on either side of the central element are subdivided into four units each by the alterna-

**4.55 Trondheim. Stiftsgården. 1774–1778.**

**4.56 Drottningholm. Chinese Pavilion. C. J. Cronstedt and C. F. Adelcrantz. 1763–1768.**

tion of two triangular and two segmental pediments over the windows. From this relatively decorous exterior one passes to an interior enriched with lively stucco ornament.

If we turn from Norway to Sweden we encounter a different aspect of late eighteenth-century taste, that of fascination with Chinese art and design. The Swedish East India Company was established in 1731, with its headquarters in Gothenburg, and Chinese goods were pouring into Sweden as into other European countries. Sir William Chambers, who in 1774 became a knight in the Order of the Polar Star, was the son of a Scottish merchant in Gothenburg and as a youth sailed on his father's ships to China. In 1757 he published *Designs for Chinese Buildings,* which was a source of ideas for Carl Fredrik Adelcrantz when he designed the second Kina Slott, or Chinese Pavilion, at Drottningholm in 1763 (figure 4.56).[64] It is set in a wooded area of the park, some distance from the palace, and provided a private retreat for the royal family. It is like a tiny Palladian villa, with central block and dependencies, cheerfully decked out with Rococo and Chinese motifs. Jean Eric Rehn provided designs for some of the interiors in his light and elegant fashion. Carefully restored, it is one of the most perfectly preserved Chinese pavilions in Europe.

Among other Chinese interiors of this period in Sweden is the tower room at Tyresö in Södermanland, decorated in the 1770s. Of even more interest, perhaps, is the setting of Tyresö, for here there is much less emphasis on formal gardens and a greater preference for a country landscape in the new English manner (figure 4.57).[65] The designer was Fredrik Magnus Piper, who also did parks in the English style at Drottningholm and Haga.

A similar park was laid out at Liselund on Møn, attributed to the Dane Andreas Kirkerup, who built the charming little country house for Antoine de la Calmette in 1792–1795 (figure 4.58).[66] Its symmetrical plan and refined interiors are not apparent at first glance, the thatched roof, turret, and adjacent pond giving exactly the bucolic impression that was intended. A Chinese pavilion, Norwegian house, and gardener's lodge complete the pastoral assemblage. Liselund is perhaps the most complete expression of Romantic Naturalism in Scandinavia.

In church design, the side-entrance and centralized plans continued in popularity in the eighteenth century. At Kongsberg in Numedal the church planned by Joachim Andreas Stuckenbrock in 1739 and completed by 1761 is entered on the long side through a projecting porch that carries the bell tower (figure 4.59).[67] The interior is furnished with double balconies and an exceptionally rich complex of altar, pulpit, and organ, one above the other opposite the entrance. Later at Røros in Sør-Trøndelag the church built in 1784 by Sven Aspaas is an elongated octagon in plan, two stories high, with a central entrance tower and belfry, and galleries on three sides within. Although octagonal in plan, the Røros church is arranged on the interior as at Kalmar, with the altar on the long axis opposite the entrance, which is not apparent on the exterior (figure 4.60).[68]

Another approach was that of the cruciform plan, which Adelcrantz adopted for Adolf Fredrik's Church in Stockholm in 1768 (figure 4.61).[69] With its applied orders, pedimented windows, and details of carving, this building has a much richer exterior than the smaller Norwegian examples. Ornamental details were originally supplied by the French artists Adrien and Jean Baptiste Masreliez, who also worked at the Royal Palace in Stockholm. The altar was designed by Sweden's prominent sculptor Johan Tobias Sergel, who also designed the monument to Descartes, who was buried in the old churchyard there on his death in 1650. Adelcrantz had traveled extensively in France and Italy, and the great domes of late seventeenth-century Parisian churches and the recently completed Superga in Turin had clearly inspired him.

Adelcrantz was not alone in his admiration for the splendors of Continental churches. We have already noted that Frederik's Church in Copenhagen was planned as the climax of the short axis of the Frederiksstad project, at the end of Frederiksgade opposite the harbor. There is indeed a church there now, and the history of how it got there marks one of the most frustrating episodes in eighteenth-century Scandinavian building.[70] Eigtved, who had earlier proposed a large centralized church to be built under Christian VI, drew up several designs for the church in Frederiksstad, and these too owed much to the Continental churches that Eigtved had seen. It is perhaps worthwhile to emphasize once more that for these Protestant state churches in Sweden and Denmark, there was no hesitation in drawing upon the grandest designs of the Church of Rome. The cornerstone of Eigtved's Frederik's Church was duly laid in 1749.

Eigtved's proposal was for a round church with a massive dome and flanking towers. On

**57**

4.57 Tyresö, Södermanland.
F. M. Piper. 1770s.
(Stockholm, Nordic
Museum.)

4.58 Liselund, Møn. A. Kirkerup, attr. 1792–1795.

**58**

**4.59 Kongsberg, Numedal. Church. J. A. Stuckenbrock. Begun 1739. (Oslo, Riksantikvaren.)**

**4.60 Røros, Sør-Trøndelag. Church. S. Aspaas. 1784.**

**4.61 Stockholm. Adolf Fredrik's Church. C. F. Adelcrantz. 1768.**

his death in 1754 Thurah proposed changing the plan to a square church with a dome and no towers. Thurah had left Copenhagen for his second wife's estate of Børglum Kloster in Jutland in 1750, partly to pursue his literary work and partly because of dissatisfaction with his position after a reorganization of the official building administration in 1742. Whatever the merits of his proposal may have been, it is not surprising that the building commission sought instead to continue the church in the French academic tradition, with the Royal Danish Academy of Art newly relocated and the late Eigtved its first director. Through Saly's influence Nicholas-Henri Jardin was called from his native Paris to prepare further designs.[71]

We have already seen Jardin's work at Marienlyst. In the proposal that was approved in 1756, Jardin kept Eigtved's round domed church and flanking towers but lowered the dome to broader proportions and simplified the surfaces by omitting much detail and unifying the stories with strong giant orders. The fate of Jardin's project was linked to economics and court intrigue. By 1770 the building was far from complete, the marble pillars of the central portico standing alone, 30 feet high. Count Jo-

han Friedrich Struensee, who was then approaching the height of his power in Denmark, decided that the work had become too costly, had Jardin dismissed as architect to the king, and imposed a new constitution upon the Academy without consulting either Jardin or Saly. Funds for Frederik's Church were cut off, and Jardin resigned his professorship in the Academy and returned to France in 1771, generously proposing that his former pupil Harsdorff be his successor.[72] And so there stood the marble pillars (figure 4.62), the statue of Frederik V left gazing up Frederiksgade at the unfinished church that was to have borne his name and made a visual link between church and king. No effective attempt to complete the building was made until a century later, and that is another story.

The last eighteenth-century church to be considered has also had a somewhat unusual history. In 1785, after months of severe earth-

60

61

4.62   Copenhagen. Freder-
       ik's Church. Painting
       by C. W. Eckersberg, c.
       1817. (Copenhagen,
       Hirschsprung
       Collection.)
4.63   Reykjavik from Hóla-
       völlur. Drawing by
       Kloss, 1835. (Copen-
       hagen, Royal Library.)
4.64   Drottningholm. Court
       Theater. C. F. Adel-
       crantz. 1766. Interior.
       (Drottningholm, The-
       ater Museum.)

62

63

quakes that ruined the old Cathedral of Iceland at Skalholt, the decision was made to move the seat of the bishop to Reykjavik. The town was beginning to flourish as a port, and this part of Iceland was thought to be less subject to earthquakes and volcanic eruptions. The church there then being too small, Andreas Kirkerup was given the task of designing the new one. He began with a plan for a church built of horizontal logs, in section similar to an aisled farmhouse, thinking erroneously that this was in good Icelandic tradition.[73] Had he gone to Iceland himself, which he did not, he would have had a less romantic view. This inclination toward a vernacular building was consistent with his use of the thatched cottage motif for Liselund. His plans for a wooden church were not accepted, and the final plan was for a stone church with a tile roof (figure 4.63). Even this was not wholly satisfactory, for the tiles kept blowing off in violent winter storms, and the cathedral was much enlarged and the interior rebuilt in 1846.

Some specialized projects were also undertaken in late eighteenth-century Scandinavia. Both Adelcrantz and Jardin were involved in theater design, and two of their most interesting works have survived. At Drottningholm Queen Lovisa Ulrika's enthusiasm for theatrical performances led to the building of a theater beside the palace in 1753, for which Adelcrantz prepared drawings for remodeling in 1755.[74] This burned in 1762, and Adelcrantz designed its successor, which was completed in 1766. Restored in modern times after many years of neglect, the Drottningholm court theater is now once more in use. All the more remarkable is that over thirty of the original stage settings are extant.[75] The exterior is simple, but the interior is rich with pilasters, garlands, and a pale rose, blue, gray and yellow color scheme (figure 4.64). An entablature above the pilas-

ters is carried onto the proscenium, which forms an introduction to the stage.

In 1766 Queen Juliana Maria had Jardin convert the armory over the stables at Christiansborg to a theater.[76] Whereas at Drottningholm the seating consists of rows of benches with concealed boxes in the corners, Jardin chose a parterre and two tiers of boxes for his long narrow space (figure 4.65). He may have been thinking of the new Opéra at Versailles (1763–1770), about which he could have learned during his visit to Paris in 1763. The walls of the boxes were built at right angles to the rails as was customary in French theaters, rather than slanting in the Italian manner. Jardin's theater, with its Ionic rather than Corinthian order and lack of much surface decoration, is less exuberant than that at Drottningholm. Although the Christiansborg theater sets are gone, the interior has been restored, primarily as a museum of Danish theater history but used for occasional performances as well.

Three buildings in Stockholm should also be mentioned. In 1746 Hårleman was called upon to plan an observatory for Stockholm, which was completed in 1753 (figure 4.66).[77] In

**64**

65

65

**4.65 Copenhagen. Christiansborg Court Theater. N.-H. Jardin. 1766. Interior. (Copenhagen, Theater History Museum.)**

**4.66 Stockholm. Observatory. C. Hårleman. 1753. (Stockholm, Royal Swedish Academy of Sciences.)**

**4.67 Stockholm. Exchange. E. Palmstedt. 1767–1776.**

the years following the introduction of telescopes for astronomical observations, high towers had been popular as observing stations. Hårleman departed from this trend by building a mansion, the two lower stories for working space and the residence on the third. A solution for scientific establishments other than the conversion of houses or towers had not yet been reached.

Another familiar building type was adopted for the new Exchange in Stockholm, built in 1767–1776 by Erik Palmstedt (figure 4.67).[78] The long-standing formula of a rectangular block with side entrance and central turret that we saw in such a modest town hall as that of Sigtuna is still discernible in the Exchange, now of course on a larger scale. The lower story is rusticated. The emphatic three-bay central element with arcade below and temple-front above, using coupled columns, recalls the Frederiksstad façades, while the turret is strongly Baroque. This gave Stockholm one grand new columned façade, and the Opera House, built by Adelcrantz in 1775–1782, gave the other (figure 4.68).[79]

Tessin's original scheme for a great square across Norrbro from the Royal Palace had not materialized. When Gustavus III commissioned the Opera House, it was placed on the east side of Tessin's proposed square. It was destroyed in 1891 and replaced by the present Royal Opera House, but when built it provided a strong element of the grand effect that Tessin had intended. There was a rusticated ground story, with wall arches over the windows as well as over the central triple entrance, then a Corinthian order rising through two stories, with the three central bays projecting so that the columns were free-standing. An attic story gave the final emphasis to the central portion.

Adelcrantz was able to design a freestanding building, for which he seems to have derived inspiration from Jacques-Germain Soufflot's theater at Lyons of 1754, the plan of this having been published in 1774.[80] Soufflot's theater, the first to be freestanding in France, was planned with the then popular truncated ellipse for the auditorium, a deep stage, a grand foyer and staircases, and auxiliary room for spectators and performers. Adelcrantz adopted these, but because of site restrictions he placed the axis of the auditorium and stage north-south, with his grand entrance on the east, facing the square. He included a main foyer and also a royal foyer and a royal box at the center of the first of four tiers of boxes and galleries. The interior was finished in the French classic taste, much of the design being furnished by Jean Baptiste Masreliez.

One other note of grandeur that Tessin had not envisaged was the equestrian statue of Gustavus II Adolf that the French sculptor Pierre Hubert L'Archevêque was commissioned in 1755 to prepare for the square before the Opera House was built. It was placed facing across Norrbro toward the Royal Palace, where the stairs to the north entrance are faced with a triumphal arch motif. This may have been in response to the statue of Frederik V, just commissioned in Copenhagen. It is, however, interesting to observe that instead of the state-church symbolism of the Frederiksstad scheme, in Stockholm a national hero rather than the reigning monarch was glorified and the symbolism was purely secular.

Two special cases of town planning will close this chapter. A print by Meno Haas of 1780 gives a bird's-eye view of Christiansfeld, a Moravian settlement founded in 1772 (figure 4.69).[81] The "Herrnhutter," as they were called from the town of Herrnhut in Saxony given to their sect by Count Zinzendorf, practiced piety, good works, and celibacy, and laid out their town in orderly parallel streets with the help

**66**

**67**

of the Bohemian architect J. C. Arndt. Separate houses for the brothers and the sisters, a guest house, and a plain wooden church were the principal buildings. In granting the new settlers their permission, Christian VII had some hopes that their industries would be an economic asset, and to some extent the brotherhood earned a reputation for high quality of work. The religious fervor of the early years eventually died out, however, and in 1970 Christiansfeld became an ordinary municipality.

Finally, while we have concentrated upon the major stylistic events of the seventeenth and eighteenth centuries, there were strong forces at work that were to bring great changes in structural technology and attitudes of taste in the nineteenth century. In England the smelting of iron by coke had been developed in the 1740s, and by the end of the century steam power was being used in industrial production. The factory, as distinct from the individual workshop, was starting into prominence as a new building type, with the accompanying need for worker housing. Although forges, sawmills, glassworks, etc., were certainly not new, the iron-working estate at Fagervik in Finland was a prophetic microcosm of the "company town" (figure 4.70).[82] Water cascading into a ravine from the lake provided power for the works, a church was built in 1737, and the owner's house newly built in 1773. A street of plain wooden houses for workers completed the group, which still has the quiet rural character that the coming industrial cities could never attain.

68

4.68  **Stockholm. Opera House. C. F. Adelcrantz. 1775–1782. (Stockholm, City Museum.)**

4.69  **Christiansfeld, Jutland. Engraving by Meno Haas, 1780. (Copenhagen, National Museum.)**

4.70  **Fagervik. Painting after drawing by Z. Topelius. (Helsinki, National Museum of Finland.)**

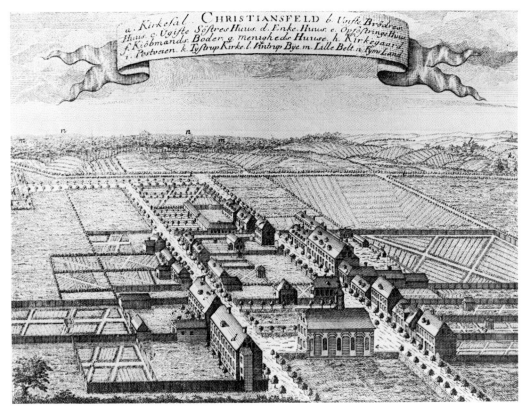

**69**

**70**

## 5 Scandinavian Neoclassicism

In the second half of the eighteenth century the vocabulary of the classical orders was used in a more sober manner than under the Baroque and Rococo tastes, largely from the impact of French classicism on the Academy in Copenhagen. At the end of the century there was another moment of reinterpretation of classical motifs. Its most eloquent Scandinavian expressions were made in Sweden, and there were similar expressions in England and America.[1] What in England is called the "Adamesque" and in America the "Federal" has been termed the "Gustavian" style in Sweden because of the strong support of the arts by Gustavus III, who reigned from 1771 to 1792.[2]

The late Gustavian period is generally dated from 1784, when Gustavus III returned to Sweden after a journey to Italy. He had been to Rome in company with the sculptor Johan Tobias Sergel, even climbing Mount Vesuvius and visiting the Forum in Rome with one of the first in Sweden to undertake archaeological investigations, Carl Frederik Fredenheim.[3]

Even before this journey, Gustavus III had called a French troupe of players to his court,

1

and he had already had a theater built at Gripsholm Castle by Erik Palmstedt.[4] The place chosen was the upper story of the southeast tower. Palmstedt's first solution was to put both stage and seating within the circle, but in 1781 this was all enlarged to the present arrangement (figure 5.1).[5] The seats are set in a semicircle, with access stairs and corridors in the thick wall of the tower. Ionic columns and engaged columns encircle the auditorium, two tiers of boxes between the columns at the back. A further remodeling in 1786 may have been inspired by *Il Teatro d'Ercolana,* the second printing of which Piranesi dedicated to Gustavus III in 1783.[6] The Gripsholm theater is therefore altogether different from those at Drottningholm and Christiansborg and is an early attempt to work in the full classical manner.

After his journey to Italy Gustavus III was all the more enthusiastic about classical antiquity. With his and others' encouragement, several architects and interior designers produced distinguished buildings in the Gustavian style. These buildings are marked by reserve and attempts at "correct" use of the orders without

and delicate interpretation of Roman and Pompeiian motifs within.

One of the first major projects was the Botanicum at Uppsala (figure 5.2).[7] A Botanic Garden had been founded at the University of Uppsala in 1657, and thanks to the efforts of the Swedish botanist Carl Linnaeus was given fresh impetus in the mid-eighteenth century. He had the patronage of his friend Carl Hårleman, who designed the Orangery c. 1745.[8] Toward the end of his life activity in the garden declined, and then in 1786 his pupil Carl Peter Thunberg as Professor of Botany moved the Botanic Garden closer to the Castle. The Swedish architect Olof Tempelman prepared a design for the institute building, a design that was altered by the French architect Louis Jean Desprez.[9] The result was a building that has in common with Thomas Jefferson's nearly contemporary Capital at Richmond, Virginia, the problem of putting a late eighteenth-century secular activity into a Roman temple. The walls of the rectangular institute building are pierced with windows that could not have been used on either a Greek or a Roman temple, but the façade has a Doric portico in valiant imitation of the Parthenon.

Far more ambitious was Desprez's project for a new palace just outside Stockholm at the

2

royal estate of Haga.[10] A rotunda, colonnades, temple fronts, and statues in niches were all intended in the design of 1791, but after the death of the king in 1792 the idea was abandoned. What was accomplished at Haga, however, was the pavilion. Tempelman enlarged an existing manor house, adding wings but keeping the wall surfaces uncluttered and the roof low behind a balustrade. This near severity does not mark the interior, where the French designer Louis Masreliez adorned the principal rooms with light-hearted paintings in the Pompeiian manner (figure 5.3).

Among the many other projects that Desprez proposed while in Sweden, not all of which were carried out, we may cite one of his church designs, that for the church at Tavastehus, now Hämeenlinna, in Finland, built 1795–1798 (figure 5.4).[11] As we see it today, it has

**5.1  Gripsholm. Theater. E. Palmstedt. 1781. Interior. (Drottningholm, Theater Museum.)**

**5.2  Uppsala. Botanicum. O. Tempelman and L. J. Desprez. 1788. (Stockholm, Antikvarisk-Topografiska Arkivet. Photo: Sigurd Curman.)**

**5.3  Haga, Uppland. Pavilion. O. Tempelman. c. 1793. Salon. (Stockholm, Royal Palace Collections.)**

been enlarged by the wings projecting from the central rotunda and the bell tower of 1837, but the basic idea is still a little Pantheon. Much simplified, using Doric columns in the porch rather than a full colonnade, the church was an early foray of Neoclassicism into Finland. The major invasion was to come later, and from another direction.

Another kind of building that was to become a concern for architects in the nineteenth century was the school. A prominent example from the late eighteenth century is the Gymnasium at Härnösand in Västernorrland, 1785–1791 (figure 5.5).[12] In the capital city of the province this turned out to be more complicated than simply an educational institution. Instead of having masters' lodgings in the same building with the classrooms, the teachers were lodged elsewhere, and the second story had a hall for the magistrates' court. Perhaps this led to the later conversion of the building to the town hall. The first plans were by the Swedish architect Per Hagmansson, and then there were modifications by Tempelman, who was responsible for the pillared porch. Once more an essentially domestic solution was found for the exterior. The Gymnasium could easily have been taken for a Gustavian manor house.

Gustavus III's enthusiasm for the antique therefore helped to stimulate some pioneering efforts toward incorporating classical ideas in contemporary design among architects active in Sweden in the 1780s and 1790s. An era more archaeologically inclined followed in the early years of the nineteenth century. This was the first of two such episodes in Scandinavian architecture, the second to follow a century later, when the principles of antiquity would be studied and interpreted in yet a different manner. In the first, forces quite apart from changing taste precipitated new opportunities in Denmark, Finland, and Norway.

5.4 Hämeenlinna. Church. L. J. Desprez. 1795–1798. (Helsinki, Museum of Finnish Architecture. Photo: A. Salokorpi.)

5.5 Härnösand, Västernorrland. Gymnasium. P. Hagmansson and O. Tempelman. 1785–1791. (Stockholm, Antikvarisk-Topografiska Arkivet.)

**4**

**5**

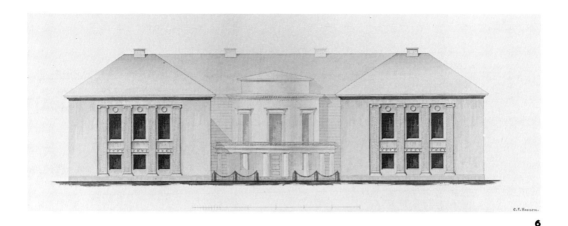

As Desprez and Tempelman had provided leadership in Sweden, Christian Frederik Hansen became the leader of Danish Neoclassicism.[13] His principal contributions were not so much the result of royal enthusiasm for a particular artistic style as of two great catastrophes in Copenhagen. He received his training in the Academy there as a pupil of Harsdorff, winning the gold medal in 1779. This award obliged him to undertake a student journey abroad, which he did late in 1782, returning in 1784. Meantime he had been appointed inspector of buildings in Holstein, where he went to begin practice in the Danish commercial town of Altona, outside Hamburg.

For the wealthy merchants he designed manors and country houses, such as Perdol, built 1788–1790 (figure 5.6).[14] The architect's drawing shows the garden façade. The round salon projected directly opposite the central entrance to the main block. From this salon corridors led to the wings and were continued along the courtyard sides, as at Clausholm. Wider pavilions at either end gave a sense of enclosure to the courtyard and made a frame for the circular salon as seen on axis. Although no longer standing, the building was an important landmark in Hansen's approach to planning and treatment of surface.

Hansen's work was to be characterized by the elements seen in the drawing for Perdol. He chose simple blocks, in this case played off against cylindrical forms, much in the manner of Ledoux. The plain wall surfaces provided a backdrop for the Ionic pilasters framing the triple windows of the pavilions. The motif was stated in a different way on the salon, with its low colonnade at the ground level and three windows above. Details were finely drawn and firmly contained. The treatment of light and shade on the drawing suggests that the salon received reflected light from the wings, and it should be compared to Eckersberg's treatment of light on the pillars of Frederik's Church. It is interesting to see how even in an architectural drawing the study of light to be so splendidly exploited by the Danish Neoclassical painters was already beginning.

Hansen's own house, which he built probably in 1792, is on Palmaillen, a long parkway lined with town houses that takes its name from the game "palla-a-maglio" (figure 5.7).[15] He built a compact three-story house with a rusticated lower portion, then a temple-front to mark the principal salon above. The staircase is circular, while in some of his other houses it is oval.

7

5.6  Perdol, Holstein. C. F.
Hansen. 1798. Drawing
by C. F. Hansen. (Copen-
hagen, Academy of Art
Library.)

5.7  Altona, Holstein. Han-
sen House. C. F. Hansen.
c. 1792. Drawing by C. F.
Hansen. (Copenhagen,
Academy of Art
Library.)

5.8  Altona, Holstein. Baur
House. C. F. Hansen.
1803–1815. Drawing by
A. Meldahl. (Copen-
hagen, Academy of Art
Library.)

8

9

10

For the interiors a richer finish was designed, a particularly fine example being that of the large salon overlooking the garden at the Georg Fr. Baur house (figure 5.8).[16] The owner, a wealthy grocer, commissioned Hansen to build eleven large houses on land he had purchased, and fortunately his own was among those that survived the bombing of Hamburg harbor during World War II. These houses are lined close together at the edge of the street in traditional urban fashion, but there are gardens behind that give a more country air, particularly to those overlooking the harbor. The deep arches over the windows of the Baur salon are expressed by arches carried on the Ionic columns of the balcony above the garden. The decorative motifs of the salon are Hansen's version of the interpretation of the antique that we have seen in the Gustavian style of Desprez and Masreliez.

While Hansen was carrying out his assignment in Altona, two disastrous events took place in Copenhagen. On the night of February 26 in 1794 Christiansborg Palace went up in flames. It was not entirely finished, and the fire must have been a sad blow not only to the royal family and other residents but to the craftsmen who saw their work destroyed as well. As we have noted, the wings surrounding the Riding Ground were spared. Then in June 1795 another fire laid waste the center of the city, including the Town Hall. Harsdorff, still teaching in the Academy, was 59 years old. The royal family bought the Amalienborg palaces for temporary residence in 1794, and Harsdorff designed the colonnade linking those on Amaliegade (figure 5.9). He died in 1799, however, before much could be done to recover the loss of the largest buildings in the city, since replacement of houses and shops had to come first.

Hansen was called back to Copenhagen for work toward rebuilding Christiansborg. He also prepared designs for the "Råd-og-domhus," the new Town Hall and Law Courts, built 1805–1815 and now housing only the courts (figure 5.10).[17] The site of the old building was abandoned and the new building placed on the west side of Nytorv. The broad façade with its impressive portico of six Ionic columns gives no hint of the wings extending behind it. Hansen departed from the traditional turreted model for a town hall and built something more like a palace for the city. He planned the entrance block with flanking chambers, then a deep vestibule or waiting room with four Doric columns, and directly beyond the courtroom, with Corinthian columns and the magistrates' niche, for all the world like the apse of a Roman basilica. This last was undoubtedly intentional. Shortly after came the Arrestbygning, or prison, with a heavily rusticated lower level and connected to the main building by a heavy arch across the street, recalling Piranesi's *Carceri*. Hansen's leaning was to Roman rather than Greek antiquity, and perhaps this caused him to choose a dark reddish stucco for exterior finish. By the time he visited Rome much of the marble had been quarried away, leaving brick the dominant color. Whatever the reason, we can see that color was one of the significant

**5.9** **Copenhagen. Amaliegade Colonnade. C. F. Harsdorff. 1794.**

**5.10** **Copenhagen. Råd-og-domhus. C. F. Hansen. 1805–1815.**

areas in which Hansen's classical cityscape differed from some others.

In 1803 a commission had been appointed for the Town Hall and Christiansborg Palace, and Hansen's proposal of 1800 for rebuilding the palace was basically accepted, leaving the two projects to be undertaken simultaneously.[18] Economy dictated that the walls remaining from the old palace should be used as much as possible, which meant that Hansen's palace was to some extent predetermined (figure 5.11). The many windows and elaborate surface ornaments of the old palace were no longer fashionable. Hansen simplified the main façade toward the Palace Square by closing openings in the two end projections, eliminating a columned portico for the main entrance, and reducing ornament to his characteristic discreet window moldings. The necessary expression of grandeur was achieved by the six-columned central temple-front rising through the two principal residence stories.

The royal apartments were located on the lower of these, with the king's suite in the east wing, the queen's in the north, and the state reception suite in the south. The west wing was not entirely rebuilt, the north and south wings being linked by a colonnade. The interiors were never fully completed, but they owed much to Hansen's awareness of French Neoclassical design, particularly through the works of Percier and Fontaine.[19] The Great Hall had a gallery supported by sixteen stately Corinthian columns and decorated with a frieze by the Danish sculptor Hermann Wilhelm Bissen (figure 5.12).

Construction proceeded slowly, the roof over the principal wing not being raised until 1809. The Napoleonic Wars had Europe in strife once more, bringing Denmark increasing

financial difficulties.[20] The palace that Lauritz de Thurah had built for Queen Sophie Magdalene at Hørsholm in 1744 was razed in 1811 for its materials.[21] By 1816 all wings were roofed, and the interiors of the royal apartments, at least, ready by 1828. As had been the case with its predecessor, however, the second Christiansborg was never entirely finished.

The Palace Chapel also had to be rebuilt, and Hansen made the same changes from Baroque to classical that he had on the palace (figure 5.13).[22] The east façade was closed up and given a four-column temple-front, while the other walls were also finished with smooth surfaces and restrained detail. Work was begun in 1810 and the dome roofed with copper in 1820. The interior was also given much simpler treatment of surface, with the galleries now minimized behind Corinthian pilasters and the Baroque ceiling replaced by a coffered dome on pendentives.

**5.11  Copenhagen. Christiansborg II. C. F. Hansen. 1803–1828. Lithograph after H. F. G. Holm. (Copenhagen, Royal Library.)**

**5.12  Copenhagen. Christiansborg II. Great Hall. (Copenhagen, National Museum.)**

13

In the meantime Copenhagen had suffered another catastrophe. Three nights of bombardment by the British in September 1807 had left much of the center city, including Vor Frue Kirke, in ruins. To Hansen fell yet another restoration, for which he began plans in 1808 (figure 5.14).[23] Construction began in 1811, and the new church was dedicated in 1829. Although built on the ruins of J. C. Krieger's church, reminder of the latter is in the austere outer walls, as is the case with the Palace Chapel. Chevet buttresses gave way to the two cylinders and dome with which Hansen built the new apse, another expression of the bold massing that he liked so much. On the east the temple-front portico is set off by the plain east wall and the simple tower rising above it. The interior is one of Hansen's strongest expressions of Roman grandeur. Rectangular piers with niches for statutes of the Apostles line the nave at the ground level, with an Ionic colonnade in the gallery. The length of the church suggested a coffered barrel vault for the nave rather than a dome, and the apse, probably designed for Thorvaldsen's statue of Christ, is lit from its dome. The effect is serene and majestic, particularly when light comes in from the south.

We may add here notice of a somewhat later building, the museum built for the works and collections of Thorvaldsen by Michael Gottlieb Bindesbøll after the return of the sculptor from Rome in 1838 (figure 5.15).[24] After several grand proposals had been made for this important new national museum, Frederik VI granted the royal carriage house, just west of the palace chapel, for the purpose. Bindesbøll added a portico on the front and an enclosing wing on the back and chose the Ionic order as fitting for Thorvaldsen's classically inspired sculptures. The sculptor's own tomb is in the center of the courtyard, and after his death in

5.13  Copenhagen. Christiansborg II. Chapel. Interior. (Copenhagen, National Museum.)

5.14  Copenhagen. Vor Frue Kirke. C. F. Hansen. 1811–1829. Watercolor by P. Christensen. (Copenhagen, National Museum.)

5.15  Copenhagen. Thorvaldsen Museum. M. G. Bindesbøll. 1838.

14

15

1844 a frieze depicting his triumphal arrival in Copenhagen was painted on the exterior by Jørgen Sonne. The building is an early and striking example of a museum devoted to the work of a single artist, and it became an important source of inspiration in Denmark's second classical period.

In this brief review of what enthusiasm for the antique meant in Sweden and Denmark we have found scattered projects in and around Stockholm and several important rebuilding projects in Copenhagen. Although the Gustavian style, especially for interiors, and Hansen's great official style each had its own distinction, neither was exercised in the service of major urban complexes. For this kind of undertaking we must turn to Finland and Norway.

While Hansen was providing a badly damaged Copenhagen with palace, church, and town hall, there was a whole new set of circumstances in the old city of Helsinki. At the instigation of Napoleon, Russia attacked Finland in February 1808, and the "Gibraltar of the North," Suomenlinna, fell ignominiously after firing only a few shots. By the Treaty of Hamina, September 17, 1809, Finland became a Grand Duchy of the Russian Empire.[25]

Czar Alexander I made an initial good impression by appointing a national legislature and declaring a Governor-General to represent him in Finland. He and his successors were, however, disinclined to see this body in action and refused to exercise their sole right to assemble it until 1863. Alexander I also moved the capital to Helsinki in 1812. The town's population was then only about 4,000, and it had suffered badly from a fire in 1808. The occasion was seized to make a new city as an expression of the new regime.

Helsinki had been founded by Gustavus Vasa in 1550 to be the maritime and commercial center of the Gulf of Finland. The first site

**5.16  Helsinki. Senate House. C. L. Engel. Begun 1818.**

**5.17  Helsinki. University. C. L. Engel. 1828–1832.**

at what is now Vanhakaupunki, three miles east, is marked by foundations of the church in a little park. The harbor facilities here proved unsatisfactory, and the present site was chosen in 1640. Never large, the town was plagued by fire and famine, and it was twice occupied by the Russians, in 1721 and in 1742. To create a major city from this unpromising start was a significant achievement.

A reconstruction committee was appointed, headed by Johan Albert Ehrenström, who developed the plan adopted in 1817. The approach to the inner harbor is past Suomenlinna and a number of islands, with one of the principal hills rising to the west and another to the north. Ehrenström planned a new church to dominate the northern height, with a great square before it and civic buildings on either side. In the more level portion between the northern and western heights he laid out the Esplanade, linking the harbor with the old north-south road. The architect he and the committee chose to carry out these plans was Carl Ludwig Engel.[26]

Engel was born in Germany and was a student together with Karl Friedrich Schinkel in Berlin. He also studied in Italy. In 1809 he went to work in Reval in Estonia and later worked in Turku where he met Ehrenström in 1814. His first large civic building in Helsinki was the Senate House, begun in 1818 (figure 5.16).[27] It was

16

17

18

19

planned as a range of four wings around a central courtyard, and it was not entirely completed until after Engel's death in 1840. The east wing facing the square set the tone of monumentality and authority that Ehrenström's plan demanded. It is four stories high, the two lower stories rusticated, the arched openings of the second level forming a base for the square-headed openings and the Corinthian order above. The central pavilion is a projecting portico of six columns, rising through the third and fourth stories, with the Throne Room (now the Senate Chamber) directly behind it on the third level. Four two-story pilasters at either end of this façade enclose the whole composition, which may reflect Hansen's Christiansborg II, begun fifteen years earlier. A notable feature of the interior is the great staircase, an ascending series of brick vaults supported by fluted Doric columns.

While the Senate House was under construction a disastrous fire occurred in Turku, providing an excuse to move the University, founded in 1640, closer to the new administration in Helsinki. Ehrenström's committee had been disbanded in 1825, leaving Engel more directly responsible to the Secretary of State in St. Petersburg and thus in a more independent position. His proposal to have the new University building in Helsinki complement rather than imitate the Senate House was fortunately accepted (figure 5.17).[28] Again we see a long four-story building, the two lower stories rusticated, a central two-story portico, and three pilastered bays at either end. The differences are subtle: square-headed openings at the lower levels, arched panels above the windows of the third, and an Ionic rather than Corinthian portico. Behind the portico rises another of Engel's great staircases, and behind this the Festival Hall, in semicircular theater form, with a giant order of fluted Corinthian columns ris-

5.18  **Helsinki. Old Church. C. L. Engel. 1826. (Helsinki, National Museum of Finland.)**

5.19  **Helsinki. Church of St. Nicholas. C. L. Engel. Begun 1826.**

ing before the gallery at the back. This room was badly damaged by bombing in World War II and has been enlarged and altered in reconstruction.

In 1824 Engel succeeded the Italian-born but Swedish-trained Carlo Francesco Bassi as Controller of Public Works, and through his direction, if not by his actual personal designs, a vigorous period of Neoclassical construction ensued, bringing churches, civic buildings, and houses to numerous towns in Finland. If some examples were less sophisticated than others, nevertheless many communities received a prompt architectural expression of the imperial regime. At Hamina, for example, Engel's church of 1837 is a round building with a dome, set in a walled enclosure.[29] Engel also built the Old Church in Helsinki in 1826, the site chosen being on Lönnrotinkatu, which runs diagonally southwest from the end of the Esplanade. The modest wooden church, embellished with pilasters, is in a park in a residential district and lays no claim to a grand setting (figure 5.18).[30]

Engel's most spectacular contribution to the new Helsinki was the church of St. Nicholas, raised to cathedral status in 1959 (figure 5.19).[31] The Senate House and University both had essentially palace façades, a solution to designing for large public buildings similar to that adopted by Hansen for the Råd-og-domhus in Copenhagen. Engel's opportunity was different, and instead of having to set his buildings into a crowded city he was able to place them in a far more ceremonial manner, flanking and defining a large open square. Now the civic pedestal was ready for a crowning monument.

Originally yellow, it now rises to a new white climax above the yellow buildings on either side below. The plan is a Greek cross, with the principal liturgical axis east-west and the main entrance on the west. The enormous stair now leading up from the north side of the square replaced Engel's colonnaded Main Guard Building (begun in 1818) in the 1840s. The four strong Corinthian porticoes stand before the four apses forming the arms of the cross, in which the galleries are supported on Ionic columns (figure 5.20).

Engel's last great secular building was the University Library, begun in 1833 (figure

20

21

5.21).[32] It is across the street from the Cathedral, and its two-story order of engaged Corinthian columns and pilasters reflects the exterior
of the Cathedral, though with an attic story
rather than pediments. The reading rooms on
the north and south of the domed central hall
may reflect the colonnaded Academy Library in
St. Petersburg.[33]

The third Scandinavian city to experience
change and development after the Napoleonic
Wars was Oslo.[34] By the Treaty of Kiel in January 1814 Frederik VI of Denmark was forced
to cede Norway to Sweden. Although the
Norwegian attempt to elect the people's own
king was unsuccessful, the constitution adopted
May 17, 1814, was agreed upon by Sweden,
and it is in fact still the basis of Norway's political structure. Charles XIII of Sweden died in
1818 and was succeeded by Karl XIV Johan,
who as Napoleon's marshal Jean Bernadotte
had been elected heir in 1810. Whereas the
new king sponsored a number of building projects in Sweden, the most dramatic impact on

**5.20  Helsinki. Church of St.
Nicholas. Interior.
(Helsinki, National Mu-
seum of Finland.
Photo: Istvan Rácz.)**

**5.21  Helsinki. University Li-
brary. C. L. Engel.
1833–1844.**

**5.22  Ulefoss, Telemark.
C. Collett. 1802–1807.
(Oslo, Riksantikvaren.
Photo: O. Vaering.)**

any individual city during his reign came to Oslo.

Classical motifs were already in use in Norway. At Ulefoss in Telemark a manor house had been built in 1802–1807 on the old estate by Christian Collett.[35] On the main façade a two-story central block with portico projects at the ground level, with pilasters between the windows of the second level, the whole section crowned by a dome. One-story extensions on either side of the central block are embellished with much shallower Tuscan pilasters and entablature. Behind these extensions two wings are added at the back of the house, also colonnaded (figure 5.22). The overall scheme is like a Palladian villa, but the clear-cut geometrical forms and the severe Doric elements belong to the new taste for the antique.

The population of Oslo was then well over 13,000, more than twice the size of Helsinki. Akershus Castle dominated the harbor from its commanding height, and there was already the Cathedral beside the market place. Norway as a separate country under the Swedish crown was in a different situation from Finland, which had merely been created a Grand Duchy. As Crown Prince, Karl Johan chose the site for the necessary Royal Palace on the northern height. The palace would thus tower over the city, balancing the fortress to the southeast (figure 5.23).[36]

His choice was applauded by the architect Hans D. F. Linstow, who began work on the palace in 1823. The original plan was for a two-storied H-shaped building, with a cross-gabled roof and temple fronts in the center. In addition there were to be four pavilions connected by colonnades. This proved to be much too costly, and the resulting building has a main block with wings to the north (figure 5.24). It has three principal stories, with basement and attic. On the south facade there is a portico

**23**

with arcaded ground story and six-columned Ionic temple-front rising through two stories above. The columns and pediments were not added until 1848, and they are therefore not visible in the lithograph of 1840.

While the palace was under construction Linstow traveled to Denmark and Germany in 1836–1837. It was then time to finish the interiors, for which the funds were ready. He was much impressed with what he saw in Germany, especially the work of Schinkel, who was then in Berlin. On his return to Oslo, Linstow had as an assistant the young German architect Heinrich Schirmer. The work of finishing the interiors was now carried forward with much stucco and polychrome in Schinkel's "Pompeiian" manner. Much was done by the theater painter P. C. F. Wergmann, the effect closer to the Gustavian style in Sweden than to the French Neoclassicism of Hansen (figure 5.25). To the latter, however, there may have been some debt in the Great Hall, which bears strong resemblance to the Great Hall at Christiansborg, finished in 1831, and which Linstow must have seen (figure 5.26).

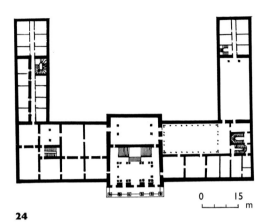

**24**

5.23   Oslo. Royal Palace.
       H. D. F. Linstow. 1823–
       1848. Lithograph, c.
       1840. (Oslo, City
       Museum.)

5.24   Oslo. Royal Palace.
       Plan. (After Kavli,
       *Norwegian Architec-*
       *ture,* p. 96.)

5.25   Oslo. Royal Palace.
       Dining Salon. (Oslo,
       Palace Archives.
       Photo: Teigens.)

5.26   Oslo. Royal Palace.
       Great Hall. (Oslo, Pal-
       ace Archives. Photo:
       Teigens.)

**25**

**26**

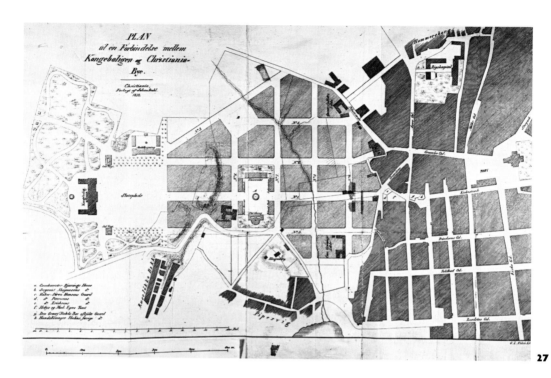

**27**

The site of the palace once chosen, in 1835 Linstow was ready with a grand plan for the city (figure 5.27).[37] He kept the land around the palace as a park covering the slopes and a great open space in front. Then down the hill toward the Cathedral he planned a boulevard, now Karl Johan Gate, with a plaza for a university at the foot of the hill and a site for a Parliament building farther south. He was not able to carry out all his ideas, but he certainly capitalized on the planning opportunity that palace builders in Copenhagen never had, and his basic scheme shapes the city still.

Linstow had a younger contemporary, Christian Henrik Grosch, who had also been born in Denmark and had studied at the Academy in Copenhagen.[38] He began teaching in the art school in Oslo in 1827 and became the state architect in 1828. His early works were in the Neoclassical tradition, probably the most severe being the Exchange of 1822–1828 (figure 5.28).[39] The clear Doric columns of its portico found another expression in the church that Grosch designed for Halden in Østfold in 1828.[40] The simple exterior surfaces and square tower recall Vor Frue Kirke in Copenhagen, which was being constructed when Grosch was a student there in 1820–1824. At Halden the aisles widen out to a transept, with a dome over the crossing, and there is a niche with a statue of Christ in the sanctuary (figure 5.29).

The most ambitious project that Grosch undertook was building for the University.[41] The first plans were drawn up in the late 1820s, and by 1840 the final scheme was adopted and construction begun. The conception was more extensive than that for the University in Helsinki, perhaps partly because a more spacious and level site was available in Oslo. Three buildings were built facing an open plaza on the north side of Karl Johan Gate (figure 5.30). On the west was placed a lecture

**29**

**5.27  Oslo. Plan by H. D. F. Linstow. 1835. (Oslo, Riksantikvaren.)**

**5.28  Oslo. Exchange. C. H. Grosch. 1826–1828.**

**5.29  Halden, Østfold. Immanuel Church. C. H. Grosch. 1828–1833. Interior. (Oslo, Riksantikvaren.)**

**5.30   Oslo. University. C. H.
Grosch. 1840–1852.
Lithograph after draw-
ing by J. Frich, c. 1850.
(Oslo, Riksantikvaren.)**

**5.31   Stockholm. Skepps-
holm Church. F. Blom.
1824–1842.**

building, in the middle a museum/collections
building together with an anatomical theater,
and on the east a library to which was added a
Festival Hall. In 1838 Grosch's original plans
had been sent to Schinkel in Berlin, and the
buildings as constructed bear some marks of his
corrections and suggestions. The majestic vestibule and staircase are similar to Schinkel's vestibule for the Altes Museum in Berlin, begun in
1823. The Festival Hall, unlike that of the University of Helsinki, was not placed on axis with
the principal entrance to the library building in
which it is located. It is built like a theater, the
decorations being supplied by Wergmann, although for all their grandeur of appearance
they were carried out in relatively inexpensive
materials.

Whereas Copenhagen, Helsinki, and Oslo
all had major building and planning projects as a
direct result of the Napoleonic Wars, Stock-

holm was not so much affected. Karl XIV Johan did indeed see to the construction of several military and administrative buildings in Stockholm and other cities, but no single architect seems to have dominated the period in Sweden.[42] For a design in the Neoclassical manner paralleling those we have been examining in other countries we may note one Swedish example by an architect who did not restrict himself to the antique for inspiration during his career.

In Stockholm Fredrik Blom designed the Skeppsholm Church, built 1824–1842 (figure 5.31).[43] This is a centralized building, octagonal on the exterior and circular on the interior, entered through porches and covered by a low dome. The present cupola is a later addition. On the interior an ambulatory is established by paired Ionic columns carrying a spacious arcade, reminiscent of Santa Costanza in Rome.

The post-Napoleonic period in Scandinavian architecture was not, however, given over solely to the Neoclassical. Blom was among the many Scandinavian architects who were exploring other possible sources of stylistic ideas. This was also a period of growing awareness of national heritage. We shall therefore turn our attention to the major traditions in vernacular architecture and then to some of the other eclectic styles.

**6**  *Vernacular Architecture in Scandinavia*

With the years when Scandinavian architects were drawing upon antiquity and the Middle Ages for much inspiration, we approach the time when Nordic building traditions would also be important sources for designers. For the student of vernacular architecture, as the term has been devised in recent years, the five Scandinavian countries offer an astonishing variety of building types, materials, and methods of construction and decoration. Lest this richness become too bewildering, the examples chosen for this chapter will be organized in a generally northward direction, beginning with the half-timbered farm buildings of Denmark and southern Sweden, proceeding to the notched log buildings of northern Sweden, Norway, and Finland, and concluding with the stone and turf buildings of the Atlantic islands and Iceland. There will also be some discussion of brick used in farm and town buildings.

In most cases the examples chosen will also be those found in the principal open air museums of the five national capitals. This is partly because these buildings are more easily accessible for study than those like them still

**6.1** **Karup Heath, Jutland (Sorgenfri, Frilandsmuseet). Farmstead. c. 1850.**

**6.2** **Lath and plaster. Drawing by Bjarne Stoklund. (Copenhagen, Dansk Historisk Faellesforening.)**

on their original and often remote sites. In addition, there has been nearly a century of investigation and care of these buildings, with the development of expertise in maintenance and interpretation that is fundamental to the study of vernacular architecture. We will therefore begin with a short review of these five museum parks.

The idea of an open air museum for buildings seems to have originated with Artur Hazelius, who began the collections of Swedish folk art in 1872 that led to the founding of the Nordic Museum in Stockholm in 1873. Although Skansen on Djurgården did not formally open until 1891, Hazelius had planned all along that there should be such a parklike setting for public visits to buildings brought there.[1] Beginning with seven or eight acres, the site expanded to seventy-five acres with 150 buildings by 1982.

In Copenhagen the motivation for the first efforts to found an open air museum was different. The Danish Folk Museum was founded by Bernhard Olsen in 1885, who had seen Swedish farmhouse interiors at the Paris Exhibition of 1878, arranged by Hazelius.[2] Olsen obtained a place in Kongens Have, the royal garden of Rosenborg Palace, in 1897 and found two buildings to place there: the dwelling house of the Halland farmstead and the loft house from Småland. These did not come from Denmark, but from areas where he felt the earliest building traditions were well preserved. The location being clearly unsuitable for any substantial development of an open air museum, land was purchased just north of Sorgenfri Castle near Lyngby, thirteen kilometers north of Copenhagen. Grown to about thirty-seven acres, Frilandsmuseet now includes about eighty buildings or groups of buildings.[3]

The third national capital in which an open air museum was founded is Oslo.[4] In 1867 some old farm buildings were moved to a site near the city. Then in 1881 Oscar II had the stave church from Gol in Hallingdal and some farm buildings moved to a park site on his estate on Bygdøy, outside Oslo. The Norwegian Folk Museum opened here in 1902. As at Skansen in Stockholm, there is an "old town" section of houses and shops as well as the farm buildings, and there is also the building housing the major folk collections.

In 1909 about twenty-five acres were set aside on Seurasaari Island at Helsinki for a collection of the rural buildings of Finland.[5] It was founded by Axel Olai Heikel of the Finnish Archaeological Commission, who had hoped to include some buildings from related cultures, but this has not materialized.

There is a zoo at Skansen, but otherwise these four open air museums have a number of features in common. There are furnishings and explanatory materials in many of the buildings, some animals are present, some typical gardens have been developed, programs of folk music and dancing and festival occur, and there are restaurants and book shops. All are visited by thousands of people every year, some just to enjoy the parks, but many to see the examples of living and working quarters of people remote in time or place.

Finally, there is the more recent Árbaer Folk Museum on a former farm site, seven kilometers from Reykjavik in Iceland.[6] The original buildings include the house and barns, a smithy, and a small turf church. Houses have been brought in from other places, and while there are no railroads in Iceland, Iceland's only locomotive is displayed here.

We begin this survey with the half-timbered type of building, dominant in Denmark from the Middle Ages for farm and town buildings.[7] This is based on vertical posts set at the corners of the building and at intervals along the walls, forming a series of sections or bays. These posts may be connected at the top by horizontal plates running the length and width of the building and also across the breadth between the intermediate posts. Rafters for the roof may rest on the side plates. The wall areas may be subdivided by horizontal timbers between the posts and then filled in with brick (figure 6.1). Another possibility is to subdivide the wall spaces with vertical lath as a basis for entwining thin withies or wattles to support an outer covering of plaster, or daub (figure 6.2). Still another possibility is to fill the wall spaces with beach stones (figure 6.3). A variety of final effects may result according to whether the timbers and/or infill are left exposed, covered, or painted.

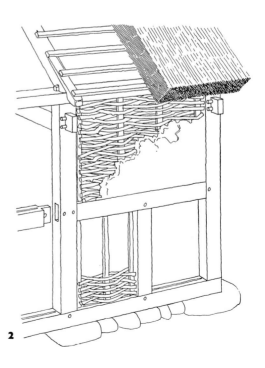

**2**

In rural building in Denmark there is also a variety of relationships between posts, horizontal members, and rafters, which constitute the elements of the building frame. The system of the fisherman's cottage from Agger in Jutland is sometimes called the "Friesian" type, since it is also to be found in the Friesian region of north Holland (figure 6.4).[8] Like the Iron Age longhouse, the main roof here is supported by a pair of longitudinal beams carried on two inner rows of posts. These posts are tied together with cross beams which are mortised through the posts and secured with pegs (figure 6.5). To the principal rafter is fastened a second shorter rafter that rests on the longitudinal beam carried on the outer wall posts. We have then what is also sometimes called a "head house," the inner row of posts being of a convenient low ceiling height. The pattern of the inner row of posts and the slight change in the slope of the outer aisles or "outshots" can be seen at the end of the farm building. At the opposite end it can be seen that the outshot was omitted on the south side of the house, making it possible to wall up between the inner row of posts and provide more window openings for the dwelling. There is as yet no chimney, smoke from the massive hearth escaping through a louver in the roof. The Agger cottage is a single long building housing the family and its livestock compactly under one roof against the weather of the North Sea coast.

Another major type of construction was the post house, in which posts in the center of the end walls rise to carry a ridge, the rafters here resting on the horizontal beams of the outer walls and on the ridge (figure 6.6). This type is found on Jutland, on the island of Funen, and on into parts of Halland and Blekinge in Sweden.[9] The example chosen here is the Lundager Farmstead from Funen, the dwelling house dated 1747 and the latest wing 1880

**3**

(figure 6.7).[10] A chimney now rises from the roof of the dwelling over the raised hearth below.[11] From the outside the farmstead appears somewhat closed, with few door or window openings. Over a period of years the four wings formed a courtyard house, another familiar type that was built in several materials in Denmark and Sweden. The dwelling room, scullery, best room, servants' room, stables for horses and sheep, cow barn, and threshing floor surround the court, a busy arena of farm and family life. C. W. Eckersberg caught the characteristic landscape in a drawing of 1817 (figure 6.8).

The thatched roofs covering these buildings were generally made of reeds or straw lashed to the purlins carried on the rafters. In a

**6.3 Agger, Jutland (Sorgen-
fri, Frilandsmuseet).
Fisherman's cottage.
19th century.**

**6.4 Agger, Jutland (Sorgen-
fri, Frilandsmuseet).
Fisherman's cottage.**

climate notable for strong winds, the "roof-
trees," short pieces of wood pegged together
and set along the ridge, were needed to hold
down the top of the thatch (figure 6.9). We
may recall the suggestion made for stabilizing
thatched roofs with poles at the experimental
Iron Age village at Lejre. In the illustration we
can also see an alternative method of filling the
gable ends, with vertical planks and batten
strips. The end of the thatching is secured and
protected by barge boards. An unusual material
is seaweed, attached to the lowest laths in bun-
dles, then piled up in layers and secured at the
tops with turfs (figure 6.10). Another possibility is heather, like seaweed useful in regions
where there is less straw available from cereal
crops.[12]

In Skåne the half-timbered courtyard farm
might also be found, such as the Ravlunda
Farmstead formerly at Skansen in Stockholm
(figure 6.11).[13] This too was built around a
court with barns, stables, woodshed, and other

5

6

6.5  Agger, Jutland (Sorgen-
     fri, Frilandsmuseet).
     Fisherman's cottage.
     Detail of frame.

6.6  Lundager, Funen (Sor-
     genfri, Frilandsmuseet).
     Farmstead. 1747. Detail
     of frame.

6.7  Lundager, Funen (Sor-
     genfri, Frilandsmuseet).
     Farmstead.

6.8  Farmstead on Møn.
     Drawing by C. W. Eck-
     ersberg, 1810. (Copen-
     hagen, State Museum of
     Art.)

**7**

**8**

9

6.9 Pebringe, Zealand (Sorgenfri, Frilandsmuseet).
Farmstead. 17th cen-
tury. Detail of gable.

6.10 Laesø (Sorgenfri, Frilandsmuseet). Farm-
stead. 1737.

6.11 Ravlunda, Skåne (formerly in Stockholm,
Skansen). Farmstead.
19th century.

6.12 Oktorp, Halland
(Stockholm, Skansen).
Farmstead. 18th
century.

10

11

12

buildings together with the dwelling, the whole complex having a single entrance. Except for windows in the dwelling, the Ravlunda Farmstead was closed on the exterior, life centering in the courtyard as at the Lundager Farmstead.[14]

From Halland in Sweden comes the Oktorp Farmstead, dating partly from the eighteenth century (figure 6.12).[15] For the stable, pigsty, and other farm buildings the bole-house type of construction was used, consisting of oak posts into which pine boards are tongued and grooved. This method was widely used in Denmark and the southern provinces of Sweden.[16] These buildings are also arranged around a courtyard, entered at one corner. The dwelling is a low building with chimneys, placed between higher buildings for storage and various farm chores. The low pitch of the roofs is an aid to conserving snow for insulation. Known as the South Scandinavian house, this type of dwelling in a single room, with hearth (and in earlier days no chimney), built-in bedsteads and benches, and a "pauper's beam," beyond which beggars and other strangers were not permit-

ted to advance, was often decorated with paintings on the walls and hanging cloths.[17]

A different kind of construction was also used at the Oktorp Farmstead, that of horizontal timbers notched together at the corners. As it happened, the first building acquired for the Danish Open Air Museum, in 1896 before the removal to Sorgenfri, was a house of this type, the farmstead from Stamhult in Halland, dating from the seventeenth century (figure 6.13).[18] The farm buildings that now form the courtyard are of plank construction and were brought in later. The roof of the dwelling is of turf, laid over a lining of birchbark, surely one of the most picturesque of roofing materials.[19] The timbers of the dwelling are oval, whereas those of the original outbuildings or "herbergs" on either side are rectangular.

This brings us to the immense subject of notched log construction in Sweden, Norway, and Finland.[20] The patterns seen here are relatively simple but could become much more complicated, both for the ways of cutting the joints and for the decorative patterns (figure 6.14).[21]

14

15

The first building to be brought to Skansen, in 1891, is the Mora Farmstead from Dalarna, which Hazelius had bought in 1891.[22] From the outside it looks very much like the forts of the American frontier, with its log buildings around a court and almost no openings to the outside. The main dwelling is on the north side of the court, the internal division into a small entrance room with chamber behind and the main room with its hearth and built-in beds being clearly defined by the projecting timbers on either side of the door (figure 6.15). On the other sides of the courtyard the farm buildings are placed close together. For protection against rotting in the soil and against marauding rodents the lowest timbers are raised well above the ground on heavy stones (figure 6.16). Dates carved on some of the buildings indicate a late sixteenth-century period of construction, and for all the vulnerability of timber buildings to fire, the Mora Farmstead bears witness to the durability of such structures. Even earlier is the most famous of the Mora farmsteads in its original location, the thirteenth-century home of Anders Zorn, one of Sweden's most prominent painters, who incorporated the original house into his estate and ultimately the Zorn Museum.[23]

For another kind of arrangement of these notched log farmsteads we may look to the characteristic groups from Setesdal in Norway. At Bygdøy several structures have been brought in and arranged in the local fashion with dwellings on one side of a road and farm buildings on the other (figure 6.17). At left in the illustration is the loft from Brottveit in Valle, probably dating from the second half of the seventeenth century. The lower level was used for the storage of food and the upper levels for clothing and valuables.[24] We observe the lower level to be built with horizontal notched logs and the two upper levels with heavy cor-

ner posts set into sills, the walls filled like the stave churches with vertical planking.

Next to the loft is the dwelling house, or *stue,* from Åmlid in Valle.[25] Here the notched log house has a protective gallery of stave construction before it, much like the exterior galleries on some of the stave churches. Within there are the two small rooms at the entrance end, as in the Mora Farmstead. The Åmlid stue, however, has a central hearth in the medieval manner, with a smoke hole in the roof above and a long beam projecting from the wall to carry the cooking pot (figure 6.18). Benches are fixed to the walls and beds built in the corners of the room. Chimneys, wooden floors, and more windows would characterize later houses. A loft from Ose and a stue from Kjelleberg complete the dwelling side of the Setesdal group, with barns and a stable across the narrow road.

17

6.16   Mora, Dalarna (Stock-
      holm, Skansen). Farm-
      stead. Loft posts.

6.17   Setesdal buildings
      (Oslo, Norwegian Folk
      Museum). c. 1700.

6.18   *Arestue på Sogneskar i*
      *Valle.* Painting by
      A. Tidemand, 1848.
      (Oslo, National
      Gallery.)

18

19

20

Like the stave churches, these buildings could be decorated with carvings, such as those on the uprights of the Kjelleberg stue gallery, reminiscent of Viking carvings (figure 6.19). For the eighteenth-century refurbishing of the fourteenth-century loft from Vastveit in Telemark, now at Skansen, a more modern pattern of acanthus was chosen (figure 6.20). The interior of the stue might be brilliantly painted, as for example at the stue from Bjørnebergs-tølen in Hemsedal, dating from 1792 and attributed to the painter Kristian Hulebak (figure 6.21).[26]

Another way to group the Norwegian farm building is often found in Numedal. At Bygdøy the examples brought from this region are set around an open space, with roads leading in and out of it from opposite corners. Among them is the Rauland stue, one of the oldest timber buildings in Norway (figure 6.22).[27] The carvings on either side of the door and the runic inscription on the lintel suggest a date in the second half of the thirteenth century. The plan is similar to that of the Åmlid stue, three rooms with originally a central hearth in the main room. A gallery across the gable end once sheltered a stair to small bed-chambers over the two smaller rooms. In contrast to the broad expanse of Danish farmsteads drawn by C. W. Eckersberg is the mountainous landscape in which the Norwegian farmsteads huddle as painted by J. C. Dahl (figure 6.23).

The Norwegian timber houses are not solely built as separate structures. In western Norway, especially in the coastal districts, a type of long building, or *lån,* has been used, which consists of two or more loft, stue, and other units joined together to form a single building with several rooms (figure 6.24). These may be built in either log or stave construction. There is some debate as to whether this kind

21

22

6.19 Kjelleberg, Valle (Oslo, Norwegian Folk Museum). Stue. Late 17th century. Door carvings.

6.20 Vastveit, Telemark (Stockholm, Skansen). Loft. 14th century. Door carvings, 18th century.

6.21 Bjørnebergstølen, Hemsedal (Oslo, Norwegian Folk Museum). Stue. 18th century. Interior. (Oslo, Norwegian Folk Museum.)

6.22 Rauland, Uvdal (Oslo, Norwegian Folk Museum). Stue. 13th century. (Oslo, Norwegian Folk Museum.)

6.23 *Hjelle in Valdres.* Painting by J. C. Dahl, 1850. (Bergen, Fine Arts Gallery.)

6.24 Habostad, Stranda (Sunnemore Museum). Stue. 19th century.

23        24

of building developed in postmedieval times by adding individual units together or whether it continues the longhouse tradition from the Iron Age.[28]

It would not be right to leave consideration of Norwegian construction in wood without mentioning the sawmills. Developed in France in the sixteenth century, the water-powered sawmill won acceptance in Holland and Norway but was strongly resisted in England.[29] In the eighteenth-century Norwegian sawmill from Åkra in Hardanger, the lower part, resting on a stone foundation, is built of notched logs, with squared timbers for the upper portion (figure 6.25). Powered by a heavy waterwheel, which is geared to move the saw blade up and down against the logs, this is a very modest forerunner of the huge wood products factories that we shall see later. In between came the larger and more permanent sawmills, such as the one at Hellefoss near Modum, painted by J. C. Dahl (figure 6.26).

In Finland there is also a strong tradition of using round or squared notched log construction for farm buildings. An early view of the Kortaniemi estate at Kittilä in Finnish Lapland shows the buildings grouped neatly around the court, several other buildings scattered on the property, with plowed fields and a hayrack (figure 6.27). This was more than an ordinary farm, for on the hilltop in the distance are located two "observatories," surely one of the northernmost scientific establishments of the day.[30] The Niemelä farm from Konginkangas in central Finland dates from the 1780s and was the first group of buildings to be set up at Seurasaari, in 1909 (figure 6.28).[31] The arrangement is less formal here. The first dwelling had also the sauna, or bathhouse, so essential in Finnish culture. In time were added an enlarged dwelling portion and dairy, cowshed, pigsty, threshing floor, and also a boathouse, since Fin-

25

6.25 **Åkra, Hardanger (Oslo, Norwegian Folk Museum). Sawmill. 18th century.**

6.26 *Hellefoss near Modum.* **Painting by J. C. Dahl, 1838. (Oslo, National Gallery.)**

6.27 **Kittilä. Kortaniemi Farmstead. Engraving by R. Outhier, 1744. (Copenhagen, Royal Library.)**

**26**

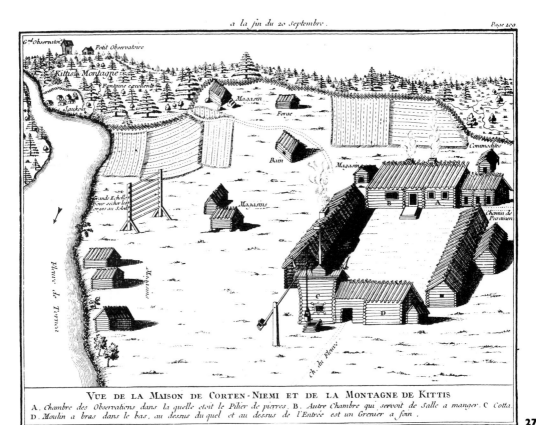

VUE DE LA MAISON DE CORTEN-NIEMI ET DE LA MONTAGNE DE KITTIS

A . *Chambre des Observations dans la quelle etoit le Pilier de pierres .* B . *Autre Chambre qui servoit de Salle a manger .* C . *Cotta .*
D . *Moulin a bras dans le bas , au dessus du quel et au dessus de l'Entrée est un Grenier a foin .*

**27**

**6.28 Konginkangas (Helsinki, Seurasaari). Niemelä Farm. 18th century.**

**6.29 Moiseinvaara, Karelia (Helsinki, Seurasaari). Farmstead. 1884. (Jay C. Henry.)**

**6.30 Karuna (Helsinki, Seurasaari). Church. 1685–1686.**

land is a country of lakes and water transport. Farms would also have one- and two-story loft houses, similar to the lofts of Norway, for the storage of clothing and for summer sleeping quarters. Many of these buildings are roofed with rough boards, the ends projecting at the ridge, as at the Mora Farmstead.

Much of the architecture of Finland that we have been observing has been close to Swedish building traditions if not actually by Swedish builders. In southeastern Finland, however, there have been closer connections with Russia, and the province of South Karelia was ceded to Russia in 1944. In 1939 the Moiseinvaara farmhouse from Suojärvi in Karelia was acquired by the museum at Seurasaari and is therefore an easily accessible example for study by Western observers (figure 6.29).[32] It may remind us of the Iron Age longhouses in that it was built to shelter the family and the cattle under one roof. The farmstead is more sophisticated, in two stories, with living, storage, and guest quarters on one side and a cowshed with

hayloft above on the other. The sauna, stable, and storage barn are separate.

There was also a tradition of church building in wood in rural areas, quite apart from the stave churches of Norway. A simple rectangular building, with no division into nave and aisles, and perhaps an entrance porch or bell tower was a common type. The church from Karuna now at Seurasaari was built in 1685–1686 and restored in 1772–1774 (figure 6.30).[33] It is covered by vertical boarding, with an entrance porch and a high steep roof. The interior is dark and crowded with pews. The paintings that once adorned it have partly been removed to museums in Helsinki. Characteristic of the Scandinavian village churches is the separate belfry (figure 6.31).

In Sweden a small number of wooden churches remain from the Middle Ages. At Granhult in Småland the church was probably begun at the end of the Romanesque period, c. 1300 (figure 6.32).[34] It began as a simple nave and chancel church, built of horizontal timbers with dovetail joints. It has a steep roof, and it originally had only very small window openings. Fragments of the late Gothic wall paintings are still visible. Additions were made beginning in the seventeenth century, and a second group of paintings dates from 1745–1754. It is a rural church, for a time abandoned and used as a granary, but then repaired between 1936 and 1950 and used for occasional services. By no means all the known early Swedish wooden churches have survived, however, and we owe considerable knowledge of those that have disappeared to the Swedish artist and antiquary Nils Månsson Mandelgren. He did for Sweden something comparable to the work of J. C. Dahl in Norway, for he went about in Småland particularly, making measurements, drawings, and notes, such as those for Bankeryd church in Småland (figure 6.33).[35]

29

30

6.31   Karuna (Helsinki, Seu-
       rasaari). Church belfry.
       1767.
6.32   Granhult, Småland.
       Church. Begun c. 1300.
       (Stockholm, Antikvar-
       isk-Topografiska
       Arkivet.)
6.33   Bankeryd, Småland.
       Church. Drawing by
       N. M. Mandelgren,
       1863. (Lund,
       Folksarkivet.)

31

32

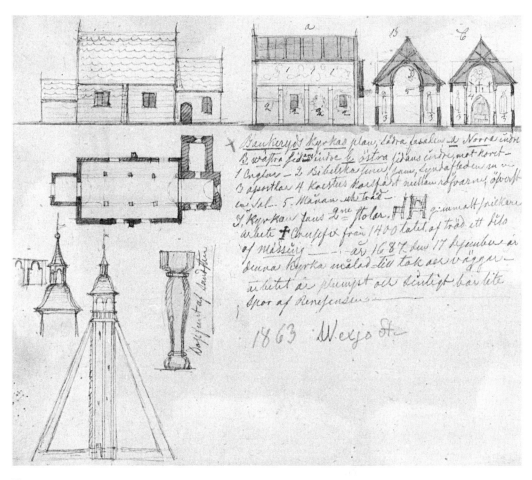

**33**

These were the basis for his publications on Swedish cultural history.

A more recent example of a Swedish village church is the one from Seglora in Västergötland, now at Skansen in Stockholm, built in 1729–1730 (figure 6.34).[36] This too is undivided internally, but is more elaborate in plan, having a polygonal apse. The exterior is covered with oak shingles painted red, as was often the custom. The bell tower at the west end and the sacristy were added in 1780–1790. On the inside the heavy horizontal timbers of the walls are whitewashed, and the low curving ceiling boards are painted with biblical scenes and acanthus borders.

A later church at Petäjävesi in Finland, 1763–1764, is more elaborate and is built of notched timbers (figure 6.35).[37] It is cruciform in plan, with galleries in the north, south, and west extensions. The interior is not painted but derives its character from the structural details so clearly exposed and from a moderate amount of blocky carving on the altar rails and gallery fronts. The four wings of the building

are covered by wooden barrel vaults, and the crossing has a gored dome. Like the houses of Halland and Blekinge, the interior is surprisingly spacious in contrast to the exterior appearance.

Before we turn to farm buildings in brick, we should take note of several distinctive types of small dwellings, some of which are, or were, used only seasonally. Prominent among these are the Lapp huts, such as the one from Frost-viken in Jämtland (figure 6.36).[38] A frame of two pairs of curving poles joined at the top by a thin ridgepole pushed through them can then be subdivided by horizontal bars and then slant-ing poles over which can be laid a covering of birchbark and turf (figure 6.37). For further protection another set of poles can be laid against the outside. In the middle of this basi-cally circular building there is a hearth, marked off by stones. With recent methods of keeping the reindeer herds these huts have generally fallen into disuse, but were characteristic of the nomadic Lapps for hundreds of years. The store-houses of the Lapp camps were mounted on one or more high poles, reached by ladders which would be set away when not in use (fig-ure 6.38). Similar storehouses are in use in Alaska today.

Then for other seasonal shelters there were the fishermen's huts, such as those from Nymindegab on the west coast of Jutland (fig-ure 6.39).[39] In the late spring farmers in this region would move to these huts, placed in groups of three to accommodate the six men needed for a boat and their wives. These huts, also no longer in use, are built like A-frame buildings of heavy slanting timbers pegged to cross-beams and thatched, the ridges secured with turfs. Beside the entrances are turf-built chimneys. A fourth unheated hut was used for storage.

On the Faroe Islands the longhouse of the Viking period was succeeded by a two-room

**35**

**6.34  Seglora, Västergötland (Stockholm, Skansen). Church. 1729–1730.**

**6.35  Petäjävesi. Church. 1763–1764.**

**36**

6.36 **Frostviken, Jämtland
(Stockholm, Skansen).
Lapp hut.**

6.37 **Lapp hut frame. (After
Manker, *Lapsk kultur*,
figure 141, p. 139.)**

6.38 **Lapp storehouse
(Stockholm, Skansen).**

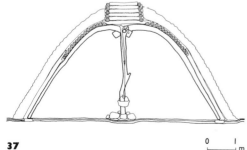

**37**

0     I
└──┴──┘ m

house, probably early in the seventeenth century.[40] One example, which is now a house museum, is Duvugarthur at Saksun on Streymoy
(figure 6.40). The original part of the house
consists of the *røgkstue* or smoke room and the
*glasstue* or window room. In the *røgkstue*, the
center of daily activity, there is a stone-framed
hearth against one wall, with louvre above but
no windows. The *glasstue* has windows, ceiling,
and a stove connected through the wall with
the hearth, and was used more as a "best
room." Stone outer walls shelter the characteristic Faroese vertical plank walls, and the roof is
thatched.

Timber was, and is, scarce. Some might be
imported, some found as driftwood, and some
from shipwrecks. The latter may sometimes be
identified by wormholes. At Saksun a "priest's
room" was added to the *glasstue*, the dark
wooden wing projecting from the whitewashed
*røgkstue*. Such a farmstead would include a
cowshed, storage sheds with dry stone walls,
and possibly a splashmill with horizontal waterwheel (figure 6.41).[41]

Certain modes of construction and arrangement give the Icelandic turf houses a special place in the group of North Atlantic
vernacular buildings, ranging from the Scottish
islands to Greenland. We have already considered the Viking foundations and the reconstruction at Stöng, noting the scarcity of wood
for building in Iceland. Two main kinds of buildings with turf have been identified from later
periods.[42] One is the building entirely of turfs,
laid to form domed or barrel-vaulted roofs.
The other is the house built of timber and covered with turf, the comparatively thin layers of
the roof widening out to form massive outer
walls. In this second group the roof might rest
on one, two, or three rafters laid over a ridgepole that would be supported just by the walls
or by one or two posts. Another type of roof

38

was built of rafters pegged together at the top
and resting on beams laid on the walls or supported by posts.

The characteristic plan of the Icelandic
farmhouse developed over a long period of
time, as the archaeological remains and the
manuscript illustrations indicate (figure 6.42).[43]
To the longhouse or *skali* of the sagas was
added a sitting room or *stofa* for a workroom
for women and also a guest room, while the
*skali* was still used for sleeping, as at Stöng.
Then by the fourteenth century a passageway
had been put between these two rooms, leading to the lavatory and bathroom, or *badstofa*,
while extra rooms were added at the ends of
the *skali* and *stofa*, with gables facing outward

**39**

**40**

41

6.39 **Nymindegab, Jutland (Sorgenfri, Frilandsmu-seet). Fishermen's huts. 19th century.**

6.40 **Saksun, Faroes. Duvu-garthur Farmstead. 18th century.**

6.41 **Mule, Bordø, Faroes (Sorgenfri, Frilandsmu-seet). Splashmill.**

6.42 **Farmstead. From the Jónsbók manuscript AM 345. (Reykjavik, Stofnun Árna Magnús-sonar á Íslandi.)**

6.43 **Laufás. Turf farm. (Reykjavik, National Museum. Photo: Gísli Gestsson.)**

42

43

**6.44** Laufás. Turf farm. Plan. (Gísli Gestsson, in Ágústsson, "Development of the Icelandic Farm," figure 14, p. 265. Courtesy Gudrun Sigurthardottir.)

**6.45** Turf wall. Drawing by Hörthur Agústsson. (Courtesy Hörthur Agústsson.)

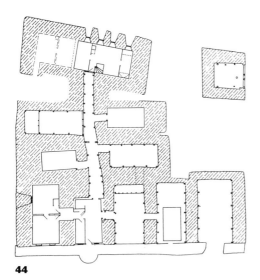

**44**

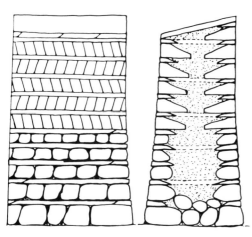

**45**

and separate entrances. These gable ends might be timbered (figure 6.43). By the seventeenth century the *badstofa* became the principal sitting and eating room, taking the place of the *stofa,* which was left out of all but the wealthiest homes. This had to do with diminishing supplies of firewood and the need to make the best use of what little heat there was, and by the eighteenth century the *badstofa* was used for sleeping as well. Then the *skali* and *stofa* were turned so that their gable ends faced outward, resulting in the ridge-farmhouse or *burstabaer* in northern Iceland (figure 6.44). In southern Iceland the *badstofa* was brought to the front of the house and the passageway shortened.

As for the turf walls themselves, they were built from turfs cut in several shapes and sizes from the sedge marshes with special tools. They were built as double skin walls of various combinations of stone and turfs with a hard-packed core of earth between (figure 6.45).[44] Herringbone patterns appearing by the fifteenth century were considered particularly attractive and added to the stability of the walls. These techniques were carried to Greenland by Icelanders settling there.[45] The interiors were lined with wooden planks set vertically, joined by tongue and groove much in the manner of the walls of Norwegian stave churches.[46] Whether the Icelandic turf houses are directly related to the "black houses" of the Scottish Hebrides is still a matter of debate.[47]

Turfs were used not solely for houses but for churches as well, though we have to rely on published accounts for descriptions of those that are lost. The first church at Reykjavik was built of turfs, to be replaced by the present cathedral in 1796.[48] We have, however, a description and drawing of the church at Thingvellir as seen by the English traveler John Barrow, Jr., in 1835 (figure 6.46).[49] Barrow

46

6.46 Thingvellir. Church.
Drawing in *The Ameri-can Magazine*, 3, no. 12
(September 1837): 461.
(Eugene, University of
Oregon Library.)

6.47 Silfrastadir (Reykja-vik, Árbaer Museum).
Church. 1842.

47

**6.48 Rømø. Kommandør-gården. 1748.**

**6.49 Rømø. Kom-mandørgården. Inte-rior. (Sorgenfri, Frilandsmuseet.)**

thought it extraordinary enough to measure and record, saying that "the extreme length was twenty-three feet, but of this eight feet were devoted to the altar, which was divided off by a partition stretching across the church, and against which was placed the pulpit. . . . The width of the church was ten feet, and the height of the walls about six feet." He went on to say that the walls "were wainscotted, and from them large wooden beams stretched from side to side. . . . The interior of the roof, the rafters of which also rested on the walls, was also lined with wood." The church was there-fore finished in the same manner as the Icelan-dic house, and Barrow found it furnished with benches but very crowded and at that time used for storage.

A later turf church that has survived was built in 1842 at Silfrastadir in northern Iceland (figure 6.47).[50] It too went out of use as a church, was moved to a nearby farmhouse, and served for a number of years as a badstofa. Then in 1950 it was moved to the Árbaer Mu-seum and reconsecrated in 1961. The sheltering function of the thick walls surrounding the tim-ber building is clearly seen here at the east end, and in this case the outer layer is of stone.

While farm building in the Scandinavian countries was almost entirely carried out in wood in the earlier periods, there did develop

a brick tradition on the Jutland peninsula. An early example is in its original location still, ac-tually on the island of Rømø off the west coast of Jutland. The Kommandørgård, or Command-er's Farm, is now the property of the Danish National Museum, which has restored the house and lets the land out for farming (figure 6.48).[51] Begun probably in 1748, it is built of brick that appears to be of Dutch rather than local manufacture. At this time there was con-tact with Friesland, whence brickmaking began to develop on the Jutland coast. The house at Rømø has undergone alterations and additions, and in the 1770s it was owned by a wealthy seafaring merchant. In the course of restoration it was found that the interior had been exten-sively decorated with paintings, the unknown painter probably coming from the mainland (fig-ure 6.49). The numerous biblical subjects sug-gest a church painter, such as the one who had worked at Møgeltønder, nearby, or the Rococo painter of Damsholte Church on Møn.

Now moved to the Open Air Museum at Sorgenfri but originally very close to Nyminde-gab is the Lønnestak Farmstead (figure 6.50).[52] It is a courtyard farmstead, built in 1803, but it is very very different from the Lundager Farm-stead (figure 6.7). Instead of opening inward to the courtyard, the principal entrances to the dwelling, barn, and stable are on the exterior, and the dwelling is in the south rather than the north wing. This represents a change in fashion, and the building was apparently the first to be built of brick this far north in Jutland. The tiles in the best room and the living room are also noteworthy as being imported from Holland. The plan allows for access to the cowshed and stable from within instead of through the courtyard, another innovation.

With the Lønnestak Farmstead we ap-proach the time when local and anonymous tra-ditions were to become codified and the

**48**

**49**

**6.50** **Lønnestak, Jutland (Sorgenfri, Frilandsmuseet). Farmstead. 1803.**

**6.51** **Proposal for a small farm. Late 18th century. (Copenhagen, Academy of Art Library.)**

**6.52** **Proposal for farm buildings. (Klein, *Landbrugets bygninger*, figure 1.)**

**6.53** **Copenhagen. Prefabricated house. 1972.**

concern of professional architects.[53] Beginning at the end of the eighteenth century, proposals for small farms were drawn up, to be followed by competitions and publications of designs up to the present (figures 6.51 and 6.52). New materials and plans, developed according to changes in agricultural practices, generally have not altered the sense of traditional appearance evident in these proposals, and there has even been room for prefabricated nostalgia (figure 6.53).

From the vernacular buildings of rural Scandinavia we should turn briefly to those of the towns. Some of the more fashionable town houses have already been noted, such as the Peterschenka House in Stockholm and the Baur House in Altona. The more modest dwellings, built of less expensive materials, are not plentiful in the larger cities for the periods before the nineteenth century and tend to be hidden away among more recent buildings. Parts of

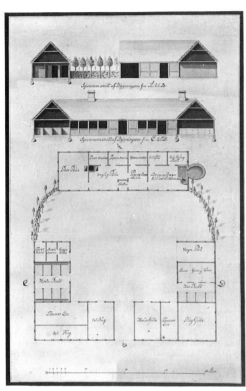

**51**

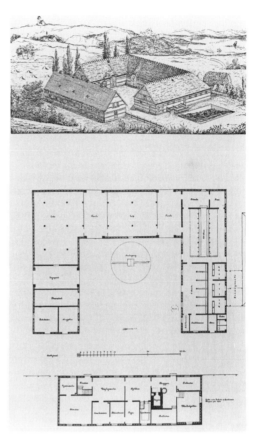

**52**

**53**

some of the smaller towns, however, retain significant numbers of their early houses so that it
is possible to get some idea of their former
character.

At Køge on the east coast of Zealand
there are several streets near the church of St.
Nicholas where old houses remain from the
sixteenth century, the town having been known
as a trading center since the eleventh century.
On Store Kirkestraede is the oldest dated timber house in Denmark, built in 1527 (figure
6.54).[54] Now only three bays wide, it was once
part of a double house. It is half-timbered with
brick nogging and a steep tiled roof with pronounced eaves flare. Inside there is just one
room, with open hearth and a door leading out
to the garden at the back. Among the larger
houses in the town is the one on Vestergade
built in 1644 (figure 6.55).[55] This is characteristic of seventeenth-century town houses all over
Denmark. It is two stories high, with an over-

**6.54  Køge, Zealand. Store
        Kirkestraede 20. 1527.**
**6.55  Køge, Zealand. Vester-
        gade 14–16. 1644.**
**6.56  Falun, Dalarna. Miners'
        houses. (Falun, Bergs-
        lagets Museum.)**

hang across the front and a high tiled roof. It
was built for a merchant, and while his means
were evidently not sufficient for a grand house
like that of Jens Bang in Ålborg, he could follow the fashion of the day and adorn the half-
timbering with brackets and carvings.

A town of a completely different nature
that still has some of its early buildings is Falun
in Dalarna.[56] The great coppermine, run by the
Kopparberg Mining Company, had been developed since 1230, the charter of the company
dating from 1347. A ton of gold, fifteen tons of
silver, and 500,000 tons of copper have come
from here, including the copper for the roof of
Versailles. Some of the small row houses for
the miners remain in the Old Town on the
west bank of the river (figure 6.56). The
houses are one story high, built of notched
logs, with their gables toward the street. The
traveler Edward Clarke reported appalling conditions of fumes in the air, saying that "the
town church is covered with copper; but a
more improper material can hardly be used; for
the sulphuric acid gas, with which the air is
powerfully impregnated, is rapidly dissolving
this copper covering."[57] In Norway, Røros in
Sør-Trøndelag was founded in 1644 as a copper
mining town, and miners' houses remain from
the seventeenth through the nineteenth centuries (figure 6.57).[58]

**55**

**56**

Over in Finland a great fire in 1827 destroyed much of the former capital of Turku, but a portion of the city on the south side of Vartiovuori Hill was spared because it was sheltered from the wind.[59] C. L. Engel's proposal for the demolition of this area in connection with his plans for rebuilding Turku fortunately did not materialize, and by 1956 the old houses were secure. They were taken over by the Historical Museum of Turku to form a handicraft as well as an open air architectural museum (figure 6.58). Called Luostarinmäki, this museum site is different from some in that the buildings have not been brought in from elsewhere but are in their original locations. Another interesting aspect is that the dwellings are accompanied by other buildings for the household, almost like small "urbansteads" instead of farmsteads, each household devoted to a particular craft: combmaker, furrier, carpenter, shoemaker, printer, baker, and several others. The buildings are raised on stone foundations and are built with corner posts and horizontal or vertical siding, with some horizontal log construction. The ropewalk set up down the middle of one long street, visible in the illustration, was necessary in a seagoing town to supply the ropes for rigging. It might be in a long building or, as here, outside.

While Luostarinmäki is now maintained as a museum, another town in Finland has a heritage of old dwellings that are still in use as private homes. Porvoo is the second oldest town in Finland, after Turku, and was founded as Borgå in 1346.[60] The Cathedral of St. Mary is the only medieval building to survive the many town fires. In 1809 Alexander I here proclaimed Finland a Grand Duchy of Russia, and the town continued to flourish commercially. In this old part of town the streets wind up and down the hillside in irregular paths and are lined with wooden one- and two-story houses

57

58

**59**

**60**

set directly on the streets (figure 6.59). There is a variety of sidings, roofs, door and window headings, and gables, and one gets a strong sense of how these nineteenth-century houses had to be crowded onto the medieval streets.

For a homogeneous community of dwellings from the early twentieth century we may look to Ålesund on the west coast of Norway.[61] The town is an important fishing and commercial center; here again what we see now is the result of a great fire, this one in 1904. Whereas the town buildings we have been considering in this chapter have been of wood or brick, Ålesund was rebuilt largely in stone. Not strictly vernacular, many of the buildings were architect-designed under a regulatory commission headed by Fredrik Naeser. The result is distinctive, however, for here are rows of houses and flats rich in Richardsonian Romanesque, Dragon Style, and Jugendstil detail (figure 6.60). In Stavanger, on the other hand, there are streets in the old part of town lined

**6.61 Stavanger, Rogaland. Houses.**

**6.62 Reykjavik. House at Laufasvegur 31. (Reykjavik, Árbaer Museum.)**

with wooden houses that preserve the early character of this seaport (figure 6.61).

While Denmark, Sweden, Finland, and Norway have had sufficient timber for domestic building, this has not been the case in Iceland. For buildings more suited to the growing towns than the turf houses, ready-cut timber was imported from Denmark late in the eighteenth century. Then toward the end of the nineteenth century, prefabricated timber houses were brought from Norway. All timber building was still very expensive, however, and an effective solution was found in corrugated iron imported from England.[62] While at first this might seem a dismal approach, the vertical wall panels resemble batten boarding, and the Icelanders paint these buildings in bright colors with contrasting trim (figure 6.62).

**62**

These rural and urban vernacular buildings survive from comparatively recent times. Farmsteads that are known to have been repeatedly rebuilt on the original foundations and remains of buildings that have been discovered in towns are among the fragmentary pieces of evidence for the centuries-old traditions of some of the house types described above. Much that has been learned from them has been adopted and transformed by some of the leading Scandinavian architects of the nineteenth and twentieth centuries.

# 7 *Eclectic and Early Modern Scandinavian Building*

The century between the Napoleonic Wars and
World War I was crowded with opportunities
and dilemmas for the Scandinavian architects.
At this time the embellishment of buildings was
dependent on imitation of admired structures
from the past. Neoclassicism was one response
to the problem of creating an official image,
whether leaning to the imperial implications of
Roman building or to the democratic implications of Greek, and there were of course models other than the classical to follow.

But this was not to be the whole story.
While Jardin was at work on Frederiks Church
and Adelcrantz was building the Drottningholm
theater, some significant technological events
were taking place in England. Such inventions as
that of the steam engine in 1768 and the
power spinning frame in 1769, to say nothing
of the smelting of iron ore by coke beginning
in the 1740s, set European industrial production on a new path. Together with the shifts in
the political alignments of Norway and Finland
and the growing tendency away from absolu-
tism toward democracy, the rise of modern industrial society brought new population

**7.1   Copenhagen. University.
P. Malling. 1831–1836.**

**7.2   Oslo. Bazaar. C. H.
Grosch. 1845–1857.
(Oslo, Riksantikvaren.)**

pressures on Scandinavian cities and new kinds of patrons of buildings.

A fully detailed account of what happened architecturally cannot be attempted here. From the 1830s up to about the turn of the twentieth century, leading Scandinavian architects turned to three other principal sources of inspiration for at least their ornamental expressions: the medieval, the Renaissance/Baroque, and local traditions. The designs resulting from their choices appeared, however, on some buildings that were anything but traditional in their functions. Among these were the rapidly growing number of industrial buildings.[1]

This chapter treats first some of the stylistic possibilities and the early factories, followed by consideration of three major projects that were begun between 1892 and 1911: the Town Hall in Copenhagen, the third Christiansborg Palace, and the Town Hall in Stockholm. It will conclude with works contemporary with these projects by certain strong artistic personalities whose individual interpretations of possible traditional sources marked a turning point in Scandinavian architectural design.

In Copenhagen, while C. F. Hansen's Christiansborg Palace was under construction, there were other projects afoot. A university, primarily for the study of theology, had been founded under Christian I in 1479 in the chapel of Vor Frue Kirke, and we have already noted Holy Trinity Church and the Round Tower with its observatory built under Christian IV. A separate building and later an anatomical theater were also added, and these were lost in the fire of 1728. Rebuilding was undertaken by J. C. Krieger, only to be destroyed in the bombing of 1807. In 1831 Peder Malling, a student of C. F. Hansen, began the present main building, completed in 1836 (figure 7.1).[2] Malling departed from the more severe classical style of Hansen by incorporating some medieval

**1**

touches in his exterior design. The tall central
entrance bay with recessed portal, window, and
lunette is capped by a gable that combines the
Roman gable-and-arch motif with stepped archivolts in the Romanesque manner. This portal
leads into a large vestibule, beyond which lies
the festival hall. Two stories of classrooms are
served by staircases in the vestibule and expressed on the exterior in three bays on either
side of the portal. This arrangement is much
like the core of C. F. Hansen's Råd-og-domhus,
but the division by pilasters, the large windows,
and the curious lunettes and gables above give
the University a much busier appearance. M. G.
Bindesbøll and the painter Constantin Hansen
were called upon for the interior decorations,
which include scenes from classical mythology
and Danish history.[3]

**2**

A much more explicit use of Romanesque motifs was made by C. H. Grosch for the Bazaar in Oslo, designed in 1839 but not entirely completed until 1857 (figure 7.2).[4] This was built to house the market and butcher stalls. The land slopes sharply down to the east back of the Cathedral, and Grosch ringed the plaza with a half circle of two-story brick buildings containing the shops, which are connected outside and inside by sheltering arcades. In 1854 he added a fire station at the southwest corner. Handsomely executed with broad arcades below and dwarf arcades in the Rheno-Lombardic Romanesque manner, the result is a unique backdrop for the Cathedral and still actively serves many of its original purposes. Grosch's primary interest in the classical manner probably led him to the Romanesque in preference to the Gothic.

For an individual dwelling, large or small, the prospective owner had these stylistic possi-

7.3   Steensgård, Langeland. G. F. Hetsch. 1836–1837. (Richardt and Secher, *Prospecter,* n.p. Copenhagen, Academy of Art Library.)

7.4   Oslo. Oscarshall. J. H. Nebelong. 1848. (Oslo, Riksantikvaren.)

7.5   "Raphael's Villa." Painting by J. Roed. c. 1840. (Copenhagen, Ny Carlsberg Glyptotek.)

3

bilities from which to choose according to means, ambition, personal preference, and the inclinations of the architect.[5] The Gothic was favored more than the Romanesque for domestic buildings. At Steensgård on Langeland a manor was rebuilt in 1836–1837 by Gustav Friedrich Hetsch, a German-born architect who had studied in Paris (figure 7.3).[6] The building already had an octagonal tower, and when finished with stringcourses, stepped gables, and parapet it emerged as a somewhat benign Rygård.

Similarly Oscarshall on Bygdøy, outside Oslo, a private castle built for Oscar I by Johan Henrik Nebelong in 1848, was designed to satisfy the king's interest in Norwegian legend and history (figure 7.4).[7] It was placed on a rocky site overlooking the Oslo Fjord and surrounded with parkland. Nebelong was a pupil of Hetsch in the Academy in Copenhagen and went to Oslo as an assistant to Linstow in 1840. Al-

4

5

6

**7.6  Oslo. Cathedral. A. Cha-**
**teauneuf. 1848–1850.**
**Interior. (Oslo,**
**Riksantikvaren.)**

**7.7  Oslo. Trinity Church.**
**A. Chateauneuf. 1849–**
**1858.**

though the compact little castle with its hexag-
onal corner tower has been compared to
contemporary German examples, the north el-
evation is also reminiscent of the so-called "Raphael's Villa" in the Villa Borghese gardens in
Rome. Since the time of Eckersberg this had
been popular with the Danish Neoclassical artists (figure 7.5).[8] Nebelong also had been in
Rome and had made drawings of the little
building, which for the Norwegian site he
translated into a little Gothic castle. The interior was decorated with paintings by Adolph
Tidemand and stucco reliefs by Christopher
Borch showing scenes of Norwegian landscape
and legend.

While individual homeowners could satisfy
nostalgic desires to live in houses decked out
with Gothic trappings, for the churches it was
another matter. Slender piers and pointed
arches evoked what was perceived as the piety
of the Middle Ages, and some church authorities moved to remodel in the Gothic manner as
well as to build afresh.

One of the more spectacular programs of
remodeling was carried out by the Hamburg
architect Alexis de Chateauneuf at the Cathedral in Oslo, 1848–1850 (figure 7.6).[9] The interior was given wooden vaults with thin applied
ribs, cast like a giant net over the old nave and
transepts. Baroque and Rococo furnishings
were removed, and the gallery received a
screen of late Gothic pointed arches. Chateauneuf's spire, added at the same time, remains,
but fashion was to change, and the church was
stripped of its Gothic revival fittings in the restorations of 1948–1950.

Chateauneuf was more fortunate in the
survival of Trinity Church in Oslo, built from
his designs in 1849–1858 (figure 7.7).[10] Placed
on a height on Akersbakken, it is now more
eclipsed by surrounding buildings than originally.
Here was an opportunity to build from the be-

ginning, and Chateauneuf chose a cruciform plan with a large central domed octagon. The latter probably reflects the octagon at Nidaros Cathedral in Trondheim and perhaps even more the Palatine Chapel at Aachen. Traceried windows, salient corner buttresses, and turrets and pinnacles complete the scheme. On the interior, clustered piers support the ribbed vaults of the aisles, and the central octagon opens out to the exterior windows. This created a far more genuinely medieval space than could be accomplished by the application of detail alone, and it was a pity that Chateauneuf did not live to see it built. It was finished by his young assistant Andreas von Hanno.

The medieval revival in church architecture continued to the end of the century, but meanwhile certain other buildings were designed in this style. In the days of Christian IV the library of the University of Copenhagen was housed in

**7**

the attic of Holy Trinity Church. In 1855 a competition was held for a new building to be built next to Peder Malling's main classroom building. M. G. Bindesbøll submitted an interesting design, but the commission went to Johan Daniel Herholdt. The library was built from 1857 to 1861 (figure 7.8).[11] By this time Henri Labrouste had built his famous Bibliothèque Sainte-Geneviève in Paris, 1843–1850, using stone and cast iron. Herholdt's library followed this model in some ways but had to be arranged differently because of the site. Across from Vor Frue Kirke, the library begins with an entrance building, with the entrance itself on Fiolstraede. The monumental vestibule and staircase give access to a suite of offices, beyond which stretches the long section for the book stacks. The exterior wall arcades and traceried oculus windows of the entrance building suggest North Italian Romanesque models,

**7.8   Copenhagen. University Library. J. D. Herholdt. 1857–1861.**

**7.9   Gothenburg. Railway Station. A. W. Edelsvärd. 1856–1858. (Gothenburg, City Museum.)**

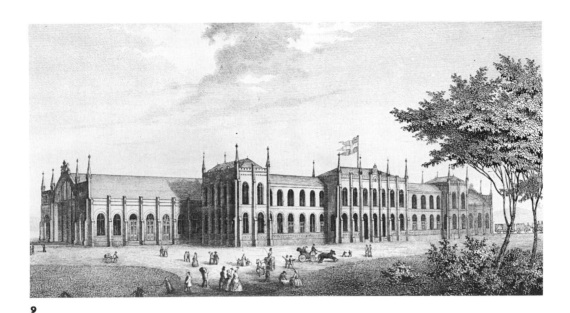

9

while the narrow vertical divisions of the library itself, with their painted moldings over the upper windows, are in sympathy with the façade of the University building. As in medieval construction, the exterior pattern of windows separated by thin wall strips corresponds to the rows of iron columns that support the interior. The churchlike effect resulting on the interior is further emphasized by the Batty Langley–like Gothic pattern of the columns. The two university buildings together have a certain grandeur outside and in that sets the tone for the authority of the educational enterprise.

An entirely different problem was posed by the coming of the railway. The first steam-powered locomotive for drawing a passenger train was put into service in England in 1825.[12] The "iron horse" also introduced a new era in the moving of goods, the earliest Danish use of the new means of transport being a line from Altona to Kiel built in 1844, then in Danish territory. Norway in 1854 and Sweden in 1856 also began short rail lines.[13] The mountainous terrain of Norway scarcely lent itself to ease of rail construction, and the many bodies of water

between the islands of Denmark were similarly inhospitable to long-distance rail lines. The earliest Scandinavian railway of any considerable length was built in Sweden over the much more continuous level land route between Stockholm and Gothenburg from 1855 to 1862. By this time a whole generation of railway stations had been constructed in England and on the Continent.

As the western terminal for this line, designed by the Swedish engineer Nils Ericson, Adolf W. Edelsvärd built the station in Gothenburg in 1856–1858 (figure 7.9).[14] The type was by now familiar, with the trains completing their journey under a long shed with arching cast iron roof, long platforms between the tracks, loading platforms and warehouse facilities on either side, and a ticket office/waiting room to accommodate passengers. The question of embellishment was being answered in a variety of ornamental styles: Greek, Italian, Egyptian, Gothic, and even Moorish. Edelsvärd chose a rather thin late Gothic set of motifs. The station was remodeled in 1877 and replaced in 1916.

**7.10  Sandvik, Vestfold.
Railway Station.
G. Bull. 1873. (Die-
trichson and Munthe,
*Holzbaukunst,* plate
13.)**

**7.11  Oslo. Parliament. E. V.
Langlet. 1866.**

A station beside a track, rather than a ter-
minus, would be planned differently. For Sandvik in Vestfold a little station was designed in
1873 by Georg Andreas Bull, who had been
the state railway architect from 1863 to 1872
(figure 7.10).[15] A central entrance with porch
and pinnacled gable led into a vestibule with
ticket office beyond and waiting rooms on either side. This was an essentially domestic design in outward appearance and characteristic
of the many small stations that were needed in
the smaller towns between the major city
terminals.

In Oslo the middle years of nineteenth-
century building were brought to a climax with
the Storting (Parliament) (figure 7.11).[16] After
more than twenty years of proposals, a design
for the Storting building was finally agreed
upon, that of the Swedish architect Emil Victor
Langlet in 1866. Built of yellow and gray brick
with granite trim, it rises boldly between Karl
Johan Gate and Stortings Gata at the end of
the esplanade leading from the Royal Palace
park. While not precisely in line with the Palace, the Parliament lies on the east side of Ak-

ersgata, which leads from Akershus park up the
hill to Gamle Aker Church. With Karl Johan
Gate leading on over the Parliament hill to the
Cathedral, the two principal axes of the city
now had the seat of the national legislative
body at their intersection. Tall modern buildings now make this difficult to perceive, but on
completion of the Parliament in 1866 the cityscape must have been quite different. Langlet
chose an H-shaped plan, with the two assembly
rooms projecting east and west from the center portion. The exterior is carried out in the
Lombard Romanesque style, the groups of single, double, and triple round-headed openings
played off against each other and against the
blind arcades and corbel tables. For the interior
Langlet turned to colorfully painted wood fin-
ishes in a combination of Gothic, "Swiss," and
ancient Norwegian motifs.

Among the later medievalizing churches
one stands out as clearly imitative, King Oscar's
Chapel at Grense-Jacobselv in Finnmark, built
by Jacob Wilhelm Norden in 1869 (figure
7.12).[17] It was built at the northern tip of Norway, just at the Russian border, in part to command respect from Russian fishermen. Built of
local stone, with its single tower, nave, short
choir, and polygonal apse it resembles medieval
Swedish parish churches and takes its name
from a visit by Oscar II in 1873.

Representative of the larger city churches
in the Gothic style is St. John's Church in Bergen, built by Herman M. Backer in 1894 (figure
7.13).[18] It is dramatically placed, high on the hill
up which climbs Vester Torv Gaten from the
market square. The view back down is as impressive as the view up. The church has the
necessary pointed openings, steep gables, and
pinnacles, but the use of some polychromed
brick and a suggestion of broad flat surfaces indicate that some changes in fashion were taking
place.

10

11

In Denmark a late expression of medieval style in church building was more Romanesque than Gothic.[19] The two great restoration projects in Norway and Sweden were for the Gothic cathedrals of Trondheim and Uppsala. In Denmark the comparable effort was for the rebuilding of the Romanesque Viborg cathedral, and Denmark, as we have seen, had a wealth of brick Romanesque churches. Martin Borch chose this tradition for the church of St. Andrew in Copenhagen, built 1898–1901 (figure 7.14).[20]

In the meantime some important developments had been taking place in thinking about Protestant church architecture. Earlier Scandinavian builders had approached the matter from the seventeenth century in such buildings as Holy Trinity Church in Kristianstad, 1617–1628, Adolf Fredrik's Church in Stockholm, 1768, and the Lutheran Church of St. Nicholas in Helsinki, 1826. Conventional symmetrical plans had been chosen, whether basilical or centralized, and the outward appearance of these churches was one of regularity, however richly ornamented. A move away from symmetry together with efforts to place more emphasis on the pulpit was already under way in England and the United States, and this had been described and illustrated by the German author K. E. O. Fritsch in 1893. The plan of St. Andrew's Church appears to be based on a "Model of a Rural Church" in that book.[21]

The church is built of red brick, with a sparing use of ornamental motifs except for the familiar paneling. The main portal leads to the nave, and there is only one aisle, on the south side behind the tower that rises south of the portal. This is the arrangement of Fritsch's "rural church" plan. On the interior the nave is covered with domical vaults, and the south aisle is separated by large round-headed arches at the lower level. Above the aisle is an open

7.12  Grense-Jacobselv, Finn-
      mark. King Oscar's
      Chapel. J. W. Norden.
      1869. (Oslo,
      Riksantikvaren.)

7.13  Bergen. St. John's
      Church. H. M. Backer.
      1894. (Oslo,
      Riksantikvaren.)

7.14  Copenhagen. St.
      Andrew's Church.
      M. Borch. 1899–1901.
      (Copenhagen, National
      Museum.)

7.15  Stockholm. Engelbrekt
      Church. L. I. Wahlman.
      1906–1914. Interior.
      (Stockholm, City
      Museum.)

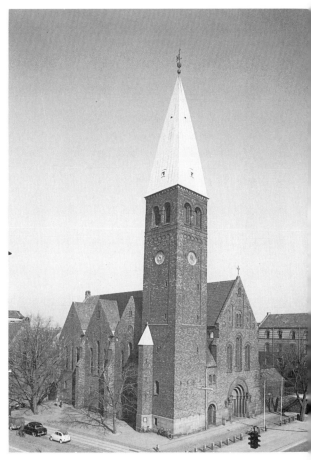

14

vaulted gallery, the effect reminiscent of San Marco in Venice or Sant' Ambrogio in Milan.

A still later interpretation of the medieval styles was made for the church commemorating the Swedish hero Engelbrekt Engelbrektsson, leader of the popular uprising in the 1430s.[22] Built from the designs of Lars Israel Wahlman in 1906–1914, it has a commanding position on a high bluff above Karlavägen in Stockholm. It is a cruciform building, with long nave and transepts and a tall tower at the southwest corner. Its brick surfaces are broad and smooth with an almost nervous delicacy of ornament at the top of the walls and the tall slender tower. Despite the conventional plan, the effect of the interior is unique, the granite piers and parabolic arches carrying the wooden roof over the nave (figure 7.15). Most striking

15

7.16 **Stockholm. National Museum. F. A. Stüler. 1849–1866. (Stockholm, National Museum.)**

7.17 **Copenhagen. Danish National Bank. J. D. Herholdt. 1866–1870. (Copenhagen, National Museum.)**

among the many paintings in the church is that of Christ Crucified above the altar, a much-transformed echo of such paintings in the medieval parish churches. The height of the nave, nearly 100 feet, keeps the massive proportions of piers and ribs from producing a cavelike effect.

Another possibility for historic style, that of the Renaissance and Baroque era, also found expression in major works in the second half of the nineteenth century. If the university buildings in Helsinki, Oslo, and Copenhagen were intended to appear as impressive halls of learning, so were the museums and theaters founded in increasing numbers in the Scandinavian cities.[23] In Stockholm the royal collections of painting and sculpture had been housed in a wing of the Royal Palace since 1793, when a plan for a separate museum came to nothing. By 1840 the matter was revived and by 1846 a

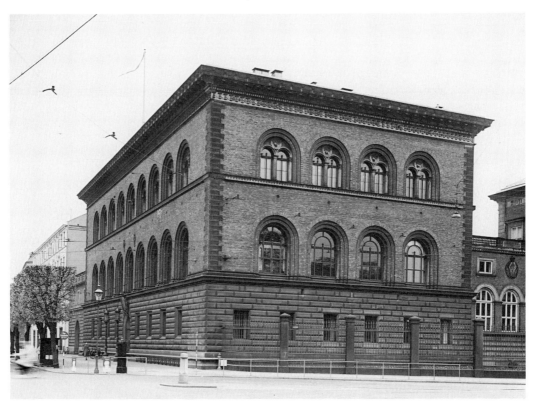

**17**

committee appointed. Several proposals were
made, approval going to that of the German
architect Friedrich August Stüler. He had studied with Schinkel and was becoming well
known as a museum designer, having recently
begun the Neues Museum in Berlin.[24] For
Stockholm the proposed National Museum was
to be a major national architectural event, the
largest project, in fact, to be undertaken since
the completion of the Royal Palace itself.

The site finally chosen is on Blasieholm,
across the harbor from the Palace. Stüler's
building, begun in 1849 and completed in 1866,
has a majestic west façade that gives some indi-
cation of the inner disposition of the building
(figure 7.16).[25] The three-bay central portion,
divided by pilasters with tall round-headed windows between, is flanked by the north and
south wings, three stories high above the base-

ment. The project was for a museum to house
galleries for painting and sculpture and also a
library. Stüler planned it to be in four wings,
the court so created crossed by a central wing.
The grand vestibule and stair hall give access to
the galleries in the wings. No corridors were
included, circulation being through the larger
and smaller galleries. Stüler had a strong sense
that such a museum should be a work of art
itself, which he tried to achieve through the
richness of red and gray limestone and a Renaissance ornamental vocabulary.[26] He also used
iron in its construction. The interior designs
were supplied by Fredrik Wilhelm Scholander,
one of Sweden's leading architects (whose proposal for the museum itself had not been accepted), and in 1896–1908 the Swedish painter
Carl Larsson designed the great frescoes above
the staircase. This was the first of the major

18

19

20

Scandinavian museums to be built as such, the collections of the Danish National Museum then as now being housed in the Prince's Palace in Copenhagen.

In an eclectical age, an architect might choose different historic styles for different buildings. Having used the Italian Romanesque for his University Library of 1855, J. D. Herholdt turned to the model of a Florentine palace for the Danish National Bank, begun in 1866 (figure 7.17).[27] Here is a compact and regular three-story building with rusticated lower story and two levels of broad arched windows, all crowned by a heavy cornice, an approach that was evidently thought appropriate for a banking establishment.

Much grander was the Royal Theater in Copenhagen, begun not far from the bank six years later. It was designed by Vilhelm Dahlerup and Ove Petersen to replace the one built by Niels Eigtved in 1748 (figure 7.18).[28] The grand façade, with its rusticated triple-arched entrance below and arched balcony above with double Ionic columns, is in the then established pattern for the European theater. Staircases lead to a foyer behind the balcony, decorated with Corinthian pilasters. The auditorium is U-shaped, with four tiers of boxes and galleries, the royal box between the proscenium and the first tier on stage right. An extensive program of remodeling for the stage and supporting facilities was carried out in 1983–1985. The simple elegance of the backstage and ballet quarters now contrasts with the exuberance of the auditorium.

Dahlerup was not solely interested in stately projects. In 1874 he designed the Pantomime Theater for the Tivoli Gardens, which had been founded by Georg Carstensen in 1843 (figure 7.19).[29] The brilliant, exotic use of Chinese motifs, so different from the Rococo elegance of the Chinese Pavilion at Drottning-

**7.21 Reykjavik. Parliament. F. Meldahl. 1881.**

**7.22 Oslo. National Gallery. A. Schirmer. 1879– 1881. Print, c. 1885. (Oslo, National Gallery.)**

holm, is well suited to the theater's setting in the pleasure gardens. It also gave Dahlerup an opportunity to depart from the more formal Renaissance manner.

One major church project was at last brought to a conclusion in this Renaissance/ Baroque group. We left Frederik's Church in Copenhagen unfinished at the time of N. H. Jardin's dismissal in 1771. Thanks to private funding the work was resumed in 1876 and completed in 1894 by Ferdinand Meldahl (figure 7.20).[30] Now instead of a ruin there is an imposing church at the end of Frederiksgade, the dome, based on that of St. Peter's in Rome, sitting rather heavily on the centralized building below. The inner circular room is divided into twelve parts along the walls, arched at the main level and rectangular windows in the drum of the dome above, all separated by pilasters, applied colonettes, and panels. The altar is placed against the wall opposite the main entrance, flanked by the pulpit and baptismal font, with seats arranged theater-fashion facing them. The overall effect is heavy, and Jardin might not be altogether pleased with the result. The use of marble and marbelized wood has given the church its other name of "The Marble Church."

21

22

**7.23   Stockholm. Royal Op-
era House. A. Ander-
berg. 1891–1898.**

While work on Frederik's Church was in progress, Meldahl had another unique assignment. In Norway the Parliament, the Storting, had existed until the constitution of 1814. Iceland's Parliament, the Althing, on the other hand, was first assembled c. 930 at the dramatic site of Thingvellir. The Althing, only briefly interrupted, met there without permanent shelter until greater independence was won from Denmark by the constitution of 1874. In 1881 the Parliament building was built beside the lake in Reykjavik, according to Meldahl's design (figure 7.21). It is like an Italian palazzo, seven bays wide and two stories high, with large round-headed windows in both levels. The material is the dark Icelandic basalt. The central entrance, with its traditional balcony for official appearances, leads to a central staircase with handsome iron balusters. The legislative chambers are on the second level, with the larger for the lower house on the north, overlooking Parliament Square. The smaller chamber is on the west, and offices occupy the east end. A recent addition on the south provides a sitting room for members of the assembly.

A much less sober palazzo design was made for the contemporary National Gallery in Oslo. As early as 1836 the Norwegian Parliament had wanted a national art collection, and indeed Linstow had drawn up a proposal for housing it. It was not until 1879 that a building to house the sculpture collections was finally begun by Adolf Schirmer (figure 7.22).[31] The original building was designed as a palazzo, two stories high, with a three-bay central portion projecting slightly and an attic story finished with guardian griffins. The fine texture of the brickwork was repeated in the additions of the south wing, 1905–1907, and the north wing, 1918–1924, both by Ingvar M. O. Hjorth.

Shortly thereafter came a series of national theaters given much grander palatial expres-

sions. In Stockholm the Opera House that Adelcrantz had built for Gustavus III in 1777–1782 was demolished in 1891 and replaced by the present Royal Opera from the designs of Axel Anderberg by 1898 (figure 7.23).[32] Some parts of the old foundations and walls were used, and the main entrance was again put on the square. Swedish granite was used to finish the walls at ground level, while the more economical rose-tinted stucco was used above. Details were carried out in Swedish limestone.

Anderberg planned the building in the traditional manner, with the axis of auditorium and stage in line with the main entrance. As it is now, there is a grand staircase beyond the vestibule, flanking staircases, and a richly decorated foyer above the vestibule. Since this is a royal theater, there is a royal staircase on the north side leading to a suite of rooms including the royal foyer, which has paintings by Prince Eugen. The royal box is here on stage left, just before the proscenium. This departure from the more frequent location, as in the Copenhagen theater, put the royal quarters on the side facing the Royal Palace. The auditorium is U-shaped, with three tiers of boxes and galleries.

At the same time, the National Theater in Oslo was being built from the designs of Henrik Bull (figure 7.24).[33] In 1891 Norway was still under the Swedish King Oscar II, and Bull undoubtedly knew the plans for the theater then under construction in Stockholm. The main entrance is again a three-part system, with an arcade below and an Ionic temple-front above. Although the original intention was to face the building with stone, economy dictated that granite could be used only for the ground level, with brick for the upper parts. On the interior Bull put the major staircases on either side of the vestibule, and as in Anderberg's Royal Opera the royal staircase, apartments,

24

and box are on stage left. The auditorium,
however, is horseshoe-shaped with two tiers of
galleries and boxes. The performing and service
areas were rebuilt in 1979–1985.

The combination of stone and stucco or
brick in these two theaters illustrates the dilemma facing Nordic architects in the late nineteenth century. A desire for "truth in
materials" led some to assert that native materials alone should be used for buildings of national significance, and stone was heavily
favored. Problems of cost led to compromises
such as those just described. In Oslo, in fact,
the first project for the National Gallery in
1876 by Heinrich Ernst Schirmer, father of
Adolf Schirmer, called for a stone façade. The

**7.24  Oslo. National The-
ater. H. Bull. 1891–
1899.**

**7.25  Stockholm. Royal Dra-
matic Theater. J. F. Lil-
jekvist. 1901–1908.**

**25**

elder Schirmer resigned from the project when his choice of material was turned down. Another problem was that of durability, since some stones proved not to weather well: the limestone of the National Museum in Stockholm very soon began to crumble. Such problems presented difficulties for those seeking to settle on the use of materials in order to develop a "national style."[34]

At the beginning of the twentieth century Scandinavian architects were exploring yet another possibility for ornamental vocabulary. Early identified as the "Art Nouveau" or "Jugendstil," its proponents were rejecting historical styles for a program of original motifs, depending for their success on references to natural forms and fluidity and sensitivity of

line.[35] In the Scandinavian countries this style was not universally adopted, but found some instances of eloquent expression.[36] For example, the Royal Dramatic Theater in Stockholm, built in 1901–1908 by Johan Fredrik Liljekvist, is planned in the traditional manner (figure 7.25).[37] The façade, however, while perpetuating the central elements that we have observed on the earlier Scandinavian theaters, does not have the arcaded gallery in the second story. It depends for its effect on the enrichment of the marble surfaces with sculpture by Carl Milles and Art Nouveau motifs. The same is true of the National Theater in Bergen, 1906–1909, designed by Einer Oscar Schou (figure 7.26).[38] Clearly owing much to the Stockholm theater then being completed, Schou's competition de-

sign proposed richer surfaces than were actually built; but placed on a rise of ground in a
park setting, the Bergen theater achieves a certain grandeur.

Perhaps more than the other Scandinavian
countries, Finland seized upon the Art Nouveau, well represented in numerous houses and
apartment blocks. One of the most interesting
nonresidential buildings is the Valtion (National)
Hotel at Imatra, built in 1903 by Usko Nyström (figure 7.27).[39] The whole setting is dramatic, as it is placed on the gorge formed by
the Vuoksi River, where the steep rapids have
been lessened by a large power station built in
the 1920s. The view downward into the rocks
remains spectacular, and Nyström's hotel with
its irregularly jutting towers and asymmetrical
window openings suits its location admirably.

One other major source of inspiration for
design in the late nineteenth century remains
to be considered, the rural Nordic traditions
that evoked even more nostalgia than the medieval or the Renaissance and Baroque. A notable example for its use for a single dwelling is
the Dunker Villa, designed for a wealthy lawyer
by H. E. Schirmer and built in 1848 or 1851 on
Malmøya near Oslo (figure 7.28).[40] The illustration by Dietrichson and Munthe shows a compact wooden building, two stories high, with a
veranda on two sides and carved detail to give
it a "Nordic" air. In Norway the inspiration is
thought to have come not so much from traditional Norwegian rural building as from Germany and Austria, hence the popular
classification of these buildings as "Swiss
Style."[41] A number of small wooden churches
were also built in Norway at this time.[42]

The restaurant became a place in addition
to the theater where those who could afford it
could be seen and entertained in splendid surroundings. In the city a palatial approach might
be taken, as at Bern's Restaurant in Stockholm,

26

7.26 **Bergen. National Theater. E. O. Schou.
1906–1909. (Oslo,
Riksantikvaren.)**
7.27 **Imatra. Valtion Hotel.
U. Nyström. 1903.**

28

29

**30**

7.28 Oslo. Dunker Villa. H. E. Schirmer. 1848 or 1851. (Dietrichson and Munthe, *Holzbau-kunst,* plate 12.)

7.29 Oslo. Frognerseteren. H. Munthe. 1890. (Die-trichson and Munthe, *Holzbaukunst,* plate 8.)

7.30 Dalen, Telemark. Ho-tel. H. L. Børve. 1894. (Bergen, University Library. Photo: K. Knudsen.)

7.31 Stockholm. Nordic Mu-seum. I. G. Clason. 1892–1907.

**31**

built in 1862 by Johan Fredrik Åbom. Those seeking enjoyment in a more nostalgic setting might dine at a restaurant built in the "Dragon Style," such as Frognerseteren, built by Holm Munthe in 1890 (figure 7.29).[43] The horizontal log walls and porches with open arcades were further romanticized by the Viking-inspired dragon heads at the roof peaks.

European efforts to provide hotels for the safety, comfort, and pleasure of travelers form a whole study in themselves.[44] Many grand buildings in Renaissance or Baroque style were constructed in the late nineteenth century, some in connection with railway stations. But there was also a growing desire to enjoy a resort hotel vacation, for which a rambling wooden structure adorned in the Dragon Style was an appealing solution. One of the most famous examples was the Dalen Hotel in Telemark, built in 1894 by Haldor Larsen Børve (figure 7.30).[45] Verandas and open porches with steeply pitched gables made for an informal airy appearance.

The Nordic Museum in Stockholm might properly be included in discussions of buildings in the Renaissance/Baroque manner. It was, however, founded in 1872 by Artur Hazelius, the founder of Skansen, and is devoted to the life of the Swedish people. Further, the aspect of the Renaissance chosen was not that of the palaces of Italy and France but rather the Netherlandish style of the early seventeenth century, a less formal and stately approach. Competition for the design began in 1883 and was finally won by Isak Gustaf Clason, under whom the museum was built from 1892 to 1907 (figure 7.31).[46] A much larger establishment was intended, with four wings around a courtyard and corner towers to resemble a castle, but the western main hall portion was the only part built. Brick was originally proposed for the exterior, but this was changed to red sandstone

with gray sandstone trim. The building is four stories high, decked out with the towers, gables, pinnacles, and surface patterns characteristic of the Northern Renaissance. The main vestibule is dark, but the three main exhibition floors rise around a central open court that gives light. Circulation is through the galleries, with stairs in the entrance portion and in the four corner towers. The court is the largest interior space among the Scandinavian museums of this period, and its effect is to unite, not separate, the exhibition wings.

Up to this point we have taken the use of iron in building construction more or less for granted. In the early years of the nineteenth century a number of theater roofs had been built with iron, largely in hopes of preventing tragic fires, and later some of the great international exposition buildings were to display its potential in design. Train sheds were also ideal subjects for iron roofs. With these we come closer to industrial buildings than to "polite" architecture, and to the philosophical rift between "architecture" and "engineering."[47]

Another appropriate use of iron was in factory construction.[48] In spite of ideological problems, factories have engaged the attention of Scandinavian architects for nearly 150 years. The English textile industry had led the way in factory design for a century when Norwegian manufacturers began such complexes as developed at Akerselva in the 1840s (figure 7.32).[49] The plain blocklike buildings of two to four stories rose in contrast to the tumbling waters of the streams needed for their water power, establishing a new aspect of the urban landscape. Because of its fire-resistant and load-bearing advantages, iron came to be used for some of the beams and pillars of construction, and also for window frames and bars. Historicism was promptly felt, as shown by C. H. Grosch's design for the canvas factory in Oslo

32

33

7.32 Akerselva, Akershus. Textile factories. Begun 1835. Lithograph, 1857. (Oslo, City Museum.)

7.33 Oslo. Canvas factory. C. H. Grosch. 1856. Xylograph, c. 1860. (Oslo, City Museum.)

7.34 Copenhagen. Carlsberg Brewery. H. C. Stilling. 1847.

34

**35**

in 1856, with its echo of Lombard Romanesque pilaster strips and corbel tables (figure 7.33).[50]

In Denmark two important industries were developing and needed factories. For J. C. Jacobsen's brewery in Copenhagen, built 1847, his own drawing was the basis for the buildings by Harald C. Stilling. Two and three stories high, with attic vents, its long walls were relieved by panels framing the window bays (figure 7.34).[51] Another brewery, Marstrands Maltmølle (later Kongens Bryghus), was built in 1865, this time from drawings by Henning Wolff (figure 7.35).[52] This was given even greater expression, with a broad arched door in the central bay, four bays with arched win-

dows at the ground level on either side, and end bays with narrow closely spaced windows in all four stories. The building was demolished in 1976, but it shows how an industrial building could be eloquent in appearance, even in the early years of industrial architectural design.

The other industry then developing in Denmark was the making of glass. After 1814 Denmark, whose glass had been made in Norway, sought her own means of production in order to avoid paying heavy duties on imports. A source of fuel was found in the peat bogs at Holme-Olstrup on Zealand, and a glassworks was begun in 1825. The oldest remaining building, from 1874, was given none of the stylistic

**36**

vocabulary of the two breweries: not all manufacturing establishments in nineteenth-century
Scandinavia were architect-designed (figure
7.36).[53]

The 1890s brought the first of the three
great Scandinavian town halls that are as much
national as civic structures. Rapid growth of the
population in Copenhagen had rendered C. F.
Hansen's Råd-og-domhus too small, and of
course its serene classicism was no longer in
fashion. In 1852 the military authorities had
abandoned the old ramparts, leaving the way
open for their demolition and new uses for the
land, badly needed because of overcrowding in
the old city. The resulting rapid expansion be-

**37**

yond the ramparts and moats was controversial and disorderly, with some park areas created but also with some poor-quality new tenement housing. The old Halmtorv, or straw market, had lain inside Vesterport, the west gate through the ramparts, and here was found the site for a new Town Hall.[54] The Tivoli Gardens had been laid out in 1843, and J. D. Herholdt's Central Railway Station had been built in 1863–1864.[55] The new Town Hall would therefore be placed between the busiest centers of the old city and its major railway.

After competitions, Martin Nyrop was chosen to be the architect. Work was begun promptly, and the building was completed in 1905 (figure 7.37).[56] Built of red brick, the main block facing the Town Hall Square rises in three stories above a basement and is finished with an attic story and battlemented roof. The main entrance is not emphasized by a projecting bay or portico, but is a broad arched opening, above which is a statue of Bishop Absalon, founder of Copenhagen. The resemblance to the Town Hall of Siena is heightened by the brick tower rising 326 feet on the northeast corner of the main block. The full plan involves two inner courts, one roofed and the other open to the sky (figure 7.38). The main entrance leads through a vaulted vestibule to the Assembly Hall, which is roofed but otherwise resembles the inner court of an Italian palazzo (figure 7.39). The cross wing on the east houses the Council Chamber in the second story. The Banqueting Hall, much like a Riddarsal, is also on the second floor, occupying the nine central bays of the front wing. Reception rooms are reached by corridors surrounding

7.37 **Copenhagen. Town Hall. M. Nyrop. 1892–1905. (James A. Donnelly.)**

7.38 **Copenhagen. Town Hall. Plan. (Hansen, *Martin Nyrop,* p. 39.)**

7.39 **Copenhagen. Town Hall. Assembly Hall. (Copenhagen, Academy of Art Library.)**

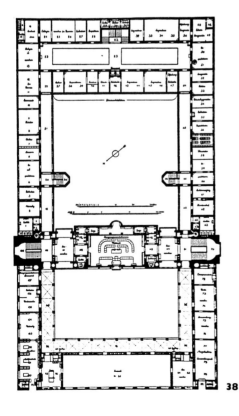

**38**

**39**

**7.40 Copenhagen. Christiansborg III.**
**T. Jørgensen. 1907–**
**1928.**
**7.41 Copenhagen. Christiansborg III. Portal.**

the Assembly Hall, and the offices in the east, south, and west wings of the second part of the building surround the open court. The plan therefore is similar to that of a great palace, with its state spaces, corridors, grand staircase, and service rooms.

Nyrop did not restrict his use of historic materials to imitations of Italian palaces. In the details of woodwork, mosaics, and fresco decorations there are numerous references to traditional Danish motifs, such as the patterns from Bronze Age lurs used on lighting fixtures. Paintings and sculptures throughout the building refer to all of Denmark, not just to Copenhagen. The whole work celebrated Danish life and culture and was completed by a great many of her finest craftsmen.[57]

Nyrop's interest in Denmark's heritage in the arts and crafts was not an isolated phenomenon. His brother Camille was a trades historian who had participated in early proposals for a Danish museum of decorative arts, which was finally accomplished in 1885.[58] This was not the first such undertaking in the Scandinavian countries and was largely inspired by the Nordic Museum in Stockholm. Schools and associations for the encouragement of native handicrafts had already been founded as early as the 1840s in response to what were viewed as threats to quality from mass-produced industrial designs.

While all this work for a new Town Hall was moving forward, elsewhere Copenhagen

suffered disfigurement and embarrassment. Fire broke out in the south wing of C. F. Hansen's Christiansborg on October 3, 1884, and by the next day the main building was in ruins. Heroic efforts saved the art collections and prevented the destruction of the Riding School, the Chapel, and Thorvaldsen's Museum. Not only were the royal State Rooms gone, but so were the chambers for Parliament and the Supreme Court. The constitution of 1848 established the Landsting, nominated by the king, and the Folketing, elected by the people. If the palace was to be reconstructed, therefore, a great many people instead of just the king would be deciding how it was to be rebuilt and by whom. Twenty years, ten legislative bills, and sixty-three proposals later, the choice fell on Thorvald Jørgensen in 1906, and the new building was more or less complete by 1928 (figure 7.40).[59]

The foundations of the previous building determined the plan, with the State Rooms, including Dining Room and Great Hall on the north of the first floor, the Throne Room in the center of the east wing overlooking the Palace Square, and the legislative chambers in the south wing. As the new building went up, many details were changed from the original plans so that it became a Baroque palace, as exemplified by the main east portal and balcony from which the Danish monarchs are proclaimed (figure 7.41). Jørgensen took advantage of the new availability of reinforced concrete for the roof and the 342-foot tower and spire. He also had much of the lower portions faced with granite, more durable than the plaster covering of the earlier palace. The old Slotsholm of Bishop Absalon's time had now grown to an elaborate ceremonial and administrative complex, still held somewhat aloof from the commercial and residential parts of the city by the surrounding canal.

**40**

**41**

42

7.42   **Stockholm. Town Hall.**
        **R. Östberg. 1909–**
        **1923. (Stockholm, City**
        **Museum.)**

7.43   **Stockholm. Town Hall.**
        **Plan. (Stockholm, City**
        **Museum.)**

7.44   **Stockholm. Town Hall.**
        **Blue Hall. (Stockholm,**
        **City Museum.)**

The academic Baroque was clearly not yet dead in Scandinavia, nor was National Romanticism. A new Town Hall was built for Stockholm in 1909–1923 by Ragnar Östberg (figures 7.42 and 7.43).[60] After ten years of discussions and competitions it was placed to command the waters of Lake Mälar across from the Old Town. Like the Town Hall in Copenhagen it is composed of traditional elements. The Stockholm building is brick with obvious references to Italian palazzo designs, an open and a covered courtyard, and a high tower placed in one corner, but there the resemblances stop.

The Town Hall is entered at the northeast corner through an archway that leads into the open courtyard, but this entrance is not a central focal point as is the entrance to the Town Hall in Copenhagen. Östberg had a different concept for the most important aspect of the building: "The *main façade* of the Town Hall, which faces *east,* and towards the old city, had been treated differently from the other façades, and is on a monumental scale. It is intended to represent the government of the City from the Middle Ages down to the present day. . . . The main façade, with its entirely vertical articulation and its row of high windows, is the external facing of the Council Chamber (the big hall where the Municipal Council meets), which corresponds to it in height and breadth."[61]

From the north entrance one looks across the courtyard to arcades that open out to a terraced garden beside the water. A broad flight of stairs, suggesting use by large numbers of people, leads up to a vestibule through the center wing. This in turn leads to the large enclosed courtyard, called the "Blue Hall," which is palatial with its marble floor and red tile walls. The name comes from the original intention to have the brick stuccoed in blue. When built, however, the hall was so effective in color with the walls of machine-made brick

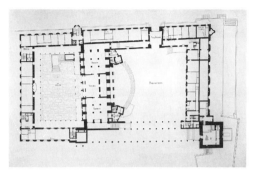

43

44

that the plan was changed to hand-chiseling the bricks to give a rougher texture (figure 7.44).[62] The staircase is grandly ceremonial although not placed symmetrically. It leads up to a balcony overlooking the Blue Hall and to the entrance to the major parts of the eastern portion of the building. The principal administrative offices are on the north side, and the Council Chamber on the east. The long reception room, with paintings by Prince Eugen, is on the south, its tall windows affording views of the city across the lake. The largest room is the Great Hall, or the "Golden Hall," in the central wing, covered with gilded mosaics depicting the history of Stockholm. The sumptuous furnishings and decorations throughout are the work of many craftmen, so that Stockholm's Town Hall is a national as well as a civic monument. For Östberg a vital part of the whole enterprise was the placing of the studios and workshops for architects, sculptors, textile designers, metalworkers, etc., on the premises as the building was under construction, thereby facilitating continual review of works in the locations for which they were being prepared.[63]

This was also a time when some Scandinavian architects were taking the ideas of National Romanticism a step further. While the

Copenhagen Town Hall was under construction, in 1896, three architecture students at the Technological Institute in Helsinki formed a partnership: Herman Gesellius, Armas Lindgren, Eliel Saarinen.[64]

Three years later they won the competition for the Finnish Pavilion at the Paris Exposition of 1900. With their prize money they built the studio-dwelling complex at Hvitträsk, a rugged lakeside site west of Helsinki, beginning in 1901 (figure 7.45).[65] As one approaches from Helsinki, the buildings are concealed by trees bordering level farmland. It is not until one has entered the complex and explored the exterior and garden that the precipitous character of the planning becomes apparent. The wooded west side of the site falls steeply to the lake below, and the dwelling rises from the rocky hillside as if it were a miniature fortress. The combination of stone, wood, and the steep roofs gives the original building a nostalgic appearance that is not borne out by the plan (figure 7.46). The living room and sitting room are dark and cavelike, the bedchambers lighter and arranged seemingly at random, and the long light studio seems in great contrast. The visitor, for Hvitträsk is now a museum, experiences

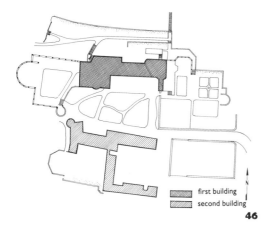

first building
second building
**46**

narrow corridors and constant changes in direction and level. There is also a wealth of furnishings designed by Akseli Gallen-Kallela and
others associated with the three architects.

Having caught public attention with the
Paris pavilion in 1900, the architects also won a
competition for the National Museum in Helsinki, built 1905–1912 (figure 7.47).[66] Plans for
such a museum were begun in the 1880s, the
first site chosen being on a hill near the Observatory, where a standard neo-Renaissance museum building was proposed. After several
years of discussion, the present site was se-
lected and a new architectural competition
opened in March 1901. The winning design reflected new thinking about museum planning
and contemporary desire for strong expressions of Finnish national character. Significantly,
two leaders of National Romanticism in other
Scandinavian countries were on the jury, Isak
Gustaf Clason of Sweden and Martin Nyrop of
Denmark.

The museum consists of two irregular,
nearly square buildings, each with an interior
courtyard, linked by the large square entrance
hall. Around one courtyard are the wings for
the several collections, with the offices in the
other. The exterior reflects but does not imitate the historic architecture of Finland. The
main entrance, on the south side, is through
the base of the tall churchlike tower. The south
wing, housing the collections of religious antiquities, has a paneled gable like that of a church.
The wings projecting east and west recall Renaissance castles, with the great round tower
similar to those of Olavlinna. Square rubble masonry and brick were chosen as characteristic
Finnish materials for the exterior.

On the interior the entrance hall is dominated by the four heavy columns supporting the
ceiling, originally closed but now with a small
domed opening. Akseli Gallen-Kallela repeated

47

here the striking paintings of subjects from the Kalevala that he had done for the Paris pavilion. Throughout, the decorative motifs are designed in the stylization of the Art Nouveau.

When in 1904 it came time to build the Railway Station in Helsinki, the competition was won by Gesellius, Lindgren, and Saarinen. Lindgren left the partnership in 1905, however, followed by Gesellius in 1907. As built from 1910 to 1920, the building is the work of Saarinen alone (figure 7.48).[67] As a terminal building its halls are perpendicular to the tracks, with the service facilities on either side of the tracks. It fronts on Kaivokatu on the northern side of the business district, but there is no avenue leading directly toward it. Consequently the oblique views obtained from most approaches together with the tall eastern clock tower suggest that the building is more asymmetrical than it is.

The projecting vestibule has a huge arched window above the actual entrances and is flanked by two pairs of sculptured figures carrying lights. The two side halls for ticket rooms and restaurant as well as the main hall are roofed with vaults in reinforced concrete, an innovation for a major public building in Finland. The broad windows in two stories are separated by narrow granite walls running the full height of the building with a unifying effect.

Specific use of traditional Finnish detail was diminished, but the design was still too much in the spirit of National Romanticism for one of the losers of the competition, Sigurd Frosterus. Strongly influenced by the work of Henry van de Velde in Holland, he had become a rationalist in his approach to planning and the use of the new materials that industrial technology was making available. After losing the Railway Station commission, Frosterus, together with like-minded architect, Gustav Strengell, wrote a pamphlet bitterly denouncing the National Romantics and calling for what he believed to be a more "honest" architecture.[68]

48

49

**7.49  Helsinki. National The-
ater. O. Tarjanne.
1902.**

**7.50  Turku. St. Michael's
Church. L. Sonck.
1894–1904. (Helsinki,
Museum of Finnish Ar-
chitecture. Photo:
A. Salokorpi.)**

A combination of National Romantic use of Finnish granite and reference to the style of the American architect H. H. Richardson is evident in the National Theater in Helsinki by Onni Tarjanne, 1902 (figure 7.49).[69] Like the theaters in Copenhagen, Stockholm, and Oslo already noted, the theater in Helsinki is in the tradition of a symmetrical façade with triple entrance on the ground level and an arcaded balcony above. The twin towers of the façade give an almost fortresslike appearance. The Baroque of the earlier Scandinavian theaters is replaced by a Romanesque scheme, with walls of granite and arcading in the medieval Finnish manner. Carvings on the capitals of the piers may show influence of Richardsonian designs, appearing by then in English and Continental publications.

Having begun this chapter with medieval motifs used for the Copenhagen University, we

may close it with the work of a Finnish architect who used medieval principles in a different
manner, Lars Sonck.[70] He was born on the
western coast of Finland and when later living
in the Åland Islands attended the Polytechnical
Institute in Helsinki. He knew the stone and
brick medieval churches of Swedish Finland and
later saw the Karelian farmhouses of eastern
Finland. Drawing upon these traditions, he developed a strong and distinctive personal style
for his churches, public buildings, and villas.

Sonck was still a student in 1893 when a
competition was announced for a major new
church in Turku. His entry won first prize in
May 1894, and the church, St. Michael's, was
completed by the end of 1904 (figure 7.50).[71] It
is basilical in plan, with a high square tower on
the south side of the west façade and lower
round towers flanking the polygonal apse.
Sonck was clearly indebted to the brick Gothic
churches of north Germany, which he saw during his travels. A large round window fills the
west façade above the triple-arched portal. At
first glance these portal openings appear to be
conventional neo-Gothic arches. But Sonck
here introduced a motif that was to characterize many of his designs: a stilted triangle, with
sides only slightly curved if at all, which gives
the effect of an arch without being one.

On the interior the nave is covered by
domical vaults in the German manner, while the
aisles are separated from the nave by short
massive columns on the first level, repeated at
the gallery level. The columns are widely
spaced and the openings into the aisles low,
giving the aisles a cavelike quality.

Then in 1899, while St. Michael's was under construction, a competition was announced
for a church to be built in a newly planned extension of Tampere. Sonck won this, calling his
entry "Aeternitas." When his plans were approved in 1902, the church was named St.

50

John's, and it became the Cathedral of Tampere in 1923 (figure 7.51).[72] Sonck had earlier made sketches for a "country church," apparently inspired by the drawings of Protestant churches in England and America by K. E. O. Fritsch.[73] From these may have come the broad massive body of the church with its major tower placed at the northwest corner. The English and American churches were built with round-headed or pointed arches, whereas Sonck used his distinctive triangular "arch" at Tampere. For the exterior he used rubble granite in tones of red and gray to provide an appropriately Finnish material. In plan the church is basically square, with a central nave rising to a high and broad ribbed vault. Galleries on three sides are carried on heavy columns similar to those of St. Michael's. Paintings, carvings, and furnishings are the work of several Finnish artists.

While St. John's in Tampere was nearing completion, Sonck successfully entered the competition for a church to be built in the Kallio suburb of Helsinki. Superbly sited at the high end of Unionkatu, it was built in 1909–1912 of granite, but now with axial symmetry and a far more restrained surface (figure 7.52).[74] On the interior the Gothic vaults of the earlier churches give way to a high semicircular barrel vault, the arcades of the gallery are broad, and the light beige color of the interior is delicately ornamented with stenciled designs. The climax of this move toward clarity in Sonck's work came with the Mikael Agricola Church in Helsinki, which we shall consider in the next chapter.

Sonck designed villas in the Karelian style and engaged in some city planning projects. He also designed some office buildings, in which changes in his style can be clearly seen.

The Telephone Building in Helsinki, 1901–1905, like St. John's has an asymmetrical façade, the four strong levels of the main building set

**7.51  Tampere. Cathedral. L. Sonck. 1902–1907. (Helsinki, Museum of Finnish Architecture. Photo: Iffland.)**

**52**

off by the left, or north, tower, similar to those of Tarjanne's National Theater (figure 7.53).[75] The granite of the Telephone Building is bolder than that of the theater, with large rough-hewn stones that Sonck chose to be in varying colors. He used his characteristic "arch" for the openings of the second level and an oculus for the fourth level of the south projection, the rest of the windows having lintels or shallow arches. The sense of this façade is Romanesque, but in a highly personal manner.

For the Finnish Mortgage Society in 1908 Sonck again provided a granite façade, but this time he chose a symmetrical scheme that echoes the façade of the National Theater.[76] The wide blocks of the triple-arched entrance are smooth, and the two-story colonnade above suggests Egyptian rather than Romanesque prototypes. The flanking sections on either side are also of smooth-cut granite, the irregularity of the ashlar the only suggestion of medieval quality.

Still more austere on the surface and almost like an organ façade with its columns is the Stock Exchange in Helsinki that Sonck built in 1911.[77] Perhaps the central columned portion was intended to establish the building as a temple of commerce. It is rather a pity that these three buildings, like the Railway Station, are so placed that their full impact as urban façades is difficult to appreciate fully. For the interior of the Stock Exchange Sonck designed a court rising through four stories, served by staircases and balconies (figure 7.54). Here is the palazzo once more, but without the historicizing motifs of the reception hall in the Town Hall in Copenhagen. Even more than on the exterior, the broad surfaces and sharply defined openings were prophetic of what was to come. A notable building, and a worthy successor to the exchanges in Copenhagen of 1619, Stockholm of 1767, and Oslo of 1826.

7.52 Helsinki. Kallio
Church. L. Sonck.
1909–1912.

7.53 Helsinki. Telephone
Building. L. Sonck.
1905. (Helsinki, Mu-
seum of Finnish Archi-
tecture. Photo:
H. Havas.)

7.54 Helsinki. Stock Ex-
change. L. Sonck. 1911.
Interior. (Helsinki, Mu-
seum of Finnish Archi-
tecture. Photo:
H. Havas.)

53

54

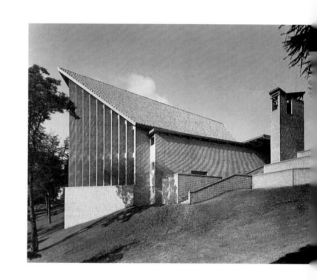

# 8  *Scandinavian Architecture since World War I*

Three years after Lars Sonck designed the Stock Exchange in Helsinki, World War I broke out in July 1914. For the next four years until the Armistice was signed in November 1918, the Scandinavian countries managed to stay out of direct military conflict. Denmark, Norway, and Sweden were, however, profoundly affected, to some extent with prosperity through the production of war materials, but increasingly with difficulty in food and supplies. In the wake of revolution in Russia, Finland declared independence in December 1917, and in December 1918 Iceland became an independent state under the Danish crown, complete independence not coming until 1944.[1]

The tensions and unrest that culminated in the war were not unlike the unrest we have observed in Scandinavian architecture during the fifteen or twenty years before 1914. Academic Historicism, National Romanticism, the Art Nouveau, and International Rationalism all had their advocates and exemplars, but in the political and social world of the early twentieth century there was no absolute standard of taste. After the war, architects were still seek-

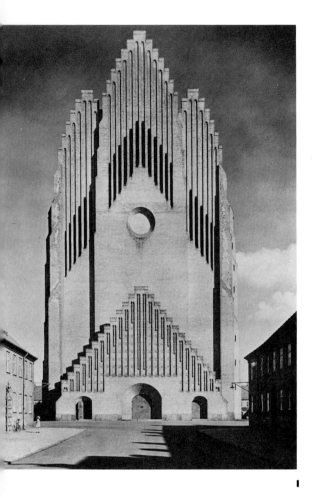

ing appropriate expressions of contemporary life in their buildings, and we may consider three major directions taken: some continuing sentiments of National Romanticism, a second Neoclassical interlude, and the increasing leadership of International Functionalism. By the outbreak of World War II much of significance had been built.

The growing desire for buildings free of direct historical references had its effect on those architects who still were using some traditional forms. Three churches built between the two world wars show how these forms could still be regarded as appropriate for individual projects if used in innovative rather than merely imitative ways. Perhaps the most astonishing of these is the Grundtvig Church in Copenhagen, built in 1920–1940 from the designs of P. V. Jensen-Klint (figure 8.1).[2] Bishop Nikolaj F. S. Grundtvig (1783–1872) was a poet and educational leader, founder of the Folk High Schools. The church was built as a memorial to him with funds raised by national subscription. The façade has a broad paneled and stepped gable covering three entrances, then a high wall with oculus and a paneled and stepped screen gable, almost like an organ façade. Similar gables are used over the side bays, as at St. Peter's Church in Malmö or the Cathedral in Århus. The apse, however, was designed with heavy buttresses such as those that by that time had been applied to Østerlars Church on Bornholm. This is all carried out in yellow brick, and the church was made to loom up over the nearby houses, also designed by Jensen-Klint, as if in a village. The interior is a direct reference to high Gothic churches, such as St. Knud's Church in Odense. Again finely crafted yellow brick was used, but even full sunlight does not compensate for the chilling effect of the unarticulated shafts of the piers and the built-in brick furniture.

While the Grundtvig Church was under construction, Lars Sonck designed two churches that reveal a turn toward Functionalism but still retain close ties to tradition. His family had moved to the Åland Islands when he was a young boy, and he had built a villa in the style of a Karelian farmhouse at Finström. Although settled from Sweden, the islands had been ceded to Finland in 1809, and this was upheld by the League of Nations in 1921. In that year the islands were granted self-government under the sovereignty of Finland, with their own Legislative Assembly and a representative to the Parliament in Helsinki. The capital, Mariehamn, had been founded by Czar Alexander II in 1861, and when in 1921 it became appropriate to build a new church there, Sonck provided the drawings. The church, built in 1927–1929, is basilical in plan, with north and south

8.1  Copenhagen. Grundt-
     vig's Church. P. V. Jen-
     sen-Klint. 1920–1940.
     (Copenhagen, National
     Museum.)
8.2  Mariehamn, Åland Is-
     lands. Church. L. Sonck.
     1927–1929.
8.3  Helsinki. Mikael Agri-
     cola Church. L. Sonck.
     1933–1935. (Helsinki,
     Museum of Finnish Ar-
     chitecture. Photo:
     Saurén.)

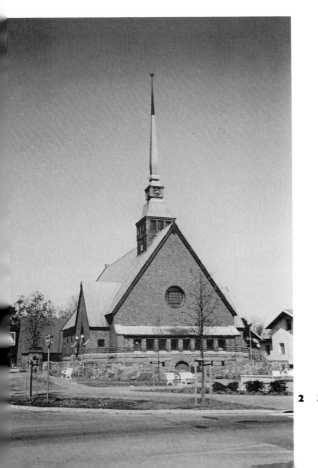

2   3

**4**

8.4   Copenhagen, Bellahøj.
Bakkehusene. T. Hen-
ningsen and I. Bentsen.
1922.

8.5   Svinninge, Zealand.
Power station. I. Bent-
sen. 1913. (Copenhagen,
Academy of Art
Library.)

porches, a shallow east apse, and a spire rising above the roof of the western vestibule (figure 8.2).[3] It is built of red brick on a granite foundation, with broad plain surfaces completely different from the Romanesque formulas of Tampere Cathedral. The interior is divided into nave and aisles by heavy piers and is covered with a painted wooden roof. A telling detail is the shape of the arch into the western bay, which appears to imitate that of St. Mikael's Church at Finström, which Sonck knew well. This is more curved than the "arch" that Sonck had used at St. Michael's in Turku, and we may ask whether it was this medieval form that Sonck had modified in the earlier church. In the church at Mariehamn, Sonck gave his beloved Åland Islands a church of considerable dignity as well as a continuation of their strong traditions.

Then in 1932 Sonck won the competition for the Mikael Agricola Church in Helsinki, built in 1933–1935 (figure 8.3).[4] The example of Grundtvig's Church in Copenhagen may have inspired this building, which was also constructed in honor of an early national religious and intellectual leader. Bishop Mikael Agricola (c. 1510–1557) had been responsible for the first books published in Finnish, an ABC book, a prayer book, and the New Testament. The single tower, nave, and sanctuary are clear shapes in unadorned red brick, the only accent being the metal belfry and spire.[5] The simplicity of the exterior is balanced by the grandeur of the interior, with cylindrical piers carrying the soaring parabolic arches of the nave. While the painted ornament of the capitals has an ancient Mediterranean flavor, the paintings on the ceilings of the aisles are biblical, after the manner of medieval Finnish painting. Structural references to medieval building details are smoothed down here in Sonck's response to Functionalism. The result is less romantic than in the Mariehamn church, and perhaps this is more suitable in the more formal urban situation.

Village traditions also found some expression in contemporary housing, notably at Bakkehusene, Bellahøj, in Copenhagen, built by Thorkind Henningsen and Ivar Bentsen in 1922 (figure 8.4).[6] The principle of such row or terrace houses was not new, as we have seen at Nyboder in Copenhagen and the houses in Møgeltønder. Henningsen and Bentsen reintroduced the principle for modern urban dwellings in these story-and-a-half houses of yellow stone, set back from the streets with small front gardens and larger private gardens at the back. The high wide roofs with ridges parallel to the streets unify the individual houses and help in the appearance of nostalgic comfort. The two sets of rows are on either side of a broad tree-lined esplanade, giving the effect of a small town.

Functionalism was not yet universally seized upon as the most appropriate architectural expression of twentieth-century society and technology. For a brief period, from about 1910 to 1930, architects in the Scandinavian countries reexamined the principles of classical antiquity in search of formulas for clarity and monumentality of design. That this search was not confined to the drawing boards but was also a matter of lively theoretical discussion is attested by numerous articles in contemporary Scandinavian architectural periodicals. The outcome was a group of buildings that has been designated as "Nordic Classicism" and that fifty years later has been the subject of fresh appraisal.[7]

The lead seems to have been taken in Denmark with Carl Petersen's Fåborg Museum of 1912–1915.[8] Its unassuming exterior belies the variation of the succession of brightly colored rooms behind it. Explicit classical references are in the coffered ceilings of the vestibule and the octagonal hall and the Ionic columns of the entrance to the latter. Otherwise Petersen was much concerned that the

**5**

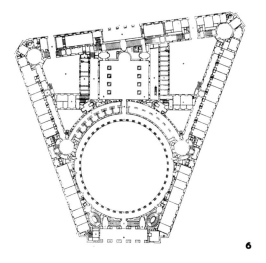

**6**

geometrical aspects of the building should present a clear, rational image. In a famous essay in 1920 he said, "A factor of the utmost importance in architecture is proportioning. . . . To achieve monumentality, it is always best that the elements which establish the scale for the whole are of sufficient size in themselves."[9]

Although it is not dominant in Petersen's pioneering museum, the columnar support is essential to what Demetri Porphyrios has called "Scandinavian Doricism."[10] For the buildings of the power station at Svinninge on Zealand in 1913, Ivar Bentsen used the echo of the column, the pilaster, in a very individual manner (figure 8.5).[11] He turned the narrow brick walls between the wide windows into pilaster strips that articulate the lower walls and are continued into the attic levels or gables in defiance of the integrity of the classical pediment. Avoiding surface ornament, but using the standard base-shaft-capital system of the normal pilaster, Bentsen dignified this industrial building with something of a temple front.

Surfaces were also reduced for the Police Headquarters in Copenhagen, begun by Hack Kampmann in 1918.[12] Kampmann was collaborating with his sons Christian and Hans Jørgen and with Aage Rafn. Rafn became the leading member of the group, especially after Hack Kampmann's death, when Holger Jacobsen and Anton Frederiksen joined the project. The irregular site resulted in a nearly triangular plan, with a portico on the shortest side and long narrow wings enclosing courtyards and cross wings (figure 8.6). The purpose of the building was to provide a new police facility, since C. F. Hansen's detention part of the Råd-og-domhus of 1805–1815 was now inadequate. The plan of the latter, however, the vestibule with Doric columns and the courtroom on the same axis terminating in the magistrate's niche, may have had something to do with the plan of the Police Headquarters. Urged by Aage Rafn, Hack Kampmann planned his building with a large circular courtyard filling the south section and three courts on the north. While the courts of the Kampmann building are open to the sky, there is an axis from the portico across the large circular court to a smaller court that also terminates in an apse. The circular court is nearly as large as the Pantheon in Rome, and is surrounded by a colonnade of coupled Doric columns based on C. F. Hansen's columns for Christiansborg. The austere exterior has little to relieve its plain walls except for the stringcourses marking the ground and uppermost stories. The façade, with a seven-arched portico and simple windows above, may contain another Roman reference, for it recalls the Tabularium (figure 8.7). The exterior is fortresslike and forbidding, and if the courtyards were to provide grace and sensitivity of proportions, these would not be evident in the open landscape of the city.

**8.6** **Copenhagen. Police Headquarters. H. Kampmann and others. 1918. Plan. (Copenhagen, Academy of Art Library.)**

**8.7** **Copenhagen. Police Headquarters.**

A distinctive early project in Sweden was for the Woodland Cemetery in Stockholm, where landscape and buildings were developed in an unusually well reasoned mortuary program. In 1912 a tract of 75 acres in the Enskede district of south Stockholm was set aside for a new cemetery, and a competition for its design was held in 1914. The first prize went to the Swedish architects Gunnar Asplund and Sigurd Lewerentz.[13] Over the next twenty years the site was developed with burial grounds, chapels, crematorium, and supporting buildings. For the landscape itself, perhaps the most compelling feature is the approach from the portals to the cross erected before the Chapel of the Holy Cross (figure 8.8). Lewerentz, who was to design other notable cemeteries, left an open space at the top of the rise

**8**

**9**

so that the visitor is under the "dome of
heaven" more truly than in any domed building.
A comparison with such ancient burial sites as
Troldkirken and Lindholm Høje seems
inescapable.

Among the buildings of the cemetery, the
Woodland Chapel by Asplund, built 1918–1920,
has drawn much attention (figure 8.9).[14] The
deep columned portico and the chapel itself are
covered together with a high hipped roof. Asplund saw Kirkerup's Liselund on Møn, which
he greatly admired. Certainly the great roof of
the chapel suggests those of south Scandinavian
farmsteads. The columns of Liselund, however,
wrap around the rear extension of a T-shaped
house, this extension being roofed separately
from the main house. The columns of the
chapel, on the other hand, form a portico, four
columns wide and three deep, before the
chapel itself. Given Asplund's interest in antiquity, the Tuscan temple as described by Vitruvius would seem to be an additional obvious
prototype. The overall proportions of the
Woodland Chapel do not correspond to those
stipulated for the Tuscan temple, but those of
the cella of the chapel are very close to the 6:5
proportions of the temple plan. On the interior
eight Doric columns support a "dome of
heaven," ornamental vocabulary is avoided, and
the impression of the entire building is of simple support and shelter, dignified and timeless.

Later, in 1935–1940, Asplund's Chapel of
the Holy Cross at the Woodland Cemetery set
a much more prominent colonnaded porch in
the landscape (figure 8.10).[15] Classical ornamental vocabulary was again omitted and monumentality was achieved by the wide spacing of
the square columns, which provides a broad
shelter swept with light and air. Within the
chapel is a broad basilica in form, its shallow
dome carried on eight round columns with simple cubical capitals. The otherwise austere

8.8   **Stockholm. Woodland
      Cemetery. G. Asplund
      and S. Lewerentz. Begun
      1915.**
8.9   **Stockholm. Woodland
      Cemetery, Woodland
      Chapel. G. Asplund.
      1918–1920.**

space is given warmth by the frescoes by Sven
Erixon.

Another way in which classical principles
might be sought was in predominant emphasis
on mass rather than on detail. Earlier in his career Gunnar Asplund had moved in this direction, notably with the Central Library in
Stockholm, 1924–1928 (figure 8.11), perhaps
inspired by Fischer von Erlach's view of the
Tomb of Hadrian in Rome.[16] Above terraces
containing shops he placed a cubical building
with a circular unit above. Unadorned windows
pierce the flat walls, with concession to ornament in the surrounds of the doorways and the
shallow terracotta frieze below the second
range of windows. The work of Ledoux and
Boullée also comes to mind here, as well as
C. L. Engel's University Library in Helsinki.
When one enters the circular main reading
room, however, the impression is entirely different from Engel's interior. Asplund's room is
a high soaring space, bookshelves lining the
walls only part of the way, with blank walls
above pierced with windows and then the
dome floating above.

A major example of Nordic Classicism in Norway is the Town Hall at Haugesund, built in 1922–1931 by Gudolf Blakstad and Herman Munthe-Kaas, using columns more explicitly (figure 8.12).[17] The town is a fishing and export center on the west coast of Norway between Stavanger and Bergen. A hillside site was chosen for the Town Hall, with a park adjacent. A rusticated gray granite lower story with small arched openings fills out the slope, and the two wings for offices rise above, finished somewhat astonishingly in pink stucco. The Council Hall is not centralized but occupies the corner uniting the two wings. On the park side its location is dramatized by three large rusticated arches at the ground level and four pairs of Doric columns rising through both principal stories, with an attic story covered by a saucer dome above. The nature of the site would cause the traditional town hall formula, symmetrical with central tower, to look lopsided. The centrality of the Council Hall is retained by its corner location, but the traditional axial view across an urban open space is not attained.

11

12

8.10 Stockholm. Woodland Cemetery, Chapel of the Holy Cross. G. Asplund. 1935–1940.

8.11 Stockholm. Central Library. G. Asplund. 1924–1928.

8.12 Haugesund, Rogaland. Town Hall. G. Blakstad and H. Munthe-Kaas. 1922–1931. (Oslo, Norwegian Museum of Architecture.)

**13**

8.13  Bergen. Torvalmennin-
        gen Square. F. Berner.
        1922–1929.

8.14  Helsinki. Parliament.
        J. S. Sirén. 1927–1931.

For another way in which the Norwegian architects attempted to put classical principles to work we may look briefly at Torvalmenningen Square in Bergen by Finn Berner, 1922–1929 (figure 8.13).[18] After a destructive fire in the center of town in 1916, Vester Torv Gatu was widened in the business district, creating a broad open space with regular business buildings rising on either side. With some arcades on the ground level and stringcourses giving classical horizontality to the stories above, this part of the old merchant city took on an aspect quite different from that of Bryggen on the water front. The broadened vista increased the dominance of St. John's Church on the hill above.

In Finland the site of the Parliament building in Helsinki, on the west side of Mannerheimintie, also precludes a grand vista (figures

8.14 and 8.15).[19] Johan Sigfred Sirén won the competition for this building in 1924. Of red granite, it sits like a palace above a high flight of stairs. Behind the Corinthian colonnade is a long vestibule with stairs at either end. In the central wing is the Delegates' Chamber, a high circular hall with tall niches for statuary in the smooth walls and a low domed ceiling above. The niches make one think of C. F. Hansen's Vor Frue Kirke. There is a large formal reception hall above the entrance hall and three wings for offices, each level designed in a different color. As in the Copenhagen and Stockholm town halls, leading Finnish artists contributed to the interior details and furnishings, using some references to traditional Finnish motifs.

Some of the other Finnish architects of this generation were traveling to Italy, and their interest in local Italian building types is reflected in their approach to composing in terms of mass. A simple blocky church building with contrasting high bell tower, such as the one that Alvar Aalto designed for the church at Muurame in 1929, for example, satisfied the desire for classical Mediterranean inspiration and was also sympathetic to the long Finnish tradition of the church and bell tower group (figure 8.16).[20] Here the façade is based on the late Roman motif of an arch penetrating the pediment. The plain white walls of the church are marked by a stringcourse below the window level, and the belfy atop the tower is set off with similar moldings. The overall impression comes from the mass of the church itself with tower rising above.

This second Neoclassical moment in Scandinavian architecture found expression in a very different manner from the first. Those devoted to eclecticism did of course continue to pick and choose among the historical styles. But some who were leaders of the Nordic Classicism movement, teaching and writing as well as designing buildings, found their efforts to understand the principles of classicism leading in another direction. Emphasis on proportion, the importance of surfaces, and simple statements of support and shelter were all factors that brought the turn to Functionalism in the 1920s.[21]

Lars Backer was one of the earliest to advocate the new style of Wright, Le Corbusier, and Mies van der Rohe, writing in 1923 that "we will shape an architecture in contact with the time we live in, natural for the materials we build with."[22] For the Ekeberg Restaurant in Oslo, 1927–1929, he used broad wall surfaces pierced by plain windows, some large expanses of glass, and wide Wrightian eaves (figure 8.17). If some vestiges of classicist detail appear on the interior, the building as a whole speaks of a change in direction.

In like manner Alvar Aalto moved to Functionalism. His tuberculosis sanatorium at Paimio, east of Turku, 1929–1933, was marked not only by the adoption of reinforced concrete as a means of aesthetic expression as well as structure but also by a significant departure from standard hospital design (figure 8.18).[23] A goodly number of hospitals had been built in the Scandinavian cities, carried out in the var-

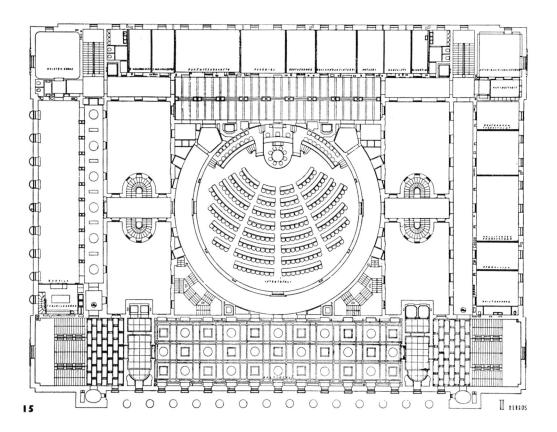

15

16

**17**

**18**

8.15 Helsinki. Parliament.
Plan. (Helsinki, Mu-
seum of Finnish
Architecture.)

8.16 Muurame. Church.
A. Aalto. 1929.

8.17 Oslo. Ekeberg Restaurant. L. Backer. 1927–
1929. (Oslo, Norwegian
Museum of Architec-
ture. Photo: Teigens.)

8.18 Paimio. Sanatorium.
A. Aalto. 1929–1933.
(Helsinki, Museum of
Finnish Architecture.)

8.19 Oslo, Blindern. University. F. Bryn and J. El-
lefsen. 1929–1935.
(Oslo, Norwegian Mu-
seum of Architecture.
Photo: Teigens.)

**19**

**20**

ious historical styles. They tended to be massive, symmetrical buildings, in some cases hardly distinguishable from school or hotel buildings, and indeed there were certain similarities of function between these building types.[24] At Paimio, the remote forested site was chosen according to then current practices in the treatment of tuberculosis. Instead of a blocky mass, Aalto built the sanatorium with long tall wings, asymmetrically placed, for patients' rooms and for social areas, connected by the administrative offices. While the exterior is severe, it is closely surrounded by the natural forest, a relationship that was to become a hallmark of Aalto's work. On the interior he also characteristically planned many details for circulation, lighting, heating, and ventilation with an ingenuity that reminds one of Thomas Jefferson.

Another institution to have a building program in the early days of Functionalism was the University of Oslo, which built a new campus at Blindern, on the edge of the city, in 1929–1935 (figure 8.19).[25] The buildings designed by Finn Bryn and Johan Ellefsen show the classicist details of the first designs giving way to more severity as the work progressed, still with symmetrical planning. The plain brick walls are pierced with rows or groups of windows that furnish all the exterior pattern except for discreet stringcourses at the basement and attic levels. If these façades are compared with those of the Haugesund Town Hall, for example, we can see that even within the decade, architects were taking bolder approaches to the use of fenestration for the total aesthetic effect.

While all these approaches to a Nordic Classicism were being undertaken, a very serious problem was being addressed in the Scandinavian countries, that of housing, especially low-cost urban housing. The Swedish government, for example, sent a delegation to the Interallied Housing and Town Planning Congress in London in 1920. The published report stated the case firmly: "there has been a real shortage of dwellings since the War—a shortage which it becomes more necessary every day to make good if the industrial productive power of Sweden is again to be restored to its full capacity."[26] State and municipal subsidies for housing were already in effect in Sweden, and in Denmark a Government Housing Fund was established in 1922.

The demand in the cities was for large blocks of flats that would be economical to build, provided with developing systems of indoor plumbing and central heating, and preferably grouped around open spaces. The long multistoried blocks by Povl Baumann and Kay Fisker depended for their aesthetic effect on the rhythms and proportions of doors and windows, but monotony was difficult to avoid.[27] Then ten years after the London congress came the Stockholm Exhibition of 1930.

Planned to display industrial art, crafts for the home, and new designs for houses and apartments, it was proposed by the Swedish Crafts Council in 1927. Gunnar Asplund was on the original committee and in 1928 became the principal architect.[28] A waterside location had been chosen on Djurgårdsbrunnviken, east of the center of the city. For the exhibit areas Asplund departed from the usual format of separate halls and created a series of wide and narrow spaces, using slender supports and generous walls of glass. Festive colors were enhanced by flags and balloons. Knowing the work of the Continental leaders of Functionalism, especially that of Le Corbusier, Asplund set forth this new international style in Scandinavia so that it could not be, and was not, ignored (figure 8.20).

In the decade before the outbreak of World War II the Scandinavian architects continued their efforts to devise better housing on

**8.20 Stockholm. Exhibition. G. Asplund. 1930. (Stockholm, City Museum.)**

a modest scale.[29] In Sweden Hakon Ahlberg developed the "lamella" block for workers in the Stockholm gas works at Hjorthagen (figure 8.21).[30] In this a long narrow building was planned so that all rooms in each unit could have direct sunlight, the blocks being only 23 feet wide. Again a certain monotony was inevitable in groups of such buildings, which Povl Baumann and Knud Hansen tried to relieve with the balconies of their Storgården in Copenhagen, 1935 (figure 8.22).[31] These balconies were also in response to fire regulations. They are indeed repetitious when seen from a distance, but on closer view many such buildings will reveal the variety of their residents' tastes in colorful awnings and flower boxes.

Meanwhile in Finland Alvar Aalto had also designed housing for the workers at the Sunila factory (figure 8.23).[32] Here the blocks are not parallel to each other, as at Hjorthagen, but are placed at slightly different angles. The site chosen is a forested hillside, with the buildings scattered here and there among the abundant trees. Aalto also broke up the south façades of most of the blocks with terraces formed by

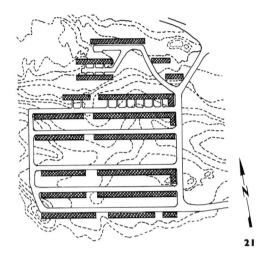

21

8.21 Stockholm, Hjort-
    hagen. "Lamella"
    houses. H. Ahlberg.
    1930s. Plan. (After
    Paulsson, *Scandinavian
    Architecture,* figure
    74, p. 223.)

8.22 Copenhagen.
    Storgården. P. Bau-
    mann and K. Hansen.
    1935.

8.23 Kotka. Sunila housing
    estate. A. Aalto.
    1936–1939.

8.24 Copenhagen, Gentofte.
    Lassen House. M. Las-
    sen. 1934. (Copen-
    hagen, Academy of Art
    Library.)

22

23

24

setting back the upper floors. This solution to multiple housing seems more personal because the blocks are comparatively small and appear more like row houses than apartment buildings.

In its report of 1920 the Swedish delegation to London acknowledged that individual industrial workers were unlikely to be able to afford their own houses. Those more affluent, however, also applied the principles of Functionalism to individual dwellings. In Denmark, Mogens Lassen had clearly been thinking about the work of Le Corbusier when he designed several villas, including his own in the Gentofte suburb of Copenhagen in 1935 (figure 8.24).[33] Built of ferro-concrete, it is whitewashed to set off the clear planes of the walls and the sharp window openings. It is four stories high, the top being a roof garden, open to the sky.

Similarly Ove Bang developed the ideas of Le Corbusier in Norway, as for example in the villa at Ullern in Oslo, built in 1937–1938 for the shipowner Ditlev-Simonsen (figure 8.25).[34] The glazed areas of the lower level are recessed in a sheltering, almost cavelike way, while the severity of the upper wall is offset by the stone wall of the terrace. Behind the principal block, seen in the illustration, extends a bedroom wing. The plan is convenient, and symmetry has been avoided.

Even more personal is Villa Mairea at Noormarkku in Finland, designed by Alvar and Aino Aalto in 1939 (figure 8.26).[35] This is one of the most famous recent examples of a collaboration between architect and client. The villa was built for Harry Gullichsen, head of the Ahlström industrial group, to which the Sunila factory belongs. Named for Mairea Gullichsen, it is the third residence on the Ahlström estate, which includes the old sawmill. Three purposes were fused into the final design: a family home, a gallery for a growing art collection, and a meeting place for cultural gatherings.

25

8.25　Oslo, Ullern. Villa Ditlev-Simonsen. O. Bang. 1937–1938. (Oslo, Norwegian Museum of Architecture. Photo: Teigens.)

8.26　Noormarkku. Villa Mairea. A. and A. Aalto. 1938–1939.

8.27　Århus, Jutland. University. K. Fisker, C. F. Møller, and P. Stegmann. 1931–1946. (Copenhagen, Academy of Art Library.)

**26**

**27**

**8.28 Oslo. City Hall. A. Arneberg and M. Poulsson. 1931–1950.**

**8.29 Oslo. City Hall. Plan. (After Kavli, *Norwegian Architecture*, p. 117.)**

Generous use of glass walls and of supporting posts on the first level creates a flow of space without and within, and a warm personal atmosphere is achieved in the use of many contrasting and complementary kinds of stone, tile, and wood. Many experimental details and refinements were included here, made possible by the wealth of the owners, but the architects expressed hope that some of these could be adopted at reasonable cost for the benefit of all homes.[36]

Principles of Functionalism were of course widely applied in major projects other than housing. In 1931 Kay Fisker, together with C. F. Møller and Povl Stegmann, won the competition for the University at Århus.[37] The irregular site was designed into a park by C. Th. Sørensen, into which the individual buildings are set without formality. Unity was sought by having the principal buildings aligned north-south, with their roofs pitched at 30 degrees (figure 8.27). Construction went on over a period of

several years until the professors' houses, student residences, and classroom buildings were completed by 1946. In this unpretentious group of buildings important accents are given by the octagonal assembly hall and the tower of the library. Altogether the university might be called an "academical park" in the spirit of Thomas Jefferson's "academical village."

At the same time the fourth great municipal/national building in Scandinavia was under construction. The City Hall in Oslo, designed by Arnestein Arneberg and Magnus Poulsson, was begun in 1931 and completed in 1950 (figure 8.28).[38] Its twin towers rise high over the waters of the Pipervik at the head of the Oslo Fjord, a commanding position like that of the Town Hall in Stockholm. The immediately surrounding area of the city was redesigned to regularize some of the streets and clear the building site. New buildings were restricted to six stories in height so that the City Hall has no nearby competition for attention. The plain red brick walls make a background for fountains and other sculptures by Norwegian artists. The patterns of windows and stringcourses emphasize the horizontality of the lower south block and the verticality of the office wings. In its external appearance the City Hall has none of the palazzo-like historical references of its counterparts in Copenhagen and Stockholm.

The organization of the interior is similar to those two buildings in the inclusion of a large Festival Hall rising in two stories in the lower portion (figure 8.29). A grand staircase leads to the second level containing the Banqueting Hall, gallery, registry rooms, and board room. The Council Chamber occupies the north wing connecting the office towers. As is the case in the other two Nordic capitals, the Oslo City Hall is richly furnished with paintings, sculptures, tapestries, and other works by the country's leading artists, making it a monument

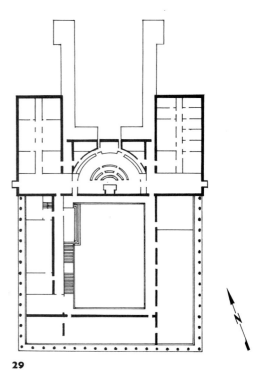

**29**

to national as well as civic artistic pride.

For an industrial building we may consider the Sunila wood pulp factory near Kotka on the Gulf of Finland (figures 8.30 and 8.31).[39] Designed by Alvar Aalto in 1936–1939 and enlarged in 1951–1954, the entire complex included the workers' housing that we have already noted. For the factory itself Aalto made use of a rocky site with a good deep harbor. From the storage pond for logs from the great system of lakes in Finland to the docks, the various sections of the factory descend the slopes. The bold masses of the brick or concrete buildings rise directly from the rocks and the native vegetation. The Sunila factory was a powerful declaration that industrial architecture need no longer depend on even the most stylized historical references, as at Svinninge, but could exhibit its own authority.

A final example from the 1930s is the design for the Copenhagen Airport at Kastrup, the competition having been won by Vilhelm Lauritzen in 1936 (figure 8.32).[40] In the first days of air travel a terminal had been built here in 1925, but the rapid development of this new means of transportation made a new facility necessary a decade later. Like the railway station, the airport presented a new challenge to architects. A long narrow building, such as Lauritzen designed, seemed then a reasonable solution, making a relatively short distance for passengers to cross between the entrance to the terminal and the aircraft, and vice versa. Whereas trains were entered by numerous doors from long platforms, aircraft were entered through single doors and could be lined up on the departure side of the terminal. Many changes in the technologies of air travel have taken place since the 1930s, and indeed Lauritzen was called upon for the remodeling of his building into the present one in the 1950s. His original building was lightly constructed, with

long clean lines, considerable flexibility in planning of the interior spaces, and ample use of glass.

With the outbreak of World War II in September 1939, much that was being hoped and planned in the Scandinavian countries came to be delayed by the many effects of the war, including invasion and occupation. The uneasy peace in 1945 did not entirely restore the status quo. The German occupation of Denmark was of course ended, but Iceland, which had been under the Danish crown since 1380, established its independence as the Iceland Republic in June 1944. The territories of Norway were not affected, but Finland lost Karelia in the southeast and also Petsamo on the Arctic coast to Russia.[41]

Much rebuilding and new building followed upon the cessation of hostilities. Several developments are especially notable in response to the new challenges. Among the architects moving away from strict Functionalism, for example, was Knut Knutsen, who built the Norwegian Embassy in Stockholm in 1952 (figure 8.33).[42] At first glance it appears to be a spacious, irregularly planned residence set into a gentle slope. It is in fact the home of the Ambassador as well as the official office building. The domestic quarters have their principal rooms looking across the bay toward the park on Djurgården, while the office wing is set farther back from the main boulevard. The open planning and provision for large gatherings of people recall the Villa Mairea with its special purposes, while the studied proportions of the windows, heavily framed in wood, and the pronounced cornices recall the Prairie Style in American building. Knutsen himself, following some of the principles of Frank Lloyd Wright and Alvar Aalto, wrote of closeness to nature in materials and of spaces organized so that buildings might be harmonious and with a humanistic content.[43]

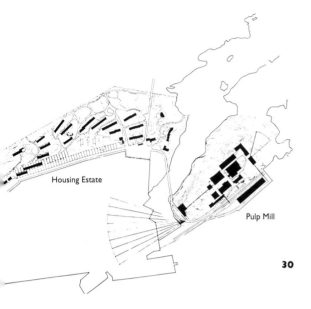

Housing Estate

Pulp Mill

30

8.30　Kotka. Sunila Cellulose
　　　Factory. A. Aalto. Be-
　　　gun 1936. Site plan.
　　　(Helsinki, Museum of
　　　Finnish Architecture.)

8.31　Kotka. Sunila Cellulose
　　　Factory.

**31**

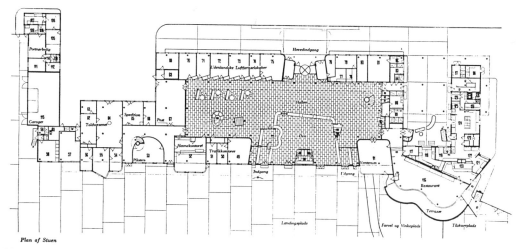

Plan af Stuen

**32**

**33**

Similarly the Danish architect Jørn Utzon sought a closer relation of his buildings to the natural environment than had characterized Functionalism. A particularly notable project was the Kingohusene housing estate near Helsingør, developed in 1957–1960. Economically built houses of yellow brick are here grouped around irregular courtyards on a hilly site so that wide glass areas look out onto a landscape view.[44]

An even more decisive effort to deal with forces of the environment was made by the English-born Ralph Erskine in Sweden. In the 1960s he experimented with designs for housing in the subarctic conditions of northern Sweden. His recommendation for "town plans which allow considerable south exposure of buildings and windows to encourage positive solar gain" reminds us of the characteristic south porch of the medieval Swedish church, placed on the warmest and most sheltered side. Erskine also noted that "while buildings have to be heated in the cold they have to be cooled in the heat," saying that certain techniques could be used in both extremes of climate.[45]

The search for a humane approach extended to several of the multiple-dwelling projects in postwar Scandinavia. An early example in Denmark is the Bellahøj community in Copenhagen, for which a competition was won by Mogens Irming and Tage Nielsen in 1945 (figure 8.34).[46] The apartment blocks, begun in 1950 and designed by several different architects, were built as much smaller units than the lamella blocks and placed for the maximum use of sunlight. The whole community includes two groups of these "point houses," as they are called, separated by a park containing an open air theater and a restaurant. A lake at the south end is balanced by the community center on the north, where the church, school, library, and theater are grouped together, reflecting

8.32  **Copenhagen. Kastrup Airport. V. Lauritzen. 1937–1939. Plan. (Copenhagen, Academy of Art Library.)**

8.33  **Stockholm. Norwegian Embassy. K. Knutsen. 1952.**

**8.34 Copenhagen, Bellahøj. Housing estate. M. Irming and T. Nielsen. 1945–1956. Site plan. (Copenhagen, Academy of Art Library.)**

**8.35 Helsinki, Tapiola. Apartment blocks. V. Revell. 1958. (Helsinki, Museum of Finnish Architecture. Photo: H. Havas.)**

the emphasis on communal life that was intended. Ample space between the housing blocks and considerable planting help to create a parklike setting, and the whole project was designed with families with small children in mind.

Bellahøj is a residential suburb of Copenhagen. In Finland in 1952 several housing and welfare organizations founded the Housing Foundation, a building society for a new satellite town as a western suburb of Helsinki. The result was Tapiola, already planned in part, for which Aarne Ervi won the competition for further planning.[47] The purpose was to create a nonprofit community with an administrative, shopping, and cultural center (also designed by Ervi), and groups of housing of different types: single residences, terrace houses, and flats (figure 8.35). Three groups were planned, separated by natural forested areas, each to have its own school and shopping facilities. What makes the Tapiola project different from many others is the grouping of the buildings in a community deliberately planned to house people of widely varying occupations and incomes.

By the time these communities were being built, the "garden city" idea as such was already

*Bellahøjvej*

**34**

**35**

half a century old. In 1898 Ebenezer Howard published *Tomorrow: A Peaceful Path to Real Reform,* reissued in 1902, slightly revised, as *Garden Cities of Tomorrow.*[48] Controversial and slow to exert wide influence, Howard's fundamental concept was that of a town surrounded by agricultural land and having its homes and simple gardens supported by its own local industries. This is of course different from the "garden suburbs" just described. Planning for better urban housing was also of concern in Sweden, as we have seen, and Lewis Mumford's *Culture of Cities* aroused enough interest to warrant a Swedish edition in 1942.[49] An attempt in 1955 at such a subcommunity is at Vällingby outside Stockholm, designed by Sven Backström and Leif Reinius (figure 8.36).[50] Here business and industries were included with the residential quarters and community facilities. As it has

turned out, most of the residents have come to work elsewhere, usually in the city of Stockholm, making this attempt less successful than the first "garden city" at Letchworth, England, of 1903.[51]

One of the most admired community complexes is the civic center at Säynätsalo in south central Finland, built by Alvar Aalto in 1950–1952 (figure 8.37).[52] The town, on an island in Lake Paijänne, was founded by the Enzo-Gutzeit wood products company, and Aalto won the 1949 competition for a center to house Council Chamber, town offices, library, and some staff residences. The buildings are grouped around a court, all on a sloping site. The court is raised to the second level by fill from the excavations and may be reached by a conventional stair at the southeast corner or a dramatic boarded earth set of steps at the

36

**8.36 Stockholm. Vällingby.
S. Backström and
L. Reinius. 1955. Air
view. (Stockholm, City
Museum. Photo: Oscar
Bladh.)**

**8.37 Säynätsalo. Civic Cen-
ter. A. Aalto. 1950–
1952.**

**8.38 Otaniemi. Technical
University. A. Aalto.
Begun 1949.**

**37**

**38**

**8.39 Roskilde, Zealand. Viking Ship Museum. C. T. Sørensen. 1966–1968.**

**8.40 Bergen. Bryggens Museum. O. Maurseth. 1974.**

southwest corner. At this time Aalto was building in brick, and the combination of the broad expanse of walls and the glass and wood elements of window walls and pergolas creates seemingly countless views, all closely linked to the surrounding forest. Wood and brick are boldly juxtaposed in the Council Chamber, where the great timber trusses are left exposed. The Säynätsalo center is small but monumental, as if it were the urban version of a Finnish courtyard farmstead.

We have already looked at two twentieth-century university projects, those at Århus and Blindern. A third example that has attracted much attention is the Technical University at Otaniemi, west of Helsinki. For this a competition was announced late in 1948, when Alvar Aalto was in the United States in connection

**40**

with his designs for the Baker Dormitory at MIT.[53] Since 1942 he had been involved with plans for the town of Säynätsalo, and the projects for Otaniemi and Säynätsalo were closely linked to events in Aalto's personal life. His first wife, Aino, who collaborated with him, was able during her last illness to contribute to the competition designs for Otaniemi. The first prize, awarded several months after her death early in 1949, was made in both their names. Then when Aalto turned his attention once more to Säynätsalo in 1949 he was assisted by Elissa Mäkiniemi, a young architect in his office, who became his second wife in 1952.

At Otaniemi the plans were for the main auditorium and adjacent buildings for the general departments, the Geodetic Institute, and the School of Architecture.[54] The site chosen was formerly a private estate, with broad parklands already partly landscaped. As the project was finally developed, the auditorium dominates the high area, with the classroom buildings descending in terrace fashion (figure 8.38). The auditorium, also planned for conferences, was originally intended to be wedge-shaped, but as built it is a quadrant and resembles a Greek theater outside because of the terraced windows lighting the simple but striking interior. As at Säynätsalo, the warmth of red brick prevails, except in the School of Architecture for which Aalto used a thin cladding of Carrara marble. The student dormitories, designed by other architects, are placed in a more wooded area to the east of the main complex, and the library, a long rectangular block, is in a grove of trees on the west. This leaves the wide open

41

8.41 Reykjavik. Hallgrims
Church. G. Samúelsson.
1946–1986.

8.42 Otaniemi. Chapel.
K. and H. Siren. 1954–
1957. (Photo: Jay C.
Henry.)

42

terraces between, giving a sense of breadth and expansion unusual in Aalto's work.

In addition to the universities as educational institutions, a number of museums have been built in the Scandinavian countries since World War II. Among those built for quite special purposes are the Viking Ship Museum in Roskilde and the Bryggens Museum in Bergen. Both are planned so that the visitor sees a "working" facility, in contrast to earlier museums in which collections were simply displayed on walls or in cases.

That the Roskilde Fjord had been blocked at Skuldelev had long been known, but it was not until 1957 and 1959 that the Danish National Museum underwater excavations revealed five Viking ships as the cause of the blockage. After they were salvaged, in thousands of pieces, in 1962 a closed competition was held for a museum, and the winning design was by Erik Chr. Sørensen.[55] The building was constructed from 1966 to 1968 and is a long low structure set at the edge of the water. Built of glass and concrete, it is a distinctive landmark in the lower part of the city (figure 8.39). Window walls on the north and south light the exhibition area, where the fragments of the ships are being mounted on full scale metal frames. From walkways at different levels the visitor can see the work being done and gain impressions of the size and shape of the ships. Sørensen himself spoke of his concern that the regularity and broad surfaces of the building should set them off effectively.[56]

Another special case developed in Bergen, where excavations from 1955 to 1972 revealed extensive remains of the twelfth-century town on the sloping land south of St. Mary's Church. To shelter the reconstructed remains of several buildings on the site, the Bryggens Museum was built by Oivind Maurseth in 1974 (figure 8.40).[57] Like the Viking Ship Museum it is com-posed of clear geometrical elements of walls and windows, but here of brick, and with the internal sections clearly marked by vertical projections on the exterior. The site includes an outdoor area where masonry foundations of the medieval buildings are exposed. Wood predominates for the interior, where the visitor is led by a series of ramps to the rear portion housing reconstructed wooden dwelling remains and thence to the area for the display of artifacts.

Scandinavian churches built since World War II show some striking transformations of traditional elements together with innovative designs. Perhaps the one longest in building and certainly the one making the most impact on the landscape is Hallgrimskirkja in Reykjavik (figure 8.41).[58] From the beginning in 1946 it has dominated the height of Skólavörduhaed and can be seen from nearly everywhere in the city. The tower and transepts were completed in 1974, and the church was finally consecrated in 1986. The State Architect Gudjón Samúelsson sought to evoke Iceland's glaciers and columns of basalt while providing a traditional setting for Christian worship. Curiously enough, even without the projected stained glass windows the severe interior is warmer than that of Grundtvig's Church in Copenhagen. The church is named for the Reverend Hallgrim Pétursson, the seventeenth-century religious poet. If we reflect on the other churches honoring national leaders, Engelbrekt in Stockholm, Grundtvig in Copenhagen, and Mikael Agricola in Helsinki, it is only fitting that Iceland should have chosen to so honor a figure from her great literary tradition.

For an entirely different approach, at Otaniemi we find the Chapel of the Technical University set on a forested hill near the student dwelling quarters (figure 8.42).[59] Built by Kaija and Heikki Siren in 1954–1957, it is a

8.43 Randers, Jutland. St.
Clement's Church.
I. and J. Exner and K.
E. Larsen. 1963.
(Photo: T. and P.
Pedersen.)

8.44 Bodø, Sør-Hälogoland.
Church. G. Blakstad
and H. Munthe-Kaas.
1956.

8.45 Tromsdalen, Nord-Häl-
ogaland. Church. J. I.
Hovig. 1959–1966.
(Oslo, Norwegian Mu-
seum of Architecture.
Photo: Teigens.)

**44**

simple rectangular building of red brick, with a
high upper window wall on the west and the
roof sloping to a window wall on the east. Slat-
ted screens and bell tower emphasize the
woodland setting. The entire east wall of glass
means that the woods outside serve as an ever-
changing backdrop for the altar, according to
season and weather. Although expressed in a
different architectural idiom, the setting, the
small size, the simplicity of its means, and the
sense it gives of personal quiet all give this little building much in common with Asplund's
Woodland Chapel.

Another use of a glazed east wall was
made at St. Clement's Church in Randers on
Jutland in 1963 (figure 8.43).[60] This is built dramatically on a hillside, the main auditorium en-

**45**

tered from the higher ground. The parish
rooms are in the level below, and the tall windows of the east wall serve both levels. Again a
view over a park landscape forms a backdrop
to the altar. The three architects Inger Exner,
Johannes Exner, and Knud Erik Larsen chose a
wedge-shaped plan so that the interior of the
church widens out to the altar. Most of the liturgical furnishings were designed especially for
this place. The organ is by the Danish builder
Frobenius, built by deal, as are the other
wooden furnishings. The altar is of Norwegian
marble, and like the organ case is composed of
straight lines and flat surfaces, far removed
from the Baroque and Rococo furnishings of
earlier churches. The Romanesque baptismal
font is mounted on a plain stainless steel base.

Certain parts of Scandinavia suffered more
damage than others during World War II.
Among them were the Norwegian port towns
that were attacked by German bombers while
they were centers for Allied shipping. Bodø in
Sør-Hälogoland, above the Arctic Circle, thus
lost its church on May 27, 1940. The present
one was finally begun in 1956, designed by Gudolf Blakstad and Herman Munthe-Kaas (figure
8.44).[61] More than thirty years after designing
the Haugesund Town Hall, they again used familiar patterns, but this time in the overall conception of the building rather than in surface
detail. The church on the exterior appears to
be a five-aisled basilica, together with the traditional separate belfry, carried out with modern
materials in almost stark simplicity. The interior,
with a high barrel-vaulted ceiling and no internal posts, is similarly uncluttered.

Another Norwegian church drawing on
tradition in a different way was built by Inge
Hovig at Tromsdalen in Nord-Hälogaland in
1959–1966 (figure 8.45).[62] This building is triangular in cross section, with a cross rising to the
peak of the west gable. The nave roof de-

8.46 Tampere. Kaleva
Church. R. Paatelainen
and R. Pietilä. 1964–
1966.

8.47 Copenhagen. SAS-
Royal Hotel. A. Jacob-
sen. 1959–1960.

creases in height in several stages, and then the apse rises behind it. The spaces between the slanting roof-wall panels are glazed. The two steep masses of nave and apse remind one of the steep shapes of the stave churches, here reduced to a very simple statement, like a piece of architectural sculpture. Stairs in the west gable lead up to a gallery and down to a lower level for the parish rooms. In spite of acoustical difficulties coming from its length and height, the church has attracted much attention. It is also called the Ishavkatedral, or the cathedral of the icy sea, appropriate to its northern location.[63]

Another sculptural shape is the Kaleva Church in Tampere, built by Reima Pietilä and Raili Paatelainen in 1964–1966 (figure 8.46).[64] Its white tiled walls rise boldly from the ground, with dramatic contrasts in sunlight and artificial light at night. The plan, basically an irregular pentagon like that of St. Clement's Church in Randers, is said to represent a fish, an important Christian symbol. The interior has the same soaring quality, lighted by tall narrow windows on the sides. Unlike St. Clement's the church does not terminate in a large window wall, but rather has a single tall narrow window, filled with a sculpture by Pietilä called *The Shattered Cane*. The interior fittings, including the organ case, are of Finnish pine, left in its natural color.

The number of distinctive commercial and industrial buildings constructed since 1945 is equally formidable. The few examples to be introduced here have been chosen for the contrasts they offer to earlier buildings with similar purposes. One very great contrast is that between the romantic wooden hotel in a small community, such as the Dalen Hotel in Telemark of 1894, and the concrete and glass city skyscraper such as the SAS-Royal Hotel in Copenhagen. Designed by Arne Jacobsen and built

**47**

**48**

in 1959–1960, the latter is a major landmark (figure 8.47).[65] It consists of two parts, a long horizontal two-story building, faced with gray-green enameled steel plates, and an eighteen-story hotel tower with gray-green glass and aluminum panels. What might seem too severe is modified by the play of reflections from adjacent buildings and the sky. The lower section, which was built first, was designed to house the downtown SAS terminal as well as the hotel lobby and a series of shops surrounding it at the street level. Within the lobby the black marble walls set off the spiral staircase to the restaurant, while light and the relief of plants were given by a conservatory. The latter was of course in the best tradition of the grand hotels. The long series of windows gives the guest rooms panoramic views over the city. Throughout, the carpets, furniture, curtains, and accessories were also designed by Jacobsen, continuing a distinguished tradition of work by

Scandinavian architects in the decorative arts. Vilhelm Dahlerup, J. H. Nebelong, G. F. Hetsch, P. V. Jensen-Klint, Kay Fisker, Alvar Aalto, and others have made notable contributions in furniture, glass, metalwork, ceramics, and textiles, from the historically inspired objects of the nineteenth century to the "Scandinavian Modern" of wares popular all over the world today.[66]

By the same architect we have another major business building in Copenhagen, the Danish National Bank, for which Jacobsen won the competition in 1961 (figure 8.48).[67] It was begun in 1965 and finished after his death by his associates Hans Dissing and Otto Weitling in 1978. Six stories high, with two basement levels, its exterior rises in long marble slabs behind a high wall that surrounds the whole site. There is only one entrance, an unpretentious one on Havnegade. Two major surprises await the person entering for the first time, however.

A huge vestibule rises with tall windows on the street side, an open stair partly filling the wall opposite the door; and a high blank wall stands on the interior side, through which there is a passage to the banking offices. From this almost grim introduction one passes to the center of the bank, which is built around a patio filled with planting.

The vestibule was intended to have its decorative scheme restricted to the architectural elements. By 1977, however, it was apparent that as built the hall seemed too cold and severe. The Danish weaver Kim Naver designed five red and gold tapestries for the deep niches of the first level, having the sections of gold increasing toward the stair wall to heighten the effect of opening light and perspective.[68]

Finally, three recent designs for factories involve products for which we have noted earlier facilities. The first is the rope yard at Lesjöfors in Sweden, built by Lennart Bergström in 1960 (figure 8.49).[69] For a seafaring nation rope is still as essential as it was in the heyday of Luostarinmäki at Turku. Bergström designed the necessary long building like a tent, with five

**8.48** Copenhagen. Danish National Bank. A. Jacobsen. 1964–1978.

**8.49** Lesjöfors, Värmland. Rope yard. L. Bergström. 1960. (Photo: Lennart Olsson/TTO.)

8.50    Copenhagen. Carlsberg
        Bottling Works. S. E.
        Kristensen. 1967–
        1969. (Photo: S. E.
        Kristensen.)
8.51    Holme-Olstrup, Zea-
        land. Holmegård Glass-
        works. S. E.
        Kristensen. 1971–
        1972.

major bays marked by posts supporting the
roof and with eleven glazed peaks as skylights.
The building stretches across the landscape in a
dramatic manner.

Then it became necessary to build an extension of the bottling plant at the Carlsberg
brewery, carried out by Svenn Eske Kristensen
in 1967–1969 (figure 8.50).[70] The site to be
used posed a special dilemma: it sits next to
the garden of the J. C. Jacobsen house, now
used as a "mansion of honor" for distinguished
scholars. To avoid placing windows overlooking
the garden and also to avoid monotony, Kristensen designed the side facing the garden with
four curving terraces, each with a walkway outside the windows and outer brick walls to
shield the view toward the garden. Planting
was included to enhance the views of the terraces from the working areas.

Having provided the Carlsberg breweries
with a new bottling works, Kristensen turned
his attention to a factory to supply the bottles.
For the Holmegård glassworks an addition was
needed, and Kristensen's designs resulted in the
new buildings of 1971–1972 (figure 8.51).[71]
Steel frames and outer cladding made for wide
interior spaces, flexibility in planning, and dramatic exterior shapes. The contrasts of shapes
and surfaces on the exterior is matched by the
contrasts of sound within. (Like many Scandinavian manufacturing plants, the Holmegård
works is open to visitors.) The characteristic
crash tinkle of rejected pieces in the art glass
area is mild compared to the thunderous racket
of beverage bottles descending through the
processing racks of the commercial area.

Perhaps it may seem surprising that a history of architecture in the Scandinavian countries should conclude with a factory. Let us
remember, however, that building in the
Nordic countries began, as at Ulkestrup, with
the most elementary shelters for human activ-

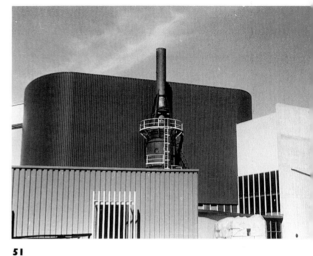

51

ity. Fragments of tools and weapons, made of
less perishable materials than was clothing, indicate the production of goods for use at the
very outset of human habitation in this region.
To the shelters for meeting individual physical
needs were added shelters for individual and
communal social and spiritual needs, and these
fundamental human requirements have not
changed over 10,000 years.

According to many factors, builders in the
Scandinavian countries have found numerous
ways in which to meet these needs. Some have
been indigenous, some imitative, and some innovative. Asko Salokorpi has pointed out the
difficulty in defining what is "Finnish" about architecture in twentieth-century Finland.[72] This
review of building in the Nordic countries since
prehistoric times should indicate that "Scandinavian architecture" as a whole is difficult to de-
fine if one is seeking a common stylistic
approach. We do better, I think, to use "Scandinavian architecture" as a regional designation
and then enjoy and learn from the great
breadth of building activity that it represents.

# Note on Alphabetizing

In the appendix, bibliography, and index, the extra letters in Danish, Norwegian, and Swedish are treated alphabetically as if spelled out: *å* as *aa*, *ä* as *ae*, and *ø* and *ö* as *oe*. These letters normally appear at the end of the alphabet in Scandinavian dictionaries, encyclopedias, bibliographies, and the like. English-speaking readers should bear this in mind when consulting sources in the Scandinavian languages. Conversely, readers in the Nordic countries will find names of persons and places listed here as indicated above, instead of in the arrangement more familiar to them.

# Appendix: Architects and Builders

This list covers architects and builders of the Scandinavian buildings included in the text, with their dates if known. Citations are to dictionary and encyclopedia articles and principal monographs that treat their work. Dictionaries and encyclopedias are abbreviated as follows:

**MEA** Adolf K. Placzek, ed., *Macmillan Encyclopedia of Architects*, 4 vols. (New York: The Free Press, 1982)

**NK** Leif Østby, et al., eds., *Norsk kunstnere leksikon*, 3 vols. (Oslo: Universitetsforlaget, 1982–1987)

**SK** Gösta Lilja, Bror Olsson, and S. Artur Svensson, eds., *Svenskt konstnärs lexikon*, 5 vols. (Malmö: Allhems Förlag, 1952–1967)

**TB** Ulrich Thieme and Felix Becker, *Allgemeines Lexicon des bildenden Kunstler . . .*, 37 vols. (Leipzig: W. Engelmann, 1907–1950)

**TBV** Hans Vollmer, ed., *Allgemeines Lexicon der bildenden Kunstler des XX. Jahrhunderts*, 6 vols. (Leipzig: E. A. Seemann, 1953–1962)

**WK** Merete Bodelsen and Povl Engelstoft, eds., *Weilbach's konstnerlexikon*, 3 vols. (Copenhagen: Aschehoug, 1947–1952)

**WWA** James M. Richards, ed., *Who's Who in Architecture* (London: Weidenfeld and Nicolson, 1977)

Åbom, Johan Fredrik, 1817–1900

Aalto, Aino, 1894–1949

Aalto, Alvar, 1899–1976
MEA 1:1–13; TBV 1:1; WWA 131–136; Pearson 1978; Miller 1984; Schildt 1984

Adelcrantz, Carl Fredrik, 1716–1796
MEA 1:34; SK 1:24–25; TB 1:80–81; Fogelmarck 1957

Ahlberg, Hakon, 1891–1984
MEA 1:36–37; TBV 1:16

Ahrenberg, Jakob, 1847–1914
TB 1:143–144; TBV 1:18

Anderberg, Axel, 1860–1937

Arndt, J. C.

Arneberg, Arnstein, 1882–1961
NK 1:76–79; TBV 1:66

Aspaas, Sven, 1736–1816
NK 1:91–92; TB 2:184

Asplund, Erik Gunnar, 1885–1940
MEA 1:110–112; TBV 1:73; WWA 26–27; Maré 1955; Wrede 1980; Caldenby and Hultin 1986

Backer, Herman Major, 1856–1932
NK 1:125; TBV 1:90

Backer, Lars, 1892–1930
TBV 1:90

Backström, Sven, b. 1903
TBV 1:91

Bang, Ove, 1895–1942
  NK 1:147–149; Blakstad and Munthe-Kaas 1943
Bassi, Carlo Francesco, 1772–1840
  TB 3:13; WWA 30–31
Baumann, Povl, 1878–1963
  MEA 1:156; TBV 1:135; WK 1:60
Bentsen, Ivar, 1876–1943
  TBV 1:173; WK 1:82–83
Berg, Axel, 1856–1929
  WK 1:86–87
Bergström, Lennart
Berner, Finn, 1891–1947
Binck, Jakob, fl. c. 1560–1569
  SK 1:181; TB 4:36–37; WK 1:98–100
Bindesbøll, Michael Gottlieb
  MEA 1:211–212; TB 4:38; WK 1:100–102;
  Wanscher 1903; Bramsen 1959
Blakstad, Gudolf, 1893–1985
  NK 1:247–250; TBV 1:225
Blasius, Leonhard, fl. 1640–1644
  TB 4:104; WK 1:116–117
Blom, Fredrik, 1781–1851
  SK 1:107; TB 4:130
Børve, Haldor Larsen, 1857–1933
  NK 1:374–375
Bonneuil, Etienne de
  SK 1:216; TB 4:313
Borch, Martin, 1852–1937
  TB 4:338–339; WK 1:134–137
Boy, William, c. 1520–1592
  SK 1:228–229; TB 4:490–491
Brandenburger, Ernst, d. 1713
  WK 1:143
Brockam, Heinrich, fl. 1690
Bryggman, Erik, 1891–1955
  MEA 1:318; TBV 1:339; WWA 58
Bryn, Finn, 1890–1975
  NK 1:337–338; TBV 1:339
Bull, Georg Andreas, 1829–1917
  NK 1:349–351; TB 5:215
Bull, Henrik, 1864–1953
  NK 1:351–352; TB 5:215
Bussert, Morten, d. 1552
  SK 1:256; WK 1:171

Chateauneuf, Alexis de, 1799–1853
  MEA 1:410; NK 1:395–396; TB 6:425–426; Lange
  1965
Cicignon, Johan Caspar von, d. 1698
  NK 1:413–415
Clason, Isak Gustav, 1856–1930
  MEA 1:422–423; SK 1:310; TB 7:57; TBV 1:448;
  WWA 74; Edestrand and Lundberg 1968
Cöllen, Heinrich von, fl. 1512–1592
  TB 7:304
Collett, Christian Ancher, 1771–1833
  NK 1:419–420
Coucheron, Wyllem, d. 1689
  NK 1:427–428
Cronstedt, Carl Johan, 1709–1799
  SK 1:323–324; TB 8:161

Dahlberg, Erik, 1625–1703
  SK 2:16–20; TB 8:276–277
Dahlerup, Vilhelm, 1836–1907
  TB 8:278–279
Desprez, Louis Jean, 1737–1804
  SK 2:50–53; TB 9:147–149
Dieskau, Hans von, fl. 1541–1563
  WK 1:254
Dieussart, François, d. 1711
  WK 1:252
Dissing, Hans, b. 1926
Döteber, Christian Julius
  SK 2:67; TB 9:378
Donatus
  SK 2:59–60; TB 9:431
Düren, Adam von
  TB 10:60

Edelsvärd, Adolf Wilhelm, 1824–1919
  SK 2:72; TB 10:338
Ehrensvärd, Augustin, 1710–1772
  SK 2:86–88
Eigtved, Niels, 1701–1754
  MEA 2:19; TB 10:416–417; WK 1:283–285
Ellefsen, Johan, 1895–1969
  TBV 2:30
Engel, Johan Carl Ludwig, 1778–1840
  MEA 2:26–27; TB 10:529; Meissner 1937; Wick-
  berg 1970

Lange, Philip de, 1704–1766
   TB 22:329; WK 2:214–215
Langlet, Emil Victor, 1824–1898
   NK 2:708–710; SK 3:456; TB 22:346–347
Larsen, Knud Erik, b. 1929
Lassen, Mogens, 1901–1987
   WK 2:241
Lauritzen, Vilhelm, 1894–1984
   TBV 3:185–186; WK 2:245–246
La Vallée, Jean de, 1620–1696
   TB 22:471–472; WWA 84
La Vallée, Simon de, d. 1642
Lewerentz, Sigurd, 1885–1975
   MEA 2:698–699; SK 3:503; TBV 2:223; WWA
   184–187; Ahlin 1987
Liljeqvist, Johan Fredrik, 1863–1932
   SK 3:515; TBV 3:231
Lindgren, Armas, 1874–1929
   MEA 3:12; TB 23:245; TBV 3:236; Nikula 1988
Linstow, Hans Ditlev F., 1787–1851
   NK 2:774–780; TB 23:158

Malling, Peder, 1781–1865
   TB 23:597; WK 2:332–333
Markelius, Sven Gottfrid, 1889–1972
   MEA 3:107–108; SK 4:85; TBV 3:327; WWA 201
Mathiesen, Albertus, d. 1668
   TB 24:264
Maurseth, Oivind, b. 1928
   NK 2:804–805
Meldahl, Ferdinand, 1827–1908
   TB 24:357; WK 2:365–367; Stemann 1926
Møller, Carl Oscar, 1857–1933
   SK 4:163; TB 25:8
Møller, Christian Friedrich, 1898–1988
   SK 4:163; TB 25:8
Møller, Erik, b. 1909
   TBV 3:405; WK 2:419–420
Munthe, Holm, 1848–1898
   NK 2:1017–1019
Munthe-Kaas, Herman, 1890–1977
   NK 2:1022–1023; TBV 3:449

Nebelong, Johan Henrik, 1817–1871
   MEA 3:272; NK 3:21–24; TB 25:371; WK 2:438–
   439

Nielsen, Tage, b. 1914
   WK 2:467
Norden, Jacob Wilhelm, 1824–1892
   NK 2:266
Nyrop, Martin, 1849–1921
   MEA 3:309–310; TB 25:545; WK 2:483–486;
   WWA 235; Beckett 1919
Nyström, Per Axel, 1793–1868
   SK 4:290–291; TB 25:546
Nyström, Usko, 1861–1923
   TB 25:546

Östberg, Ragnar, 1866–1945
   MEA 4:329–330; SK 5:812–813; TB 25:573–574;
   TBV 3:508; WWA 238–239
Opbergen, Antonius van, 1543–1611
   TB 25:547; WK 2:507–508

Paatelainen, Raili, b. 1926
Paeschen, Hans von, fl. 1561–1582
   TB 26:112; WK 2:520–521
Pahr, Domenicus
   SK 4:348; WWA 242
Pahr, Franciscus
   SK 4:348; WWA 242
Palmstedt, Erik, 1741–1803
   SK 4:363; TB 26:186; WWA 247; Setterwall 1945
Petersen, Carl, 1874–1923
   MEA 3:407; TB 26:482
Petersen, Ove, 1830–1892
   TB 26:485; WK 2:565–566
Pietilä, Reima, b. 1923
Piper, Fredrik Magnus, 1746–1824
   MEA 3:420; SK 4:430; TB 27:77
Poulsson, Magnus, 1881–1958
   NK 3:231–239; TBV 3:618

Rafn, Aage, 1890–1953
   TB 27:565; TBV 4:12; WK 3:11–12
Rawert, Jørgen Henrik, 1751–1823
   NK 2:228; TB 28:55–56; WK 3:29–30
Rehn, Jean Eric, 1717–1793
   TB 28:95–96; Wahlberg 1983
Reinius, Leif, b. 1907
   TBV 4:42

# Notes

## 1 Prehistoric Scandinavia

1. The brief historical summaries given in this chapter are based on a vast literature of prehistoric studies. For general discussions of European prehistory the following may be consulted: Renfrew, *Before Civilization;* Clark, *World Prehistory;* and Phillips, *Prehistory of Europe.* The detailed accounts of archaeological investigations in Scandinavia are generally to be found in reports and journals in the Scandinavian languages. Useful introductory summaries in English, with bibliography, may be found in Stenberger, *Sweden;* Hagen, *Norway;* Kivikoski, *Finland;* and Klindt-Jensen, *Denmark before the Vikings.*

As for the dates in this chapter on prehistoric architecture, the traditional "BC" has been adopted, the dates themselves being those used by the National Museum in Copenhagen. This is admittedly an arbitrary choice, but it has been taken in order to spare the reader the complexities of what is in fact an enormous controversy. Consulting Renfrew, Clark, and Phillips on the subject of carbon-14 dating alone will reveal the extent of the problem. For a discussion of the Danish chronology see Tauber, "Radiocarbon Chronology," which predates the recalibration discussions of the later 1970s. A more recent summary of the whole matter is to be found in Ottaway, *Archaeology, Dendrochronology and the Radiocarbon Calibration Curve.*

Finally, since archaeological sites are perhaps not as easy for the would-be visitor to find as extant buildings in town or countryside, the reader is referred to two guidebooks for Denmark. Munksgaard, *Denmark: An Archeological Guide,* is in English. Thorvildsen and Kehler, *Med Arkaeologen Danmark rundt,* is in Danish. Both are supplied with maps and organized and indexed so as to be easy to use.

2. Becker, "Late Paleolithic Finds."

3. Becker, "En 8000-Årig stenalder boplads," and Clark, *Earlier Stone Age Settlements,* pp. 102–105.

4. See Skaarup, *Stengade;* Brogaard, Lund, and Nørregård-Nielsen, *Danmarks Arkitektur. Landbrugets huse,* p. 16; Iwar Anderson, "Contribution"; and Drury, ed., *Structural Reconstruction,* pp. 1–5.

5. Winther, *Troldbjerg,* and Klindt-Jensen, *Denmark,* pp. 45–46.

6. Stenberger, *Sweden,* pp. 40–42. For fuller accounts see Florin, "Bauernhöfe und Fischerdörfer," and Florin, *Vråkulturen.*

7. Hagen, *Norway,* p. 60, and Reimers and Anker, "Trearkitektur," pp. 357–359.

8. Gjessing, *Circumpolar Stone Age,* pp. 46–54, and Hagen, *Norway,* pp. 370–371.

9. Ibid., pp. 73–74 and figure 22.

10. Kivikoski, *Finland*, pp. 36–37. For discussion of the later pyramidal tents of the Lapps, see Manker, *Lapsk kultur*, pp. 106–119, and Erixon, *Svensk byggnads kultur*, pp. 36–47.

11. The earlier view is set forth in Glob, "Barkaer," and Glob, *Danish Prehistoric Monuments*, pp. 72–75. The view that Barkaer is more probably a burial site is given in Madsen, "Earthen Long Barrows," pp. 3–6.

12. Stenberger, *Sweden*, pp. 42–44, and Glob, *Danish Prehistoric Monuments*, pp. 53–75.

13. Ibid., p. 65.

14. Elton, *Saxo Grammaticus*, pp. 13–14.

15. Stenberger, *Sweden*, pp. 45–47, and Glob, *Danish Prehistoric Monuments*, pp. 77–100.

16. Becker, "Grav eller temple?," and Glob, *Danish Prehistoric Monuments*, pp. 95–96.

17. Becker, "Hal og hus," and Lomborg, "Vadgård."

18. Glob, *Mound People*, pp. 127–131, and Larsen, "Gravhøje."

19. Stenberger, *Sweden*, pp. 107–109.

20. Becker, "To landsbyer," and Glob, *Danish Prehistoric Monuments*, pp. 240–242.

21. Stenberger and Klindt-Jensen, eds., *Vallhager*, 2:140–154, 997–998, and 1033–1064; and Stenberger, *Sweden*, pp. 140–143.

22. Todd, *Northern Barbarians*, pp. 95–112.

23. Myhre, "Gårdsanlegget på Ullandhaug"; Reimers and Anker, "Trearkitektur," pp. 358–361; Myhre, "Development of the Farm House"; and Myhre, "Views on the Building Techniques."

24. Glob, *Danish Prehistoric Monuments*, pp. 236–241.

25. Stenberger, *Sweden*, p. 138, and Cohen, *Viking Fortresses*, pp. 59–60.

26. Hagen, *Studier i jernalderens gårdssamfunn*, pp. 136–139, and Hagen, *Norway*, pp. 138–139.

27. Clark, *World Prehistory*, figure 68, p. 140; and Meist and Paasche, *Hannoverisches Wendland*, pp. 32–35.

28. Because so much has been written about Viking ships, settlements, and art, only a few general works are noted here. Among those readily available in English with good bibliographies are Jones, *History of the Vikings*; Foote and Wilson, *The Viking Achievement*; Magnus Magnusson, *Vikings!*; Randsborg, *Viking Age in Denmark*; Wilson, *The Vikings and Their Origins*; Sawyer, *Kings and Vikings*; and Logan, *The Vikings in History*. A detailed discussion of Viking art may be found in Wilson and Klindt-Jensen, *Viking Art*, while numerous good color photographs of Viking artifacts are included in Graham-Campbell and Kidd, *The Vikings*, and Magnus Magnusson, *Viking: Hammer of the North*. Two earlier works that may also be consulted are Brøndsted, *The Vikings*, and Arbman, *The Vikings*. More recent are the publications of two series of lectures and symposia, *Vikings in the West*, edited by Eleanor Guralnick, 1982, and *The Vikings*, edited by R. T. Farrell, 1982. Included in the latter is "Norsemen in America: A Select Bibliography 1950–1980," compiled by Louis A. Pitschmann.

29. Hamilton, *Excavations at Jarlshof*, pp. 102–111; Small, "The Norse Building Tradition in Shetland," pp. 248–150; and Crawford, *Scandinavian Scotland*, pp. 140–141.

30. Sverri Dahl, *Fornar toftir i Kvívík*; Sverri Dahl, "Survey of Archaeological Investigations"; Jones, *History of the Vikings*, pp. 269–272; Sverri Dahl, "Norse Settlement," pp. 66–71; Thorsteinsson, "Development of Faroese Settlements"; and Logan, *The Vikings in History*, pp. 58–61.

31. Roussell, "Stöng"; Roussell, "Det nordiske hus i vikingetid"; Eldjárn, "Viking Archaeology in Iceland"; Foote and Wilson, *The Viking Achievement*, pp. 149–158; Ingólfsson, "Saga-Age Farmhouse"; and Logan, *The Vikings in History*, pp. 61–70. See also Thór Magnússon, "Viking Age Settlement of Iceland." For the

dating of Stöng, a technique was used that perhaps does not often come to mind: tephrochronology, or dating by means of layers of airborne volcanic materials. See Eldjárn, "Two Medieval Farm Sites."

32. Nørlund, *Viking Settlers*; Roussell, *Farms and Churches*; Jones, *Norse Atlantic Saga*, pp. 50–54; Krogh, *Viking Greenland*, pp. 52–69; Albrethson, "Development of the Norse Farm"; and Logan, *The Vikings in History*, pp. 71–80.

33. An early description of this discovery is in Helge Ingstad, *Westward to Vinland*. The official excavation report is in Anne Stine Ingstad, *Discovery of a Norse Settlement*. For other commentary see Magnus Magnusson, *Viking Expansion Westward*, pp. 125–148, and Wahlgren, *Vikings and America*, pp. 122–125.

34. Magnus Magnusson, *Vikings!*, p. 244.

35. Ramskou, *Lindholm Høje*, and Foote and Wilson, *Viking Achievement*, pp. 150–152.

36. West, "Anglo-Saxon Village of West Stow," and Anne Stine Ingstad, *Discovery of a Norse Settlement*, pp. 185–192, 210–215.

37. Foote and Wilson, *Viking Achievement*, pp. 191–231; Randsborg, *Viking Age in Denmark*, pp. 71–96; Skovgaard-Petersen, "The Historical Context"; and Blindheim, "Emergence of Urban Communities."

38. Ramskou, *Hedeby*; Foote and Wilson, *Viking Achievement*, pp. 210–213; Magnus Magnusson, *Vikings!*, pp. 67–71; and Randsborg, *Viking Age in Denmark*, pp. 85–90. A recent report on the extensive excavations undertaken at Hedeby is Schietzel, *Stand der siedlungsarchäologischen Forschungen in Haithabu*.

39. James and Jameson, eds., *Journal of Jasper Danckaerts*, p. 63.

40. Benson, ed., *Peter Kalm's Travels*, 1:272.

41. Foote and Wilson, *Viking Achievement*, pp. 220–229.

42. De Paor, "Viking Towns of Ireland," and Murray, *Viking and Early Medieval Buildings*, pp. 1–2.

43. Harbison, *Archaeology of Ireland*, pp. 76–89, and Murray, "Houses and Other Structures." For an account of the controversy over the portion of the excavations known as the Wood Quay Site, see Bradley, ed., *Viking Dublin Exposed*.

44. Hall, *Excavations at York*.

45. Ibid., pp. 67–76.

46. The examples at West Stow have already been mentioned. See also Davison, "The Late Saxon Town of Thetford," pp. 191–192.

47. Tienhoven, "Information."

48. A large body of literature on the Viking camps has developed since the beginning of excavations at Trelleborg under Poul Nørlund in 1934. His own publication of the site, *Trelleborg*, and Cohen, *Viking Fortresses*, are major works in English. A discussion not only of Fyrkat but of all four of the camps, their relation to each other, and the many theories and speculations about them is given, along with extensive bibliography, in Olsen, Schmidt, and Roesdahl, *Fyrkat*, including English summaries, 1:205–241 and 2:185–207. The Roman foot, or more precisely a "reduced" Roman foot, has been assumed to be the basic unit of measurement for these camps. It has recently been suggested that this unit was instead the "Northern rod" (Huggins, Rodwell, and Rodwell, "Anglo-Saxon and Scandinavian Building Measurements," pp. 38–52).

49. Roesdahl, "Aggersborg," p. 119.

50. Schmidt, "Trelleborg House Reconsidered."

51. Roesdahl, "Aggersborg," pp. 118–119.

52. Harvey, *Medieval Architect*, pp. 19–21.

53. Vitruvius, *Ten Books*, pp. 22–27, and Vegetius, *Military Institutions*, pp. 82–85.

## 2 The Middle Ages

1. Derry, *History of Scandinavia*, pp. 36–63.

2. Ekhoff, *Svenska stavkyrkor*, pp. 148–179, and Lagerlöf and Stolt, *Hemse kyrkor*, pp. 181–191. The latter is one of the volumes in the inventory series called *Sveriges Kyrkor,* a province by province official survey of the churches of Sweden, including their structural history (and that of their predecessors), their liturgical furnishings (even if now in museums or other locations), and their paintings and sculptures. Begun in 1912, the individual parts of the volumes are being issued irregularly and are being written by authorities in the various fields of Swedish church art and architecture. In some cases there are English, French, or German summaries, and in some cases there are also figure captions in English. References to other parts in this series will be indicated by *SK*.

3. Anders Bugge, *Norwegian Stave Churches*, pp. 15–18, and Gunnar Bugge, *Stave Churches in Norway*, pp. 20–21.

4. Ekhoff, *Svenska stavkyrkor*, pp. 79–128, and also pp. 66–70 for fragments of similar eleventh-century planks at St. Andrew's Church, Greensted, Essex.

5. For notes on early Danish wooden churches see Elna Møller and Olaf Olsen, "Danske traekirker"; Krins, *Frühen Steinkirchen Dänemarks*, pp. 126–134; and Hugo Johannsen and Claus M. Smidt, *Danmarks Arkitektur. Kirkens huse*, pp. 10–13. The early wooden churches in Sweden are discussed in Ekhoff, *Svenska stavkyrkor*; Lundberg, *Byggnadskonsten i Sverige*, pp. 169–172; Andreas Lindblom, *Sveriges konsthistoria*, 1:45–52; and Ullén, *Medeltida träkyrkor I (SK)*, pp. 225–229.

6. A recent account of the stave churches with an extensive bibliographical note is Håkon Christie, "Stavkirkene-Arkitektur." For discussions of the stave churches in English see Anders Bugge, *Norwegian Stave Churches;* Kavli, *Norwegian Architecture*, pp. 15–22; Dan Lindblom, *Stave Churches in Norway;* Anker and Aron Andersson, *Art of Scandinavia,* 1:200–447; and Gunnar Bugge, *Stave Churches in Norway.*

7. Dietrichson, *Norske stavkirker,* pp. 212–226; Anker and Aron Andersson, *Art of Scandinavia,* 1:201–225; Håkon Christie, "Stavkirkene-Arkitektur," pp. 212–213, 249–250 n7; and Gunnar Bugge, *Stave Churches in Norway,* pp. 52–53.

8. Detailed analyses of this system may be found in Aune, Sack, and Selberg, "The Stave Churches of Norway," and Gunnar Bugge, *Stave Churches in Norway,* pp. 7–18.

9. Dietrichson, *Norske stavkirker,* pp. 314–326; Anker and Aron Andersson, *Art of Scandinavia,* 1:273–274; and Gunnar Bugge, *Stave Churches in Norway,* pp. 66–67.

10. Dietrichson, *Norske stavkirker,* pp. 280–287; Anker and Aron Andersson, *Art of Scandinavia,* 1:225–235; Håkon Christie, "Stavkirkene-Arkitektur," pp. 149–153; and Gunnar Bugge, *Stave Churches in Norway,* pp. 64–65.

11. Dietrichson, *Norske stavkirker,* pp. 337–345.

12. The various theories are reviewed in Olsen, *Hørg, hov og kirke;* Anker and Aron Andersson, *Art of Scandinavia,* 1:386–394; and Håkon Christie, "Stavkirkene-Arkitektur," pp. 197–219. Theories of pagan origin for the mast type of stave church are largely based on the discovery in 1926 of postholes beneath the present church at Gamla Uppsala, together with the famous description of the "nobilissimum templum" at Uppsala by Adam of Bremen in the 1070s (Jones, *History of the Vikings,* pp. 326–327). There have been attempts to reconstruct this "temple," such as that by Conant (*Carolingian and Romanesque Architecture,* pp. 35–36), based on that by Lindqvist (*Gamla Uppsala Fornminnen*). Given that the remains are scanty at best, that Adam of Bremen was writing from hearsay rather than from his own observation, and that when the "temple" was built in the mid-eleventh century Christian churches had already been built in Scandinavia, is it not possible that the Gamla Uppsala building was not a prototype but a copy?

13. Moltke and Elna Møller, *Danmarks Kirker. Københavns Amt (DK),* 3:1267–1268. This volume is in

the Danish counterpart to the inventory series *Sveriges Kyrkor* described in note 2 above, beginning 1933. When it is not otherwise apparent, reference to other volumes in this series will be indicated by *DK* following the title. For Roskilde see also Bolvig, *Bykirker*, p. 182.

14. Exner, *Landsbykirker*, pp. 83–84, and Horskjaer, ed., *Danske kirker*, 13:201–203. The latter reference should not be confused with the *Danmarks Kirker* series. It is much smaller in size, also geographically arranged, well illustrated, and includes bibliographical references.

15. A general history of the wall paintings of this period is Nørlund, *Danmarks romanske kalkmalerier*. A guide to the medieval church paintings including the Gothic is found in Saxtorph, *Jeg ser på kalkmalerier*. The National Museum in Copenhagen has announced a forthcoming series on the church paintings, *Danske kalkmalerier*, to be published in seven volumes. The paintings at Råsted were analyzed for their possible relation to religious drama by Lise Gotfredsen in *Råsted kirke—spil og billede*.

16. Exner, *Landsbykirker*, p. 116, and Horskjaer, ed., *Danske kirker*, 11:263–264. For the portal sculptures see Mackeprang, *Jydske granitportaler*, pp. 211–217.

17. Bennett, *Botkyrka kyrka (SK)*.

18. Muri, *Norsk Kyrkjer*, pp. 87–88.

19. Kristjánsson, *Churches of Iceland*, pp. 6–13.

20. Nørlund, *Viking Settlers*, p. 30.

21. Ibid., pp. 34–40.

22. Moltke and Elna Møller, *Danmarks Kirker. Københavns Amt*, 3:1285–1299.

23. Exner, *Landsbykirker*, p. 104, and Horskjaer, ed., *Danske kirker*, 2:15–20.

24. Lundberg, *Byggnadskonsten*, pp. 205–221; Cornell, *Svenska konstens historia*, 1:17–19; and Krins, *Frühen Steinkirchen* pp. 34–37.

25. Rydbeck, *Lunds domskyrkas byggnadshistoria*, pp. 15–48; Wrangel, *Lunds Domkyrkas konsthistoria*, pp. 141–201; and Hugo Johannsen and Claus M. Smidt, *Danmarks Arkitektur. Kirkens huse*, pp. 24–28.

26. Johnny Roosval, *Baltiska nordens kyrkor*, pp. 44–47.

27. Rydbeck, "Italienske inflytande"; Graebe, *Kyrkorna i Vä (SK)*, pp. 11–117; and Lundberg, *Byggnadskonsten*, pp. 231–235.

28. Horskjaer, ed., *Danske kirker*, 17:19–49; Bolvig, *Bykirker*, pp. 166–171; Villadsen, *Ribe Domkirke*; and Elna Møller, *Danmarks Kirker. Ribe Amt*, 1/2:61–84 and 3/4:145–272.

29. Lidén, *Mariakirken*, pp. 23–66; Anker and Aron Andersson, *Art of Scandinavia*, 2:158–160; Lidén and Magerøy, *Norges kirker. Bergen*, 1:9–50; and Lidén, "Middelalderens steinarkitektur," pp. 40–41.

30. Gerhard Fischer, *Domkirken i Stavanger*; Anker and Aron Andersson, *Art of Scandinavia*, 2:153; and Lidén, "Middelalderens steinarkitektur," pp. 85–88.

31. Gerhard Fischer, *Domkirken i Trondheim*, 1:43–98; Gerhard Fischer, *Nidaros Domkirke*; Lysaker, *Domkirken i Trondheim*; and Lidén, "Middelalderens steinarkitektur," pp. 69–84.

32. Krins, *Frühen Steinkirchen Dänemarks*, pp. 73–84; Horskjaer, ed., *Danske kirker*, 14:324–327.

33. Lundberg, *Byggnadskonsten*, pp. 370–371; Cornell, *Svenska konstens historia*, 1:46–49; Swartling, "Cistercian Abbey Churches"; and Anker and Aron Andersson, *Art of Scandinavia*, 2:176–178.

34. Conant, *Carolingian and Romanesque Architecture*, pp. 126–134.

35. Hermansen and Nørlund, *Danmarks Kirker. Sorø Amt*, 1:107–137; Horskjaer, ed., *Danske kirker*, 4:14–24; and Bolvig, *Bykirker*, pp. 182–189.

36. Hermansen and Nørlund, *Danmarks Kirker. Sorø Amt*, 1:17–53; Horskjaer, ed., *Danske kirker*, 4:38–49; and Bolvig, *Bykirker*, pp. 219–227.

37. Frölén, *Nordens befästa rundkyrkor;* Anker and Aron Andersson, *Art of Scandinavia,* 2:142–149; Hugo Johannsen and Claus M. Smidt, *Danmarks Arkitektur. Kirkens huse,* pp. 53–55; and Johan Lange, *Vaern og våben,* pp. 103–115.

38. Norn, Schultz, and Skov, *Danmarks Kirker. Bornholm,* pp. 383–431; Horskjaer, ed., *Danske kirker,* 19:97–101; and Exner, *Landsbykirker,* p. 120. The other three are Nylars, Nykirke, and Ols, described in Norn, Schultz, and Skov, *Danmarks Kirker. Bornholm,* pp. 199–222, 244–274, and 335–362.

39. For Bjernede see Hermansen and Nørlund, *Danmarks Kirker. Sorø Amt,* 1:351–363; Horskjaer, ed., *Danske kirker,* 4:64–69, and Exner, *Landsbykirker,* p. 25. For Thorsager see Horskjaer, ed., *Danske kirker,* 13:226–229, and Exner, *Landsbykirker,* p. 99.

40. Carl M. Smidt, *Kalundborg;* Bencard, "Om Kalundborg kirke"; Horskjaer, ed., *Danske kirker,* 2:20–28; and Bolvig, *Bykirker,* pp. 70–72.

41. A painting of Kalundborg by Johan Thomas Lundbye, 1837, now in the State Museum of Art, Copenhagen, shows the cathedral without its central tower.

42. Moltke and Elna Møller, *Danmarks Kirker. Københavns Amt,* 3:1267–1332; Horskjaer, ed., *Danske kirker,* 3:29–37; and Bolvig, *Bykirker,* pp. 182–189.

43. Lorenzen, *Danske cistercienserklosters bygningshistorie,* pp. 1–18 and 62–95; Moltke and Møller, *Danmarks Kirker. Sønderjylland,* 2:1050–1095; Horskjaer, ed., *Danske kirker,* 18:37–46; and Exner, *Landsbykirker,* pp. 67–68.

44. See Johnny Roosval, *Baltiska nordens kyrkor.*

45. Horskjaer, ed., *Danske kirker,* 7:30–42, and Bolvig, *Bykirker,* pp. 150–154.

46. Horskjaer, ed., *Danske kirker,* 14:33–53; Vibeke Michelsen and Licht, *Danmarks Kirker. Århus Amt,* 1:125–383; and Bolvig, *Bykirker,* pp. 269–273.

47. Hermansen, Roussell, and Steenberg, *Danmarks Kirker. København,* 1:9–12, and Claus M. Smidt, *Vor Frue Kirke,* pp. 9–10.

48. Hermansen, Roussell, and Steenberg, *Danmarks Kirker. København,* 1:13–30, and Claus M. Smidt, *Vor Frue Kirke,* pp. 11–15.

49. Johnny Roosval, *Baltiska nordens kyrkor,* pp. 128–130.

50. Rinne, *Åbo Domkyrka,* pp. 12–26; Nils E. Wickberg, *Finnish Architecture,* pp. 24–27; Gardberg, "Åbo Domkyrka"; and Richards, *800 Years,* pp. 27–29.

51. Boëthius and Romdahl, *Uppsala Domkyrka;* Lundberg, *Byggnadskonsten,* 1:486–497; Andreas Lindblom, *Sveriges konsthistoria,* 1:173–179; and Cornell, *Svenska konstens historia,* 1:115–117.

52. Ibid., pp. 115–116; English translation in Bumpus, *Cathedrals,* p. 178.

53. Johnny Roosval, *S. Nikolai eller Storkyrkan (SK),* pp. 206–263.

54. Gunnar Svahnström, *Visby Domkyrka (SK),* pp. 113–195.

55. Gunnar Svahnström and Karin Svahnström, *Visby Domkyrka (SK),* pp. 140–148.

56. Lundmark, *Tingstäde kyrka (SK).*

57. Romdahl, *Linköpings domkyrka,* pp. 11–127, and Cnattingius et al., *Linköpings domkyrka (SK),* pp. 242–275.

58. Gerhard Fischer, *Domkirken i Trondheim,* 1:99–358.

59. Gerhard Fischer, *Domkirken i Stavanger,* pp. 49–81, and Lidén, "Middelalderens steinarkitektur," pp. 85–88.

60. Sverri Dahl, "Extracts from a Lecture on Kirkjubøur," and Jessen, "Magnus-Katedralen."

61. In this account of Scandinavian architecture no attempt is made to deal fully with the multitudinous problems of conservation. Here at Kirkjubøur out in the North Atlantic, at least, one might expect a minimum of difficulty, but this is not the case. The shell mortar is being attacked by acid rain from the Continent, causing the structure to become increasingly

unstable and raising questions about how to safe-guard and use this much-beloved building.

62. Roussell, *Farms and Churches*, pp. 119–126, and Krogh, *Viking Greenland*, pp. 93–99.

63. Berthelson, *Studier i Birgittinerordens byggnad-skick*, pp. 9–20, and Iwar Anderson, *Vadstena gård och kloster*, 1:136–148.

64. Horskjaer, ed., *Danske kirker*, 13:138–139, and Exner, *Landsbykirker*, p. 54.

65. Saxtorph, *Jeg ser på kalkmalerier*. Additional il-lustrations can be found in Broby-Johansen, *Det danske Billedbibel*, and Franceschi and Hjort, *Kalkmal-erier fra danske landsbykirker*. The first of a projected iconographical study of the Danish paintings is Ban-ning, ed., *Catalogue of Wall-Paintings*.

66. Erichs and Wilcke-Lindqvist, *Kyrkor i Närding-hundra härad (SK)*, pp. 221–267. An account of the Swedish paintings, with extensive bibliography, is in Söderberg, *Svenska kyrkomålningar*.

67. A discussion of the baldachin paintings, with bib-liography, is in Wichström, "Maleriet i høymiddel-alderen," pp. 263–270.

68. Sárkány, "Finströms kyrka." See also the general discussion in Kronqvist, "Mittelalterliche Kirchen-architektur."

69. For an extensive bibliography of the literature on medieval Scandinavian churches, 1950–1982, see "Kirkearkaeologisk litteratur i Norden."

70. The following articles that summarize these studies, with bibliography, are in Barley, ed., *European Towns*: Nyberg, "Denmark," pp. 65–81; Lidén, "Ur-ban Archaeology in Norway," pp. 83–101; and Am-brosiani and Hans Andersson, "Urban Archaeology in Sweden," pp. 123–126.

71. Lebech, *Danske købstaeder*, 1:127–128, and Hart-mann and Villadsen, *Danmarks Arkitektur. Byens huse. Byens plan*, pp. 13–15.

72. Ekhoff and Janse, *Visby stadsmur*, and Wåhlin, *Visby*, pp. 34–42.

73. Hvidt, Ellehøj, and Norn, eds., *Christiansborg*, 1:1–47, and Jørgensen, Lund, and Nørregård-Nielsen, *Danmarks Arkitektur. Magtens bolig*, pp. 17–18. See also Hahr, *Nordiska Borgar*, pp. 27–132, and Tuulse, *Burgen des Abenlands*, pp. 197–204.

74. Ramsing, *Københavns historie*, 1:7–12.

75. Martin Olsson, ed., *Stockholms Slotts historia*, 1:31–60. For the early stone walls of Stockholm's Old City see Hansson, *Stockholms stadsmurar*, pp. 86–171. The painting *Vädersolstavlan* is the earliest known view of Stockholm.

76. The earlier defenses in Norway are discussed in Gerhard Fischer, *Norske kongeborger*. For a full ac-count of King Håkon Håkonsson's building in Bergen, see Gerhard Fischer and Dorothea Fischer, *Norske Kongeborger. Bergenhus*. A summary is found in Lidén, "Middelalderens steinarkitektur," pp. 109–113.

77. King Håkon Håkonsson was a friend of King Henry III of England, whose master builder was Henry of Reynes, the architect of Westminster Ab-bey. There has been speculation that Henry of Reynes was the builder of Håkon's Hall (Simpson, *Castle of Bergen*).

78. Kronqvist, *Åbo slott*, and Gardberg, *Åbo slott*.

79. Nils E. Wickberg, *Finnish Architecture*, pp. 34–35, and Olof af Hällström, *Sveaborg*.

80. Rydbeck, *Glimmingehus*, pp. 3–30, and Kjellberg, *Skåne*, 3:61–81.

81. For a brief history of the development of Euro-pean town halls from the twelfth to the fifteenth centuries see Pevsner, *History of Building Types*, pp. 53–62.

82. Tidemand-Dal, "Gildhuset i Naestved"; Sestoft, *Danmarks Arkitektur. Arbejdets bygninger*, pp. 21–22; and Aage Andersen, *Middelalderbyen Naestved*, pp. 85–86.

### 3 The Renaissance in Scandinavia

1. Derry, *History of Scandinavia*, pp. 86–95.

2. The Netherlandish works are discussed in Hitchcock, *Netherlandish Scrolled Gables*, pp. 33–47.

3. Roussell, ed., *Danske slotte*, 1:353–370. The sixteenth-century Danish manor houses are discussed in Hahr, *Nordiska Borgar*, pp. 151–174.

4. Eriksen, *Om vaelske gavle*; Norn, *Hesselagergaard*; and Roussell, ed., *Danske slotte*, 8:7–20.

5. Ibid., 8:128–155.

6. Hahr, "Torup"; Lundberg, "Torups Slott"; Kjellberg and Svensson, eds., *Slott och herresäten, Skåne*, 1:343–365; and Söderberg, *Manor Houses*, p. 38.

7. Norn, *Christian III's borge*, 1:82–91, and Söderberg, *Riksfästen*, pp. 177–200.

8. Strömbon, *Gripsholm*, pp. 18–62; Westlund, *Gripsholm under Vasatiden*; Wollin, "Gripsholmsföreningen och restaureringen"; Malmborg, ed., *Gripsholm*; and Malmborg, *Kungliga slotten* 2:9–84.

9. Andreas Lindblom, *Vadstena*; Unnerbäck, *Vadstena slott*; and Söderberg, *Riksfästen*, pp. 286–320.

10. Martin Olsson, *Kalmar slotts historia*, and Söderberg, *Riksfästen*, pp. 79–138.

11. Martin Olsson, *Kalmar slotts kyrkor*, pp. 34–48. See also Hahr, *Architektenfamilie Pahr*, pp. 56–92.

12. Hahr, *Uppsala slott*, and Söderberg, *Riksfästen*, pp. 232–265.

13. Andreas Lindblom, *Stockholms slott*; Malmborg, *Kungliga slotten*, 1:112–132; and Martin Olsson, ed., *Stockholms slotts historia*, 1:61–86.

14. Kloster and Gerhard Fischer, *Rosencrantz Tower*, and Lexow, "Arkitektur 1536–1814," pp. 13–15.

15. Ibid., p. 65.

16. Beckett, *Frederiksborg*, pp. 1–249; Weilbach, *Frederiksborg Slot*; Roussell, ed., *Danske slotte*, 1:83–86; and Honnens de Lichtenberg, "Frederik II's Frederiksborg."

17. Wanscher, *Kronborgs historie*; Christensen, *Kronborg*; Weilbach, *Kronborg Castle*; Norn, *Kronborg*; and Roussell, ed., *Danske slotte*, 1:11–52. The earliest stages of Kronborg and possible sources for the design of its walls in the late fourteenth century are discussed in Langberg, "Castle of Elsinore." A brief discussion of the work of individual builders and sculptors under Frederik II is in Skovgaard, *King's Architecture*, pp. 17–25. For eighteenth-century views and comments see Thurah, *Danske Vitruvius*, 2:67–75 and plates 28–30. For discussion of Thurah and of his great publication see below, chapter 4.

18. Beckett, *Uraniborg*; Martin Olsson, *Uraniborg*, pp. 3–23; and Jern, *Uraniborg*. Tycho Brahe set forth his idea of the site for astronomical observations as follows: "First of all, the place should be in a high locality from where there is a free view round the whole horizon, without woods or mountains or other buildings intervening. It is also preferable that it is a solitary place, free from the commotion of the common herd, where it is possible to enjoy philosophical tranquility," in Raeder, Strömgren, and Strömgren, trans. and eds., *Tycho Brahe's Description*, p. 121.

19. Allgulin, *Hans van Steenwinckel d.ä.*, pp. 39–60.

20. Kidd, ed., *Documents*, p. 199. For the Reformed liturgies and church furnishings see Hamberg, *Tempelbygge*, pp. 149–230, and Johannsen and Claus M. Smidt, *Danmarks Ariktektur. Kirkens huse*, pp. 110–135.

21. Moltke and Elna Møller, *Danmarks Kirker. Frederiksborg Amt*, 3:2023–2118; Exner, *Landsbykirker*, pp. 90–91; and Horskjaer, ed., *Danske kirker*, 3:252–256.

22. Christian A. Jensen and Hermansen, *Danmarks Kirker. Praestø Amt*, 1:294–300.

23. Skovgaard's *King's Architecture* is the most extensive account in English of the architectural activities of Christian IV. See also Wanscher, *Christian IV's bygninger*, Stein, "Christian IV," and Heiberg, ed., *Christian IV and Europe*, pp. 462–505.

24. Hvidt, Ellehøj, and Norn, eds., *Christiansborg*, 1:170.

25. Among the major publications on Frederiksborg are Thurah, *Danske Vitruvius*, 2:3–60 and plates 4–18; Wanscher, *Christian IV's bygninger*, pp. 41–62; Steenberg, *Christian IV's Frederiksborg*; and Roussell, ed., *Danske slotte*, 1:83–110. For gardens at Frederiksborg see Hakon Lund, *Kongelige lysthaver*, pp. 108–120. For the Chapel see Moltke and Elna Møller, *Danmarks Kirker. Frederiksborg Amt*, 3:1673–1778.

26. The original fountain was seized as booty by the Swedes in 1660 and is now at Drottningholm.

27. Skovgaard, *King's Architecture*, pp. 45–51.

28. Bligaard, "Privy Passage."

29. Molesworth, *Account of Denmark*, quoted in Skovgaard, *King's Architecture*, p. 67.

30. Thurah, *Danske Vitruvius*, 1:43–54 and plates 24–34; Wanscher, *Christian IV's bygninger*, pp. 64–72, 80–84, 89–98, and 150–154; and Heiberg, ed., *Christian IV and Europe*, pp. 471–473. For the gardens at Rosenborg see Lund, *Kongelige lysthaver*, pp. 15–40.

31. Thurah, *Danske Vitruvius*, 3:68–69 and plate 41.

32. Ibid., 1:61–63 and plates 53–55; Wanscher, *Christian IV's bygninger*, pp. 114–123; and Sestoft, *Danmarks Arkitektur. Arbejdets bygninger*, pp. 28–30.

33. Christian IV's desire to encourage trade with India led him to send the merchant Ove Giedde to Ceylon, near where the Danish trading post of Tranquebar was founded in 1620. This is the source of the name for the faience pattern designed for the Royal Copenhagen Porcelain Manufactory by Christian Joachim in 1914. The Danish buildings in Tranquebar are discussed in Pedersen, "Tranquebars danske huse."

34. Lorenzen, ed., *Christian IV's Byanlaege*, pp. 73–75, and Lebech, *Nyboder*.

35. Langberg, ed., *Hvem Byggede Hvad*, 1:24–25.

36. Lorenzen, *Jens Bangs Stenhus*, pp. 12–25.

37. Cederström, *Kristianstad*; Lorenzen, ed., *Christian IV's Byanlaege*, pp. 160–173; Sandblad, *Skånsk stadsplanekonst*, pp. 283–287; and Eimer, *Stadtplanung*, pp. 154–155.

38. Lorenzen, ed., *Christian IV's Byanlaege*, pp. 83–96; Lebech, *Christianshavn*, pp. 12–24; Eimer, *Stadtplanung*, pp. 157–158; and Hartmann and Villadsen, *Danmarks Arkitektur. Byens huse. Byens plan*, pp. 22–23.

39. Lorenzen, ed., *Christian IV's Byanlaege*, pp. 254–281, and Gerhard Fischer, *Oslo under Eiksberg*, pp. 31–48.

40. Sinding-Larsen, *Akershus*, 1:51–125 and 2:9–146; Arno Berg, *Akershus slott*, 2:20–80; Stenseng, *Akershus Castle*; and Mamen, *Akershus*.

41. Moltke and Elna Møller, *Danmarks Kirker. København Amt*, 3:1504–1526.

42. Lundborg, *Heliga Trefaldighetskyrkan*, pp. 25–82, and Wanscher, *Christian IV's bygninger*, pp. 105–113.

43. The suggestion has been made that Christian IV designed the chapel at Roskilde himself, on the grounds that Lorenz van Steenwinckel would have been unlikely to put a column so awkwardly in the center of the room (Skovgaard, *King's Architecture*, p. 79). The columns of the cross aisle at Holy Trinity Church in Kristianstad interrupt this central space in the same manner, however, and in neither building was the affected area likely to be used for processions.

44. Friis, *Orgelbygning i Danmark*, pp. 37–41. No satisfactory history of the organ cases built for the Renaissance and Baroque churches in the Scandinavian countries has been written. The organ works themselves have rarely survived, the casings now generally housing rebuilds or entirely new instruments.

45. Steenberg, *Danmarks Kirker. København*, 2:3–70; Horskjaer, ed., *Danske kirker*, 1:86–90; and Bolvig, *Bykirker*, pp. 93–100.

46. Steenberg, *Danmarks Kirker. København*, 2:225–250 and 265–288; Horskjaer, ed., *Danske kirker*, 1:172–177; and Bolvig, *Bykirker*, pp. 118–121.

47. Steenberg, *Danmarks Kirker. København*, 2:251–265; Steenberg, *Rundtaarn;* Stein, "Rundetaarns gaade"; and Svendsen, *Rundtårn opklaret.*

48. Johnson, *Swedish Settlements on the Delaware.*

49. Masson, *Queen Christina,* pp. 127–132. In September of 1649 Descartes was invited to Stockholm to instruct the queen in his new philosophy. Wherever his lodgings may have been, appearances in the drafty old castle at five o'clock in the morning led to his illness and death the following February.

50. Andreas Lindblom, *Sveriges konsthistoria,* 2:360–361.

51. Sirén, *Gamla Stockholmshus,* 1:11–13, and Andreas Lindblom, *Sveriges konsthistoria,* 1:359–360 and 399.

52. Söderberg, *Närke. Västmanland,* pp. 381–403.

53. Sirén, *Gamla Stockholmshus,* 1:28–34; Silfverstolpe, "Riddarhuspalatset," pp. 85–196; Karling, "Simon de La Vallée."

54. Lexow, "Arkitektur 1536–1814," pp. 55–58.

55. Lundmark, *Sankt Jakobs Kyrka (SK),* pp. 229–310.

56. Flodin, *Tyresö kyrka (SK),* pp. 25–51.

## 4 Scandinavian Baroque and Rococo

1. Krabbe, *Kastellet,* pp. 17–109.

2. Anderson, *Karlskrona,* pp. 13–36, and Eimer, *Stadtplanung,* pp. 483–509. Count Erik Dahlberg was a military engineer whose topographical drawings are a valuable source of information about Swedish and Finnish buildings in the late seventeenth century. The drawings were engraved and published in three volumes as *Suecia antiqua et hodierna,* 1693–1714. For his interest in city planning see Eimer, *Stadtplanung,* pp. 395–409 and 510–532.

3. Fett and Schnitler, eds., *Norsk Kunsthistorie,* 1:206, and Henry Berg, *Trondheim før Cicignon,* p. 17.

4. Engqvist, *Sønderjyske byen,* pp. 84–95.

5. Josephson, *Tessin,* 2:109–118, and Eimer, *Stadtplanung,* pp. 541–562.

6. Nordenstreng, *Fredrickshamn,* pp. 19–27.

7. Silfverstolpe and Stavenow, *Drottningholm;* Malmborg, *Drottningholm;* and Malmborg, *Kungliga slotten,* 2:183–241. For the gardens see Ahlberg, *Svenska trädgaardskonsten,* 1:77–85, and Karling, *Trädgårdkonstens historia i Sverige,* pp. 408–414.

8. Thurah's illustration is similar to a painting of Sophie Amalienborg at Ledreborg, both of which are dated long after the Copenhagen palace was destroyed. Both views probably had a common source, now lost. See comments by Lund in Thurah, *Danske Vitruvius,* 3:350–351, and Linvald, *Sophie Amalienborg,* pp. 8–10. For the gardens see Lund, *Kongelige lysthaver,* pp. 41–54.

9. Weilbach, *Charlottenborg,* pp. 3–55; Roussell, ed., *Danske slotte,* 2:253–270; and Thurah, *Danske Vitruvius,* 1:54–56. For the gardens see Lund, *Kongelige lysthaver,* pp. 257–260.

10. Josephson, *Tessin i Danmark,* pp. 25–84. For a shorter account see Josephson, *Tessin,* 1:80–85.

11. Ironically it was a small theater built close to the Sophie Amalienborg in 1689 that caught fire during its second performance and caused the burning of the palace as well. The episode is described in Overskou, *Danske Skueplads,* 1:117.

12. Lindblom, *Stockholms slott,* pp. 42–68; Josephson, *Tessin,* 2:70–98; Martin Olsson, ed., *Stockholms slotts historie;* and Setterwall, *The Royal Palace, Stockholm.* A more recent study that reexamines the project in detail and includes reproductions of Tessin's drawings and an analytical catalogue is Kommer, *Nicodemus Tessin der Jüngere und das Stockholmer Schloss.* For Rehn's work on the interiors see Wahlberg, *Jean Eric Rehn,* pp. 31–61.

13. Josephson, *Tessin,* 1:49–52. In 1687 as Royal Architect Tessin visited Versailles, where Le Nôtre himself showed him the gardens. In 1705 he offered a design for the rebuilding of the Louvre, but it was

not accepted (ibid., 1:72–73 and 97–106).

14. Weilbach, *Frederiksberg slot*, pp. 28–51; Nystrøm, *Frederiksbergs historie;* Roussell, ed., *Danske slotte,* 2:281–322; and Thurah, *Danske Vitruvius,* 2:110–114. For the park and gardens see Lund, *Kongelige lysthaver,* pp. 61–107.

15. Steenberg, *Danmarks Kirker. København,* 3:341–370; Horskjaer, ed., *Danske kirker,* 1:49–51; and Bolvig, *Bykirker,* pp. 82–84.

16. Barrow, *Excursions,* p. 192.

17. Hvidt, Ellehøj, and Norn, eds., *Christiansborg,* 1:81–84.

18. Ibid., 1:98–99. For the Castle Chapel see Birgitte-Boggild Johannsen, *Danmarks Kirker. København,* 5:22–35 and 67–81.

19. Thurah, *Danske Vitruvius,* 2:62–67; Steenberg, *Fredensborg;* Helsted, *Dronning Juliane Marie og Fredensborg slot;* Roussell, ed., *Danske slotte,* 1:131–164; and Steenberg, "Fredensborg Interiorer." See also Lund, *Kongelige lysthaver,* pp. 121–205.

20. Ehbisch also designed two pulpits for the Copenhagen Palace chapel, one of which was built (Hvidt, Ellehøj, and Norn, eds., *Christiansborg,* 1:157–161, figures 176 and 177). For the Fredensborg chapel see Moltke and Elna Møller, *Danmarks Kirker. Frederiksborg Amt,* 2:797–821, and Jørgen Høj Madsen, "Fredensborg slotskirke."

21. Hopstock and Tschudi-Madsen, *Rosendal,* and Lexow, "Arkitektur 1536–1814," pp. 58–60.

22. Andrén, *Skokloster.* For the gardens see Karling, *Trädgårdskonstens historia i Sverige,* pp. 468–478.

23. Langberg, *Clausholms bygningshistorie,* and Roussell, ed., *Danske slotte,* 14:77–98.

24. The organ in the chapel was probably originally built in the sixteenth century, by an unknown builder, and rebuilt in the seventeenth century. During restoration of the instrument in 1964 the bellows were found to have been lined with fragments of music,

some of which turned out to be parts of a cycle of *Magnificat* settings by the German organist and composer Jacob Praetorius (1586–1651) (Friis, *Orgelbygning,* pp. 87–89).

25. Wrangel, *Tessinska Palatset,* pp. 5–25; Siren, "Tessinska palatset"; and Josephson, *Tessin,* 2:176–180.

26. Schiøtt, "Frederik III's Biblioteks og kunstkammerbygning."

27. Rosell and Bennett, *Kalmar Domkyrka (SK),* pp. 9–164.

28. Steenberg, *Danmarks Kirker. København,* 2:484–503; Thurah, *Danske Vitruvius,* 1:80–83; Horskjaer, ed., *Danske kirker,* 1:189–195; and Bolvig, *Bykirker,* pp. 122–125.

29. Josephson, *Tessin i Danmark,* pp. 121–135. The altar was based on Bernini's altar in SS. Domenico e Sisto in Rome, of which Tessin had made a sketch (ibid., figure 89).

30. Friis, *Orgelbygning,* pp. 84–87. During restoration in 1965 it was found that the organ was leaning away from the tower. Arnolt Schlick had warned against such dangers in his treatise on organ building of 1511 (quoted in Berry, "Arnolt Schlick's Spiegel," p. 80).

31. Steenberg, *Danmarks Kirker. København,* 3:24–67; Thurah, *Danske Vitruvius,* 1:84; Horskjaer, ed., *Danske kirker,* 1:227–231; and Bolvig, *Bykirker,* pp. 107–110.

32. For a brief discussion of Continental Protestant architecture before the seventeenth century see Donnelly, *New England Meeting Houses,* pp. 20–35.

33. Lexow, "Arkitektur 1536–1814," p. 43, and Muri, *Norske Kyrkjer,* p. 210.

34. Arno Berg, *Vor Frelsers Kirke,* and Muri, *Norske Kyrkjer,* pp. 43–44.

35. Thurah, *Danske Vitruvius,* 1:27–43 and plates 8–23, and Roussell, ed., *Danske slotte,* 2:26–40. A full account of the first Christiansborg project is given in

Hvidt, Ellehøj, and Norn, eds., *Christiansborg*, 1:181–258, with a summary in English, pp. 395–401.

36. Jørgensen, Lund, and Nørregård-Nielsen, *Danmarks Arkitektur. Magtens bolig*, pp. 56–61.

37. Langberg, *Danmarks bygningskultur*, 1:276 and figure 256, and Hvidt, Ellehøj, and Norn, eds., *Christiansborg*, 1:167–198.

38. Thurah, *Danske Vitruvius*, 1:90, and plates 48–52.

39. Ibid., 1:41–42, and plates 17–21, and Birgitte-Boggild Johannsen, *Danmarks Kirker. København*, 5:99–175. The pulpit was designed by Louis-Augustus LeClerc. For the organ by Lambert Daniel Kastens see Friis, *Orgelbygning*, pp. 128–130. See also Hvidt, Ellehøj, and Norn, eds., *Christiansborg*, 1:292–297.

40. Donnelly, "Theaters in the Courts," pp. 328–340.

41. The text of the proclamation of March 31, 1738, is translated in Marker and Marker, *Scandinavian Theatre*, p. 69: ". . . no play actors, rope dancers, conjurers, or those who run so-called games of chance shall be found in Denmark or Norway, nor shall their plays and routines anywhere be performed or exercised."

42. Thurah, *Danske Vitruvius*, 1:64–68 and plates 49–64, and Hermansen, Roussell, and Steenberg, *Danmarks Kirker. København*, 1:113–136.

43. Thurah, *Danske Vitruvius*, 1:53–54 and plates 30–34, and Roussell, ed., *Danske slotte*, 2:57–66.

44. Overskou, *Danske Skueplads*, 2:27–47.

45. Thurah, *Danske Vitruvius*, 3:64 and plate 32.

46. Ibid., 1:57–59 and plates 44 and 47; 3:45 and plate 14.

47. Ibid., 1:53–54 and plates 21–25; Roussell, ed., *Danske Slotte*, 2:141–190; Viggo Sten Møller, *Amalienborg*; and Elling, *Amalienborg Interiors*.

48. Weilbach, *Architekten Lauritz Thura*, pp. 173–185. Baptized Laurids Thurah, he adopted the later version of his name after receiving letters of nobility in 1740. Weilbach's biography remains the principal source for Thurah's life and work. For an account of the preparation and publication of *Den Danske Vitruvius* and its place in Thurah's career, see the comments by the editor of the 1967 edition, Hakon Lund, appended to each volume, in Danish, French, and German. Lund also wrote on each of the buildings, clarifying Thurah's remarks and commenting on the later histories of the buildings.

49. Meldahl and Johansen, *Kongelige akademi*, pp. 8–69; Poulsen, Lassen, and Danielsen, eds., *Dansk Kunst Historie*, 3:11–21; and Pevsner, *Academies of Art*, pp. 155–156.

50. Meldahl and Johansen, *Kongelige akademi*, pp. 69–71.

51. Thurah, *Danske Vitruvius*, 1:85–87 and plates 90–95.

52. Hvidt, Ellehøj, and Norn, eds., *Christiansborg*, 1:197.

53. Thurah, *Danske Vitruvius*, 1:91 and plate 107, and Elling, "Arkitekten Philip de Lange."

54. Christian A. Jensen and Hermansen, *Danmarks Kirker. Praestø Amt*, 2:1008–1013; Exner, *Landsbykirker*, pp. 30–31; and Horskjaer, ed., *Danske kirker*, 6:269–270.

55. Donnelly, *New England Meeting Houses*, pp. 91–108.

56. Lindblom, *Sveriges konsthistoria*, 2:613.

57. Hirn, *Sveaborg*, and Hällström, *Sveaborg*.

58. Stavenow, *Hårleman*, pp. 149–157. For later proposals for further remodeling of Svartsjö by the Swedish-born English architect Sir William Chambers, see Harris, *Sir William Chambers*, pp. 87–88 and plates 127 and 128.

59. Roussell, ed., *Danske slotte*, 1:301–326.

60. Ibid., 1:53–66, and Hartmann and Villadsen, *Dan-*

marks Arkitektur. Byens huse. Byens plan, pp. 103–105. For the Marienlyst gardens see Lund, *Kongelige lysthaver*, pp. 243–252.

61. Weilbach, *Arkitekten C. F. Harsdorff*, pp. 153–163, and Hartmann and Villadsen, *Danmarks Arkitektur. Byens huse. Byens plan*, pp. 107–109. The attentive observer will note, however, that the Ionic capitals of these pilasters are presented with their rolls to the street, rather than with their volutes in the normal fashion.

62. Lexow, "Arkitektur 1536–1814," pp. 78–80.

63. Ibid., pp. 98–110.

64. Malmborg, *Kungliga slotten*, pp. 242–252. The first pavilion of 1753 was built as a birthday gift for Queen Lovisa Ulrica and, becoming unsound, was demolished in 1763 to make way for the present building. Much of the queen's collection of Chinese furnishings and objects of art remain there. An extensive account of both buildings, the collections, the landscaping, and the restorations is given in Setterwall, Fogelmarck, and Gyllensvärd, *Chinese Pavilion*. See also Wahlberg, *Jean Erik Rehn*, pp. 75–79, and Hardy, "Historic Houses: Fantasy at Kina Slott."

65. Karling, *Tyresö Slott*, and Söderberg, *Södermanland*, 2:255–271.

66. Roussell, ed., *Danske slotte*, 5:397–406, and Jørgensen, *Danmarks Arkitektur. Enfamiliehuset*, pp. 25–28. An extensive account of such gardens in Denmark is by Elling, *Romantiske Have*.

67. Muri, *Norske Kyrkjer*, pp. 69–71, and Lexow, "Arkitektur 1536–1814," pp. 48–49. Lexow calls attention to the work by the German mathematician Leonhard Christoph Sturm, *Architectonisches Bedenken*, which was known and used in Norway. See also Bugge and Alsvik, eds., *Norges Kirker. Kongsberg Kirke*, pp. 59–78.

68. Muri, *Norske Kyrkjer*, pp. 97–98, and Ødegaard, *Om Kjerke på Røros*.

69. Mannström, *Adolf Fredriks Kyrka (SK)*, pp. 62–75,

and Fogelmarck, *Carl Fredrik Adelcrantz*, pp. 147–160 and 389–392.

70. Meldahl, *Frederikskirken*, pp. 52–65.

71. Langberg, *Danmarks bygningskultur*, 1:5–8, and Lund and Millech, eds., *Danmarks bygningskunst*, pp. 277–291.

72. Weilbach, *Arkitekten C. F. Harsdorff*, pp. 58–71.

73. Hiort, "Andreas Kirkerup's Islandske kirke."

74. Beijer, *Court Theatres*, p. 7. The original architect is not known, but a member of the Bibiena family of designers has been suggested as a possibility (Donnelly, "Theaters in the Courts," pp. 333–334).

75. Fogelmarck, *Carl Fredrik Adelcrantz*, pp. 189–195 and 303–313; Malmborg, *Kungliga slotten*, 1:253–258; and Eklund and Stribolt, *Bollhuset och Dramaten*, pp. 8–15. Beijer's *Court Theatres* illustrates a large collection of drawings for the buildings and the sets, with commentary. On the staff of the Royal Library in Stockholm, in 1921 Beijer recognized the importance of the building and its contents, then stored in warehouse fashion, and led efforts for restoration.

76. Neiiendam, *Hofteatret*, pp. 8–12.

77. Stavenow, *Carl Hårleman*, pp. 197–199, and Alm, "Stockholms observatorium."

78. Setterwall, "Stockholms börsbyggnad," and Setterwall, *Erik Palmstedt*, pp. 52–89.

79. Fogelmarck, "Gustav III's Opera"; Fogelmarck, *Carl Fredrik Adelcrantz*, pp. 200–212 and 433–453; Hilleström, *The Royal Opera*, pp. 10–12; and Eklund and Stribolt, *Bollhuset och Dramaten*, pp. 16–19.

80. Dumont, *Parallèle*, and Pevsner, *History of Building Types*, pp. 76–77.

81. Høy, *Christiansfeld*, pp. 4–11, and Gorssen, *Christiansfeld*. This was of course not the only Herrnhutter colony founded in order to escape persecution in Germany. As early as 1731 Count Zinzendorf was in Copenhagen to arouse initial interest in such a settle-

ment, and in 1741 under his patronage the town of Bethlehem in Pennsylvania was founded. See Murtagh, *Moravian Architecture*, pp. 22–93.

82. Rácz, *Rokoko och klassicism*, p. 242 and plate 29, and Richards, *800 Years*, p. 60.

## 5 Scandinavian Neoclassicism

1. For comparable developments in England and America see Summerson, *Architecture in Britain*, pp. 247–291, and Whiffen and Koeper, *American Architecture*, pp. 100–124.

2. Cornell, *Svenska konstens historia*, 2:7–14, and Söderberg, *Manor Houses*, pp. 179–234.

3. Bain, *Gustavus III*, 1:269–270.

4. Setterwall, *Palmstedt*, pp. 165–180; Bjurström, "Gripsholmsteaterns salong"; and Beijer, "Les Théâtres," pp. 222–224.

5. For a discussion of Palmstedt's experience and probable resources see Donnelly, "Theaters in the Courts," pp. 339–340.

6. Beijer, "Les Théâtres," pp. 217–218. The dedication reads "alle maesta di Gustavo III, re di Svezia."

7. Ekberg, *Uppsala slott*, pp. 65–83.

8. Stavenow, *Hårleman*, pp. 216–217.

9. Wollin, *Desprez i Sverige*, pp. 84–89.

10. Ibid., pp. 59–82, and Malmborg, *Kungliga slotten*, 2:85–130.

11. Wollin, *Desprez i Sverige*, pp. 161–166.

12. Bucht, *Härnösands historia*, 1:384–390.

13. Jakstein, *Landbaumeister Christian Friedrich Hansen*; Langberg, *Omkring C. F. Hansen*; Wietek, *C. F. Hansen*; and Jørgensen, "Copenhagen School of Classicism," pp. 6–21.

14. Brogaard, Lund, and Nørregård-Nielsen, *Danmarks Arkitektur. Landbrugets huse*, pp. 176–177.

15. Jakstein, *Landbaumeister Christian Friedrich Hansen*, pp. 23–24.

16. Jørgensen, *Danmarks Arkitektur. Enfamiliehuset*, p. 34.

17. Jakstein, "C. F. Hansens Rat-und-Arresthaus," and Jørgensen and Porphyrios, eds., "Neoclassical Architecture," pp. 46–51.

18. Weilbach, *C. F. Hansens Christiansborg*. For the full account of the second Christiansborg see Hvidt, Ellehøj, and Norn, eds., *Christiansborg*, 2:2–186.

19. Percier and Fontaine, *Recueil de décorations intérieures*.

20. Derry, *History of Scandinavia*, pp. 199–206.

21. Thurah, *Danske Vitruvius*, 2:77–97 and plates 36–53.

22. Horskjaer, ed., *Danske kirker*, 1:29–31; Bolvig, *Bykirker*, pp. 77–78; Hvidt, Ellehøj, and Norn, eds., *Christiansborg*, 2:27–32; and Birgitte-Boggild Johannsen, *Danmarks Kirker. København*, 2:177–202.

23. Hermansen, Roussell, and Steenberg, *Danmarks Kirker. København*, 1:151–184; Horskjaer, ed., *Danske kirker*, 1:195–201; and Bolvig, *Bykirker*, pp. 103–105. Attention has been drawn to some of the possible French sources for Hansen's ideas for rebuilding (Langberg, *Omkring C. F. Hansen*, pp. 30–34). See also Wohlert, "C. F. Hansen's Domkirke," and Jørgensen and Porphyrios, eds., "Neoclassical Architecture," pp. 38–41.

24. Wanscher, *Arkitekten G. Bindesbøll*, pp. 15–29; Millech and Fisker, *Danske arkitekturstrømninger*, pp. 26–30; Langberg, *Danmarks bygningskultur*, 2:106–109; Bramsen, *Gottlieb Bindesbøll*, pp. 49–97; Jørgensen, "Thorvaldsen's Museum"; and Jørgensen and Porphyrios, eds., "Neoclassical Architecture," pp. 42–45.

25. Derry, *History of Scandinavia*, pp. 206–209.

26. Meissner, *Carl Ludwig Engel*, pp. 39–41; Wickberg, "Engels stilhistoriska ställning"; Nils E. Wickberg, "Tillhundraårsminnet"; and Nils E. Wickberg, *Senaatintori*, pp. 121–123. The latter is the most extensive account in English of the history of the Senate Square and its buildings (the text is also in

Finnish, Swedish, and German), and includes color reproductions of a number of Engel's drawings for the entire project, published for the first time. See also Knapas, "Eastern and Western Neoclassicism," and Pöykkö, "Helsinki's Neo-Classical Center."

27. Nils E. Wickberg, Senaatintori, pp. 125–126.

28. Meissner, Carl Ludwig Engel, pp. 59–61; Nils E. Wickberg, Finnish Architecture, pp. 74–75; and Nils E. Wickberg, Senaatintori, pp. 127–130.

29. Lindberg, Finlands kyrkor, pp. 38–39.

30. Lindberg, Finlands kyrkor, p. 55; Meissner, Carl Ludwig Engel, p. 45; and Nils E. Wickberg, Senaatintori, p. 134.

31. Lindberg, Finlands kyrkor, pp. 55–56; Meissner, Carl Ludwig Engel, pp. 78–83; and Nils E. Wickberg, Senaatintori, pp. 132–134.

32. Meissner, Carl Ludwig Engel, pp. 64–66; Nils E. Wickberg, Finnish Architecture, pp. 76–77; and Nils E. Wickberg, Senaatintori, pp. 130–131.

33. Although the Library of the Academy of Sciences in St. Petersburg, built in 1718–1734, had burned in 1747, it had been recorded in an elaborate publication of 1741, Palaty Sanktpeterburgskoi Imperatoskoi Academii. The interior was a great hall with a two-story colonnade surrounding the walls, which had book shelves in two stories. Engel's colonnade is a giant order, but his inspiration for the reading room may well have come from his knowledge of the Russian example.

34. Derry, History of Scandinavia, pp. 210–218.

35. Fett et al., Ulefos, and Hamran, "Det nye Norge," pp. 15–17. Recent studies have changed the former attribution to Jørgen Henrik Rawert (ibid., pp. 123–124).

36. Kielland, Paleet i Oslo; Kavli, The Royal Palace in Oslo; Kavli and Hjelde, Slottet i Oslo, pp. 1–35; Hamran, "Det nye Norge," pp. 31–44; and Kavli and Hjelde, Kongens Slott.

37. Fett and Schnitler, eds., Norsk kunsthistorie,

2:235–238.

38. Anders Bugge, Arkitekten Stadskonduktor Chr. H. Grosch, pp. 31–44 and 75–80.

39. Ibid., pp. 91–94, and Hamran, "Det nye Norge," pp. 45–46.

40. Anders Bugge, Arkitekten Stadskonduktor Chr. H. Grosch, pp. 97–110; Muri, Norske Kyrkjer, p. 31; and Hamran, "Det nye Norge," pp. 46–48.

41. Fett and Schnitler, eds., Norsk kunsthistorie, 2:241–243; Anders Bugge, Arkitekten Stadskonduktor Chr. H. Grosch, pp. 131–153; and Hamran, "Det nye Norge," pp. 50–59.

42. Lindblom, Sveriges konsthistoria, 3:685–719.

43. Wollin, Skeppsholmskyrkan (SK), pp. 71–113.

## 6 Vernacular Architecture in Scandinavia

1. Uldall, "Open Air Museums"; Peter Michelsen, "The Outdoor Museum"; Arnö-Berg and Biörnstad, eds., Skansens hus, pp. 14–30; and Alexander, Museum Masters, pp. 240–275.

2. Peter Michelsen, "The Origin and Aim of the Open-Air Museum."

3. Peter Michelsen, Frilandsmuseet, pp. 17–59.

4. Uldall, "Open Air Museum," pp. 68–69.

5. Ailonen and Kinnunen, Seurasaari Open Air Museum.

6. Hermansson, "Árbaer Museum," and The Árbaer Museum.

7. There is a considerable literature on half-timber construction, including work done in England, Germany, and Holland. A useful discussion of the Scandinavian "bindingsvaerk" or "korsvirke" may be found in Lund and Millech, eds., Danmarks bygningskunst, pp. 54–59. See also Stoklund, Bondegård og byggeskik, pp. 28–37; Lundberg, Trä gav form, pp. 123–125; and Brogaard, Lund, and Nørregård-Nielsen, Danmarks Arkitektur. Landbrugets huse, pp. 30–33.

8. Christian Axel Jensen, *Dansk bindingsvaerk;* Stoklund, *Bondegård,* pp. 40–44; Peter Michelsen, *Frilandsmuseet,* pp. 208–210; and Vensild, "Højremshuse i Nord-og-Nordvest-Jylland."

9. Lund and Millech, eds., *Danmarks bygningskunst,* pp. 50–52, and Stoklund, *Bondegård,* pp. 37–41.

10. Peter Michelsen, *Frilandsmuseet,* pp. 130–135.

11. For a study of chimneys and ovens see Peter Michelsen, *Ildsteder.*

12. For thatching see Erixson, "Halmtakstyper i Sverige"; Stoklund, *Bondegård,* pp. 50–54; and Brogaard, Lund, and Nørregård-Nielsen, *Danmarks Arkitektur. Landbrugets huse,* pp. 33–35.

13. Berlin, "Ravlundsgården." The Ravlunda Farmstead unfortunately burned in 1970, and a farmstead from Hög in Skåne has been erected in its place.

14. For bibliography on the folk buildings of Skåne see Lundqvist, *Svensk konsthistorisk bibliografi,* pp. 154–155.

15. Arnö-Berg and Biörnstad, eds., *Skansens hus,* pp. 144–153.

16. For the bole-house techniques see Steensberg, "Bulhus"; Stoklund, *Bondegård,* pp. 44–46; Lundberg, *Trä gav form,* pp. 92–108; and Håkon Christie, *Middelalderen bygger,* pp. 41–54.

17. For the use of wall paintings and hangings in the Swedish farmhouses see Plath, *Decorative Arts of Sweden,* pp. 5–8 and 169–212.

18. Peter Michelsen, *Frilandsmuseet,* pp. 72–77.

19. A vivid account of how such roofs could be put to use other than for shelter also gives insight into early nineteenth-century conditions in Sweden: "We found a clean and excellent inn at Tännäs. A cooling and delicious delicacy presented itself to our parched palates upon our arrival here, and in a place where we should last have looked for it: this was nothing less than a whole crop of turnips growing upon the top of the house, and covering all the roof of the inn. Garden vegetables are hardly ever seen in Sweden; and with the exception of a few potatoes, we had been so long strangers to any thing of this kind, that pine-apples could not have been more grateful. We all ate of them greedily, both in their crude state and boiled; telling our host not to be anxious in procuring for us any other provisions" (Clarke, *Travels,* 10:156).

20. No attempt will be made here to include all possible bibliographical sources. A general survey is given in Valonen, "Knuttimring." For Sweden see Erixon, *Svensk byggnads kultur;* Hallerdt, *Timmerhus;* and Lundberg, *Trä gav form,* pp. 18–31. For Norway see Kavli, *Norwegian Architecture,* pp. 22–29; Gunnar Bugge and Norberg-Schulz, *Stav og laft,* pp. 29–80; Håkon Christie, *Middelalderen bygger,* pp. 33–40; and Gjaerder, "Om stavverk og lafteverk."

21. Erixon, "North European Technique" and Erixon, "Är den Nordamerikanska timringstekniken överförd fran Sverige?"

22. Arnö-Berg and Biörnstad, eds., *Skansens hus,* pp. 343–366.

23. Boëthius, *Anders Zorn.*

24. Stigum, "Loft," and Reimers and Anker, "Trearkitektur, pp. 400–410. For a discussion of changing elements in Norwegian houses as related to historical factors see Lloyd, "The Norwegian Laftehus."

25. Stigum and Arne Berg, "Stove," and Reimers and Anker, "Trearkitektur," pp. 386–400.

26. For a discussion of the Norwegian painters of these interiors see Hauglid, *Native Art of Norway,* pp. 63–106.

27. Reimers and Anker, "Trearkitektur," pp. 386–390, and Visted and Stigum, *Vår gamle bondekultur,* 1:46–153.

28. Arne Berg, "The Joining of Individual Houses," and Myhre, "Development of the Farm House."

29. For the early history of sawmills see Bishop, *History of American Manufactures,* 1:93–94.

30. The illustration is from Reginald Outhier, *Journal d'un voyage au nord.* Outhier had accompanied the French astronomer Pierre Louis Moreau de Maupertuis on an expedition to Lapland in 1736–1737, sent by Louis XV to measure the length of a degree of the meridian. The work was undertaken at the observatory at Kittilä.

31. Nikander, "Byar och gårdar," pp. 117–146, and Valonen, *Zur Geschichte der finnischen Wohnstuber.*

32. Vilkuna, "Den karelska gården," and Nils E. Wickberg, *Finnish Architecture,* pp. 56–57.

33. Heikel, *Karuna Kyrka,* and Lindberg, *Finlands kyrkor,* p. 97.

34. Ullén, *Granhults och Nottebäcks kyrkor (SK),* pp. 277–296, and Ullén, *Medeltida träkyrkor I (SK),* pp. 19–30.

35. Ibid., pp. 112–113.

36. Wallin, *Seglora Kyrka,* pp. 9–17 and 35–77, and Arnö-Berg and Biörnstad, eds., *Skansens hus,* pp. 510–534. The Seglora church has two features in common with churches built by the Swedish settlers in the New World. In 1647 John Printz, Governor of New Sweden, wrote in a report to the Swedish West India Company, "Again, I have caused a church to be built in New Gothenburg, decorating it according to our Swedish fashion, so far as our resources and means would allow," in Myers, ed., *Narratives of Early Pennsylvania,* p. 122. This would suggest paintings similar to those in the Seglora church. Then in 1698 the Swedish community in Philadelphia built Gloria Dei Church, which also has a polygonal apse. See Morrison, *Early American Architecture,* pp. 508–510.

37. Petterson, *Petäjäveden vanhau kirkon puolesta,* pp. 56–57.

38. Manker, *Lapsk kultur,* pp. 106–155, and Erixon, *Svensk byggnads kultur,* pp. 48–59. The use of curved poles for the frame is thought to have preceded the familiar "cruck" construction in English building. See Innocent, *Development of English Building Construction,* pp. 10–14; Crossley, *Timber Building in England,* pp. 109–112; and Clifton-Taylor, *Pattern of English Building,* p. 35.

39. Michelsen, *Frilandsmuseet,* pp. 199–201. In this group the hut in the foreground is original, brought to the Open Air Museum in 1910, and distinctive in being the first building acquired from Danish territory proper.

40. Stoklund, "Røgstue og glasstue"; Thorsteinsson, "Faroese House Constructions"; Stoklund, "Røykstova and Glasstova"; and Stoklund, "Houses and Culture."

41. The splashmill illustrated here is another Faroese example, from Sandur, moved to the Open Air Museum in 1961–1965. A dwelling similar to the one at Saksun, a kiln, and a storehouse complete the group there. An especially hazardous part of the enterprise was to lower the stones of the dwelling from Múla on Borthoy down a 60-foot cliff to the ship below. (Peter Michelsen, *Frilandsmuseet,* pp. 229–234.)

42. Sigurdsson, "The Turf Farm"; Ágústsson, "Inner Construction"; and Ágústsson, "Building through the Centuries," pp. 97–101.

43. Nilsson, "Den sentida bebyggelsen"; Eldjárn, "Two Medieval Farm Sites"; and Ágústsson, "Development of the Icelandic Farm."

44. Gestsson, "The Use of Stone and Turf in the Icelandic Houses."

45. Roussell, *Farms and Churches,* pp. 24–27 and 138.

46. Ágústsson, "Inner Construction," pp. 181–183.

47. Fenton, "The Longhouse in Northern Scotland."

48. Hiort, "Andreas Kirkerup's Islandske kirke," pp. 126–167.

49. Quoted in *The American Magazine,* 3, no. 12 (September 1837): 461.

50. Jökulsson, "Árbaer Museum and Church."

51. Jespersen, *Kommandørgården,* and Ester Ander-

sen and K. Roland Hansen, "Kommandørgården på Rømø."

52. Stoklund, "Frilandsmuseets gård fra Lønnestak."

53. Klein, *Landbrugets bygninger;* Langberg, *Danmarks bygningskultur,* 2:44–53; and Brogaard, Lund, and Nørregård-Nielsen, *Danmarks Arkitektur. Landbrugets huse,* pp. 58–67.

54. Langberg, *Danmarks bygningskultur,* 1:115, and Hartmann and Villadsen, *Danmarks Arkitektur. Byens huse,* p. 55.

55. Langberg, *Danmarks bygningskultur,* 1:185.

56. Tunander, *Falun.*

57. Clarke, *Travels,* 10:556–557.

58. Lexow, "Arkitektur 1536–1814," pp. 101–102, and Ødegaard, *Røros.*

59. Sahlberg, *Handicraft Museum.*

60. Richards, *800 Years,* pp. 94–96.

61. Tschudi-Madsen, "Veien hjem," pp. 92–94.

62. Ágústsson, "Building through the Centuries," pp. 102–103, and Árnason, "New Lease on Life."

## 7 Eclectic and Early Modern Scandinavian Building

1. An extensive account of this period in European architecture is given in Hitchcock, *Architecture: Nineteenth and Twentieth Centuries,* pp. 93–151; the work of Scandinavian builders is discussed on pp. 40–42. See also Paulsson, *Scandinavian Architecture,* pp. 177–184; Andreas Lindblom, *Sveriges konsthistoria,* 3:800–828; Langberg, *Danmarks bygningskultur,* 2:103–142; Faber, *History of Danish Architecture,* pp. 112–126; Lund and Millech, eds., *Danmarks Bygningskunst,* pp. 333–378; and Hamran, "Det nye Norge," pp. 99–122.

2. Werlauff, *Udsigt over Kiøbenhavns Universitets-Bygnings,* and Jørgensen, Lund, and Nørregård-Nielsen, *Danmarks Arkitektur. Magtens bolig,* pp. 116–119.

3. Wanscher, "Constantin Hansen."

4. Anders Bugge, *Arkitekten Stadskonduktor Chr. H. Grosch,* pp. 172–177, and Hamran, "Det nye Norge," pp. 71–72.

5. Jørgensen, *Danmarks Arkitektur. Enfamiliehuset,* pp. 38–63, and Brogaard, Lund, and Nørregård-Nielsen, *Danmarks Arkitektur. Landbrugets huse,* pp. 178–182.

6. Roussell, ed., *Danske slotte,* 8:319–322, and Brogaard, Lund, and Nørregård-Nielsen, *Danmarks Arkitektur. Landbrugets huse,* pp. 178–179. The illustration is from Richardt and Secher, *Prospecter af danske herregaarde,* n.p.

7. Hjelde, *Oscarshall,* pp. 11–34, and Hamran, "Det nye Norge," pp. 72–75.

8. Jørgensen, *Danmarks Arkitektur. Enfamiliehuset,* pp. 48–84.

9. Guenther Lange, *Alexis de Chateauneauf,* pp. 49–51, and Hamran, "Det nye Norge," pp. 94–95.

10. Guenther Lange, *Alexis de Chateauneuf,* pp. 51–53; Muri, *Norske Kyrkjer,* pp. 45–46; and Hamran, "Det nye Norge," pp. 96–97.

11. Millech and Fisker, *Danske arkitekturstrømninger,* pp. 103–109, and Millech, *J. D. Herholdt.*

12. Meeks, *The Railroad Station,* pp. 26–55, and Pevsner, *History of Building Types,* pp. 225–230.

13. Derry, *History of Scandinavia,* pp. 228 and 264. For discussion of the early Danish railway stations see Sestoft, *Danmarks Arkitektur. Arbejdets bygninger,* pp. 81–83 and 116–123.

14. Paulsson, *Scandinavian Architecture,* pp. 172–194. Hahr expressed dissatisfaction with the station as remodeled, calling the façade a "very inexpressive mantle" (*Architecture in Sweden,* p. 75).

15. Tschudi-Madsen, "Veien hjem," pp. 61–67.

16. Haffner, *Stortingets Hus,* pp. 74–128, and Hamran, "Det nye Norge," pp. 80–90.

17. Muri, *Norske Kyrkjer,* pp. 247–248.

18. Tschudi-Madsen, "Veien hjem," pp. 30–31.

19. Hugo Johannsen and Claus M. Smidt, *Danmarks Arkitektur. Kirkens huse*, pp. 171–175.

20. Millech and Fisker, *Danske arkitekturstrømninger*, pp. 222–224, and Horskjaer, ed., *Danske kirker*, 1:134–135.

21. Fritsch, *Kirchenbau des Protestantismus*, p. 208. Fritsch found this plan in A. W. N. Pugin's *Present State of Ecclesiastical Architecture*, where it appeared as the first of four ideal plans for not Protestant but Roman Catholic churches, Pugin by this time having become a Catholic. Although Borch could have known Pugin's book, it is more likely that he saw the plan published by Fritsch. In the German author's book there is a substantial section on "evangelical" churches in Denmark, Norway, and Sweden, which must have been appealing to Scandinavian readers (pp. 409–450).

22. Grut, "Engelbrektskyrkan," and Wahlman, *Engelbrektskyrkan*.

23. For discussion of the immediately preceding French and German museums see Pevsner, *History of Building Types*, pp. 120–129, and also for theaters, pp. 82–84.

24. Plageman, *Das Deutsche Kunstmuseum*, pp. 117–126.

25. Ibid., pp. 145–149.

26. Ringbom, *Stone, Style and Truth*, pp. 72–74.

27. Millech and Fisker, *Danske arkitekturstrømninger*, pp. 109–111.

28. Langberg, *Danmarks bygningskultur*, 2:146–148; Jørgensen, Lund, and Nørregård-Nielsen, *Danmarks Arkitektur. Magtens bolig*, pp. 162–163; and Skriver, "Royal Theatre."

29. Engberg, *Pantomimeteatret*, pp. 9–16; Lund and Millech, eds., *Danmarks Bygningskunst*, p. 379; and Jørgensen, Lund, and Nørregård-Neilsen, *Danmarks Arkitektur. Magtens bolig*, p. 162.

30. For discussions of Meldahl and his contemporaries see Stemann, *F. Meldahl og hans venner*, and Millech and Fisker, *Danske arkitekturstrømninger*, pp. 165–206. See also Horskjaer, ed., *Danske kirker*, 1:44–47, and Bolvig, *Bykirker*, pp. 84–85.

31. Willoch, *Nasjonal galleriet*, pp. 25–35 and 88–94, and Ringbom, *Stone, Style and Truth*, p. 74.

32. Sachs, *Modern Opera Houses*, 1:53–54; Eklund and Stribolt, *Bollhuset och Dramaten*, pp. 36–43; and Stribolt, *Stockholms 1800-talsteatrar*, pp. 287–357.

33. Sachs, *Modern Opera Houses*, 1:51–52; Tschudi-Madsen, *Henrik Bull*, pp. 45–53; and Skriver, "National Theatre in Oslo."

34. This matter is discussed at some length in Ringbom, *Stone, Style and Truth*.

35. Hitchcock, *Architecture: Nineteenth and Twentieth Centuries*, pp. 281–306.

36. In Denmark the architectural expression of the Art Nouveau was limited (Faber, *History of Danish Architecture*, pp. 142–145), but the impact of this style in the decorative arts was strong. See Viggo Sten Møller, *Dansk kunstindustrie*, 2:11–24. For the Norwegian architectural Art Nouveau see Tschudi-Madsen, "Veien hjem," pp. 81–94. For the Swedish see Andreas Lindblom, *Sveriges konsthistoria*, 3:922–124. For the Finnish see Moorhouse, Carpetian, and Ahtola-Moorhouse, *Helsinki Jugendstil Architecture*, and John Boulton Smith, *Golden Age of Finnish Art*, pp. 117–199.

37. Lindegren, "Kungliga Dramatiske teatern," and Eklund and Stribolt, *Bollhuset och Dramaten*, pp. 44–68.

38. Tschudi-Madsen, "Veien hjem," pp. 80–90.

39. Richards, *800 Years*, p. 133.

40. Hamran, "Det nye Norge," pp. 105–106.

41. Addison, *Romanticism and the Gothic Revival*, pp. 117–126, and Hamran, "Det nye Norge," pp. 102–104.

42. Ibid., pp. 98–102. For the Finnish wooden churches see Petterson, *Suomalainen piukirkko.*

43. Tschudi-Madsen, "Veien hjem," pp. 68–69.

44. Pevsner, *History of Building Types,* pp. 169–192.

45. Tschudi-Madsen, "Veien hjem," pp. 56–60.

46. Curman, "Nordiska museets byggnad"; Edestrand and Lundberg, *Isak Gustaf Clason,* pp. 32–43; and Ringbom, *Stone, Style and Truth,* pp. 130–132.

47. Giedion, *Space, Time and Architecture,* pp. 211–218.

48. Ibid., pp. 181–196.

49. Hamran, "Det nye Norge," pp. 117–120.

50. Anders Bugge, *Arkitekten Stadskonduktor Chr. H. Grosch,* p. 184. For industrial buildings in Denmark from 1807 to 1914 see Sestoft, *Danmarks Arkitektur. Arbejdets bygninger,* for an interesting and well-illustrated account.

51. Ibid., pp. 77–78.

52. Millech and Fisker, *Danske arkitekturstrømninger,* p. 114; Lund and Millech, eds., *Danmarks Bygningskunst,* pp. 377–381; and Sestoft, *Danmarks Arkitektur. Arbejdets bygninger,* pp. 83–84.

53. Ibid., p. 73.

54. Knud Jensen, *Fra Halmtorvet till Rådhusplads,* and Hartmann and Villadsen, *Danmarks Arkitektur. Byens huse,* pp. 35–38.

55. Fisker, "Omkring Herholdt."

56. Cervin, "The City Hall at Copenhagen"; Beckett, *Københavns raadhus;* Stein Eiler Rasmussen, *Nordische Baukunst,* pp. 7–16; Millech and Fisker, *Danske arkitekturstrømninger,* pp. 207–252; Funder, *Arkitekten Martin Nyrop,* pp. 34–52; and Jørgensen, Lund, and Nørregård-Nielsen, *Danmarks Arkitektur. Magtens bolig,* pp. 78–81.

57. The future architect of the Stockholm Town Hall, Ragnar Östberg, saw the Copenhagen building in 1896 and later wrote of his impression: "The town hall in Denmark, for example, seemed to typify the exuberant vitality of the Danish people. The equipoise and repose of the structure amid the lively play of the lines, the rich lustre of the red brick,— this was at once Scandinavian and characteristically Danish, symbolizing as it were, the sturdy self-reliance of the one who, after much toil and trouble, builds a cosy home on his own soil" (Östberg, *The Stockholm Town Hall,* p. 15).

58. Holger Rasmussen, ed., *Dansk Folkemuseum,* pp. 8–11.

59. The history of projects and quarrels, political as well as architectural, that finally resulted in the third Christiansborg is set forth in Hvidt, Ellehøj, and Norn, eds., *Christiansborg,* 2:187–327, with English summary, pp. 362–371.

60. Stein Eiler Rasmussen, *Nordische Baukunst,* pp. 17–29. From the considerable literature on the Town Hall in Stockholm the most important account in English is by the architect himself: *The Stockholm Town Hall.* See also Strömbon, "The new townhall of Stockholm," David Dahl, "Stockholms stadshus," and Easton, "The Stadshus at Stockholm."

61. Östberg, *The Stockholm Town Hall,* pp. 31–32.

62. Ibid., p. 38.

63. Ibid., pp. 28–30.

64. Saarikivi, Niilonen, and Ekelund, *Art in Finland,* pp. 118–120; Ulf Hård af Segerstad, *Modern Finnish Design,* pp. 7–71; Salokorpi, *Modern Architecture in Finland,* pp. 5–14; Mikkola, *Architecture in Finland,* pp. 5–16; and Hausen, Mikkola, and Amberg, *Saarinen in Finland.*

65. Pallasmaa, ed., *Hvitträsk.*

66. Kopisto, *Suomen Kansallismuseo,* and Nikula, *Armas Lindgren,* pp. 153–154.

67. Christ-Janer, *Eliel Saarinen,* pp. 30–34, and Hausen, Mikkola, and Amberg, *Saarinen in Finland,* pp. 42–48 and 71–76.

68. Saarikivi, Niilonen, and Ekelund, *Art in Finland*, p. 120, and Salokorpi, *Modern Architecture in Finland*, pp. 9–11.

69. Ringbom, *Stone, Style and Truth*, pp. 148–152. For a discussion of Richardsonian influence in the Scandinavian countries see Eaton, *American Architecture Comes of Age*, pp. 143–207.

70. Treib, "Lars Sonck," and Kivinen, Korvenmaa, and Salokorpi, *Lars Sonck*, pp. 7–11.

71. Ibid., pp. 35–45.

72. Nils E. Wickberg, *Finnish Architecture*, pp. 104–106; Kivinen, *Tampereen tuomiokirkko*, pp. 61–90; Kivinen, Korvenmaa, and Salokorpi, *Lars Sonck*, pp. 45–62; and Ringbom, *Stone, Style and Truth*, pp. 226–227.

73. Fritsch, *Kirchenbau des Protestantismus*, pp. 513–530. Fritsch made a distinction between Anglican churches in England and America and those of other Protestant denominations. His plan of St. James Congregational Church in Newcastle-upon-Tyne, by T. Lewis Banks, 1884, is thought to be the inspiration for Sonck's plan of St. John's (figure 1007, p. 521). This plan had appeared in *Building News* of 1885, but Sonck would have been more likely to have used Fritsch's book.

74. Treib, "Lars Sonck," pp. 234–236, and Kivinen, Korvenmaa, and Salokorpi, *Lars Sonck*, pp. 81–85.

75. Ibid., pp. 63–67, and Ringbom, *Stone, Style and Truth*, pp. 179–180.

76. Kivinen, Korvenmaa, and Salokorpi, *Lars Sonck*, p. 75, and Ringbom, *Stone, Style and Truth*, pp. 240–241.

77. Nils E. Wickberg, *Finnish Architecture*, pp. 117–118, and Kivinen, Korvenmaa, and Salokorpi, *Lars Sonck*, pp. 75–81.

## 8 Scandinavian Architecture since World War I

1. For the Scandinavian countries in World War I see Derry, *History of Scandinavia*, pp. 303–304.

2. Marstrand, *Grundtvigs Mindekirke*, pp. 28–29; Fisker, "Den Klintske skole," pp. 48–53; Millech, "På Bjerget, Grundtvigs Kirke"; Bolvig, *Bykirker*, pp. 87–89; and Jelsbak, ed., *Grundtvigs Kirke*, pp. 7–26.

3. Kivinen, Korvenmaa, and Salokorpi, *Lars Sonck*, pp. 108–111.

4. Sonck, "Mikael Agricola Kyrkan i Helsingfors," and Kivinen, Korvenmaa, and Salokorpi, *Lars Sonck*, pp. 113–117.

5. The spire, carrying a gold cross, rises 103 meters above sea level. Special equipment built into the tower made it possible to lower it considerably during World War II.

6. Millech and Fisker, *Danske arkitekturstrømninger*, pp. 300–301; Faber, *New Danish Architecture*, pp. 76–77; and Stephenson, *Arkitekten Thorkild Henningsen*, pp. 52–59. See also Jørgensen, *Danmarks Arkitektur. Enfamiliehuset*, pp. 64–78, for workers' housing in Denmark. The work of Heinrich Tessenow in Germany, and particularly his publication *Hausbau und dergleichen* (1916), is discussed by Kenneth Frampton in "The Classical Tradition," pp. 167–168.

7. In 1980 the Museum of Finnish Architecture began organizing an exhibition, "Nordic Classicism," for which it collaborated with the other Nordic architectural museums. The catalogue (Paavilainen, ed., *Nordic Classicism*) contains essays by leading scholars of Scandinavian architecture and is a significant contribution to the study of this development. In 1982 the catalogue was published as the exhibition was on view in Copenhagen, Helsinki, Oslo, and Stockholm. In the same year another major study of classicism appeared: Porphyrios, ed., *Classicism Is Not a Style*. See also Elling, *Klassiske København;* Millech and Fisker, *Danske arkitekturstrømninger*, pp. 283–306; Langberg, *Danmarks bygningskultur*, 2:177–208; Faber, *History of Danish Architecture*, pp. 150–164; and Lund

and Millech, eds., *Danmarks Bygningskuħst*, pp. 383–406.

8. Swane, *Faaborg Museum;* Hiort, "Museet i Faaborg"; Stephenson, *Arkitekten Carl Petersen*, pp. 34–63; Paavilainen, ed., *Nordic Classicism*, pp. 67 and 70–71; and Langkilde, *Nyklassicismen*.

9. From "Contrasts," publ¡shed in *Architekten*, 1920, quoted in Paavilainen, ed., *Nordic Classicism*, pp. 45–48.

10. Porphyrios, ed., *Classicism*, pp. 23–35.

11. Fisker, "Den Klintske skole," pp. 60–61; and Millech, "Nordvestsjaellands Elektricitetsvaerk."

12. Kampmann, "Politigaarden"; Wanscher, "Politigaarden"; Bröchner, "Copenhagen's New Scotland Yard"; Rafn, "The Police Headquarters in Copenhagen"; Rasmussen, *Nordische Baukunst*, pp. 103–113; and Langkilde, "Politigaarden." Kampmann is quoted as saying, "I love putting up pillars . . . but they have got to be decent pillars and not like Palladio's who made them all imitations, plastered boardings" (Rafn, "Police Headquarters," p. 199, and Jørgensen, "Hack Kampmann").

13. Caldenby and Hultin, eds., *Asplund*, pp. 41–46; Ahlin, *Sigurd Lewerentz*, pp. 38–49 and 116–118; Cruickshank, ed., *Erik Gunnar Asplund*, pp. 97–113; and Treib, "Woodland Cemetery."

14. Holmdahl, Lind, and Ödeen, eds., *Gunnar Asplund Architect*, pp. 41–42 and 94–97; Maré, *Gunnar Asplund*, pp. 20–21; and Caldenby and Hultin, *Asplund*, pp. 23, 44, and 68–71.

15. Holmdahl, Lind, and Ödeen, eds., *Gunnar Asplund Architect*, pp. 76–81; Wrede, *Architecture of Gunnar Asplund*, pp. 45–46 and 120–129; and Cruickshank, ed., *Erik Gunnar Asplund*, pp. 97–113.

16. Tynell, "Stockholms stadsbibliotek"; Holmdahl, Lind, and Ödeen, eds., *Gunnar Asplund Architect*, pp. 42–43; Maré, *Gunnar Asplund*, pp. 21–24; Wrede, *Architecture of Gunnar Asplund*, pp. 100–124; and Caldenby and Hultin, *Asplund*, pp. 28–29 and 92–101. The Tomb of Hadrian is illustrated in Fischer von Er-

lach's *Entwurff einer historischen Architectur*, Book 2, plate VIII. The building in the background of Book 4, no. 11 is also a cylindrical structure rising from a rectilinear base, set on a hill much as is the Stockholm library.

17. Blakstad and Munthe-Kaas, "Haugesund rådhus," Norberg-Schulz, "Fra nasjonalromantikk," pp. 38–42, Norberg-Schulz, *Modern Norwegian Architecture*, pp. 41–43, and Pontvik, "Haugesund rådhus."

18. Berner, "Torvalmenningen," and Paavilainen, ed., *Nordic Classicism*, p. 115.

19. Veijola, "Riksdagshuset"; Sirén, "Finland's New House of Parliament"; Nils E. Wickberg, *Finnish Architecture*, pp. 126–129; and Paavilainen, ed., *Nordic Classicism*, pp. 83–85.

20. Lindberg, *Finlands kyrkor*, p. 184; Pearson, *Alvar Aalto*, pp. 50–53; Quantrill, *Alvar Aalto*, pp. 37–50; and Schildt, *Alvar Aalto*, pp. 44–45 and 283.

21. Lundahl, ed., *Nordisk Funktionalism*, is a collection of essays on this aspect of architecture in the Scandinavian countries, similar to the volume on *Nordic Classicism*.

22. Lars Backer in *Byggekunst* 7 (1925), quoted in Norberg-Schulz, "Fra nasjonalromantikk," p. 46.

23. Alvar Aalto, "Sanatorium i Penmar"; Nils E. Wickberg, *Finnish Architecture*, pp. 132–134; Pearson, *Alvar Aalto*, pp. 84–93; and Quantrill, *Alvar Aalto*, pp. 51–55. See also Salokorpi, "Currents and Undercurrents."

24. See Pevsner, *History of Building Types*, pp. 153–158, for discussion of nineteenth- and early twentieth-century hospitals.

25. Norberg-Schulz, "Fra nasjonalromantikk," pp. 66–68.

26. *Housing Question in Sweden*, p. 49.

27. Faber, *History of Danish Architecture*, pp. 156–158, and Hartmann and Villadsen, *Danmarks Arkitektur. Byens huse. Byens plan*, pp. 161–166.

28. Shand, "Stockholm, 1930"; Holmdahl, Lind, and Ödeen, eds., *Gunnar Asplund Architect*, pp. 54–58; Maré, *Gunnar Asplund*, pp. 27–31; Rasmussen, *Nordische Baukunst*, pp. 122–128; Caldenby and Hultin, *Asplund*, pp. 29–31 and 35–39; and Fant, "Gunnar Asplund."

29. Paulsson, *Scandinavian Architecture*, pp. 192–202. See also Silk, *Sweden Plans for Better Housing*; Hartmann and Villadsen, *Danmarks Arkitektur. Byens huse. Byens plan*, pp. 167–178; Norberg-Schulz, "Fra nasjonalromantikk," pp. 94–103; and Norberg-Schulz, *Modern Norwegian Architecture*, pp. 73–85.

30. Paulsson, *Scandinavian Architecture*, pp. 220–224. See also Hitchcock, *Architecture: Nineteenth and Twentieth Centuries*, pp. 374–375, for the Siemenstadt Estate by Walter Gropius in 1930, a prototype for such housing blocks all over Europe.

31. "Københavnske etagehus," *Arkitekten* 40, no. 4 (1939):51–72; Rasmussen, *Nordische Baukunst*, pp. 158–163; and Millech and Fisker, *Danske arkitekturstrømninger*, pp. 332–334.

32. Pearson, *Alvar Aalto*, pp. 138–140; Richards, *800 Years*, pp. 148–149; and Quantrill, *Alvar Aalto*, pp. 70–72.

33. Faber, *History of Danish Architecture*, p. 172, and Jørgensen, *Danmarks Arkitektur. Enfamiliehuset*, pp. 140–141.

34. Blakstad and Munthe-Kaas, *Arkitekt Ove Bang*; Norberg-Schulz, "Fra nasjonalromantikk," pp. 75–79; and Norberg-Schulz, *Modern Norwegian Architecture*, pp. 61–65.

35. Koppel, "Villa Mairea"; Giedion, *Space, Time and Architecture*, pp. 645–649; Pearson, *Alvar Aalto*, pp. 168–175; and Quantrill, *Alvar Aalto*, pp. 83–91.

36. Aino Alto and Alvar Aalto, "Mairea."

37. Langkilde, *Arkitekten Kay Fisker*, pp. 53–59; Faber, *History of Danish Architecture*, pp. 186–189; and Møller, *Aarhus Universitets Bygninger*.

38. Arneberg and Poulsson, *Oslo rådhus*; "Oslo rådhus," *Byggekunst* 9–10 (1950):145–174; Norberg-Schulz, "Fra nasjonalromantikk," pp. 29–35, especially for the proposals and competitions; and Norberg-Schulz, *Modern Norwegian Architecture*, pp. 34–37.

39. "Sunila sulfatcellulosafabrik," *Arkitekten Finland* (1938, no. 10), 145–160; Nils E. Wickberg, *Finnish Architecture*, pp. 139–141; and Giedion, *Space, Time and Architecture*, pp. 640–645.

40. Lauritzen, "Bygningerne ved Københavns Lufthavn."

41. For the consequences of Scandinavian involvement in World War II, see Derry, *History of Scandinavia*, pp. 328–355.

42. Kavli, *Norwegian Architecture*, pp. 120–122; Norberg-Schulz, "Fra gjenreisning," pp. 13–14; and Norberg-Schulz, *Modern Norwegian Architecture*, pp. 92–93.

43. Knutsen, "Menneskit i sentrum," p. 129.

44. *Architectural Digest* 30, no. 9 (September 1960):347–348; Faber, *History of Danish Architecture*, pp. 218–219; and Jørgensen, *Danmarks Arkitektur. Enfamiliehuset*, pp. 156 and 161.

45. *Architectural Design* 47, nos. 11–12 (1977):783–790, and Erskine, "Architecture in a Cold Climate."

46. Paulsson, *Scandinavian Architecture*, pp. 234–238; Langkilde, "Bellahøj"; and Hartmann and Villadsen, *Danmarks Arkitektur. Byens huse. Byens plan*, pp. 180–188.

47. Nils E. Wickberg, *Finnish Architecture*, pp. 226–233; Ervi, "Bybyggerne bag Tapiola"; Ålander, *Viljo Revell*, pp. 40–51; Tempel, *New Finnish Architecture*, pp. 60–98; and Hertzen and Spreiregen, *Building a New Town*.

48. Howard, *Garden Cities*.

49. Mumford, *Stadskultur*.

50. Smith, *Sweden Builds*, pp. 94–113; Paulsson, *Scandinavian Architecture*, pp. 234–236; and Åström, *City Planning in Sweden*, pp. 67–74.

51. For a discussion of "garden cities" and "new towns" see Hitchcock, *Architecture: Nineteenth and Twentieth Centuries,* pp. 405 and 420–421, and Giedion, *Space, Time and Architecture,* pp. 782–785.

52. Nils E. Wickberg, *Finnish Architecture,* pp. 146–147; Pearson, *Alvar Aalto,* p. 219; and Quantrill, *Alvar Aalto,* pp. 128–136.

53. Pearson, *Alvar Aalto,* pp. 203–217.

54. Skriver, "Den tekniske højskoles hovedbygning"; Borràs, *Arquitectura Finlandisa;* Pearson, *Alvar Aalto,* pp. 216–217; and Quantrill, *Alvar Aalto,* pp. 121–127.

55. Olsen and Crumlin-Pedersen, "The Skuldelev Ships"; Faber, *New Danish Architecture,* pp. 146–147; and Jørgensen, Lund, and Nørregård-Nielsen, *Danmarks Arkitektur. Magtens bolig,* pp. 178–179.

56. *Arkitekten* 45, no. 13 (1963):245–249.

57. *Byggekunst* (1977):22–26, and Herteig, *Handbook,* pp. 11–13.

58. Yates, "A Monument to Faith."

59. Tempel, *New Finnish Architecture,* pp. 182–183, and Bruun and Popovits, eds., *Keija and Heikki Siren,* pp. 20–43.

60. Lund, "Skt. Clemens Kirke"; Horskjaer, ed., *Danske kirker,* 13:31–32; Faber, *New Danish Architecture,* pp. 213–215; Bolvig, *Bykirker,* p. 62; and Johanssen and Smidt, *Danmarks Arkitektur. Kirkens huse,* pp. 186–189. St. Clement's Church is also mentioned in a series of essays on church architecture, furnishings, and liturgy edited by one of the architects, Johannes Exner, and Tage Christiansen, *Kirkebygning og teologi,* p. 260.

61. Jor, *Kirker i en ny tid,* pp. 43–48.

62. Ibid., pp. 65–67; Muri, *Norske Kyrkjer,* pp. 256–257; and Norberg-Schulz, "Fra gjenreisning," p. 39.

63. I have seen icebergs in the fjords of southern Greenland of nearly identical shape. Were such natural formations Hovig's inspiration for the Tromsdalen church?

64. Brochmann, "Kaleva Kirken," and Connah, *Writing Architecture,* pp. 174–180.

65. Skriver, "SAS Air Terminal"; Skriver, "Royal-Hotel-Copenhagen"; and Faber, *New Danish Architecture,* pp. 158–161. For Arne Jacobsen see Pedersen, *Arkitekten Arne Jacobsen;* Faber, *Arne Jacobsen;* Kastholm, *Arne Jacobsen;* and Dyssegaard, *Arne Jacobsen: A Danish Architect.*

66. A detailed study of architects as decorative designers would be an enormous but fascinating undertaking. They have been represented in several exhibitions of Scandinavian design, including a recent one at the Cooper-Hewitt Museum in New York City. For critical essays by Scandinavian experts and a good bibliography, see the exhibition catalog edited by David R. McFadden, *Scandinavian Modern Design 1880–1890.*

67. Skriver, "Arne Jacobsens Nationalbank," and Jørgensen, Lund, and Nørregård-Nielsen, *Danmarks Arkitektur. Magtens bolig,* pp. 113–115.

68. Woldbye, "Kim Naver's Wall Hangings."

69. Larsson, ed., *New Architecture in Sweden,* p. 312.

70. Kristensen, "Udvidelse af tappehall."

71. Erik Berg, "Udvidelse af Kastrup," and Sestoft, *Danmarks Arkitektur. Arbejdets bygninger,* pp. 176–177.

72. Salokorpi, "Currents and Undercurrents."

# Bibliography

Ålander, Kyösti, ed. *Viljo Revell.* New York: Praeger, 1966.

Aalto, Aino, and Alvar Aalto. "Mairea," *Arkitekten* 36 (1939):134–137.

Aalto, Alvar. "Sanatorium i Pemar," *Arkitekten* 30 (1933):79–91.

Åström, Kell. *City Planning in Sweden.* Trans. Rudy Feichtner. Stockholm: The Swedish Institute, 1967.

Addison, Agnes. *Romanticism and the Gothic Revival.* New York: Robert R. Smith, 1936.

Ágústsson, Hörthur. "Building through the Centuries," in Nordal and Kristinsson, eds., *Iceland 874–1974,* pp. 97–107.

Ágústsson, Hörthur. "Development of the Icelandic Farm from the 'Landnam' until the 20th Century," in Myhre, Stoklund, and Gjaerder, eds., *Vestnordisk byggeskikk,* pp. 255–267.

Ágústsson, Hörthur. "Inner Construction of the Icelandic Turf House," in Myhre, Stoklund, and Gjaerder, eds., *Vestnordisk byggeskikk,* pp. 172–185.

Ahlberg, Hakon. *Svenska trädgaardskonsten.* 2 vols. Stockholm: Nordisk Rotogravyr, 1930–1931.

Ahlin, Janne. *Sigurd Lewerentz, Architect 1885–1975.* Cambridge, Mass., and London: MIT Press, 1987.

Ailonen, Riitta, and Ritva Kinnunen. *Seurasaari Open Air Museum, Helsinki.* Helsinki: Museovirasto, 1978.

Albrethson, Svend Erik. "Features of the Development of the Norse Farm on Greenland," in Myhre, Stoklund, and Gjaerder, eds., *Vestnordisk byggeskikk,* pp. 269–297.

Alexander, Edward P. *Museum Masters.* Nashville: American Association for State and Local History, 1983.

Allgulin, Torsten. *Hans van Steenwinckel d.ä.* Uppsala: Appelbergs Boktryckeri, 1932.

Alm, Henrik J. "Stockholms observatorium," *Samfundet Sankt Eriks Årsbok* (1930):130–173.

Almqvist, Bo, and David Green, eds. *Seventh Viking Congress.* Dublin: Royal Irish Academy, 1976.

Ambrosiani, Björn, and Hans Andersson. "Urban Archaeology in Sweden," in Barley, ed., *European Towns,* pp. 103–126.

Andersen, Aage. *Middelalderbyen Naestved.* Centrum, 1987.

Andersen, Ester, and K. Roland Hansen. "Kommandørgården på Rømø," *Fra Nationalmuseets Arbejdsmark* (1954):46–62.

Andersen, Knut, et al. "Maglemose hytterne ved Ulkestrup Lyng," *Nordiske Fortidsminder,* Series B, vol. 7 (1982):86–102.

Anderson, Iwar. "A Contribution to the Problem of Transitional Forms between the Primitive Hut and the House Proper," in Stenberger and Klindt-Jensen, eds., *Vallhager,* 2:1008–1032.

Anderson, Iwar. *Vadstena gård och kloster.* 2 vols. Stockholm: Almqvist & Wiksell, 1972.

Anderson, William. *Karlskrona; gator och byggnader.* Lund: Borelius, 1930.

Andrén, Erik. *Skokloster.* Stockholm: Nordisk Roto-gravyr, 1948.

Anker, Peter, and Aron Andersson. *The Art of Scandinavia.* 2 vols. London: The Hamlyn Publishing Group Limited, 1970.

*The Árbaer Museum.* Reykjavik, 1981.

Arbman, Holger. *The Vikings.* New York: Praeger, 1961.

Árnason, Örnófur. "New Lease on Life for Old Reykjavik Neighborhoods," *Atlantica and Iceland Review* (1979, no. 1):10–13.

Arneberg, Arnstein, and Magnus Poulsson. *Oslo rådhus.* Oslo: Aschehoug, 1933.

Arnö-Berg, Inga, and Arne Biörnstad, eds. *Skansens hus och gårdar.* Stockholm: Nordic Museum, 1980.

Aune, Peter, Roland L. Sack, and Arne Selberg. "The Stave Churches of Norway," *Scientific American* 249, no. 2 (August 1983):96–105.


Bain, Robert N. *Gustavus III and His Contemporaries.* 2 vols. London: Kegan Paul, 1894.

Banning, Knud, ed. *A Catalogue of Wall-Paintings in the Churches of Medieval Denmark 1100–1600. Scania, Halland, Blekinge.* 4 vols. Copenhagen: Akademisk Forlag, 1982.

Barley, Maurice W., ed. *European Towns, Their Archaeology and History.* London: Academic Press, 1977.

Barrow, John. *Excursions in the North of Europe.* London: John Murray, 1834.

Becker, Charles J. "Grav eller tempel? En kultbygning fra yngre stenalder ved Herrup, Vestjylland," *Fra Nationalmuseets Arbejdsmark* (1968):17–28.

Becker, Charles J. "Hal og hus i yngre bronzealder," *Fra Nationalmuseets Arbejdsmark* (1972):5–16.

Becker, Charles J. "Late Paleolithic Finds from Denmark," *Proceedings of the Prehistoric Society* 37, part 2 (December 1971):131–139.

Becker, Charles J. "New Finds of Houses from the Viking Period in Denmark," in Myhre, Stoklund, and Gjaerder, eds., *Vestnordisk byggeskikk,* pp. 146–148.

Becker, Charles J. "To landsbyer fra tidlig jernalder i Vestjylland," *Fra Nationalmuseets Arbejdsmark* (1945):39–50.

Becker, Charles J. "En 8000-Årig stenalder boplads i Holmegaards Mose," *Fra Nationalmuseets Arbejdsmark* (1945):61–72.

Beckett, Francis. *Arkitekten Martin Nyrop.* Copenhagen, 1919.

Beckett, Francis. *Frederiksborg. Slottet's historie.* Copenhagen: Hagerups Forlag, 1914.

Beckett, Francis. *Københavns raadhus, opført 1893–1905.* Copenhagen: A. Bang, 1908.

Beckett, Francis. *Uraniborg og Stjaerneborg.* Copenhagen: A. Marcus, 1921.

Beijer, Agne. *Court Theatres of Drottningholm and Gripsholm.* New York: Benjamin Blom, Inc., 1972.

Beijer, Agne. "Les Théâtres de Drottningholm et de Gripsholm," *Revue de la Société d'Histoire du Théâtre* 8 (1956):215–227.

Bekker-Nielsen, Hans, Peter Foote, and Olaf Olsen, eds. *Eighth Viking Congress.* Odense: Odense University Press, 1981.

Bencard, Mogens. "Om Kalundborg kirke," *Fra Holbaek Amt* (1960):74–104.

Bennett, Robert. *Botkyrka kyrka (Sveriges Kyrkor).* Stockholm: Almqvist & Wiksell, 1975.

Benson, Adolph B., ed. *Peter Kalm's Travels in North America.* 2 vols. New York: Dover Publications, Inc., 1966.

Berg, Arne. "The Joining of Individual Houses to form a Longhouse, lån, in Western Norway," in Myhre, Stoklund, and Gjaerder, eds., *Vestnordisk byggeskikk,* pp. 186–194.

Berg, Arno. *Akershus slott i 1600–1700 årene.* 2 vols. Oslo: Cappelen, 1950–1951.

Berg, Arno. *Vor Frelsers kirke.* Oslo: Land og Kirke, 1950.

Berg, Erik. "Udvidelse af Kastrup og Holmegaards Glassvaerker A/S, Fensmark," *Arkitektur* 17, no. 3 (1973):106–111.

Berg, Henry. *Trondheim før Cicignon.* Trondheim, 1951.

Berg, Knut, ed. *Norges kunsthistorie.* 7 vols. Oslo: Gyldendal Nordisk Forlag, 1981–1983.

Berlin, U. "Ravlundsgården och dess gamla miljö," *Fa-*

*taburen* (1949):35–60.

Berner, Finn. "Torvalmenningen," *Byggekunst* 5 (1923):17–24.

Berry, Elizabeth Irene. "Arnolt Schlick's Spiegel der Orgelmacher und Organisten." Ph.D. dissertation, University of Oregon, 1968.

Berthelsen, Bertil. *Studier i Birgittinerordens byggnadskick.* Stockholm: Kungl. Vitt. Hist. och Ant. Akademien *Handlingar* no. 63 (1947).

Bishop, James L. *A History of American Manufactures.* 3 vols. 3d rev. ed. Philadelphia: Edward Young and Co., 1865.

Bjerknes, Kristian B. *Fra hov til stavkirke.* Bergen: J. W. Eides, 1948.

Bjurström, Per. "Gripsholmsteaterns salong," *Konsthistorisk Tidskrift* 21 (1952):49–58.

Blakstad, Gudolf, and Herman Munthe-Kaas. *Arkitekt Ove Bang.* Oslo, 1943.

Blakstad, Gudolf, and Herman Munthe-Kass. "Haugesund rådhus," *Byggekunst* 14 (1932):27–33.

Bligaard, Mette. "The Privy Passage and the Audience House," *Leids Kunsthistorisch Jaarboek* 2 (1983):55–68.

Blindheim, Charlotte. "The Emergence of Urban Communities in Viking Age Scandinavia," in Farrell, ed., *Vikings,* pp. 42–69

Boëthius, Gerda. *Anders Zorn och hans hembygd.* Stockholm, 1941.

Boëthius, Gerda, and Axel L. Romdahl. *Uppsala Domkyrka 1258–1435.* Uppsala: Almqvist & Wiksell, 1935.

Bolvig, Axel. *148 danske bykirker.* Copenhagen: Gyldendal Nordisk Forlag, 1974.

Borch, Martin. "St. Andreaskirken," *Arkitekten* (1900–1901):185–192.

Borràs, Maria Lluisa. *Arquitectura Finlandisa en Otaniemi.* Barcelona: Ediciones Poligrafa, S.A., 1971.

Bradley, John, ed. *Viking Dublin Exposed: The Wood Quay Saga.* Dublin: The O'Brien Press, 1984.

Brahe, Tyge. *Tycho Brahe's Description of His Instruments and Scientific Work.* Translated and edited by Hans Raeder, Elis Strömgren, and Bengt Strömgren. Copenhagen: Munksgaard, 1946.

Bramsen, Henrik. *Gottlieb Bindesbøll, Liv og Arbejder.* Copenhagen: Høst, 1959.

Broby-Johansen, Rudolf. *Det danske Billedbibel i Kalkmalerier.* Copenhagen: Gyldendal Nordisk Forlag, 1947.

Brochmann, Odd. "Kaleva Kirken i Tammerfors," *Arkitektur* 12, no. 2 (April 1968):94–100.

Bröchner, Georg. "Copenhagen's New Scotland Yard," *Architectural Review* 61, no. 364 (March 1927):84–86.

Brøndsted, Johannes. *The Vikings.* Trans. Kalle Skov. Baltimore: Penguin Books, 1965.

Brogaard, Peter, Hakon Lund, and Hans Edward Nørregård-Nielsen. *Danmarks Arkitektur. Landbrugets huse.* Copenhagen: Gyldendal Nordisk Forlag, 1980.

Bruun, Erik, and Sara Popovits, eds. *Keija and Heikki Siren.* Helsinki: Otava, 1976.

Bucht, Gösta. *Härnösands historia.* 2 vols. Härnösand: Aktiebolaget W. Aström, 1935–1954.

Bugge, Anders. *Arkitekten Stadskonduktor Chr. H. Grosch.* Oslo: H. Aschehoug, 1928.

Bugge, Anders. *Norwegian Stave Churches.* Trans. Ragnar Christophorson. Oslo: Dreyers Forlag, 1953.

Bugge, Anders, and Henning Alsvik, eds. *Norges Kirker. Kongsberg Kirke.* Oslo: Land og Kirke, 1962.

Bugge, Gunnar. *Stave Churches in Norway.* Oslo: Dreyers Forlag, 1983.

Bugge, Gunnar, and Christian Norberg-Schulz. *Stav og laft i Norge.* Oslo: Norske Arkitekturs Landsforbund, 1969.

Bumpus, T. Francis. *The Cathedrals of Norway, Sweden and Denmark.* New York: James Pott & Co., 1908.

Caldenby, Claes, and Olof Hultin, eds. *Asplund.* New York: Rizzoli International Publications Inc., 1986.

Cederström, Eugène. *Kristianstad i äldre tider.* Kristianstad: L. Littoren, 1923.

Cervin, Olof Z. "The City Hall at Copenhagen," *Architectural Record* 18 (October 1905):283–299.

Christensen, Charles. *Gamle bygninger på Slotsholmen.* Copenhagen, n.d.

Christensen, Charles. *Kronborg.* Copenhagen: G. E. C. Gad, 1950.

Christie, Håkon. *Middelalderen bygger i tre.* Oslo: Universitetsforlaget, 1974.

Christie, Håkon. "Old Oslo," *Medieval Archaeology* 10

(1966):45–58.

Christie, Håkon. "Stavkirkene-Arkitektur," in Knut Berg, ed., *Norges Kunsthistorie,* 1:139–251.

Christie, Håkon. "Stavkirkene som tradisjonsbaerer og fornyere i middelalderens norske byggemiljø," in Myhre, Stoklund, and Gjaerder, eds., *Vestnordisk byggeskikk,* pp. 68–79.

Christ-Janer, Albert. *Eliel Saarinen.* Foreword by Alvar Aalto. Chicago: University of Chicago Press, 1948.

Clark, Grahame. *The Earlier Stone Age Settlement of Scandinavia.* Cambridge: Cambridge University Press, 1975.

Clark, Grahame. *World Prehistory in New Perspective.* 3d ed. Cambridge: Cambridge University Press, 1977.

Clarke, Edward D. *Travels in Various Countries of Europe Asia and Africa.* 20 vols. London: Cadell & Davies, 1810–1824.

Clifton-Taylor, Alec. *The Pattern of English Building.* London: B. T. Batsford Ltd., 1962.

Cnattingius, Bengt, Ralph Edenheim, Sune Ljungstedt, and Marian Ullén. *Linköpings domkyrka.* Stockholm: Almqvist & Wiksell International, 1987.

Cohen, Sidney L. *Viking Fortresses of the Trelleborg Type.* Copenhagen: Rosenkilde and Bagger, 1965.

Conant, Kenneth J. *Carolingian and Romanesque Architecture.* Baltimore: Penguin Books, 1959.

Connah, Roger. *Writing Architecture.* Cambridge, Mass.: MIT Press, 1990.

Cornell, Henrik. *Den svenska konstens historia.* 2 vols. Rev. ed. Stockholm: Bokförlaget Aldus/Bonniers, 1966.

Crawford, Barbara E. *Scandinavian Scotland.* Leicester: Leicester University Press, 1987.

Crossley, Fred H. *Timber Building in England.* London: B. T. Batsford Ltd., 1951.

Cruickshank, Dan, ed. *Erik Gunnar Asplund.* London: The Architect's Journal, 1988.

Curman, Sigurd. "Nordiska museets byggnad," *Nordisk Tidskrift* (1908):1–29.

Curman, Sigurd, and Johnny Roosval, eds. *Sveriges Kyrkor. Stockholm.* Vol. 1. Stockholm: Svenska Bokhandelscentralen A.-B., 1928.

Dahl, David. "Stockholms Stadshus," *Arkitekten* 26 (1924):179–192.

Dahl, Sverri. "Extracts from a Lecture on Kirkjubøur," in Niclasen, ed. *Fifth Viking Congress,* pp. 188–192.

Dahl, Sverri. *Fornar toftir i Kvívík.* Torshavn, 1951.

Dahl, Sverri. "The Norse Settlement of the Faroe Islands," *Medieval Archaeology* 14 (1970):60–73.

Dahl, Sverri. "A Survey of Archaeological Investigations in the Faroes," in Small, ed., *Fourth Viking Congress,* pp. 135–141.

Dahlberg, Eric. *Suecia antiqua et hodierna.* Stockholm, 1693–1714.

Danstrup, Johan, ed. *Kulturhistorisk Leksikon for nordisk middelalder.* Copenhagen: Rosenkilde and Bagger, 1956.

Davison, Brian K. "The Late Saxon Town of Thetford," *Medieval Archaeology* 11 (1967):189–195.

De Paor, Liam. "The Viking Towns of Ireland," in Almqvist and Green, eds., *Seventh Viking Congress,* pp. 29–37.

Derry, Thomas K. *A History of Scandinavia.* Minneapolis: University of Minnesota Press, 1979.

Dietrichson, Lorenz. *De norske stavkirker.* Christiania and Copenhagen: Alb. Cammermeyers Forlag, 1892.

Dietrichson, Lorenz, and Holm Hansen Munthe. *Die Holzbaukunst Norwegens.* Berlin: Schuster & Bufleb, 1893.

Donnelly, Marian C. *The New England Meeting Houses of the Seventeenth Century.* Middletown: Wesleyan University Press, 1968.

Donnelly, Marian C. "Theaters in the Courts of Denmark and Sweden from Frederik II to Gustav III," *Journal of the Society of Architectural Historians* 43, no. 4 (December 1984):328–340.

Drury, Paul J., ed. *Structural Reconstruction: Approaches to the Interpretation of the Excavated Remains of Buildings.* B.A.R. British series, 110 (1982).

Dumont, Pierre Martin. *Parallèle de plans des plus belles salles de spectacles.* Paris, 1774.

Dyssegaard, Søren. *Arne Jacobsen: A Danish Architect.* Copenhagen: Ministry of Foreign Affairs, 1971–1972.

Easton, J. Murray. "The Stadshus at Stockholm," *Architectural Review* 55, no. 326 (January 1924):1–6.

Eaton, Leonard K. *American Architecture Comes of Age.* Cambridge, Mass., and London: MIT Press, 1972.

Edestrand, Hans, and Erik Lundberg. *Isak Gustaf Clason.* Stockholm: Norstedt, 1968.

Eimer, Gerhard. *Die Stadtplanung im schwedischen Ostseereich 1600–1715.* Stockholm: Svenska Bokförlaget, 1961.

Ekberg, G. *Uppsala slott och Botanska trädgården.* Uppsala, 1949.

Ekhoff, Emil. *Svenska stavkyrkor.* Stockholm: Cedarquists Grafiska Aktiebolag, 1914–1916.

Ekhoff, Emil, and Otto Janse. *Visby Stadsmur.* Stockholm: Wahlström & Widstrand, 1936.

Eklund, Hans, and Barbro Stribolt. *Bollhuset och Dramaten. Kungliga teaterbyggen.* Stockholm, 1978.

Eldjárn, Kristján, ed. *Third Viking Congress.* Reykjavik, 1958.

Eldjárn, Kristján. "Two Medieval Farm Sites in Iceland and Some Remarks on Tephrochronology," in Small, ed., *Fourth Viking Congress,* pp. 10–19.

Eldjárn, Kristján. "Viking Archaeology in Iceland," in Eldjárn, ed., *Third Viking Congress,* pp. 25–38.

Elling, Christian. *Amalienborg Interiors: Christian VII's Palace, 1750–1800.* Copenhagen: Gyldendal Nordisk Forlag, 1945.

Elling, Christian. "Arkitekten Philip de Lange," *Arkitekten* (November 1930):225–272.

Elling, Christian. *Det Klassiske København.* Copenhagen: Thaning & Appel, 1944.

Elling, Christian. *Den Romantiske Have.* Copenhagen: Gyldendal Nordisk Forlag, 1942.

Elton, Oliver, trans. *The First Nine Books of the Danish History of Saxo Grammaticus.* London: David Nutt, 1894.

Engberg, Harald. *Pantomimeteatret.* Copenhagen: Boghallen, 1959.

Engfors, Christina, ed. *Lectures and Briefings from the International Symposium on the Architecture of Erik Gunnar Asplund.* Stockholm: Swedish Museum of Architecture, 1986.

Engqvist, Hans H. *Sønderjyske byen.* Copenhagen: J. Gellerup, 1951.

Engqvist, Hans H., et al., eds. *Bygnings arkaeologiske studier* 3 (1986).

Erichs, Molte, and Ingeborg Wilcke-Lundqvist, eds. *Kyrkor i Närdinghundra härad, västra delen. Sveriges Kyrkor. Uppland.* Vol. 3, no. 3. Stockholm, 1953.

Eriksen, Svend. *Om vaelske gavle.* Copenhagen: Arkitektens Forlag, 1956.

Erixon, Sigurd. "Är den Nordamerikanska timringstekniken överförd fran Sverige?," *Folkliv* 19 (1955–1956):36–65.

Erixon, Sigurd. "Halmtakstyper i Sverige," *Folkliv* 12 (1948–1949):53–86.

Erixon, Sigurd. *Moragårdens tillkomst.* Stockholm, 1939.

Erixon, Sigurd. "The North European Technique of Corner Timbering," *Folkliv* 1 (1937):13–66.

Erixon, Sigurd. "Some Primitive Constructions and Types of Lay-out with Their Relation to European Rural Building Practice," *Folkliv* 1 (1937):124–155.

Erixon, Sigurd. *Svensk byggnads kultur.* Stockholm: Institutet för Folklivsforskning, 1947.

Erskine, Ralph. "Architecture in a Cold Climate," *RIBA Journal* 87, no. 10 (October 1980):22–23.

Ervi, Aarne. "Bybyggerne bag Tapiola," *Arkitektur* 6, no. 2 (April 1962):43–54.

Exner, Johan. *400 danske Landsbykirker.* Copenhagen: Gyldendal Nordisk Forlag, 1968.

Exner, Johannes, and Tage Christiansen, eds. *Kirkebygning og teologi.* Copenhagen: G. E. C. Gad, 1965.

Faber, Tobias. *Arne Jacobsen.* Trans. E. Rockwell. New York: Praeger, 1964.

Faber, Tobias. *A History of Danish Architecture.* Trans. Frederic R. Stevenson. Copenhagen: Det Danske Selskab, 1963.

Faber, Tobias. *New Danish Architecture.* Teufen: Verlag Arthur Niggli, 1962.

Fant, Ake. "Gunnar Asplund and the 1930 Exhibition," in Engfors, ed., *Lectures and Briefings,* pp. 49–55.

Farrell, Robert T., ed. *The Vikings.* London: Phillimore, 1982.

Fenton, Alexander. "The Longhouse in Northern Scotland," in Myhre, Stoklund, and Gjaerder, eds.,

*Vestnordisk byggeskikk*, pp. 231–240.

Fett, Harry, et al. *Ulefos. En norsk herregård.* Oslo: 1940.

Fett, Harry, and Carl W. Schnitler, eds. *Norsk Kunsthistorie.* 2 vols. Oslo: Gyldendal Nordisk Forlag, 1925.

Finsen, Helge, and Esbjørn Hiort. *Gamle stenhus i Island fra 1700-talet.* Copenhagen: Arkitektens Forlag, 1977.

Fischer, Gerhard. *Domkirken i Stavanger.* Oslo: Dreyers Forlag, 1964.

Fischer, Gerhard. *Domkirken i Trondheim.* Oslo: Land og Kirke, 1965.

Fischer, Gerhard. *Nidaros Domkirke.* Trondheim: Land og Kirke, 1969.

Fischer, Gerhard. *Norske Kongeborger.* Oslo: Cappelen, 1951.

Fischer, Gerhard. *Oslo under Eiksberg 1050–1950.* Oslo: Aschehoug, 1950.

Fischer, Gerhard, and Dorothea Fischer. *Norske kongeborger. Bergenhus.* Oslo: Gyldendal Nordisk Forlag, 1980.

Fischer von Erlach, Johann Bernhard. *Entwurff einer historischen Architectur.* Vienna, 1721.

Fisker, Kay. "Den Klintske skole," *Arkitektur* 7, no. 2 (April 1963):37–80.

Fisker, Kay. "Omkring Herholdt," *Arkitekten* (1943):49–64.

Flodin, Barbro. *Tyresö kyrka. Sveriges Kyrkor. Södermanland.* Vol. 3, no. 3. Stockholm, 1979.

Florin, Sten. "Bauernhöfe und Fischerdörfer aus der Dolmen- und Gangräberzeit Schweden," in Reinerth, ed., *Haus und Hof,* pp. 34–40.

Florin, Sten. *Vråkulturen.* Stockholm: Kungl. Vitt. Hist. och Ant. Akademien, 1958.

Fogelmarck, Stig. *Carl Fredrik Adelcrantz Arkitekt.* Stockholm: Almqvist & Wiksell, 1957.

Fogelmarck, Stig. "Gustav III's Opera," *Samfundet Sankt Eriks Årsbok* (1949):95–150.

Foote, Peter, and David M. Wilson. *The Viking Achievement.* London: Sidgwick & Jackson, 1970.

Frampton, Kenneth. "The Classical Tradition and the European Avant-garde," in Paavilainen, ed., *Nordic Classicism,* pp. 161–173.

Franceschi, Gerard, and Øystein Hjort. *Kalkmalerier fra dansk landsbykirker.* Copenhagen: Rhodos, 1969.

Friis, Niels. *Orgelbygning i Danmark.* Copenhagen: Dan Fog, 1971.

Fritsch, K. E. O. *Der Kirchenbau des Protestantismus von der Reformation bis zur Gegenwart.* Berlin, 1893.

Frölén, Hugo F. *Nordens befästa rundkyrkor.* Stockholm: L. Frölén, 1910–1911.

Funder, Lise. *Arkitekten Martin Nyrop.* Copenhagen: Gyldendal Nordisk Forlag, 1979.

Gardberg, Carl J. "Åbo Domkyrka—några synpunkter," in Karling, Lagerlöf, and Svanberg, eds., *Nordisk medeltid,* pp. 232–245.

Gardberg, Carl J. *Åbo slott under den äldre vasatiden.* Helsinki, 1959.

Gestsson, Gísli. "The Use of Stone and Turf in the Icelandic Houses within Historical Times," in Myhre, Stoklund, and Gjaerder, eds., *Vestnordisk byggeskikk,* pp. 162–172.

Giedion, Sigfried. *Space, Time and Architecture.* 5th rev. ed. Cambridge, Mass.: Harvard University Press, 1967.

Gjaerder, Per. "Om stavverk og lafteverk," in Myhre, Stoklund, and Gjaerder, eds., *Vestnordisk Byggeskikk,* pp. 31–67.

Gjessing, Gutorm. *Circumpolar Stone Age.* Acta Arctica Fasc. 2. Copenhagen: Munksgaard, 1944.

Glob, Poul V. "Barkaer. Danmarks aeldste landsby," *Fra Nationalmuseets Arbejdsmark* (1949):5–16.

Glob, Poul V. *Danish Prehistoric Monuments.* Trans. Joan Bulman. London: Faber & Faber, 1971.

Glob, Poul V. *The Mound People.* Trans Joan Bulman. Ithaca: Cornell University Press, 1970.

Gorssen, Hans. *Christiansfeld.* Christiansfeld: Turisforeningen, 1972.

Gotfredsen, Lise. *Råsted kirke—spil og billede.* Århus: Akademisk Forlag, 1975.

Graebe, Henrik. *Kyrkorna i Vä. Sveriges Kyrkor. Skåne.* Vol. 3, no. 1. Stockholm, 1971.

Graham-Campbell, James, and Dafydd Kidd. *The Vikings.* London: British Museum Publications Limited, 1980.

Grut, Torben. "Engelbrektskyrkan," *Ord och Bild* (1916):513–528.

Guralnick, Eleanor, ed. *Vikings in the West.* Chicago, 1982.

Hällström, Olof af. *Sveaborg Viapori Suomenlinna.* Ryngsted Kyst: Anders Nyborg, A/S, 1986.

Haffner, Vilhelm. *Stortingets Hus.* Oslo: Gyldendal Nordisk Forlag, 1953.

Hagen, Anders. *Norway.* London: Thames and Hudson, 1967.

Hagen, Anders. *Studier i jernalderens gårdssamfunn.* Oslo: Universitets oldsaksamling, 1953.

Hahr, August. *Architecture in Sweden.* Stockholm: Alb. Bonniers Boktryckeri, 1938.

Hahr, August. *Die Architektenfamilie Pahr.* Strassburg: Heitz, 1908.

Hahr, August. *Nordiska Borgar.* Uppsala: J. A. Lindblads Forlag, 1930.

Hahr, August. "Torup," in Hahr, ed., *Skånska borgar,* 7–8 (1918):23–49.

Hahr, August. *Uppsala slott och dess rikssal.* Stockholm: Wahlström & Widstrand, 1932.

Hall, Richard. *The Excavations at York.* London: The Bodley Head, 1984.

Hallendorf, Carl, ed. *Sveriges Riddarhus.* Stockholm: Aktibolaget Historiska Förlaget, 1926.

Hallerdt, Björn. *Timmerhus.* Falu: Nya Boktryckeri Aktiebolag, 1965.

Hamberg, Per Gustaf. *Tempelbygge för Protestanter.* Stockholm: Svenska Kyrkans Diokonstyrelses Bokförlag, 1955.

Hamilton, John R. C. *Excavations at Jarlshof, Shetland.* Edinburgh: Her Majesty's Stationery Office, 1956.

Hamran, Ulf. "Det nye Norge bygger Norsk arkitektur 1814–1870," in Knut Berg, ed., *Norges kunsthistorie,* 4:7–125.

Hansen, Henning. *Martin Nyrop.* Copenhagen, 1919.

Hansson, Hans. *Stockholms stadsmurar.* Stockholm, 1956.

Harbison, Peter. *The Archaeology of Ireland.* New York: Charles Scribner's Sons, 1976.

Hardy, James Hathaway. "Historic Houses: Fantasy at Kina Slott," *Architectural Digest* 37, no. 4 (May 1980):174–180.

Harris, John. *Sir William Chambers.* London: A. Zwemmer Ltd., 1970.

Hartmann, Sys, and Villads Villadsen. *Danmarks Arkitektur. Byens huse. Byens plan.* Copenhagen: Gyldendal Nordisk Forlag, 1979.

Harvey, John. *The Medieval Architect.* London: Wayland Publishers, 1972.

Hauglid, Roar, ed. *Native Art of Norway.* Oslo: Dreyers Forlag, 1965.

Hauglid, Roar. *Norske stavkirker.* Oslo: Dreyers Forlag, 1969.

Hausen, Marika, Kirmo Mikkola, and Anna-Luisa Amberg. *Saarinen in Finland.* Helsinki: Museum of Finnish Architecture, 1984.

Heiberg, Steffen, ed. *Christian IV and Europe.* Copenhagen: Foundation for Christian IV Year, 1988.

Heikel, Axel Olai. *Karuna Kyrka.* Helsinki: Seurasaaren Ulkomuseo, 1922.

Helsted, Dyveke. *Dronning Juliane Marie og Fredensborg slot.* Copenhagen: Thaning & Appel, 1958.

Hermansen, Victor, and Poul Nørlund. *Danmarks Kirker. Sorø Amt.* Copenhagen: G. E. C. Gad, 1936–1938.

Hermansen, Victor, Aage Roussell, and Jan Steenberg. *Danmarks Kirker. København.* Vol. 1. Copenhagen: G. E. C. Gad, 1945–1958.

Hermansson, Nanna. "Árbaer Museum. Preserving the Old Amidst the New," *Atlantica & Iceland Review* 14, no. 2 (1976):24–29.

Herteig, Asbjorn C. *Handbook to the Cultural History of the Middle Ages.* Bergen: Bryggens Museum, 1978.

Hertzen, Heikki von, and Paul D. Spreiregen. *Building a New Town: Finland's New Garden City, Tapiola.* Cambridge, Mass.: MIT Press, 1971.

Hilleström, Gustav. *The Royal Opera Stockholm.* Trans. Alan Blair. Stockholm: The Royal Opera House, 1960.

Hiort, Esbjørn. "Andreas Kirkerup's Islandske kirke. Af Reykjavik's Domkirkes bygnings-historie," *Architectura* 2 (1980):126–144.

Hiort, Esbjørn. *Housing in Denmark since 1930.* London: The Architectural Press, 1952.

Hiort, Esbjørn. "Museet i Faaborg og nyklassicism i Norden," in Nielsen, ed., *Ikke bare om Norden.*

Hirn, Marta. *Sveaborg genom tva sekler.* Borga: W. Soderström, 1948.

Hitchcock, Henry-Russell. *Architecture: Nineteenth and Twentieth Centuries*. Baltimore: Penguin Books, 1958.

Hitchcock, Henry-Russell. *Netherlandish Scrolled Gables of the Sixteenth and Early Seventeenth Centuries*. New York: New York University Press, 1978.

Hjelde, Gunnar. *Oscarshall. Lystslottet pa Bygdøy*. Oslo: Dreyers Forlag, 1978.

Høy, F. C. *Christiansfeld*. Christiansfeld, 1923.

Holmdahl, Gustav, Sven Ivar Lind, and Kjell Ödeen, eds. *Gunnar Asplund Architect 1885–1940*. Stockholm: AB Tidskriften Byggmästaren, 1959.

Honnens de Lichtenberg, Hanne. "Frederik II's Frederiksborg," *Leids Kunsthistorisch Jaarboek* 2 (1983):37–53.

Hopstock, Carsten, and Stephan Tschudi-Madsen. *Rosendal. Baroni og bygning*. Oslo: Universitetsforlaget, 1969.

Horskjaer, Erik, ed. *De Danske kirker*. 20 vols. Copenhagen: G. E. C. Gad, 1966–1973.

*Housing Question in Sweden*. Stockholm: Norstedt, 1920.

Howard, Ebenezer. *Garden Cities of To-Morrow*. Ed. Francis J. Osborn. Cambridge, Mass.: MIT Press, 1965.

Huggins, Peter, Kristy Rodwell, and Warwick Rodwell. "Anglo-Saxon and Scandinavian Building Measurements," in Drury, ed., *Structural Reconstruction*, pp. 21–65.

Hvidt, Kristian, Svend Ellehøj, and Otto Norn, eds. *Christiansborg Slot*. 2 vols. Copenhagen: Arnold Busk, 1975.

Ingólfsson, Adalsteinn. "A Saga-Age Farmhouse Reconstructed at a South-Icelandic Excavation Site," *Atlantica & Iceland Review* 18, no. 1 (1980):25–27.

Ingstad, Anne Stine. *The Discovery of a Norse Settlement in America*. Oslo: Universitetsforlaget, 1977.

Ingstad, Helge. *Westward to Vinland*. Trans. Erik J. Friis. London: Jonathan Cape, 1969.

Innocent, Charles F. *The Development of English Building Construction*. Cambridge: Cambridge University Press, 1916.

Jakstein, Werner. "C. F. Hansens Rat-und-Arrest-haus," *Wasmuths Monatshefte für Baukunst* 10 (1926):222–239.

Jakstein, Werner. *Landbaumeister Christian Friedrich Hansen*. Neumünster in Holstein: Karl Wachholtz Verlag, 1937.

James, Bartlett B., and J. Franklin Jameson, eds. *Journal of Jasper Danckaerts 1679–1686*. New York: Charles Scribner's Sons, 1913.

Jelsbak, Jens, ed. *Grundtvigs Kirke*. Copenhagen: Krohns Bogtrykkeri, 1977.

Jensen, Christian A. *Dansk bindingsvaerk fra Renaessancetiden*. Copenhagen: G. E. C. Gad, 1933.

Jensen, Christian A., and Victor Hermansen. *Danmarks Kirker. Praestø Amt*. 2 vols. Copenhagen: G. E. C. Gad, 1933–1935.

Jensen, Knud. *Fra Halmtorvet til Rådhusplads*. Copenhagen, 1957.

Jern, Carl H. *Uraniborg*. Lund: Studentlitteratur, 1976.

Jespersen, Svend. *Kommandørgården on the Island of Rømø*. Copenhagen: National Museum, 1955.

Jessen, Curt von. "Magnus-Katedralen," in Langberg, ed., *Hvem Byggede Hvad*, 2:311–312.

Jökulsson, Illugi. "The Árbaer Museum and Church," *Atlantica*, n.d., pp. 8–13.

Jørgensen, Lisbet Balslev. "The Copenhagen School of Classicism," *Architectural Design* 57, no. 3/4 (1987):6–21.

Jørgensen, Lisbet Balslev. *Danmarks Arkitektur. Enfamiliehuset*. Copenhagen: Gyldendal Nordisk Forlag, 1979.

Jørgensen, Lisbet Balslev. "Hack Kampmann," *Architectural Review* 172, no. 1035 (January 1983):58–62.

Jørgensen, Lisbet Balslev. "Thorvaldsen's Museum. A National Monument," *Apollo* 96, pt. 1 (July-September 1972):198–205.

Jørgensen, Lisbet Balslev, Hakon Lund, and Hans Edvard Nørregård-Nielsen. *Danmarks Arkitektur. Magtens bolig*. Copenhagen: Gyldendal Nordisk Forlag, 1980.

Jørgensen, Lisbet Balslev, and Demetri Porphyrios, eds. "Neoclassical Architecture in Copenhagen and Athens," *Architectural Design* 57, no. 3/4 (1987):2–81.

Johannsen, Birgitte-Boggild. *Danmarks Kirker*.

*København*. Vols. 23, 24, and 25. Copenhagen: G. E. C. Gad, 1983.

Johannsen, Hugo, and Claus M. Smidt. *Danmarks Arkitektur. Kirkens huse*. Copenhagen: Gyldendal Nordisk Forlag, 1981.

Johnson, Amandus. *The Swedish Settlements on the Delaware*. 2 vols. Philadelphia: University of Pennsylvania Press, 1911.

Jones, Gwyn. *History of the Vikings*. New York: Oxford University Press, 1968.

Jones, Gwyn. *The Norse Atlantic Saga*. London: Oxford University Press, 1964.

Jor, Finn. *Kirker i en ny tid*. Oslo: Land og Kirke, 1966.

Josephson, Ragnar. *Tessin i Danmark*. Stockholm: A. B. Bonniers Förlag, 1924.

Josephson, Ragnar. *Tessin. Nicodemus Tessin d.y. Tiden—Mannen—Verket*. 2 vols. Stockholm: Norstedt, 1930–1931.


Kampmann, Hack. "Politigaarden i København," *Arkitekten* 21 (1919):277–283.

Karling, Sten, ed. *Ålands medeltida kyrkor*. Stockholm: Almqvist & Wiksell, 1973.

Karling, Sten. "Simon de La Vallée," *Ord och Bild* 44 (1935):401–406.

Karling, Sten. *Trädgårdskonstens historia i Sverige*. Stockholm: Albert Bonniers Förlag, 1931.

Karling, Sten. *Tyresö Slott*. Stockholm, 1933.

Karling, Sten, Erland Lagerlöf, and Jan Svanberg, eds. *Nordisk medeltid*. Stockholm Studies in History of Art 13. Stockholm: Almqvist & Wiksell, 1967.

Kastholm, Jørgen. *Arne Jacobsen*. Copenhagen: Høst, 1968.

Kavli, Guthorm. *Norwegian Architecture*. Oslo: Dreyers Forlag, 1958.

Kavli, Guthorm. *The Royal Palace in Oslo*. Oslo: Dreyers Forlag, 1970.

Kavli, Guthorm, and Gunnar Hjelde. *Kongens Slott*. Oslo: Dreyers Forlag, 1973.

Kavli, Guthorm, and Gunnar Hjelde. *Slottet i Oslo*. Oslo: Dreyers Forlag, 1973.

Kidd, Beresford. *Documents Illustrative of the Continental Reformation*. Oxford: At the Clarendon Press, 1911.

Kielland, Thor B. *Paleet i Oslo*. Oslo: Gyldendal Nordisk Forlag, 1939.

"Kirkearkaeologisk Litteratur i Norden 1950–1982," *Hikuin* 9 (1983):245–278.

Kivikoski, Ella. *Finland*. New York: Praeger, 1967.

Kivinen, Paula. *Tampereen tuomiokirkko*. Porvoo and Helsinki, 1986.

Kivinen, Paula, Pekka Korvenmaa, and Asko Salokorpi. *Lars Sonck 1870–1956*. Helsinki: Museum of Finnish Architecture, 1977.

Kjellberg, Sven T. *Skåne*. 3 vols., in Kjellberg and Svensson, eds., *Slott och herresäten*.

Kjellberg, Sven T., and S. Artur Svensson, eds. *Slott och herresäten i Sverige*. 18 vols. Malmö: Allhem, 1966–1971.

Klein, August. *Landbrugets bygninger*. Copenhagen: R. Klein, 1893.

Klindt-Jensen, Ole. *Denmark before the Vikings*. New York: Praeger, 1967.

Kloster, Robert, and Gerhard Fischer. *The Rosencrantz Tower*. Trans. Toni Ramholt. Bergen: A. Garnaes, 1966.

Knapas, Rainer. "Eastern and Western Neoclassicism in Finland," *Journal of the Society of Architectural Historians* 38, no. 2 (May 1979):124–129.

Knutsen, Knut. "Mennesket i sentrum," *Byggekunst* (1961):129.

Kommer, Björn R. *Nicodemus Tessin der Jüngerer und das Stockholmer Schloss*. Heidelberg: Carl Winter, Universitäts Verlag, 1974.

Kopisto, Sirkka. *Suomen Kansallismuseo*. Helsinki: Museovirasto, 1981.

Koppel, Nils. "Villa Mairea," *Arkitekten* 42, no. 7 (1940):93–99.

Krabbe, Herluf. *Kastellet gennem 300 år*. Copenhagen: Martins Forlag, 1964.

Krins, Hubert. *Die frühen Steinkirchen Dänemarks*. Hamburg, 1968.

Kristensen, Svenn Erik. "Udvidelse af tappehall for Carlsberg Bryggerierne," *Arkitektur* 14, no. 5 (October 1970):224–227.

Kristjánsson, Rev. Gunnar. *Churches of Iceland*. Reykjavik: Iceland Review, 1988.

Krogh, Knud J. *Viking Greenland*. Copenhagen: National Museum, 1967.

Kronqvist, Iikka. *Åbo slott under medeltiden.* Helsinki, 1947.

Kronqvist, Iikka. "Die mittelalterliche Kirchenarchitektur im Finland," in *Finska Forminnesföreningens Tidskrift* 48, no. 1 (1948):7–80.

Lagerlöf, Erland, and Bengt Stolt. *Hemse Kyrkor. Sveriges Kyrkor. Gotland.* Vol. 6, no. 3. Stockholm, 1969.

Lagerlöf, Erland, and Gunnar Svahnström. *Gotlands Kyrkor.* Uddevalla: Rabén and Sjögren, 1966.

Langberg, Harald. "The Castle of Elsinore, Castel S. Angelo in Rome, and St. Birgitta of Sweden," in *Quaderni dell'Istituto di storia dell'Architettura* 1–10 (1983–1987):129–134.

Langberg, Harald. *Clausholms bygningshistorie.* Copenhagen: 1958.

Langberg, Harald. *Danmarks bygningskultur.* 2 vols. Copenhagen: Gyldendal Nordisk Forlag, 1955.

Langberg, Harald, ed. *Hvem Byggede Hvad.* 3 vols. Copenhagen: Politikens Forlag, 1968–1971.

Langberg, Harald. *Omkring C. F. Hansen.* Copenhagen: V. Prior, 1950.

Lange, Guenther. *Alexis de Chateauneuf.* Hamburg: Verlag Weltarchiv, 1965.

Lange, Johan. *Vaern og våben i kirker og klostre.* Copenhagen: Rhodos, 1987.

Langkilde, Hans Erling. *Arkitekten Kay Fisker.* Copenhagen: Arkitektens Forlag, 1960.

Langkilde, Hans Erling. "Bellahøj," in Langberg, ed., *Hvem Byggede Hvad,* 1:39–41.

Langkilde, Hans Erling. *Nyklassicismen i købstaederne.* Copenhagen: Arkitektens Forlag, 1986.

Langkilde, Hans Erling. "Politigaarden," in Langberg, ed., *Hvem Byggede Hvad,* 1:220–222.

Larsen, Carsten U. "Gravhøje på Sjaelland," *Fra Nationalmuseets Arbejdsmark* (1989):143–158.

Larsson, Marten J., ed. *New Architecture in Sweden.* Stockholm: Svenska Arkitektens Riksforbund, 1961.

Lauritzen, Vilhelm. "Bygningerne ved Københavns Lufthavn," *Arkitekten U* 42(1940):107–115.

Lebech, Mogens. *Christianshavn paa halvveien.* Copenhagen: Burmaster & Wain, 1955.

Lebech, Mogens. *Danske købstaeder for to hundrede år.* 2 vols. Copenhagen, 1961.

Lebech, Mogens. *Nyboder i opgang og nedgang.* Copenhagen: Foreningen Fremtiden, 1962.

Lexow, Jan Hendrick. "Arkitektur 1536–1814," in Knut Berg, ed., *Norges kunsthistorie,* 3:7–119.

Lidén, Hans-Emil. *Mariakirken; romansk kirkebygningskunst i Bergen.* Bergen, 1961.

Lidén, Hans-Emil. "Middelalderens steinarkitektur i Norge," in Knut Berg, ed., *Norges kunsthistorie,* 2:7–125.

Lidén, Hans-Emil. "Urban Archaeology in Norway," in Barley, ed., *European Towns,* pp. 83–101.

Lidén, Hans-Emil, and Ellen-Marie Magerøy. *Norges Kirker. Bergen.* 2 vols. Oslo: Gyldendal Nordisk Forlag, 1980–1983.

Lindberg, Carolus. *Finlands kyrkor.* Helsinki: Förlag Bildkonst, 1935.

Lindblom, Andreas. *Stockholms slott genom seklerna.* Uppsala: Almqvist & Wiksell, 1925.

Lindblom, Andreas. *Sveriges konsthistoria från fortid til nutid.* 3 vols. Stockholm: Nordisk Rotogravyr, 1944–1947.

Lindblom, Andreas. *Vadstena.* Stockholm: Norstedt, 1925.

Lindblom, Dan. *Stave Churches in Norway.* Trans. Stella and Adam Bittleston. London: Rudolf Steiner Press, 1969.

Lindegren, Axel Johan. "Kungliga Dramatiska teatern och dess konstnärlige utsmyckning," *Ord och Bild* (1908):129–160.

Lindqvist, Sune. *Gamla Uppsala Fornminnen.* Stockholm: Wahlström & Widstrands Förlag, 1949.

Linvald, Steffen. *Sophie Amalienborg og Dronningens Have.* Copenhagen: Uffe Petersen Schmidt, 1958.

Lloyd, John. "The Norwegian Laftehus," in Oliver, ed., *Shelter and Society,* pp. 33–48.

Logan, F. Donald. *The Vikings in History.* Totowa, N.J.: Barnes and Noble Books, 1983.

Lomborg, Ebbe. "Vadgård. Ein Dorf mit Häusern und einer Kultstätte aus der älteren nordischen Bronzezeit," in Mitscha-Märheim, Friesinger, and Kerchler, eds., *Festschrift,* 2:414–432.

Lorenzen, Vilhelm, ed. *Christian IV's Byanlaege og Bygningsarbejdere.* Copenhagen: Høst, 1937.

Lorenzen, Vilhelm. *De danske cistercienserklosters byg-*

*ningshistorie.* Copenhagen: G. E. C. Gad, 1941.

Lorenzen, Vilhelm. *Jens Bangs Stenhus.* Copenhagen: Gyldendal Nordisk Forlag, 1947.

Lund, Hakon. *De kongelige lysthaver.* Copenhagen: Gyldendal Nordisk Forlag, 1977.

Lund, Hakon, and Christian Küster. *Architekt Christian Frederik Hansen, 1756–1845.* Hamburg: Altonaer Museum, 1968.

Lund, Hakon, and Knud Millech, eds. *Danmarks bygningskunst.* Copenhagen: H. Hirschsprungs Forlag, 1963.

Lund, Nils-Ole. "Skt. Clemens Kirke i Randers," *Arkitekten* 8, no. 3 (June 1964):124–134.

Lundahl, Gunilla, ed. *Nordisk Funktionalism.* Copenhagen: Arkitektens Forlag, 1980.

Lundberg, Erik. *Byggnadskonsten i Sverige under medeltiden 1000–1400.* Stockholm: Nordisk Rotogravyr, 1940.

Lundberg, Erik. "Torups Slott. En Byggnadshistorisk undersökning," *Skånes Hembygningsförening Årsbok* (1933):103–122.

Lundberg, Erik. *Trä gav form.* Stockholm: Norstedt, 1971.

Lundborg, Matheus. *Heliga Trefaldighetskyrkan i Kristianstad.* Kristianstad: Kristianstads Boktryckeri Aktiebolag, 1928.

Lundmark, Efraim. *Sankt Jakobs Kyrka.* Stockholm, 1930.

Lundmark, Efraim. *Tingstäde kyrka. Sveriges Kyrkor. Gotland.* Vol. 1, no. 2. Stockholm, 1923.

Lundqvist, Maja. *Svensk konsthistorisk bibliografi.* Lund: Carl Bloms Boktryckeri, 1967.

Lysaker, Trygve. *Domkirken i Trondheim.* Oslo: Land og Kirke, 1973.


McFadden, David R., ed. *Scandinavian Modern Design 1880–1890.* New York: Abrams, 1982.

Mackeprang, Mogens B. *Jydske Granitportaler.* Copenhagen: Høst, 1948.

Madsen, Jørgen Høj. "Fredensborg slotskirke—undersøgelse og restaurering," *Fra Nationalmuseets Arbejdsmark* (1975):60–74.

Madsen, Torsten. "Earthen Long Barrows and Timber Structures: Aspects of the Early Neolithic Mortuary Practice in Denmark," *Proceedings of the Pre-*

*historic Society* 45 (1979):301–320.

Magnusson, Magnus. *Viking Expansion Westward.* New York: Henry Z. Walch, Inc., 1973.

Magnusson, Magnus. *Viking: Hammer of the North.* New York: Galahad Books, 1980.

Magnusson, Magnus. *Vikings!* New York: E. P. Dutton, 1980.

Magnusson, Thór. "The Viking Age Settlement of Iceland," *Atlantica and Iceland Review* 18, no. 3 (1980):32–37.

Malmborg, Boo von. *Drottningholm.* Stockholm: Rabén & Sjögren, 1966.

Malmborg, Boo von, ed. *Gripsholm. Ett slott och des konstkatter.* Stockholm: Ehlius, 1956.

Malmborg, Boo von. *De kungliga slotten.* 2 vols., in Kjellberg and Svensson, eds., *Slott och herresäten.*

Mamen, Hans Christian, ed. *Akershus.* Oslo: Gyldendal Nordisk Forlag, 1981.

Manker, Ernst. *Lapsk kultur.* Acta Lapponica 4. Stockholm: H. Geber, 1944.

Mannström, Oscar. *Adolf Fredriks Kyrka och S. Olovs kapell. Sveriges Kyrkor. Stockholm.* Vol. 5, no. 1. Stockholm, 1924.

Maré, Eric de. *Gunnar Asplund.* London: Art and Technics, 1955.

Marker, Frederick J., and Lise-Lone Marker. *The Scandinavian Theatre. A Short History.* Totowa, N.J.: Rowman and Littlefield, 1975.

Marstrand, Jacob. *Grundtvigs Mindekirke paa Bispeberg.* Copenhagen: Gyldendal Nordisk Forlag, 1932.

Masson, Georgina. *Queen Christina.* London: Secher & Warburg, 1968.

Meeks, Carroll L. V. *The Railroad Station.* New Haven: Yale University Press, 1956.

Meissner, Carl. *Carl Ludwig Engel.* Forschungen zur deutschen Kunstgeschichte 20. Berlin, 1937.

Meist, Paul-Friedrich, and Wilhelm Paasche. *Hannoverisches Wendland.* Hannover, 1981.

Meldahl, Ferdinand. *Frederikskirken i Kjøbenhavn.* Copenhagen: Thieles Bogtrykkeri, 1896.

Meldahl, Ferdinand, and Peter Johansen. *Det Kongelige akademi for de skjønne kunsten 1700–1904.* Copenhagen: Hagerup, 1904.

Michelsen, Peter. *Frilandsmuseet.* Copenhagen: National Museum, 1973.

Michelsen, Peter. *Ildsteder og Opvarming på Frilands-museet.* Copenhagen: National Museum, 1968.

Michelsen, Peter. "The Origin and Aim of the Open-Air Museum," in Rasmussen, ed., *Dansk Folkemu-seum,* pp. 227–244.

Michelsen, Peter. "The Outdoor Museum and Its Ed-ucational Program," in National Trust, *Historic Pre-servation Today,* pp. 201–217.

Michelsen, Vibeke, and Kield de Fine Licht. *Danmarks Kirker. Århus Amt.* Vol. I. Copenhagen: G. E. C. Gad, 1968.

Mikkola, Kirmo. *Architecture in Finland in the 20th Century.* Trans. David Miller. Helsinki: Humari, 1981.

Millech, Knud. *J. D. Herholdt og Universitets biblioteket i Fiolstraede.* Copenhagen: E. Paluden, 1961.

Millech, Knud. "Nordvestsjaellands Elektricitets-vaerk," in Langberg, ed., *Hvem Byggede Hvad,* 2:271–273.

Millech, Knud. "På Bjerget, Grundtvigs Kirke," in Langberg, ed., *Hvem Byggede Hvad,* 1:227–233.

Millech, Knud, and Kay Fisker. *Danske arkitek-turstrømninger 1850–1950.* Copenhagen, 1951.

Miller, William C. *Alvar Aalto: An Annotated Bibliogra-phy.* New York: Garland Publishing, Inc. 1984.

Mitscha-Märheim, Herbert, Herwig Friesinger, and Helga Kerchler, eds. *Festschrift für Richard Pittioni.* 2 vols. Vienna: Franz Deutiske, 1976.

Møller, Christian F. *Aarhus Universitets Bygninger.* Århus: Universitetsforlaget, 1977.

Møller, Elna. *Danmarks Kirker. Ribe Amt.* 2 vols. Co-penhagen: Nationalmuseets Forlag, 1979.

Møller, Elna, and Olaf Olsen. "Danske traekirker," *Fra Nationalmuseets Arbejdsmark* (1961):35–58.

Møller, Viggo Sten, ed. *Amalienborg.* Copenhagen: Rhodos, 1932.

Møller, Viggo Sten. *Dansk kunstindustrie.* 2 vols. Co-penhagen: Rhodos, 1969–1970.

Moltke, Erik, and Elna Møller. *Danmarks Kirker. Fred-eriksborg Amt.* 3 vols. Copenhagen: G. E. C. Gad, 1967–1987.

Moltke, Erik, and Elna Møller. *Danmarks Kirker. Københavns Amt.* 3 vols. Copenhagen: G. E. C. Gad, 1951.

Moltke, Erik, and Elna Møller. *Danmarks Kirker. Sønderjylland.* 4 vols. Copenhagen: G. E. C. Gad, 1945–1961.

Moorhouse, Jonathan, Michael Carpetian, and Leena Ahtola-Moorhouse. *Helsinki Jugendstil Architecture 1895–1915.* Helsinki: Otava, 1987.

Morrison, Hugh. *Early American Architecture.* New York: Oxford University Press, 1952.

Mumford, Lewis. *Stadskultur.* Trans. Leif Björk and Åke Malmström. Stockholm, 1942.

Munksgaard, Elisabeth. *Denmark: An Archaeological Guide.* London: Faber & Faber, 1970.

Muri, Sigurd. *Norske Kyrkjer.* Oslo: Det Norske Sam-laget, 1971.

Murray, Hilary. "Houses and Other Structures from the Dublin Excavations," in Bekker-Nielsen, Foote, and Olsen, eds., *Eighth Viking Congress,* pp. 37 68.

Murray, Hilary. *Viking and Early Medieval Buildings in Dublin.* B.A.R. British Series 119. Oxford, 1983.

Murtagh, William J. *Moravian Architecture and Town Planning.* Chapel Hill: University of North Carolina Press, 1967.

Myers, Albert Cook, ed. *Narratives of Early Pennsylva-nia, West New Jersey, and Delaware 1630–1707.* New York: Charles Scribner's Sons, 1912.

Myhre, Bjørn. "Development of the Farm House dur-ing the Iron Age and the Middle Ages," in Myhre, Stoklund, and Gjaerder, eds., *Vestnordisk bygges-kikk,* pp. 195–217.

Myhre, Bjørn. "Gårdsanlegget på Ullandhaug," *Arkeo-logisk Museum i Stavanger Skrifter* 4 (1980).

Myhre, Bjørn. "Views on the Building Techniques of Farm Houses from the Iron Age and Early Middle Ages in SW Norway," in Myhre, Stoklund, and Gjaerder, eds., *Vestnordisk byggeskikk,* pp. 98–118.

Myhre, Bjørn, Bjarne Stoklund, and Per Gjaerder, eds. *Vestnordisk byggeskikk gjennom to tusen år.* Sta-vanger: Arkeologisk Museum, 1982.


National Trust for Historic Preservation. *Historic Pre-servation Today.* Charlottesville: University of Vir-ginia Press, 1965.

Neiiendam, Robert. *Hofteatret og Teatermuseet ved Christiansborg.* Rev. ed. Copenhagen: Teatermu-seet, 1971.

Niclasen, Bjarni, ed. *Fifth Viking Congress.* Torshavn, 1968.

Nielsen, Erling, ed. *Ikke bare om Norden.* Copenhagen, 1975.

Nikander, Gabriel. "Byar och gårdar," *Det Svenska Finland* I (1919–1921):117–146.

Nikula, Riita. *Armas Lindgren 1874–1929 Arkkitehti.* Helsinki: Museum of Finnish Architecture, 1988.

Nilsson, Albert. "Den sentida bebyggelsen på Islands landsbygd," in Stenberger, ed., *Forntida gårdar,* pp. 269–306.

Nørlund, Poul. *Danmarks romanske kalkmalerier.* Copenhagen: Høst, 1944.

Nørlund, Poul. *Trelleborg.* Trans. John R. B. Gosney. Copenhagen: Gyldendal Nordisk Forlag, 1948.

Nørlund, Poul. *Viking Settlers in Greenland.* London: Cambridge University Press, 1936.

Norberg-Schulz, Christian. "Fra gjenreisning til omverdenskrise, Norsk arkitektur 1945–1980," in Knut Berg, ed., *Norges kunsthistorie,* 7:7–92.

Norberg-Schulz, Christian. "Fra Nasjonalromantikk til funksjonalisme. Norsk arkitektur 1914–1940," in Knut Berg, ed., *Norges kunsthistorie,* 6:7–111.

Norberg-Schulz, Christian. *Modern Norwegian Architecture.* Oslo: Universitetsforlaget, 1986.

Nordal, Johannes, and Valdimar Kristinsson, eds. *Iceland 874–1974.* Reykjavik: Central Bank of Iceland, 1975.

Nordenstreng, Sigurd. *Fredrikshamn såsom befäst gränsort och stapelstad.* Vasa: F. W. Unggrens Boktryckeri, 1909.

Norn, Otto. *Christian III's borge.* 2 vols. Copenhagen: Høst, 1949.

Norn, Otto. *Hesselagergaard og Jacob Binck.* Copenhagen: Arkitektens Forlag, 1961.

Norn, Otto. *Kronborg.* Copenhagen: Schønbergske Forlag, 1954.

Norn, Otto, Christian G. Schultz, and Erik Skov. *Danmarks Kirker. Bornholm.* Copenhagen: G. E. C. Gad, 1954.

Nyberg, Tore. "Denmark," in Barley, ed., *European Towns,* pp. 65–81.

Nystrøm, Eiler. *Frederiksbergs Historie.* 3 vols. Copenhagen: Gyldendal Nordisk Forlag, 1942.

O'Callaghan, Edmund B., ed. *Documents Relative to the Colonial History of the State of New York.* 15 vols. Albany, 1853–1887.

Ødegaard, Sverre. *Om Kjerke på Røros.* Røros, 1984.

Ødegaard, Sverre. *Røros.* Oslo, 1984.

Östberg, Ragnar. *The Stockholm Town Hall.* Stockholm: Norstedt, 1929.

Østby, Leif. *Norges Kunsthistorie.* Oslo: Gyldendal Nordisk Forlag, 1977.

Oliver, Paul, ed. *Shelter and Society.* New York: Praeger, 1969.

Olsen, Olaf. *Hørg, hov og kirke.* Aarboger for Nordisk Oldkyndighed 1965. Copenhagen, 1966.

Olsen, Olaf, and Ole Crumlin-Pedersen. "The Skuldelev Ships," *Acta Archaeologica* 38 (1967):73–174.

Olsen, Olaf, Holger Schmidt, and Else Roesdahl. *Fyrkat. En jysk vikingeborg.* 2 vols. Copenhagen: H. J. Lynge og Son, 1977.

Olsson, Martin. *Kalmar slotts historia.* 2 vols. Stockholm: Kungl. Vitt. Hist. och Ant. Akademien, 1944.

Olsson, Martin. *Kalmar slotts kyrkor.* Sveriges Kyrkor. Småland. Vol. 3, no. 1. Stockholm, 1968.

Olsson, Martin, ed. *Stockholms slotts historia.* 3 vols. Stockholm: Norstedt, 1940–1941.

Olsson, Martin. *Uraniborg og Stjärnborg.* Stockholm: Wahlström & Wikstrand, 1928.

Olsson, Sven, ed. *Falun. Stad i Trä.* Falun, 1975.

Ottaway, B. S., ed. *Archaeology, Dendrochronology and the Radiocarbon Calibration Curve.* Edinburgh, 1983.

Outhier, Reginald. *Journal d'un voyage au nord, en 1736 & 1737.* Paris, 1744.

Overskou, Thomas. *Den danske Skueplads i dens Historie.* 7 vols. Copenhagen: Thieles Bogtrykkeri, 1854–1876.

Paavilainen, Simo, ed. *Nordic Classicism.* Helsinki: Museum of Finnish Architecture, 1982.

*Palaty Sanktpeterburgskoi Imperatorskoi Akademii nauk Biblioteki i Kunstkameri.* St. Petersburg, 1741.

Pallasmaa, Juhani, ed. *Hvitträsk: The Home as a Work of Art.* Helsinki: Museum of Finnish Architecture, 1987.

Paulsson, Thomas. *Scandinavian Architecture.* London: Leonard Hill Ltd., 1958.

Pearson, Paul David. *Alvar Aalto and the International*

*Style*. New York: Whitney Library of Design, 1978.

Pedersen, Johan. *Arkitekten Arne Jacobsen*. Copenhagen: Arkitektens Forlag, 1957.

Pedersen, Karl Peder. "Tranquebars danske huse: en bygningshistorie skitse," in Engqvist et al., eds., *Bygningsarkaeologiske studier*, pp. 73–86.

Penn, William, attr. *Information and Directions . . .* London, 1684.

Percier, Charles, and Pierre F. L. Fontaine. *Recueil de décorations intérieures*. Paris, 1801.

Petterson, Lars. *Petäjäveden vanhau kirkon puolesta*. Helsinki, 1951.

Petterson, Lars. *Suomalainen piukirkko*. Helsinki: Museum of Finnish Architecture, 1990.

Pevsner, Nikolaus. *Academies of Art Past and Present*. Reprint ed. New York: Da Capo Press, 1976.

Pevsner, Nikolaus. *A History of Building Types*. Princeton: Princeton University Press, 1976.

Phillips, Patricia. *The Prehistory of Europe*. London: Book Club Associates, 1980.

Phleps, Hermann. *Die norwegischen stabkirchen*. Karlsruhe: Bruderverlag, 1958.

Pitschmann, Louis A. "Norsemen in America: A Select Bibliography, 1950–1980," in Farrell, ed., *The Vikings*, pp. 231–235.

Plageman, Volker. *Das Deutsche Kunstmuseum 1790–1870*. Munich: Prestel-Verlag, 1967.

Plath, Iona. *The Decorative Arts of Sweden*. New York: Charles Scribner's Sons, 1948.

Pontvik, Alexis. "Haugesund rådhus og drommen om Italia." *Byggekunst* 70, no. 2 (1988):156–167.

Porphyrios, Demetri, ed. *Classicism Is Not a Style*. New York: Academy Editions, 1982.

Poulsen, Vagn, Erik Lassen, and Jan Danielsen, eds. *Dansk Kunst Historie*. 5 vols. Copenhagen: Politikens Forlag, 1972–1975.

Pöykkö, Kalevi. "Helsinki's Neo-Classical Center," *Apollo* 115, no. 243 (May 1982):354–360.

Quantrill, Malcolm. *Alvar Aalto: A Critical Study*. New York: Schocken Books, 1983.

Rácz, Istvan. *Rokoko och klassicism*. Helsinki: Otava, 1968.

Raeder, Hans, Elis Strömgren, and Bengt Strömgren, trans. and eds. *Tycho Brahe's Description of His Instruments*. Copenhagen: Munksgaard, 1946.

Rafn, Aage. "The Police Headquarters in Copenhagen," *Artes* 4 (1936):157–206.

Ramsing, Holger U. *Københavns historie og topografi i middelalderen*. 3 vols. Copenhagen: Munksgaard, 1940.

Ramskou, Thorkild. *Hedeby*. Copenhagen: Munksgaard, 1962.

Ramskou, Thorkild. *Lindholm Høje*. Copenhagen: National Museum, 1960.

Randsborg, Klaus. *The Viking Age in Denmark*. New York: St. Martin's Press, 1980.

Rasmussen, Holger, ed. *Dansk Folkemuseum & Frilandsmuseum*. Copenhagen: National Museum, 1966.

Rasmussen, Steen Eiler. *Nordische Baukunst*. Berlin: E. Wasmuth, 1940.

Reimers, Egill, and Peter Anker. "Trearkitektur bygd og by," in Knut Berg, ed., *Norges kunsthistorie*, 1:356–427.

Reinerth, Hans, ed. *Haus und Hof im nordischen Raum*. Leipzig, 1937.

Renfrew, Colin. *Before Civilization*. New York: Alfred A. Knopf, 1974.

Resen, Peder Hansen. *Atlas Danicus*. Copenhagen, 1677.

Richards, James M. *800 Years of Finnish Architecture*. Newton Abbot: David and Charles, 1978.

Richards, James M. "Hvitträsk," *Architectural Review* 139, no. 828 (February 1966):152–154.

Richardt, Ferdinand, and Tyge A. Secker. *Prospecter af danske herregaarde*. 20 vols. Copenhagen: C. A. Reitzel, 1845–1870.

Ringbom, Sixten. *Stone, Style and Truth*. Helsinki: Finska Fornminnesföreningen, 1987.

Rinne, Junanni. *Åbo Domkyrka*. Helsinki: Otava, 1929.

Roesdahl, Else. "Aggersborg in the Viking Age," in Bekker-Nielsen, Foote, and Olsen, eds., *Eighth Viking Congress*, pp. 107–222.

Romdahl, Axel. *Linköpings domkyrka 1232–1932*. Gothenberg: O. Isacsons Boktryckeri, 1932.

Roosval, Albin, ed. *Svenska slott och herresäten*. N.s. 3 vols. Stockholm: V. Petterson, 1934.

Roosval, Johnny. *Den baltiska nordens kyrkor*. Uppsala:

J. A. Lundblads Förlag, 1924.

Roosval, Johnny, ed. *S. Nikolai eller Storkyrkan i Stockholm*. Stockholm: A.-B. Gunnar Tisells Tekniska Förlag, 1924.

Rosell, Ingrid, and Robert Bennett. *Kalmar Domkyrka. Sveriges Kyrkor. Småland.* Vol. 3, no. 4. Stockholm: Almqvist & Wiksell International, 1989.

Roussell, Aage, ed. *Danske slotte og herregårde.* 20 vols. Copenhagen: Hassing, 1963–1968.

Roussell, Aage. *Farms and Churches on the Mediaeval Norse Settlements of Greenland.* Meddelelser om Grønland 89 (1941).

Roussell, Aage. "Det nordiske hus i vikingetid," in Stenberger, ed., *Forntida gårdar,* pp. 193–200.

Roussell, Aage. "Stöng. Thjórsárdalur," in Stenberger, ed., *Forntida gårdar,* pp. 72–97.

Rubow, Jørn. *C. F. Hansens arkitektur.* Copenhagen: G. E. C. Gad, 1936.

Rydbeck, Otto. *Glimmingehus.* Stockholm: Wahlström & Wikstrand, 1947.

Rydbeck, Otto. "Italienske inflytande på skånsk kyrkobyggnadskonst," Kungl. Vitt. Hist. och Ant. Akademien *Handlingar* 39, no. 2 (1936).

Rydbeck, Otto. *Lunds domkyrkas byggnadshistoria.* Lund: C. W. K. Gleerup, 1932.

Saarikivi, Sakari, Kerttu Niilonen, and Hilding Ekelund. *Art in Finland.* Helsinki: Otava, 1952.

Sachs, Erwin O. *Modern Opera Houses and Theatres.* 3 vols. London: Batsford, 1896, 1897, 1898; reprint ed., New York: Arno Press, 1981.

Sahlberg, Irja. *The Handicraft Museum at Luostarinmäki.* Turku: The Historical Museum, 1976.

Salokorpi, Asko. "Currents and Undercurrents in Finnish Architecture," *Apollo* 115, no. 243 (May 1982):388–393.

Salokorpi, Asko. *Modern Architecture in Finland.* London: George Weidenfeld and Nicolson, Ltd., 1970.

Sandblad, Nils Gösta. *Skånsk stadsplanekonst och stadsarkitektur.* Lund and Copenhagen, 1949.

Sárkány, Tamás. "Finströms kyrka," in Karling, ed., *Ålands medeltida kyrkor,* pp. 115–134.

Sawyer, Peter H. *Kings and Vikings: Scandinavia and Europe AD 700–1100.* London and New York: Methuen & Co. Ltd., 1982.

Saxtorph, Niels M. *Jeg ser på kalkmalerier.* Copenhagen: Politikens Forlag, 1970.

Schietzel, K. *Stand der siedlungsarchäologischen Forschungen in Haithabu.* Neumünster: Karl Wachholtz, 1981.

Schildt, Göran. *Alvar Aalto: The Early Years.* New York: Rizzoli, 1984.

Schiøtt, Frederik C. "Frederik III's Biblioteks og kunstkammerbygning," *Arkitekten* 10 (1907–1908):261–277.

Schmidt, Holger. "The Trelleborg House Reconsidered," *Medieval Archaeology* 17 (1973):52–77.

Sestoft, Jørgen. *Danmarks Arkitektur. Arbejdets bygninger.* Copenhagen: Gyldendal Nordisk Forlag, 1979.

Setterwall, Åke C. E. *Erik Palmstedt, 1741–1803.* Stockholm: Norstedt, 1945.

Setterwall, Åke C. E. *The Royal Palace, Stockholm.* Trans. William Cameron. Stockholm: Norstedt, 1948.

Setterwall, Åke C. E. "Stockholms börsbyggnad," *Samfundet Sankt Eriks Årsbok* (1934):151–184.

Setterwall, Åke C. E., Stig Fogelmarck, and Bo Gyllensvärd. *The Chinese Pavilion at Drottningholm.* Malmö: Allhems Förlag, 1974.

Shand, Philip Morton. "Stockholm, 1930," *Architectural Review* 68 (August 1930):66–95.

Sigurdsson, Gisli. "The Turf Farm: Now a Relic of the Past," *Atlantica & Iceland Review* 9, no. 1 (1971):33–41.

Silfverstolpe, G. M. "Riddarhuspalatset," in Hallendorf, ed., *Sveriges Riddarhus,* pp. 85–196.

Silfverstolpe, G., and Åke Stavenow. *Drottningholm,* in Albin Roosval, ed., *Svenska slott,* n.s. 1:401–480.

Silk, Leonard. *Sweden Plans for Better Housing.* Durham, N.C.: Duke University Press, 1948.

Simpson, W. Douglas. *The Castle of Bergen and the Bishop's Palace at Kirkwall.* Edinburgh, 1961.

Sinding-Larsen, Peter A. Holger. *Akershus.* 2 vols. Oslo: Oppi, 1924–1925.

Sirén, Johan S. "Finland's New House of Parliament," *Architecture* 70 (October 1934):195–202.

Sirén, Osvald. *Gamla Stockholmshus af Nicodemus Tessin d. Ae.* 2 vols. Stockholm: Norstedt, 1912.

Sirén, Osvald. "Tessinska palatset," *Ord och Bild* 22

(1913): 385–395.

Skaarup, Jørgen. *Stengade. Meddelelser fra Langelands Museum 1975.* Rudkøping: Langelands Museum, 1975.

Skovgaard, Joakim A. *A King's Architecture.* London: Hugh Evelyn, 1973.

Skovgaard-Petersen, Inge. "The Historical Context of the First Towns in Northern and Eastern Europe," in Bekker-Nielsen, Foote, and Olsen, eds., *Eighth Viking Congress,* pp. 9–18.

Skriver, Poul Erik. "Arne Jacobsens Nationalbank," *Arkitektur* 16, no. 4 (1972):133–140.

Skriver, Poul Erik. "The National Theatre in Oslo," *Arkitektur DK* 1987, no. 3 (July 1987):124–127.

Skriver, Poul Erik. "Royal-Hotel-Copenhagen," *Arkitektur* 4, no. 6 (December 1960):209–248.

Skriver, Poul Erik. "The Royal Theatre in Copenhagen," *Arkitektur DK* 1987, no. 3 (July 1987):100–115.

Skriver, Poul Erik. "SAS Air Terminal," *Arkitektur* 3, no. 2 (April 1959):45–53.

Skriver, Poul Erik. "Den tekniske højskoles hovedbygning, Otaniemi, Helsinki," *Arkitektur* 11, no. 2 (April 1967):49–61.

Small, Alan, ed. *Fourth Viking Congress.* Aberdeen: University of Aberdeen, 1965.

Small, Alan. "The Norse Building Tradition in Shetland," in Myhre, Stoklund, and Gjaerder, eds., *Vestnordisk Byggeskikk,* pp. 241–253.

Smidt, Carl M. *Kalundborg.* Copenhagen: Gyldendal Nordisk Forlag, 1936.

Smidt, Claus M. *Vor Frue Kirke.* Copenhagen: Poul Kristensen Hening, 1980.

Smith, G. E. Kidder. *Sweden Builds.* New York: Albert Bonnier, 1950.

Smith, John Boulton. *The Golden Age of Finnish Art.* 2d rev. ed. Helsinki: Otava, 1985.

Söderberg, Bengt G. *Manor Houses and Royal Castles in Sweden.* Malmö: Allhems Förlag, 1975.

Söderberg, Bengt G. *Närke. Västmanland,* in Kjellberg and Svensson, eds., *Slott och herresäten.*

Söderberg, Bengt G. *Riksfästen och Residens,* in Kjellberg and Svensson, eds., *Slott och herresäten.*

Söderberg, Bengt G. *Södermanland.* 2 vols. In Kjellberg and Svensson, eds., *Slott och herresäten.*

Söderberg, Bengt G. *Svenska kyrkomålningar från medeltiden.* Stockholm: Natur och Kultur, 1951.

Sonck, Lars. "Mikael Agricola Kyrkan i Helsingfors," *Arkitekten* 32, no. 12 (1935):180–182.

Stavenow, Åke. *Carl Hårleman.* Uppsala: Almqvist & Wiksell, 1927.

Steenberg, Jan. *Christian IV's Frederiksborg.* Hillerød, 1950.

Steenberg, Jan. *Danmarks Kirker. København.* Vols. 2 and 3. Copenhagen: G. E. C. Gad, 1960–1972.

Steenberg, Jan. *Fredensborg.* Copenhagen: G. E. C. Gad, 1969.

Steenberg, Jan. "Fredensborg Interiorer," *Fra Nationalmuseets Arbejdsmark* (1961):59–66.

Steenberg, Jan. *Rundtaarn.* Copenhagen: Rhodos, 1962.

Steensberg, Axel. "Bulhus," in Danstrup, ed., *Kulturhistorisk Leksikon* 2 (1957).

Stein, Meir. "Christian IV—A 'Renaissance Man,'" *Apollo* 120, no. 6 (December 1984):368–379.

Stein, Meir. "Rundetaarns gaade, en ny forklaring," *Arkitekten* 26, no. 10 (May 1984):204–206.

Stemann, Helge. *F. Maldahl og hans venner.* Copenhagen: H. Hagerups Forlag, 1926.

Stenberger, Mårten, ed. *Forntida gårdar i Island.* Copenhagen: Munksgaard, 1943.

Stenberger, Mårten. "Öland under äldre Järnaldern," Kungl. Vitt. Hist. och Ant. Akademien *Monografier* 19 (1933).

Stenberger, Mårten. *Sweden.* New York: Praeger, 1962.

Stenberger, Mårten, and Ole Klindt-Jensen, eds. *Vallhager: A Migration Period Settlement on Gotland/Sweden.* 2 parts. Copenhagen: Munksgaard, 1955.

Stenseng, Arne. *Akershus Castle.* Trans. Christopher Norman. Oslo: Grøndahl & Søn, 1950.

Stephenson, Hakon. *Arkitekten Carl Petersen.* Copenhagen: Arkitektens Forlag, 1979.

Stephenson, Hakon. *Arkitekten Thorkild Henningsen.* Copenhagen: Arkitektens Forlag, 1979.

Stigum, Hilmar. "Loft," in Danstrup, ed., *Kulturhistorisk leksikon* 10 (1965).

Stigum, Hilmar, and Arne Berg. "Stove," in Danstrup, ed., *Kulturhistorisk leksikon* 17 (1972).

Stikvoort, J. M. *Nederlands Openluchtmuseum.* Arnhem, 1982.

Stoklund, Bjarne. *Bondegård og byggeskik før 1850*. Copenhagen: Dansk Historisk Faellesforening, 1969.

Stoklund, Bjarne. "Frilandsmuseets gård fra Lønnestak," *Fra Nationalmuseets Arbejdsmark* (1968):27–44.

Stoklund, Bjarne. "Houses and Culture in the North Atlantic Isles," *Ethnologica Scandinavia* (1980):113–132.

Stoklund, Bjarne. "Røgstue og glasstue," *Fra Nationalmuseets Arbejdsmark* (1966):31–32.

Stoklund, Bjarne. " 'Røykstova' and 'Glasstova': The Development of the Faroese Dwelling House Considered in a West Nordic Context," in Myhre, Stoklund, and Gjaerder, eds., *Vestnordisk byggeskikk,* pp. 218–230.

Stribolt, Barbro. *Stockholms 1800-talsteatrar*. Stockholm: Stockholms Kommun Liber Forlag, 1982.

Strömbon, Sixten, ed. *Gripsholm. Slottet och des samlingar 1537–1937*. Stockholm: Nordisk Rotogravyr, 1937.

Strömbon, Sixten. "The New Townhall of Stockholm," *Burlington Magazine* 43 (1923):208–214.

Sturm, Leonhard Christoph. *Architectonisches Bedenken von Protestantischen Kleinen Kirchen figur und Einsichtung*. Hamburg, 1712.

Summerson, John. *Architecture in Britain 1530–1830*. Baltimore: Penguin Books, 1954.

Svahnström, Gunnar. *Visby Domkyrka. Sveriges Kyrkor. Gotland*. Vol. 175. Stockholm: Almqvist & Wiksell International, 1978.

Svahnström, Gunnar, and Karin Svahnström. *Visby Domkyrka. Sveriges Kyrkor. Gotland*. Vol. 202. Stockholm: Almqvist & Wiksell International, 1986.

Svendsen, Peter Juhl. *Rundtårn opklaret: katedralens mysterium*. Copenhagen: Sphinx, 1987.

Swane, Leo. *Faaborg Museum*. Copenhagen: G.E.C. Gad, 1932.

Swartling, Ingrid. "Cistercian Abbey Churches in Sweden and 'the Bernardine plan,' " in Karling, Lagerlöf, and Svanberg, eds., *Nordisk medeltid,* pp. 193–198.

Tauber, Henrik. "Radiocarbon Chronology of the Danish Mesolithic and Neolithic," *Antiquity* 46 (1972):106–110.

Tempel, Egon. *New Finnish Architecture*. Stuttgart: Verlag Gerd Hatje, 1968.

Thiis-Evenson, Thomas. *Henrik Bull*. Oslo: Norsk Arkitektur Museum, 1975.

Thorsteinsson, Arne. "Faroese House Construction from the Viking Period until the 19th Century," in Myhre, Stoklund, and Gjaerder, eds., *Vestnordisk byggeskikk,* pp. 149–161.

Thorsteinsson, Arne. "On the Development of Faroese Settlements," in Bekker-Nielsen, Foote, and Olsen, eds., *Eighth Viking Congress,* pp. 189–202.

Thorvildsen, Elise, and Stephan Kehler, eds. *Med Arkaeologen Danmark rundt*. Copenhagen: Politikens Forlag, 1966.

Thurah, Lauritz de. *Den Danske Vitruvius*. 3 vols. Copenhagen: Ernst Heinrich Berlings Bogtrykkerii, 1746. Reprint ed., edited by Hakon Lund. Copenhagen: Thaning & Appel, 1967.

Tidemand-Dal, C. J. "Gildhuset i Naestved," *Byggeforum* (1947):165.

Tienhoven, Cornelius van. "Information Relative to Taking up Land in New Netherland," in O'Callaghan, *Documents,* 1:368.

Todd, Malcolm. *The Northern Barbarians 100 B.C.–A.D. 300*. London: Hutchinson University Library, 1975.

Treib, Marc. "Lars Sonck: From the Roots," *Journal of the Society of Architectural Historians* 30, no. 3 (October 1971):225–237.

Treib, Marc. "Woodland Cemetery—A Dialogue of Design and Meaning," *Landscape Architecture* 76, no. 2 (March/April 1986):42–49.

Tschudi-Madsen, Stephan. *Henrik Bull*. Trans. Sandra Hamilton. Oslo: Universitetsforlaget, 1983.

Tschudi-Madsen, Stephan. "Veien hjem. Norsk arkitektur 1870–1914," in Knut Berg, ed., *Norges kunsthistorie,* 5:7–108.

Tunander, Ingemar. *Falun, staden vid Kopparberget*. Falun, 1954.

Tuulse, Armin. *Burgen des Abendlandes*. Vienna: Anton Schroll, 1958.

Tynell, Knut. "Stockholms stadsbibliotek," *Arkitektur* (1922):146–154.

Uldall, Kai. "Open Air Museums," *Museum* 10, no. 1 (1957):68–83.

Ulf Hård af Segerstad. *Modern Finnish Design.* London: George Weidenfeld and Nicolson, Ltd., 1969.

Ullén, Marian. *Granhults och Nottebäcks kyrkor. Sveriges Kyrkor. Småland.* Vol. 2, no. 4. Stockholm, 1972.

Ullén, Marian. *Medeltida träkyrkor. Sveriges Kyrkor.* Vol. 192. Stockholm, 1983.

Unnerbäck, Eyvind. *Vadstena slott 1545–1554.* Stockholm, 1966.

Valonen, Niilo. "Knuttimring," in Danstrup, ed., *Kulturhistorisk Leksikon* 8 (1963).

Valonen, Niilo. *Zur Geschichte der finnischen Wohnstuber.* Helsinki: Suomalais-Ugrilainen Seura, 1963.

Vegetius, Flavius Renatus. *The Military Institutions of the Romans.* Trans. John Clark. Harrisburg, Pa.: The Military Service Publishing Company, 1944.

Veijola, V. "Riksdagshuset," *Arkitekten* 28, no. 11 (1931):65–100.

Vensild, Henrik. "Højremshuse i Nord-og-Nordvest-Jylland i historisk tid," in Myhre, Stoklund, and Gjaerder, eds., *Vestnordisk byggeskikk,* pp. 119–129.

Vilkuna, K. "Den karelska gården," *Arkitekten* 43 (1941):140–145.

Villadsen, Villads. *Ribe Domkirke.* Ribe: Historisk Samfund for Ribe Amt, 1974.

Vilppula, Hilkka. *Guide to the Open Air Museum.* Helsinki: Seurasaarisäätio, 1964.

Visted, Kristofer, and Hilmar Stigum. *Vår gamle bondekultur.* 2 vols. 3d ed. Oslo: Cappelen, 1971.

Vitruvius, Marcus Pollio. *The Ten Books on Architecture.* Trans. M. H. Morgan. Cambridge, Mass.: Harvard University Press, 1914.

Wåhlin, Hans. *Visby.* Stockholm: Norstedt, 1938.

Wahlberg, Anna Greta. *Jean Eric Rehn 1717–1793.* Lund: Signum, 1983.

Wahlgren, Erik. *The Vikings and America.* London and New York: Thames and Hudson, 1976.

Wahlman, Lars I. *Engelbrektskyrkan i ord och bild.* Stockholm: 1932.

Wallin, Sigurd. *Seglora Kyrka på Skansen.* Stockholm: Cederquists Grafiska Aktiebolag, 1918.

Wanscher, Vilhelm. *Arkitekten G. Bindesbøll.* Copenhagen: K. Koster, 1903.

Wanscher, Vilhelm. *Christian IV's bygninger.* Copenhagen: P. Haase og Søn, 1947.

Wanscher, Vilhelm. "Constantin Hansen 1804–80 et les peintures du vestibule de L'université de Copenhague," *Artes* 4 (1936):1–27.

Wanscher, Vilhelm. *Kronborgs historie.* Copenhagen: Dreyers Forlag, 1939.

Wanscher, Vilhelm. "Politigaarden," *Architekten* (1924):69–72.

Wanscher, Vilhelm. *Rosenborgs historie 1606–1634.* Copenhagen: P. Haase og Søn, 1930.

Weilbach, Frederik. *Architekten C. F. Harsdorff.* Copenhagen: Hannas, 1928.

Weilbach, Frederik. *Architekten Lauritz Thura.* Copenhagen: Hannas, 1924.

Weilbach, Frederik. *C. F. Hansens Christiansborg.* Copenhagen: Nyt Nordisk Forlag, 1935.

Weilbach, Frederik. *Charlottenborg.* Copenhagen: Nyt Nordisk Forlag, 1933.

Weilbach, Frederik. *Frederiksberg Slot och Frederiksberg Have.* Copenhagen: Nyt Nordisk Forlag, 1936.

Weilbach, Frederik. *Frederiksborg Slot.* Copenhagen: Gyldendal Nordisk Forlag, 1923.

Weilbach, Frederik. *Kronborg Castle.* Trans. Nina Sabra and P. Boisen. Helsingør: K. Brammer, 1950.

Werlauff, Erich Christian. *Udsigt over Kiøbenhavns Universitets-Bygnings.* Copenhagen: J. H. Schultz, 1836.

West, Stanley E. "The Anglo-Saxon Village of West Stow: An Interim Report of the Excavation," *Medieval Archaeology* 13 (1969):1–20.

Westlund, Per-Olof. *Gripsholm under Vasatiden.* Kungl. Vitt. Hist. och Ant. Akademiens *Handlingar* 67 (1948).

Whiffen, Marcus, and Frederick Koeper. *American Architecture 1606–1976.* Cambridge, Mass.: MIT Press, 1981.

Wichström, Anne. "Maleriet i høymiddelalderen," in Knut Berg, ed., *Norges kunsthistorie,* 2:252–314.

Wickberg, Nils E. *Carl Ludwig Engel.* Berlin, 1970.

Wickberg, Nils E. "Engels Stilhistoriska ställning," *Arkitekten* 35 (1938):65–70.

Wickberg, Nils E. *Finnish Architecture.* Helsinki: Otava, 1959.

Wickberg, Nils E. *Senaatintori.* Helsinki: Anders Nyborg A/S, 1981.

Wickberg, Nils E. "Tillhundraårsminnet av Engels död," *Arkitekten* 37 (1940):4–7.

Wietek, Gerhard, ed. *C. F. Hansen 1756–1845.* Neumünster: Karl Wachholtz Verlag, 1982.

Wijnblad, Carl. *Bygnings konsten.* 2 vols. Stockholm: Kongl. Boktrycheriet Peter Momman, 1755 and 1756.

Willoch, Sigurd. *Nasjonal galleriet gennom hundrede år.* Oslo: Gyldendal Nordisk Forlag, 1937.

Wilson, David M. *The Vikings and Their Origins.* 2d ed. New York: A & W Publishers, Inc., 1980.

Wilson, David M., and Ole Klindt-Jensen. *Viking Art.* Ithaca: Cornell University Press, 1966.

Winther, Jens. *Troldbjerg.* 2 vols. Rudkøbing: Langelands Museum, 1933 and 1935.

Wohlert, Vilhelm. "C. F. Hansen's Domkirke," *Architectura* 2 (1980):49–54.

Woldbye, Vibecke. "Kim Naver's Wall Hangings for Denmark's National Bank." Trans. Carol L. Schroeder. *Haandarbejdets Fremme* 18, no. 1 (1979–1980):1–2.

Wollin, Nils G. *Desprez i Sverige.* Stockholm: Bokförlag A.-B. Thule, 1939.

Wollin, Nils G. "Gripsholmsföreningen och restaureringen på 1890-talet," Kungl. Vitt. Hist. och Ant. Akademiens *Handlingar* 71 (1950):148–219.

Wollin, Nils G. *Skeppsholmskyrkan eller Karl Johans Kyrka i Stockholm.* Sveriges Kyrkor. Stockholm. Vol. 9, no. 1.

Wrangel, Ewert. *Lunds domkyrkas konsthistoria.* Lund: Berlinska Boktrickeriet, 1923.

Wrangel, Fredrik Ulrik, greve. *Tessinska Palatset.* Stockholm: 1912.

Wrede, Stuart. *The Architecture of Gunnar Asplund.* Cambridge, Mass.: MIT Press, 1980.

Yates, Ann. "A Monument to Faith," *Iceland Review* 26, no. 4 (1987):13–18.

# Index